# DELUSIONS OF INTELLIGENCE

## Enigma, Ultra, and the End of Secure Ciphers

In 1974, the British government admitted that its WWII secret int
organization had read Germany's ciphers on a massive scale. The intel
from these decrypts influenced the Atlantic, the Eastern Front and
mandy. Why did the Germans never realize the Allies had so thoroughly p
etrated their communications? As German intelligence experts conducte
numerous internal investigations that all certified their ciphers' security, the
Allies continued to break more ciphers and to plug their own communication
leaks. How were the Allies able to so thoroughly exploit Germany's secret
messages? How did they keep their tremendous success a secret? What flaws
in Germany's organization allowed this counterintelligence failure and how
can today's organizations learn to avoid similar disasters?

This book, the first comparative study of WWII SIGINT (signals intelligence), analyzes the characteristics that allowed the Allies SIGINT success
and that fostered the German blindness to Enigma's compromise.

R. A. Ratcliff, who currently lives and consults in the hills above Silicon
Valley, has taught history and rhetoric at the University of California at
Berkeley and the University of San Francisco and has lectured at the National
Security Agency's intelligence school. In addition to working in the high
tech industry, Dr. Ratcliff has written articles for *Cryptologia*, *Intelligence and
National Security*, and the NSA's internal newsletter.

# Delusions of Intelligence

## ENIGMA, ULTRA, AND THE END OF SECURE CIPHERS

### R. A. Ratcliff

CAMBRIDGE
UNIVERSITY PRESS

CAMBRIDGE UNIVERSITY PRESS
Cambridge, New York, Melbourne, Madrid, Cape Town, Singapore, São Paulo

Cambridge University Press
40 West 20th Street, New York, NY 10011-4211, USA

www.cambridge.org
Information on this title: www.cambridge.org/9780521855228

First published 2006

Printed in the United States of America

A catalog record for this publication is available from the British Library.

Library of Congress Cataloging in Publication Data

Ratcliff, R. A. (Rebecca Ann), 1963–
Delusions of intelligence : Enigma, Ultra and the end of secure ciphers / R. A. Ratcliff.
    p.   cm.
Includes bibliographical references and index.
ISBN 0-521-85522-5 (hardcover)
1. Enigma cipher system.   2. ULTRA (Intelligence system)   3. World War,
1939–1945 – Cryptography.   4. World War, 1939–1945 – Electronic intelligence –
Great Britain.   5. World War, 1939–1945 – Electronic intelligence – Germany.   I. Title.
D810.C88R37   2006
940.54'8743 – dc22        2005036466

ISBN-13   978-0-521-85522-8 hardback
ISBN-10   0-521-85522-5 hardback

*For Chris,*
*Nick, and Alec*
*who slowed progress on the book*
*and have made life marvelous*

# CONTENTS

# LIST OF ILLUSTRATIONS

# GLOSSARY OF TERMS USED

| | |
|---|---|
| **Admiralty** | British Royal Navy (the Marine generally used this term) |
| **Arlington Hall** | A former girl's school that housed the main American naval decryption effort near Washington, D.C. |
| **B-Dienst** | The Marine observation (Beobachtung) service responsible for intercepting radio signals |
| **Bombe** | Electromechanical deciphering machine first designed by Polish cryptanalysts to discover the daily settings of the Enigma |
| **BP** | Bletchley Park, the primary location of GC&CS and the cracking of Enigma |
| **Colossus** | British-designed protocomputer used primarily to crack the Geheimschreiber |
| **cribs** | Known message texts or phrases used as possible solutions for unknown texts |
| **cryptology** | The development of codes and ciphers (cryptography) and the cracking of the same (cryptanalysis); the study of codes and ciphers |
| **decrypt** | A signal that has been decrypted by the enemy |
| **depths** | More than one message being encrypted at the same or nearly the same setting; a breach of standard security procedures and an excellent entry point for cryptanalysts |
| **D/F** | Direction Finding – the process of locating the source of a (usually radio) signal through triangulation |
| **discriminant** | A group of letters placed in front of the encrypted text to indicate the setup used (e.g., the alignment of the |

|  |  |
|---|---|
|  | Enigma rotors) at the start of the message's encipherment and hence the degree of secrecy of the message or to distinguish one type or section of traffic from another |
| **Enigma** | Commercial name, used by both Germans and Allies, for the (portable) electromechanical enciphering machine used by the branches of the German Wehrmacht, SS, and railroads |
| **Enigma M** | The Marine's version of the Enigma machine |
| **Fish** | British cover name for German radioteletype non-Morse intercepts and ciphering machines, specifically the Siemens Geheimschreiber T-52 series (code-named Sturgeon) and the Lorenz SZ 40/42 machines (code-named Tunny) |
| **Geheimschreiber** | Electromechanical enciphering machine used by the Germans for messages sent by wire (i.e., nonradio) |
| **Heer** | German Army |
| **Huff/Duff** | High Frequency Direction Finding (D/F) |
| **Inspk. 7** | OKH/Inspektorate 7/VI, which included the Heer's cryptanalytic unit |
| **Index** | A room-size index card catalog of crucial terms and people mentioned in decrypted Enigma signals |
| **indicator** | One or more letter or figure groups placed somewhere in the message to indicate the key or subtractor used |
| **intercept** | Radio signals "caught" by the enemy's interceptors, usually for location through D/F or for decryption |
| **key** | The setting for a cipher (e.g., Enigma machine) in a particular network for a specific period, commonly one day (hence, daily key) |
| **Luftwaffe** | German Air Force |
| **Magic** | American code name for decrypts from Purple |
| **Marine** | German Navy |
| **Metox** | A German radar warning device |
| **MI6** | Military Intelligence department 6 – responsible for external intelligence (comparable to the modern CIA) |
| **MND** | Marine Nachrichtendienst, the information service of the German Navy |

| | |
|---|---|
| **OKW** | Oberkommando der Wehrmacht (Wehrmacht high command) |
| **one-time pad** | A code based on sheets of substitutions to be used once only. Highly secure |
| **Purple** | American code name for the high-grade Japanese diplomatic cipher machine used just before and during the war |
| **re-encodements** | Signals encrypted in more than one Enigma net (repeats) |
| **rotors** | The turning wired wheels inside electromechanical cipher machines, such as Enigma, which created a set of electrical paths and the machine's enciphering component |
| **RSHA** | Reichssicherheit Haupt Amt (Primary Reich Security Bureau), the Nazi government security and intelligence agency that eventually absorbed the Wehrmacht's Abwehr |
| **Shark** | Allied code name for the Enigma M used for U-boat communications |
| **Sigaba** | American high-grade electromechanical cipher machine, more advanced than Enigma |
| **sigint** | Signals intelligence or any intelligence from signals, including D/F, Traffic Analysis, and decrypts |
| **SLUs** | Special Liaison Units, the teams responsible for protecting and transmitting Ultra Intelligence to battlefield commanders |
| **TA** | Traffic Analysis, the tracking of signals, usually undecrypted, by origin, length, and number, and comparing this information with past experience to project bombing raids, offensives, and retreats |
| **TICOM** | Target Intelligence Committee, Anglo-American teams sent into German territory around the end of the war to gather documents and personnel with information on intelligence, cryptology, and technological developments |
| **Triton** | German code name for the Enigma M used for U-boat communications |
| **Typex** | British electromechanical cipher machine, more advanced than Enigma |

| | |
|---|---|
| **Ultra** | Allied code name for intelligence derived from Enigma decrypts |
| **WAVES, WRENS, WAAFS** | The women's auxiliary forces who assisted in cracking Enigma, often running the Bombes |
| **Walze** | Rotors in the German Enigma machines |
| **Watch** | The group of people at BP staffing an eight-hour shift of translating, typing, and analyzing Ultra |
| **Wehrmacht** | German Armed Forces (i.e., Marine, Heer, Luftwaffe, etc.; for most ex-officers, this term excludes the Nazi military and paramilitary groups such as the SS and Waffen SS) |
| **X-B-Dienst** | Division of B-Dienst responsible for decryption of enemy codes and ciphers |

# ACKNOWLEDGMENTS

True knowledge comes from the exchange of ideas. No author researches and writes a book without help from many sources – I am no exception. My work rests not just on the foundations of the literature cited, but on the help, ideas, and enthusiasm of numerous people. As the research for this book took me across two continents, numerous archives, and many years, I had help and encouragement from strangers, colleagues, and friends. I cannot attempt to thank all of them, but here, briefly and incompletely, is an attempt to thank some of those helping hands.

I am greatly indebted to the Center for Cryptologic History at the National Security Agency (NSA), its NSA Scholar-in-Residence program, and its staff. David Hatch brought me into the program, opened all kinds of vital doors, and introduced me to some of America's cryptologic geniuses. I had regular help on matters both small and significant from all the staff of the CCH and the National Cryptologic Museum, including Larry Sharp, Rowena Clough, and the late Dave Mowry, who also commented on drafts of this work.

My year at NSA also provided the wisdom and insights of two excellent sigint specialists and historians. Dr. Thomas Johnson has a likely unparalleled knowledge of American intelligence history and practice that I hope will inform our leaders as well as it has me. Robert J. Hanyok has shared his enthusiasm for history and sigint and spent many hours confirming details and procuring photos. Both of these experts have shaped my thinking and writing about cryptology and sigint. Thank you.

I owe much to Wladyslaw Kozaczuk and the late Sir Harry Hinsley for their works and correspondence. Arthur Levinson, Sir Edward Thomas, Alan Stripp, Peter Calvocoressi, and Ralph Bennett all spoke eloquently of Bletchley. The late Cecil and Nancy Phillips provided useful details on the American side. Robert Harris saved me hours in the Public Record Office and kindly kindled interest with his novel *Enigma*. David J. Alvarez connected me with the journal *Intelligence and National Security* (*INS*) and NSA. Whitfield Diffie, Judith Field, and the British Society for the History of Mathematics prodded me to explore Enigma's mathematics. Brian McCue offered radar and U-boat help and a most marvelous small-world moment. My thanks to Stephen J. Kelley and *Cryptologia*'s Louis Kruh for their interest and information.

Jürgen Rohwer gave me access to his archives and the Bibliothek für Zeitgeschichte and answered numerous questions about German historians, life in the Marine, and the German perspective on Enigma and Ultra. Ralph Erskine and Steve Budiansky pointed out important documents and gave me access to their own writings on World War II sigint. Wesley K. Wark read a very early version of this work and gave me excellent guidance. Mary Sutphen also offered comments on several chapters.

David Kahn has always been most generous with his time, knowledge, and materials. Although I have tried consciously not to lean too heavily on his excellent foundations, I owe a great debt to his works on cryptology, Enigma, and German intelligence.

Several grants made the research for this work possible, including the NSA residence program, a grant from the Department of Education for initial research and advanced German, and University of California, Berkeley, grants for research, travel, and writing. Sections of Chapter 6 appeared in the journal *Intelligence and National Security*, and I acknowledge their permission to include that material here.

Thanks also to my UCB connections, particularly Deborah Cohen, Takiyoshi Nishiuchi, Patricia Reilly, and Maxine Fredericksen. I still owe much to my doctoral committee: David Cohen, Margaret Anderson, Anthony Adamthwaite, Reginald Zelnick, and the late Art Quinn, who is greatly missed.

Throughout my research, I received crucial assistance from the personnel of several libraries and archives: the Mitarbeitern of the Bibliotek für Zeitgeschichte; the staffs of the Bundes-Militärarchiv and the Auswärtiges Amt's archive; the reference librarians at the PRO; and the staff and volunteers at NSA's National Cryptologic History Museum.

My greatest debt of all is to Timothy P. Mulligan of National Archives and Records Administration. The use of technology in archives has improved the researcher's lot tremendously; but no technology, however advanced, can provide a researcher with the depth of information, years of lessons in German naval matters, and numerous gentle nudges toward crucial documents that Tim has provided for more than a decade. Archivists such as he are a national resource, and they are retiring unreplaced. In the midst of its rush to acquire all things electronic, NARA's administration should not neglect this most valuable resource of all.

For the actual writing, I was aided by Sonja Aschenbrenner and Tanja Fassel managing Schnabel and Schnuffel, by quiet spots in Stevens Hall, NARA, and Cañada College, by my antique printer's forbearance, and by Chris Gellrich's support and technical assistance. Dr. (med.) Birgit Jödicke not only introduced me to German and provided decades of friendship, including ein Patenkind (Lisa Joanna), she also cast her professional translator's eye over my work (any remaining errors are, of course, mine).

The support and encouragement from family and friends has made this work both possible and a joy. Thanks and appreciation to my parents, who still keep an eye out for all things Enigma-related; to the best siblings ever, Rosemary and Jamie; and to S. G. Hamlen, whose support, encouragement, and keen editorial eye made all the difference and who recommended the Groupthink book ages ago. Jonathan Klein, Anne Wright, and Chris Gellrich kindly agreed to read everything with fresh eyes. I remain forever grateful to James E. Ratcliff, Jr., for mentioning that story about the Poles cracking some code during the war and for subsequently reading everything I passed him on the subject – including the numerous iterations of this work. Thanks Dad.

Finally, thanks to Lewis Bateman for initially adopting the book, and to Eric Crahan and, especially, Frank Smith of Cambridge University Press, who waited patiently through my mergers and acquisitions for the final product.

R. A. Ratcliff
May 2005

# THE TRAITOR IN OUR MIDST

## Enigma's Decipherment and Ultra Intelligence

...it is contended that very few Armies ever went to battle better
informed of their enemy ...
– Brig. E. T. Williams' report on British use of signals intelligence,
October 1945

In 1974, after decades of secrecy, the British government finally admitted its World War II intelligence service had read thousands of German messages encrypted by the Enigma machine cipher.[1] The intelligence derived from these decrypted messages traveled under the code name "Ultra" (for Ultra Secret) and influenced nearly all of the major battles in the Western theater. Now readers can find histories of Ultra's role in battles across the Atlantic, North Africa, the skies over Britain, and occupied Europe.[2]

Less public attention has been spent on how the Allies obtained these signals decrypts. Many early accounts of the breaking of Enigma have proved to be incomplete or erroneous and have been superseded as more information appeared in the 1980s and 1990s. Now, through various sources, the public can learn the history of Enigma's development and downfall.

Enigma emerged after the end of the First World War as one of several similar electro-mechanical enciphering ideas emerging in the U.S. and Europe. The Dutch inventor, Hugo Alexander Koch, apparently saw his secret-writing machine idea as a tool for a business world needing a relatively uncomplicated yet effective method for protecting commercial secrets. He sold the rights to his enciphering machine patent to

German manufacturer, Arthur Scherbius.[3] Scherbius' firm produced the Enigma in the 1920s and trumpeted the machine as portable and easy to use yet statistically highly secure: over 15 million, million ($15 \times 10^{12}$) possible substitutions for each letter typed into the machine. In 1926, the German Marine (navy)[4] adopted the Enigma cipher machine, with modifications, as its primary cipher system.[5] Soon the Heer (army) followed suit.[6] Over the next several years, German cryptologists improved the cipher machines to tighten their security against decipherment. By the beginning of World War II, each of the branches of the German military, the police, the railway, civilians, and the Nazi Party were using their own variations of Enigma.

Although the Germans continued to believe their signals impregnable, the Allies captured and stole cipher key settings, found and exploited Enigma's weaknesses, built a rudimentary computer, and broke into virtually every German cipher net. For the first time in history, not just individual codes but an entire system of encipherment was broken.[7]

This successful assault on Enigma's secrets began in the 1930s. Polish intelligence[8] attacked the machine analytically, reconstructing Enigma's internal and rotor wirings from the signals they received. With these reconstructed wirings and a few key documents turned over by a spy, Polish cryptanalysts built their own Enigma facsimiles. They linked several of the reconstructed rotors together to create "Bombes," electromechanical aids capable of checking possible solutions far more quickly than humans. When Adolf Hitler's attack threatened, the Poles passed their decrypting techniques and Enigma models on to the British and the French. The poles soon fled the advancing German army, only to continue working from France until the Germans occupied Vichy France in November 1942. By 1939, the British had organized a section of the Government Code and Cypher School (GC&CS) at Bletchley Park (or BP) to work exclusively on radio intercepts. There, in 1940, the first British Bombes came into service.[9]

In addition to developing new electromechanical and electronic aids, the Allies exploited the Enigma machine's mechanical and linguistic weaknesses, finding shortcuts to its solution.[10] As the analysts began reading one cryptosystem, they often found clues to other key settings, for example, by tracking weather reports on different networks. The lack of coordination between different arms of the Wehrmacht required that whole messages sometimes be repeated verbatim in several different cipher keys. When the Allies had a "crib"[11] or a possible text for a message repeated to several commands, they could give it as a "menu" (or potential solution) to the Bombes. With such practices, Bletchley's analysts frequently could decrease their deciphering time.

The most frequently and consistently cracked keys were those of the Luftwaffe.[12] From its first cracking in early 1940, the general Luftwaffe key, "Red," provided almost constant reading material for BP through the war's end. During the Battle of Britain, Polish and Bletchley Park cryptanalysts began reading the main German Air Force (Luftwaffe) key regularly in time to assist Fighter Command.[13] The Allies read the Luftwaffe keys in North Africa from the first day of their introduction, 1 January 1942. The continuity offered by reading the Luftwaffe keys virtually every day for years helped keep Bletchley Park ahead of changes in this and other Enigma nets.[14]

The German Army (Heer and Wehrmacht) keys were cracked after the Luftwaffe's but before the more difficult Naval Enigma (Enigma M), which the Bletchley Park team first broke in August 1941.[15] The Enigma M keys proved the most sophisticated and far more secure than the Luftwaffe and Army keys because of several changes and improvements to the Marine machine. Nonetheless, Bletchley Park read the Home Waters key from 1 August 1941 through the end of the war. The most crucial alteration to Enigma M came in February 1942 when the Marine instituted a four-rotor Enigma for the U-boat cipher Triton (Shark to the Allies). Only nine months later, in December 1942, did Bletchley begin reading Shark again, first with occasional delays, but by late March 1943 with little interruption.[16]

As the number of Enigma networks proliferated, Bletchley's cryptanalysts only increased their successes. A report of work in mid-November 1944 reported breaking 77 percent of Luftwaffe traffic, 18 percent of Army traffic (during a difficult call signs upgrade), 35 percent of SS traffic, and 24 percent of railway ciphers. In March 1944, Bletchley reported work on more than one hundred thousand messages, not including Naval Enigma. Bletchley Park's cryptanalysts solved keys for more than 50 percent of this selection, including 62 percent of Luftwaffe traffic and 30 percent of Heer traffic.[17] At times, the intercepts were solved almost immediately. Often, however, a lack of cribs, tightening of operator security, or Enigma machine modification would increase Bletchley Park's deciphering delay from hours to days or months.

By 1945, Bletchley Park had identified and attacked most versions of Enigma, defeating more than 200 separate networks of keys, albeit many irregularly or temporarily. The Ultra Secret intelligence from these decrypted signals passed to the Allied military commands under tight security, often attributed to a (notional) secret agent working in German command offices and code-named "Boniface." Commanders could use Ultra information only if they had a second source as a cover story, for example, a POW's interrogation, or a fix on a signal through direction finding (D/F). This secret intelligence at times allowed the Allies to avoid waiting U-boats, anticipate surprise attacks, and send their own troops to the Germans' most vulnerable points.

In a massive Index, each shift at Bletchley Park cross-referenced the information acquired from each decrypted Enigma signal. One could track a particular U-boat or a particular general, and through the succeeding actions speculate on upcoming offensives or the whereabouts of other, not-yet-located divisions or ships. For example, the ship *Schorndorf* was sunk with Ultra's help, not through her own enciphered signals, which were infrequent and not solved, but rather through the deciphered signals ordering two U-boats to support her. With the Index's extensive anthology, the Allies could track components that might not be momentarily important, yet could lead to bigger fish.

## A Fatal Blindness

Yet as the Allies pieced together thousands of supply requests, status reports, and direct orders emerging in Enigma decrypts, the Germans seemed not to notice the enemy's intelligence collection. German cryptologic experts touted the high security and reliability of the Enigma ciphers and attributed information leaks to every other possible source, even their own radio operators. Through numerous investigations during the war, intelligence bureaus confirmed Enigma's security and announced the enemy could not regularly read the machine's ciphers.

Even after the war, confidence in Enigma persisted. A Polish book published in 1967 claimed that young cryptologists working for Polish intelligence before and during World War II had solved Enigma. As word of the book crossed Germany, ex-Wehrmacht officers dismissed its claim of cryptological triumph as "wishful thinking." Not even the historical community considered following up on the tale.[18]

In 1970, the former head of the German Marine's B-Dienst (Beobachtung or Observation Service), Captain Heinz Bonatz, wrote his own history of Germany's intelligence successes.[19] He described the German military and government embracing the latest communications technology, combining Enigma and radios with striking results. In the rapid conquest of country after country, they had relied heavily on nearly constant signals to coordinate the rapid attacks, "which overwhelmed France and might have overwhelmed Britain."[20] Knowing their radio messages would be overheard by enemy ears even long before the war, they had adopted Enigma as the most modern enciphering system of the time.

Bonatz directly answered the claim of Enigma's compromise. He acknowledged that the Allies had seized cipher machines from captured U-boats but insisted nonetheless that the Allies did not and could not have read German ciphers regularly. He explained that "all necessary measures were taken to guarantee the cipher's security, in case a machine should fall into the hands of the enemy."[21]

As further proof, the former B-Dienst chief declares that the Allies "would not have let [Enigma's compromise] go unmentioned." After the war, he had had "numerous conversations with the former enemy's specialists," which had confirmed "that the [Marine Enigma] was secure against break-in and the German naval radio signals could not be read." He was certain the Allies would never have remained silent about such a triumph. "Besides," he continues, "this [ability to read Enigma-encrypted signals] would have been visible in their own sigint [signals intelligence]," which Bonatz's agency had deciphered.[22] Thus, in 1970, after published Polish claims and U.S. admissions of successes solving machine ciphers, Bonatz still entertained no doubts of Enigma's security. The sheer weight of the Allies' continued silence convinced him.

In 1974, the publication of *The Ultra Secret* stating, with approval from a high-level wartime commander, that the Allies had cracked Enigma completely reversed the German position.[23]

## A Puzzlement

Why were the revelations of Ultra so astonishing? Why did they catch not only former intelligence officers but the most distinguished historians of cryptology by surprise? How could the Allies use so much secret information from Enigma-encrypted signals and not make the Germans suspect their source?

This book considers the answers to these questions and draws lessons about security, specifically in cryptology and communications. This wartime saga also offers guidelines for setting up an organization for failure or for success in exploiting emerging technologies. Here is the story of the Germans using a sophisticated, technologically advanced communications system and yet losing their grip on both gathering enemy intelligence and securing their own communications. This story also describes the largely British organization whose primarily civilian staff constantly challenged their own and the enemy's security and, in so doing, had unprecedented and so far unequaled success.

German intelligence had its own share of cryptographic and cryptanalytic successes, many of which Captain Bonatz and others touted after the war. Early on, German cryptanalysts had considerable success against the codes of Britain, France, the United States, and the Soviet Union. Given their own success at cracking ciphers, why, as the war progressed, did the Germans never seriously consider their main high-grade cipher system as the source of so many of their problems? An enormous percentage of their enciphered signals depended on a single cipher system. Did they ever consider how completely their communications system could be compromised? How could the Germans have never recognized that Enigma had been broken? How did the Allies manage both to break this "secure" system and to keep the secret of their success so completely for thirty years? Why were the Germans so certain of their machine's security?

Both Enigma's compromise and the extraordinary success of Ultra stem from technical and cultural grounds. Technologically, the world stood on a different plane from our postwar years. Radio was a still new tool for communicating across distances without wires. Computers considered obsolete decades ago seemed a practical impossibility in the 1930s. In the age of punch cards and tabulators, the sheer number of

Enigma's possible letter substitutions with its appearance of randomness implied extraordinary security.

The Allies' remarkable success against this sophisticated electromechanical enciphering machine was first a feat of mathematical and cryptanalytic brilliance. But this triumph goes beyond the actual breaking of the cipher machine. More important than technology, the organization and basic assumptions of the opposing intelligence systems shaped the success of one side and the defeat of the other. In the rapidly changing cryptologic war, intelligence agencies had to adapt quickly to succeed. The Allied agencies managed to do this. German intelligence did not.

This contrast in adaptability stems from the opposing signals intelligence organizations. The structures and cultures in these organizations shaped the ability of intelligence personnel to adapt and respond quickly to the constant changes in the enemy's ciphers. The men and women in intelligence entered the war, began their attacks on enemy ciphers, and considered their own ciphers' compromise, all within the confines of their organization's assumptions about cryptology. Thus, to understand Enigma's defeat, as well as Ultra's success, requires knowing the construction and functioning of the opposing agencies.

We cannot simply dismiss the failure of German intelligence as a direct result of Hitler's National Socialism or some single act of Allied genius or German idiocy. Rather the strengths of the Enigma cipher machine and the flaws of the German signals intelligence organizations combined to create a blind spot that the well-coordinated Allied agencies eagerly exploited.

Finally, Bonatz's words epitomize his peers' attitude toward World War II signals intelligence and Enigma's security during the war and into the present. These intelligence officers maintained a stubborn belief in Enigma's absolute security in the face of considerable evidence to the contrary. The Germans missed numerous clues, overlooked several obvious signs, and succumbed to their own wishful thinking about Enigma. Even their numerous security investigations failed to reveal the weaknesses in the Enigma system, let alone the hemorrhage of information passing to the Allies from Ultra. Their refusal to simply acknowledge mistakes, let alone enlist help to investigate them, would ruin German signals intelligence.

## Learning from Defeat

In the end, as we all know, the Germans lost the war. The general public has long attributed both this loss and the war more generally to the evils of National Socialism. So, some may ask, why bother looking at the security investigations of defeated sigint bureaus? Because Nazism played only a minimal role in the signals intelligence war and certainly not a deciding one. The real story is both more mundane and far more important for us today. Ordinary people made the difference. Their belief in possibility and impossibility decided whether they defeated the enemy. They have much to teach the modern user of communications and cryptology.

Although the Allied cracking of Enigma has inspired numerous personal accounts as well as historical analyses of Ultra, modern security enthusiasts will learn more from tracing the causes of Enigma's failure. We can see strong parallels between today and the 1930s and 1940s. Like the commanders in World War II, we must grapple with the advances and perils of more mobile communications. Whether we know it or not, our numerous communications devices – from cell phones to the Internet – all use some form of cryptology. The twenty-first century need for secure communications does not stop with national intelligence staff but extends to companies of every size, their IT experts and financial transactions, right down to the average Internet user.

A similar revolution in communications before and during the Second World War also launched new technologies, new specialties, new business practices, and, of course, new problems. This revolution arose from a convergence of new technologies and industrial methods: wireless radio, electricity, mechanization, mass production, and automation. Cryptography moved from book codes and ciphers to machine ciphers. In turn, cryptanalysis would create new specialties, first in electromechanics and eventually in computer science. Moreover, cryptanalysis in the Second World War would produce rooms full of new machines, enormous production systems, and an appreciation for the ephemeral nature of even machine-based cryptologic security.

Today's technology may be more advanced than shortwave radios and Enigma, but we face the same issues of protecting communications from unwanted eavesdroppers and recognizing when security has failed. Knowing the dramatic outcome of two different methods of exploiting these new technologies will help us avoid the pitfalls into which German signals intelligence tumbled. This work examines these various snares, including arrogance and complacency about security, as well as the cultural and structural pressures, such as rigid signaling procedures, that limited the success of German organizations and their staffs.

Using recently declassified archival materials, this book compares the organization and practices of the German intelligence agencies with those of the spectacularly successful western Allies. A thorough examination of the various German organizations and their operations explains why no one could acknowledge that their main cipher network had been completely compromised. In contrast, the British increasingly exploited signals intelligence successfully and foiled German signals intelligence by improving cipher security throughout the war.

This work arose from the examination of German, American, and British wartime and postwar documents now housed in the U.S. National Archives, London's Public Record Office, and Germany's Auswärtiges Amt (Bonn) and Bundes-Militärarchiv (Freiburg). As the National Security Agency's (NSA) Scholar-in-Residence, I had access to these recently declassified collections, including the massive Historic Cryptologic Collection (nearly fifteen hundred boxes of documents), U.S. naval intelligence documents, collections of captured documents, POW interrogations, Target Intelligence Committee (TICOM) reports, and wartime and postwar reports. Britain's recent releases include thousands of folders of Bletchley Park memos, reports, histories, and postmortems. These documents allow a partial examination of Allied wartime communications security as a comparison to the German effort.

Through an examination of the German and Allied agencies, this book argues Enigma's defeat arose less from a technological flaw than from the systemic failure of an entire intelligence system. The first three chapters describe the particulars of Enigma and the organizations that handled both Enigma's security and the attacks on enemy systems. Turning to the Allied story, two chapters outline Allied sigint at Bletchley Park and the disguise and dissemination of the Ultra material. The Germans' concerns about Enigma's security and their investigations into the betrayal of military secrets appear in Chapter 6. Chapter 7 lays out the contrast of Allied communications security practices and responses to potential leaks. Chapters 8 and 9 analyze the underlying reasons for the two vastly different organizations and outcomes, followed by a concluding summary.

# ONE

# ENIGMA

## The Development and Use of a New Technology

It's German, therefore it must have been done according to a system.
– attributed to William Friedman, chief U.S. Army cryptanalyst

Cryptographers at the end of the First World War had a problem. The standard cryptography of the time relied on bulky books of letter codes or additive tables, and users found them awkward and time consuming. Messages were limited by the code groups – ideas and words not already contained in the codebook needed a special system to be transmitted and understood. Composing or decrypting a message by looking up each code group could take a long time. Worst of all, codebooks had no protection against physical compromise: as soon as the enemy captured a codebook, he could begin reading the code traffic.

So as they prepared for the next war, the major belligerents of the Great War turned to an emerging technology to protect their signals: machine ciphers. Electrically activated rotors and levers promised greater ease, flexibility, and security for messages destined to be signaled around the world. Even if the machines themselves fell into enemy hands, inventors claimed, the system's complexity would foil the attacks of any cryptanalyst.

All the major nations in World War II would develop and use electromechanical cryptography systems. The Japanese used the machine Americans called "Purple," the British built a Type X (Typex) rotor machine, the Americans built the formidable rotor maze Sigaba, and numerous countries used other rotor-based machines. Of them all, the most thoroughly documented case is the German Enigma. As the world now knows, Enigma's security was punctured in its first years of use by Polish mathematicians and later read by the British and the Americans throughout the war. In addition to the voluminous collection of Enigma decrypts from Bletchley Park's cryptanalysts, we now have countless German documents detailing the use, improvements, and perceived security of Enigma throughout the war. Enigma also demonstrates how a new technology can quickly move from startlingly revolutionary to so familiar that its operators fall into complacency.

Following their defeat in the Great War, Germans had discovered that Britain had trumped them in the intelligence war. From the first weeks of the war, the British had read several important German codes. In effect, as German naval leaders later complained, the Marine[1] had "played with open cards" at least through 1916.[2] The intelligence gleaned from these decrypts helped the British, if not to win the war, at least to forestall losing it before Germany did. Shortly before the great naval battle of Jutland, for example, the small cryptologic branch of the Royal Navy, called Room 40, learned the disposition and intentions of the German fleet. With this information, they helped save themselves from a surprise attack and possible annihilation.

During the Great War, the German military – the Marine in particular – had recognized that their enemy had information about German operations and intentions. Decades later, Captain Heinz Bonatz, a former head of the Marine B-Dienst (Beobachten or Observation Service), would write for his Allied captors a history of German naval intelligence in the Great War and the interwar period. Therein (and in his published account of 1970) he discusses the problems of German cryptology in 1914–1918 and the lessons that German intelligence learned from that experience.[3] He explains that the British World War I success against German naval signals rested not on cryptanalysis but on simple seizures of German codebooks. He too concedes that the British codebreaking success in 1914 had greatly handicapped German operations for much of the Great War. Although at the time the military wondered about the enemy's information sources, Bonatz explained, "the German side made random guesses and sincerely believed that the British success was due to treachery and secret agents."[4]

In his own words, Bonatz explains the underlying problem, which, we now know, plagued the Marine in both wars:

> Neither the German High Seas Fleet nor the Naval War Staff hit upon the idea that it was German naval radio traffic which supplied the British their knowledge – and this in spite of the fact that Germany too was working on radio intelligence![5]

With British post–World War I revelations of their success against German codes, the German military realized how much information their cryptographic systems had given the enemy. Germany determined not to allow an enemy such advantages in the next war.

Reeling from the revelations of Room 40's success, the German military quickly recognized that the codebook method of encryption would be inadequate for the next war.[6] Advances in radio allowed more rapid and wide-reaching communications, but the enemy could intercept and attack these signals at least as easily as they had in the previous war. The German Marine sought an encryption system that would allow rapid, protected communication and would not succumb to physical compromise. They found their solution in electromechanical cipher encryption – Enigma.

With Enigma-encrypted radio signals, Wehrmacht units could now send one another swift, secure messages necessary for the Blitzkreig-style attacks which overwhelmed Europe between 1938 and 1941. This Blitzkrieg method, in the eyes of many scholars, relied on "mechanized mobility plus air-power plus radio communications."[7] For these complex operations, the Heer, Marine, and Luftwaffe units had to communicate with each other rapidly and securely. Commanders back at headquarters needed to communicate with their far-flung troops, coordinating their movements across vast distances in the new era of mobile warfare. The U-boat fleet commander directed his U-boats roaming the Atlantic or Indian Ocean from his offices in Berlin. Hitler, in Berlin, east Prussia, or Bavaria, directed General Erwin Rommel's actions in the North African desert. Enigma gave these men the sense of security they needed to use this communication system around the world and to make the coordination of attacks possible.

1. The three rotors of the day being inserted into a military (three-rotor) Enigma machine. Note the Umkehrwalz or reflector wheel contacts on the left and the contacts on the rotors being inserted. The keyboard is the standard QWERTZ and the light bulb keyboard above is where the enciphered letters appear. (Courtesy of the National Security Agency)

## The Enigma Machine

Enigma had emerged in the early 1920s as a wonder machine to protect commercial secrets: portable, flexible, highly secure, and relatively simple to use. Developed in 1918, the basic Enigma machine enciphered letters electromechanically. Although not at all as sophisticated as the personal computers of the 1980s and 1990s and not truly random in enciphering, these machines did develop an intricate cipher presenting an apparently astronomical number of possible combinations to daunt cryptanalysts working manually.[8] Given Enigma's near randomness, Germany's cryptologic experts assured the Wehrmacht that all the

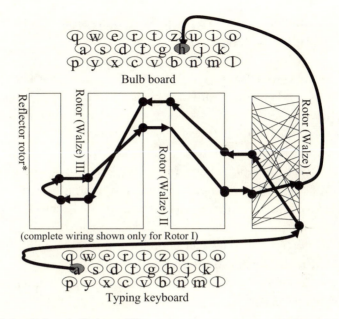

Bulb board

(complete wiring shown only for Rotor I)

Typing keyboard

* Note: Reflector rotor has only 13 wires, not 26.

BASIC ENIGMA WIRING DIAGRAM

This schematic of an unsteckered three-rotor Enigma machine shows a possible path created by pressing the letter "a" on the machine's keyboard. Pressing the "a" key sends an electric signal from the keyboard to the first ("fast") rotor or Walze at the first contact point. From there the signal travels along the rotor's internal wiring to exit at a contact corresponding to a different letter and across to the next rotor's contact.

The signal makes six more such connections, passing through rotors II, III, and the reflector and then back through III, II, and the original I. There it exits at the contact corresponding to "h" and so lights the "h" on the machine's bulb board.

The reflector rotor's thirteen wires ensure the machine enciphers and deciphers reciprocally because, for example, "j" will always connect to "f" and "f" to "j." In the standard rotors, if "j" connects to "f," "f" would not connect to "j," but rather to some third letter, so as to increase the cipher's apparent randomness. Note that after this signal's trip, the "fast" rotor would mechanically turn one step. Thus, the next time the operator pressed "a," the signal would travel a different path through rotor I (and hence through the other rotors), at the end, lighting up some letter other than "h." After twenty-six keys have been pressed, the second (medium) rotor would also turn. See later in text for other complications in the cipher's design.

usual statistical methods of cracking ciphers, such as letter frequency, would prove useless against Enigma.

Enigma had roughly the size and weight of a contemporary typewriter. It even looked a bit like a typewriter, with a regular keyboard in front and a parallel letter board of light bulbs on the top. The machine enciphered letters through a series of wires, rotors, and lights running on a battery. Each rotor had twenty-six pairs of contact points and pins, one for each letter, with internal wires connecting the letters at random. The rotors were placed on a rod with the pins of one rotor touching the contact points of the next. When the operator pressed a letter on the keyboard, an electric current passed from the keyboard to the rotors to the reversing or "reflector" rotor and back again through the rotors until it lit a light bulb under a letter on the top of the machine.[9] At least one of the rotors advanced a step each time the operator pressed a key. If the operator pressed the same letter more than once, a different cipher letter would light up each time. The first time "a" might become "p," the next time "i," the third time "b." Enigma, however, never enciphered a letter as itself, so "a," for example, would never light up the "a" on the bulb keyboard.

Enigma proved extremely flexible. Because the machine enciphered letter by letter, any word in any alphabetic language could be enciphered. (Numbers and punctuation presented an annoyance; radio signaling required that they be spelled out or given letter equivalents.) Enigma slowed down transmission of messages only by the time it took to set the machine's daily setting and to type and transcribe the plaintext and then its enciphered version. Once the radio operator had set the rotors and other variables at the beginning of the day (or whatever the setting's period), he had only to thumb the rotors to the proper starting place to begin enciphering or deciphering subsequent messages of the day.

For the 1920s, the commercial Enigma offered impressive statistical security. The original advertisement for the commercial Enigma from its Berlin manufacturer claimed that the sheer number of possible settings made the machine's ciphers impossible to crack. The commercial version created an apparently dynamic, ever-changing enciphering method with its electromechanical interchangeable rotors. These technological advances seemed to thwart such standard cryptanalytic techniques as letter frequency and brute force attacks (i.e., trying every possible combination). However, several cryptanalysts did break the original three-rotor, unsteckered commercial version, so militaries considered more sophisticated versions.[10]

The German military made numerous technological and procedural changes and upgrades to increase the machine's complexity and security. In the end, they would incorporate a range of devices from telephone plugs to electrical current alterations. Wilhelm Fenner, a chief cryptanalyst in the Wehrmacht's cipher service, "carried out the computation of the [Heer] Enigma, indicated the possibility of solution and made suggestions for the necessary improvement" to security.[11] Originally adopted by the Heer on 15 July 1928,[12] the military model of Enigma acquired a series of plugs, or Steckers, in a Steckerboard on the front of the machine. The Marine adopted the Steckerboard in 1934, as did the Luftwaffe.[13] After Fenner's changes, the Wehrmacht produced several variations of machines for the different sections of the military. These Enigma variations exploited both mechanical and procedural differences.

The mechanical differences depended on the number and type of interchangeable rotors, the Steckerboard, and eventually additional devices ranging from automatic printers to a range of devilish devices designed to scramble the letters further.[14] Before the war, all three services added two rotors (rotors IV and V) to the original three. Enigma originally held three drums at a time, chosen from the total five. The number of rotors increased to eight after the war began. During the war, the services would continue upgrading the machine. A procedural structure could include differing rotor sequences, daily settings and re-encipherment or "superenciperment,"[15] as well as additional settings for the various machine accessories.

The combination of mechanical and procedural variations produced the cipher "key." To set the machine for the first message of the day, an Enigma operator looked up the components of his key. He would first need to know which of the rotors to use for the day's basic setting (Grundstellung). Taking out the rotors for the day, he set the clip on each rotor's outer ring. (This clip adjusted the position of the notch causing the next rotor to progress.) He placed the rotors in the machine in a specified order. Then he inserted the Steckers in the correct pairings in the Steckerboard on the front of the machine. Later versions of Enigma would also require setting the Enigma Uhr, or a pluggable reflector rotor. The higher-grade Offizier signals required a superencipherment, or extra run through the Enigma on a different setting known only to command officers. Finally, having closed the windowed hatch over the rotors, the operator would select a random starting position for the rotors and encipher the resulting letters at the Grundstellung. He would then send the recipient the message indicator, the enciphered letters indicating the setting of the rotor wheels for beginning the message. This indicator changed with every signal sent.

To decipher a message, the receiving operator needed to set the machine up in precisely the same way, using the same rotor and Stecker settings. Then he set the rotors to the same starting position (denoted by the indicator) and began to type. Because of the machine's reciprocity, as he typed in the enciphered text, the plain text letters would light up on the bulb keyboard and the message slowly emerged.

Each cipher key connected a specific group of planes, U-boats, or units in a network.[16] Normally an Enigma-enciphered message remained within a network. At times, however, Berlin would send out a message to all troops, for example, Hitler's New Year's message, and so the same message would travel on several different nets. In theory, all the military services possessed the same five rotors[17] and could set their machines to the same basic setting to communicate with each other. (In practice, such communications usually went through command headquarters in Berlin.) The great number of keys, which expanded as the war grew, gave the Germans increased communications security. Each new key meant one more problem for the enemy cryptanalyst to battle. Simultaneously, the key proliferation decreased the traffic on each network and hence the chances for mistakes that could jeopardize the cipher.

## Physical Compromise Averted

With the improved military cipher machine in use, German cryptologic experts announced they had solved the vexing Great War problem of physical compromise. Even the basic three-rotor Wehrmacht Enigma had an almost inconceivable theoretical number of possible letter substitutions – $3 \times 10^{114}$ possible combinations. The true prevention of physical compromise stemmed, in German eyes, not just from their procedural precautions but from this statistical complexity. They had the universe on their side. One recent expert notes in comparison that "it is estimated that there are only about $10^{80}$ atoms in the entire observable universe. No wonder the German cryptographers had confidence in their machine!"[18] These men claimed the Allied cryptanalysts would only be able to break Enigma using pure statistical methods.[19] Because setting up the machine for each message required knowing so many variables, Enigma would not be compromised even if the enemy captured the machines. Possessing a machine would not help the enemy figure out which rotors, Steckers, or clip settings to use. Holding both the machine and the codebooks for the settings still required knowing the procedures for setting the daily key and the arrangements for each message. This huge number of statistical possibilities meant breaking a message by hand, or even with IBM or Hollerith punch card assistance, would not produce results in time for operational use.

Nonetheless the Wehrmacht's cryptologists considered the possibility of physical compromise. With thousands of Enigmas in service, they knew the enemy would capture the machines, their operators, and the attendant codebooks. To limit any insight into the machine that the enemy might gain, the Wehrmacht developed numerous safeguards.

The Wehrmacht first took steps to limit the physical compromise of Enigma. Foremost came the order to prevent functioning machines from falling into enemy hands in the first place. Presentations such as those at the German Naval Intelligence school impressed upon signal officers the danger of allowing Enigmas to fall to the enemy. All officers and radio operators had clear instructions to destroy the Enigma machines themselves when threatened with capture. Enigma manuals came with suggestions on the most effective methods for destroying the cipher machines when the enemy approached. The manual gave strongly worded and detailed instructions for disabling the machine. The machine's operator could burn the codebooks and wooden machine container using gasoline or petroleum. He could smash the pieces of the machine with rocks and bury part in the ground, part in a river. He could throw a grenade into the guts of the machine.[20] Under no circumstances was an operator to allow either a machine or its book of key settings to survive capture intact.

In spite of these often lurid guidelines, the Wehrmacht assumed that the occasional machine might fall into enemy hands and so planned accordingly. The Wehrmacht designed Grundstellungen, or basic settings, to contain any physical compromise of the machine. Each service changed their setting of the machine ever more frequently. During the 1930s, the basic settings had changed every three months, but eventually the Germans introduced new settings every month, then every day, and finally several times a day.

They designed changing codebooks, daily key settings, and indicator systems to limit the damage of any physical compromise through capture of machines and codebooks. In the event of suspected compromise, they developed emergency alterations, such as the rearrangement or shift of the daily settings. These would defeat an enemy reading Enigma by the fortuitous capture of all the cipher's elements: machines, codebooks, and procedural manuals.

Each service branch had its own method for creating the day's key, or Grundstellung. The Heer printed the components of their daily keys in monthly blocks, limiting the potential compromise to one month if both machine and settings were captured.[21] The Marine went one step further and printed Enigma monthly settings codebooks in water-soluble ink. The books themselves were to be thrown into the sea in weighted bags that would keep the sensitive materials from floating on the ocean surface into enemy hands.

All the services had emergency procedures designed to recover security after a physical compromise. In the Luftwaffe, "the usual practice upon a compromise is to use the reserve key, which is also the key for the following month." So, for example, when the Luftwaffe believed its primary key had been captured in July 1944, the key's users knew to substitute the settings for that month with the key originally designated for August.[22]

The Marine's method for containing a physical compromise relied on the "Stichwortbefehl" (keyword order). The "Stichwort" (keyword), known only to officers, served as an additive to the printed daily setting. If the Marine suspected the enemy had captured or compromised a key, headquarters issued the Stichwortbefehl, the order to move on to the next keyword additive. The officer would open a sealed envelope containing the new Stichwort, and all the compromised settings would change, effectively introducing a new monthly key at a moment's notice.[23]

Evidently the Wehrmacht command also feared enlisted men might tell their captors the procedures that governed the cipher systems. Enlisted radio operators had responsibility for only portions of the machine's daily setting. Several components needed to operate the machines remained (at least in theory) the purview of officers. Only officers knew the inner rotor settings of Enigma M.[24] Only officers knew the special commands used in cases of suspected compromise.

With these safeguards, German cryptologists insisted that Enigma dramatically reduced, indeed virtually eliminated, the dangers of physical compromise. Those who recognized that Enigma could theoretically be cracked believed even a cryptanalyst who reconstructed Enigma's mechanisms would need to test virtually all the machine's $3 \times 10^{114}$ combinations each time the setting was changed.[25] Such a process would take so long that the results would be worthless under the conditions of war. All of the German discussions of Enigma's security reiterate the cipher's strength in the face of statistical attacks.[26] The Wehrmacht command believed that for the enemy to read Enigma currently (in time to be useful), he would have to capture an intact Enigma machine, instructions for the machine's operation, and the current key settings. (Some experts believed Enigma so difficult that the enemy would be lost just by not knowing the secret of how the operator indicated the message settings at the beginning of each signal.[27])

Again and again, German experts insisted that the true prevention of physical compromise was Enigma's statistical complexity. Even if the enemy captured a complete machine and set of codebooks, the use of emergency keys or Stichwort alterations would end the enemy's advantage. Once the new settings went into effect, the enemy would again have to use trial-and-error to read the signals, an impossible task of testing millions of possibilities for every day on every key. The cryptologic experts insisted the possession of both a machine and a copy of a month's worth of daily key settings would allow the Allies to decipher no more than that month's Enigma messages. After the month ended, the enemy's cryptanalysts would have no further advantage. Thus any capture could offer the Allies only a short-term ability to read Enigma, not a permanent solution to the cipher machine. Physical possession of

Enigmas would not allow the enemy to read future Enigma-enciphered traffic.

The Wehrmacht continued to upgrade the Enigmas throughout the war. They increased the number of rotors that could be rotated into use from the original five (of which three could be used at one time) to eight. By 1942, the Marine developed a special Enigma for U-boat communications that allowed the use of four rotors at a time.[28]

Other innovations altered the rotors' movement or wiring with assorted devices designed to change the machine's drums at more random intervals. They developed a multinotched rotor that increased and varied the rotors' progression. In 1944, the Luftwaffe abruptly introduced the complicating device called the Uhr. The Uhr plugged into the machine's Steckerboard and altered the electrical current running through the plugs, creating an additional "40 (mostly non-reciprocal) Steckers... from the one plugged up for the day."[29]

The Heer created a pluggable reflector rotor, nicknamed Umkehrwalz Dora (or Uncle D in Bletchley's papers). With this development, the wirings within the reflector rotor could be completely redone with every signal, creating, in effect, multiple rotors in one. Unlike adding rotors or additional scramblers like the Uhr, the pluggable rotor could have removed all of Enigma's static qualities (except the initial connection from the keyboard). Reconstructing a rotor's inner wiring would become, if not impossible, certainly useless for future decipherment. The Umkehrwalz Dora proved impractical in the frontline conditions of the war's last year, however, and the Germans never fully exploited its potential.

The Wehrmacht appears to have considered these upgrades, along with increasingly frequent setting changes, necessary to stay ahead of potential decipherers. Through the last days of the war, all of the services continued to make changes and upgrades "which reduced and delayed decryption" and were considered sufficient for Enigma's security.[30]

Used correctly and judiciously, an Enigma will give even today's computers a challenge. In late 1944, as the Heer again tightened security and procedures, an Allied cryptanalyst called the resulting "horrors" yet more "ample confirmation of the view that the enigma machine, if properly handled, is unbreakable by any known methods."[31] The "astounding number" of possible configurations for the main three-rotor Enigma seemed enough protection itself. The Marine's four-rotor machine increased the number of theoretical combinations to $2 \times 10^{145}$.[32]

Theory, however, rarely translates directly to practice. Like other cipher machines (notably the Japanese "Purple"), Enigma's physical manifestation lowered the theoretical numbers by hardwiring in some of the choices. Among other limitations, each Enigma came with a single set of rotors, meaning that the operator could use only one of each rotor at a time. In the Marine's four-rotor machine, the fourth rotor had no notches, and so it could not move nor be interchanged with the other three rotors. The number of Umkehrwalze (reflector rotors) remained very small through the war and, in practice, added little to the machine's security. Even the promising pluggable Umkehrwalz, introduced late in the war, received only limited release in the Heer and Luftwaffe.

Even more limiting was the way in which the Germans operated Enigma. As with any cryptosystem, actual use put limits on the theoretical security a cryptologist calculates for the original design.[33] The restrictions placed on the Steckerboard, for example, diminished its complication. First, the Steckers substituted letters only in reciprocal pairs (A went to G and G to A). Second, the Enigma variations did not use Stecker pairs randomly but according to precise rules. In the Heer, the Inspektorate 7 staff's theoretical examination of the Enigma determined that ten pairings of Steckers produced the optimal variation.[34] So ten and only ten, neither more nor fewer, were used every day. Nor could Steckers ever link sequential letters. Thus sequential pairs (a and b or b and c) could be ruled out.[35]

With these and other restrictions, the number of possible configurations of the machine decreased significantly. One expert has calculated that, in practice, the number of combinations possible in the Enigma decreased from the truly astronomical number of the theory ($3 \times 10^{114}$) down to $1 \times 10^{23}$ – albeit still a daunting number.[36]

## Using Enigma

Throughout the war, Enigma and superenciphered Enigma served as the Wehrmacht's worldwide high-grade machine, the equivalent of, say,

Britain's Typex or the American Sigaba. Wehrmacht operations relied heavily on the confidentiality supplied by Enigma. Enigma machines allowed Großadmiral Karl Dönitz, Feldmarschall Hermann Göring, and Generals von Rundstedt, Keitel, and Jodl to control their widely dispersed troops directly and secretly through frequent radio contact. The secret signals furnished by Enigma allowed nearly constant control of the battle from centralized headquarters behind the lines. Using Enigma ciphers, Hitler both dispensed and required constant communiqués from his Heer generals. The signaling increased as Hitler insisted on centralizing the command of the fighting more and more as the war progressed.

In the Marine, the logistics of the wolfpack system required Admiral Dönitz's coordination of the U-boats from his headquarters and obliged the U-boat commanders to signal frequently during their sea voyages. This ability to signal (with what the Germans believed to be almost total security) fit their system of a strong vertical hierarchy. Enigma allowed them their organization and order, which to the Wehrmacht meant "laying fixed lines to the leadership, limiting assignments both above and below, and establishing the accountability."[37] Großadmiral Karl Dönitz retained direct control of the U-boat arm even after his ascent to head of the entire Marine. He sent countless signals to his U-boat commanders, frequently directing "Admonitions" and morale-boosting pronouncements to his entire U-boat fleet.

Enigma made signaling relatively easy. The most difficult aspect of setting the machine came at the beginning of each day, when the day's key had to be set, the rotors changed, the rotor clips or notches adjusted, and the plugs inserted. Once the rotors, clips, and Steckers had been arranged, enciphering a signal was not much more difficult or time consuming than typing it once more on a typewriter. Wehrmacht officers found the machine so convenient, so portable, that they could not bring themselves to reserve the machine for only high-grade (secret) traffic. Instead, Enigma carried all grades of messages, from New Year's greetings and routine supply reports and requests to virtually all U-boat orders and Heer commands' daily situation reports.[38]

Most network controllers required each of their attached units to report in every day, usually just after the daily key changed. With this "check-in" the most time-consuming element of the machine, setting the machine to the daily key, had been done. Any subsequent messages sent would require creating only the individual message indicator before typing in the plaintext, far less effort than setting the daily key or even dealing with an incoming message. Longer messages demanded little more effort than very brief signals. Enigma's advantages of ease and speed allowed signalers to be verbose and repetitive. With such a useable system, Germans employed Enigma more than was prudent.

With every additional signal came an increased chance for revealing vital information to the enemy. Wehrmacht signals encrypted with Enigma cover a large swath of the war. They came from nearly every front, covering issues of supply, intelligence, strategy, weather, personnel, bombing results, and even, briefly, death camps.[39] Some Enigma signals mentioned only the most routine aspects of fighting – daily reports on weather, fuel consumption, and the numbers of planes in service and undergoing repairs. Such routine signals are more likely to create good conditions for compromise, especially those using similar numbers on a daily basis. Routine signals often appear at the same time of day, from the same station, to the same recipient, and reporting the same type of information. Repetitive routine, particularly of mundane details, tends to lull the sender into complacency. At the same time the signals' very repetition makes them, their sender, and their contents familiar to the enemy cryptanalyst. The cryptanalyst becomes able to make rather accurate educated guesses as to a routine signal's actual content, in other words, a crib. These cribs will give him an obvious point of reentry after each change of the daily key.

In addition to these routine signals, Enigma traffic carried the highest-grade information between admirals, field marshals, and Hitler. Enigma signals even carried intelligence derived from decrypts of enemy signals. These very high-grade signals usually required an additional encipherment of some kind, known only to officers. None of these so-called superencipherments were more sophisticated than Enigma itself; indeed, some of them consisted simply of an extra enciphering on Enigma. Such a superencipherment still used the same basic rotors with the identical wiring that any other Enigma setting might use. Thus the highest-grade traffic traveled on essentially the same cipher system as the routine supply reports. Using the same system for both types of messages made high-grade signals needlessly vulnerable. If the enemy cryptanalyst could get a series of cribs based on daily supply summaries or fuel consumption reports, he could probably break into the highest-level material as well.

With the growing complexity and scope of the war, enciphered signaling mushroomed. Every day thousands of radio signals connected headquarters in Berlin, Paris, East Prussia, and Bavaria with U-boats, planes, panzers, and infantry units. To sustain cipher security, the Germans followed the standard cryptographic practice of increasing the number of keys. German intelligence believed (in large part correctly) that if only a limited number of messages were sent in a single key, the enemy would find any cipher impossible to crack. The various service branches began developing separate keys for nearly every division, every front, and every different type of unit (U-boats, raiders, heavy cruisers, and so forth), as well as for the different types and grades of signal traffic.

This ongoing division did increase the security of certain Enigma keys. By multiplying the cipher keys, the number of signals sent in a single key decreased, offering any cryptanalyst less material to work on. Moreover, separating, say, the U-boat cipher from that of the surface ships, divided the enemy cryptanalysts' interest, forcing them to attack two ciphers rather than one.

The increase in keys had one major drawback: repetition. If multiple keys carried the same text, cryptanalysts could use a break into one of these keys to crack any other key that carried the same original text. Often, the same information simply must go to a wide range of recipients. When such repetition on several keys is necessary, the standard solution calls for paraphrasing, rewriting the original language to change the actual words as well as the length of the message. Increasing the number of keys meant increasing vigilance against giving the enemy cribs, or repetitive phrases, which he could use to break into a cipher.

The Wehrmacht took other basic signaling security steps. Regulations required all cipher errors be reported to intelligence headquarters, where experts would then determine whether the mistake could have compromised Enigma. They instructed their signalers in standard security procedures and developed additional security for signaling, such as complex changing call-sign allocations for every station.

All of the German commanders seem to have recognized the importance of judicious radio use. Radio and cipher manuals were stamped with the warning "Feind Hört Mit!" (The enemy listens with you!) in dark capital letters. Official reminders included cautionary tales of soldiers whose idle radio chitchat or failure to observe proper procedure had exposed their units to attack.[40]

In theory, signaling was to be kept to a minimum. Instruction manuals strictly limited the length of signals and repeatedly emphasized the importance of restricting messages. Germans recognized radio silence as a central tenet of signal security; yet, the Wehrmacht branches could not bring themselves to observe it rigorously.[41] In practice, this basic safeguard received little attention from either the central commands or the frontline commanders. Occasionally, the various commands reiterated the importance of limiting the number and length of radio signals. As the Allied D/F locating ability appeared increasingly effective, the U-boat command called for a reduction in radio transmissions and did in fact decrease both the length and number of signals. The Germans maintained that more frequent changes of the ciphers' key settings also offset the problem of frequent signaling, but widespread adherence to centralized command largely negated the advantage of multiple ciphers. This widespread, almost continuous, use of Enigma made the cipher system increasingly vulnerable.

## Enigma's "Software" Problems

Enigma's security diminished in the hands of German cipher clerks and machine operators. These men made choices and rules for setting the machine and for creating and sending signals which greatly reduced Enigma's theoretical strengths. These regulations would make the entire cipher system vulnerable to the enemy's cryptanalysts.

When beginning a message an Enigma operator chose the starting point for the three rotors. This three-letter "message indicator" was unique to each message. The first and most devastating mistakes German procedures made with the indicators was to encipher these indicators at the same starting point (or Grundstellung) for each message and to encipher them twice. This double encipherment led to the initial break made by the Polish mathematicians in the 1930s. By 1940, most of the Enigma nets had dropped the double encipherment, but some, including a four-rotor Enigma net, continued to use the procedure for years. Sending the indicators in the clear would have given enemy cryptanalysts less of an entry into the machine's inner workings than the double encipherment allowed.[42]

Enigma's operators were supposed to choose "random" settings for their message indicators, but they often resorted to patterns such as three letters touching on the keyboard, either across the "qwertz" or along diagonals (the British nicknamed these patterns "cillies"). Some operators fell into the bad habit of choosing their girlfriends' or movie stars' initials.[43] Some service procedures attempted to cut down on human tendency toward repetition but merely eliminated one type of limitation while creating another. Certain Enigma keys, for example, restricted daily settings to including a particular plug or rotor combination only once in a month, meaning once it had been used, cryptanalysts knew it would not be a possibility for the month's remainder. In other cases, a rotor could never appear in the same position two days running or until all the other rotors had been used in that position.[44]

Clerks creating the blocks of daily settings got lazy in the course of the long war. Eventually, they began reprinting some portion of settings from previous months, say, the Stecker settings from January 1940 and the rotor order from September 1941. An enemy eagle eye, keeping careful track, could spot the reprints within a few days.[45] Some groups of nets even developed patterns of using one net's daily setting on a second net in the next month, while the second net's old settings moved to a third net. One such "quadrilateral" pattern regularly rotated the key's components (rotor order, Stecker pairings, Ringstellung or ring setting) between the same four networks for several months.[46]

Even more damaging than these patterns for daily settings were the patterns of and within signals which led to cribs. Every military uses a stereotyped language at least vaguely familiar to other militaries. Every signal has an addressee, a salutation, and a signature of some kind. Every officer must address his superiors and subordinates appropriately. German salutations and signatures were particularly long in number of letters and the language quite stereotyped. When these elements of a message always appear at the beginning or end of signals, they create excellent cribs. The security procedure of burying addresses makes finding cribs more difficult for enemy cryptanalysts. For much of the war, only the police moved these salutations from the beginning and signatures from the end of messages and buried them in the middle.[47] Only in 1943 did other Enigma networks begin adopting this practice as well.[48]

As the war dragged on, reports back to headquarters tended to fall into the same pattern. Orders for supplies, for reinforcements, for coordinated movements, all followed a predictable model increasingly familiar to the enemy. If the internal text of signals is not rearranged, if the address and signature are not buried somewhere in the middle of the message, any enemy analyst conversant with the standard order of battle and procedures could guess at least the beginning and ending of an encrypted signal. Thus the human tendency toward patterns and the familiar proved Enigma's greatest threat.

## Cryptographic Cooperation

Mechanical enciphering in the form of Enigma had provided the various German cryptologic agencies with common ground. The myriad segments of the sometimes fractious Wehrmacht all recognized the importance of swift and secure communications. To this end, all three branches of the Wehrmacht had adopted a version of the Enigma cipher machine early on. The machine drew them together.

With the adoption of Enigma for all the military branches, the Germans had begun correcting one of the worst faults in the cryptology of the great powers: total lack of cooperation. The use of Enigma forced the various branches of the Wehrmacht to cooperate in cryptography. After the original adoption of Enigma, the machine came to handle high-level messages in various versions for all the branches of the Wehrmacht and several arms of the Nazi Party by 1935. Once the entire military had some version of Enigma, the different branches and agencies could easily communicate with each other.

The Germans were so pleased with the ease and flexibility of the portable cipher system that they eventually created additional variations for communication with their allies in war – Japan and Italy.[49] Thousands of machines were issued in every theater of the war. Their relatively small size and light weight meant they could be carried by panzers and airplanes, infantry and small motorized units, in addition to U-boats and large ships. The machine's design flexibility permitted a complex system with different nets using the same machine: the same machine could be used for a message from within a single service branch, and then the rotors could be reset to encrypt or decrypt an all-Wehrmacht signal. The Marine four-rotor Enigma could mimic a three-rotor and thus both receive signals from and send signals to the Heer and Luftwaffe. This versatility allowed the Heer to coordinate its advances with the Luftwaffe's bombers and reconnaissance planes, the Luftwaffe's escorting squadrons to maintain contact with the Marine's supply convoys, and the Marine to supply the other services with its vital weather reports.

The interservice communication facilitated by Enigma meant the enemy could learn about movements and operations of one Wehrmacht service from another. The signals intelligence branches in Germany, however, preferred to think of themselves as entirely separate divisions. Beyond the use of Enigma, they rarely joined forces in either cryptography or cryptanalysis. When the Marine, for example, investigated the security of Enigma M, no one appears to have considered signals from other services as a possible source of compromise. Yet cribs and other information that assisted Bletchley cryptanalysts in breaking Porpoise, the Marine's key for the Mediterranean theater, came not from other Marine sources but from Gadfly, the key for Luftwaffenkommando Südost (Balkans).[50] Wehrmacht officers failed to recognize that by sharing a single cryptologic system, they shared the risk of enemy decryption.

## One Giant Leap Leads to Stagnation

Enigma revolutionized communication in the German military. Flexible, portable, reasonably rapid, and easy to use, the machine allowed various units an apparently secure means to coordinate their operations under conditions of rapid, mobile warfare. With Enigma, the Wehrmacht jumped beyond other powers of the early 1930s in protecting their communications system and creating cryptography that allowed extensive exploitation of radio.

Enigma's initial set of rotors went into operation in the late 1920s. These first three rotors continued in use through May 1945; they were neither replaced nor rewired. In all their upgrades to Enigma, none of the Wehrmacht branches recalled these earliest rotors. They merely added to the original set. Thus once the Poles had reconstructed the original rotors in 1932, they, and later the British, always had a partial solution of the machine's internal wirings to aid in finding the solution to new rotors.

Not that the Germans relaxed their cipher security. They constantly admonished radio and cipher machine operators. Even in the last months of the war, they devised new additions to the machine and added complications for the daily settings. They continued upgrades to the machine, such as the daunting pluggable Umkehrwalz D. Through the last chaotic months of the war, the Wehrmacht expended, as Bletchley Park commented, "remarkable energy and ingenuity over the whole field of cypher security, including … W/T signals procedure." Security procedures increased. The Heer and Luftwaffe, in particular, tightened security by altering encipherment in the middle of the message and supplying operators with random indicators rather than allowing them to choose their own.[51] These upgrades continued to threaten the success of Allied cryptanalysts right to the last weeks of the war.[52]

In the end, the changes and upgrades made in German cryptography between 1930 and the early 1940s were only small steps. The general adoption of the Steckerboard in the mid-1930s drastically changed the way the machine functioned. Only the introduction of the pluggable reflector rotor would appear as fundamental to Bletchley's cryptanalysts. The other changes really can be lumped together as upgrades, lesser modifications rather than true alterations to the machine.

Those changes and upgrades which the Wehrmacht made came in piecemeal. In virtually every case, before the upgrade went into effect, the entire network would receive word of the new rotor, encoding system, or procedural change over Enigma. The unintended recipients – cryptanalysts breaking Enigma signals at Bletchley Park – also received the warnings for upgrades.[53]

Although they were not on the distribution list for the new material, Bletchley's cryptanalysts would know when the change would happen, which Enigma users were likely to be affected, and what type of change was being made. The upgrades would only affect some nets, leaving the remainder untouched. The unaffected traffic would then assist Bletchley Park's cryptanalysts to break into the nets with the upgrades and thus unravel the wiring of a new rotor, reconstruct a new indicator procedure, or decrypt a new internal code. Rarely did more than one alteration go into effect at the same time. Usually a network or service branch introduced one change at a time, giving Bletchley Park time to focus on a single new problem before addressing the next one.

For example, message indicators had been a rich source for breaks into Enigma from the beginning. Only in late 1944 did the Heer introduce a new procedure, which "effectively [prevented] cillies, psillies and other entries [into Enigma] resulting from bad habits." This late in the cryptologic war, the upgrade did "not constitute any great loss at this stage. Of course, if this type of security measure had been taken a few years [earlier] it would have been quite a different story." By 1944, cillies had already become rare; hence, Bletchley Park had already found other breaks into the Enigma nets.[54]

Such delayed and piecemeal introduction drastically undercut the impact of the upgrades and changes. Had the Wehrmacht initiated several changes all at once – the additional rotors, new indicator methods, and the more secure operating procedures – Bletchley might well have lost their grip on Enigma.

In the early 1930s, German military cryptography had stood a giant leap ahead of its British and American counterparts. Its signal corps had tossed out their cumbersome book codes for most traffic and could now rely on a far more modern technology using electricity and moving gears. They had made a shift in thinking and in practice that Britain would not match for years.[55] Enigma had created a single unified cryptographic system for the Germans, allowing them the flexibility they would use to such effect in the invasions of 1939, 1940, and 1941. The Wehrmacht, however, would not capitalize on this advantage. The upgrades they introduced lost much, if not all, of their effectiveness through disjointed adoption. Operational and procedural mistakes counteracted the potency of advanced technologies, such as the Steckerboard, the Uhr, and the pluggable rotor (Umkehrwalz D). Moreover, German signals intelligence officers would fail to realize that unifying their cryptography required unifying their cryptographic security and their cryptanalysis system. Instead, their cryptologists would operate in isolated, fragmented, and decentralized pockets and consequently their progress in cryptology – both cryptanalytic and cryptographic – would stagnate.

TWO

# EARLY TRIUMPH

## German Intelligence Successes

... it was the precision of the work of the cryptanalysts, their diligence, and the speed with which current tasks were disposed of and every inquiry, even apparently unimportant ones, were answered, which gave the cryptanalytic section of the Chi the dominant position which it enjoyed for two decades.

– Wilhelm Fenner, head of OKW/Chi's Main Group B in his
report to Allied interrogators, 1946

Signals intelligence would have failed its purpose, if it had not also attempted, by reason of experience, to influence its own intelligence service and particularly the cipher material.... The beginnings of this influence, in our [the Marine's] case, goes back to the time of the First World War.

– Captain Heinz Bonatz, head of Marine sigint November 1941
to January 1944[1]

When a young Wehrmacht signals officer sat down at his Enigma machine and began the day's enciphering, he followed procedures designed by men far from the front lines. These men served as cryptologists in the various signals intelligence agencies and had helped propel German cryptography into the electromechanical age. They had examined various ciphering methods and settled on cipher machines as the best option. Once Enigma had been adopted, each individual cryptologic bureau had responsibility for its cipher variation's physical and cryptologic security.

In addition to this defensive duty, these bureaus had the offensive task of providing the branches of the Wehrmacht with signals intelligence from their enemies' cipher systems. Their experiences with the enemy's systems would influence their perception of Enigma's security. Moreover, the culture, structure, and priorities of their organizations would determine how they addressed problems of security and potential compromise. These organizations, their structure and culture, shaped the questions, investigations, and answers German cryptologists produced and determined the course of the signals intelligence war, its successes, and its failures.

As war approached, these intelligence bureaus had the key task of providing rapid tactical intelligence. For the offensive, rapid "blitzkrieg" Hitler planned, the Wehrmacht needed information about the enemy's strengths and tactics. The Heer, Marine, and Luftwaffe all wanted to know their potential enemies' numbers and position, their weapons capability, their order of battle. Longer-term, strategic intelligence held less interest for Wehrmacht commanders, as they planned to steamroll over their opponents with superior weapons and superior soldiers. Hitler also had little interest in long-term intelligence, instead relying on the intuition of his genius for strategic decisions. From the top down, then, the information demanded was tactical intelligence.

The service branches emphasized attacking "low-grade codes...such as the French tactical code, the Code Aeronautique and the Danish lightship code."[2] Such a focus makes sense for a military on the offense. High-grade cipher systems will carry generals' discussions and might reveal large-scale movements and long-term intentions. However, higher-grade systems are usually much harder to break, making the effort more costly in both time and resources. Tactical intelligence, on the other hand, comes from such sources as the interrogation of POWs and solution of low- and medium-grade cryptographic systems. This lower-grade intelligence provides the type of information that will have immediate and tangible results: the enemy's morale, supply situation, production capability, and current intentions and positions, and the weather.

To provide this tactical intelligence, each of the signals intelligence bureaus assumed autonomy over the intelligence of its enemy counterparts and developed a focused expertise in their own service branch's needs and targets. The military shaped their organizations to meet these goals, and the resulting bureaus found considerable success.

At the end of the Great War in 1918, Germany's signals intelligence lay in ruins.[3] The Inter-Allied Armistice Commission, created by the Versailles Treaty, had dissolved the old intelligence service and forbade Germany to develop cryptanalysis capabilities. The Commission allowed the fledgling democracy only an "Abwehr," a purely defensive, counterespionage organization, not an offensive, military intelligence organization. The cryptologic work allowed the Germans was restricted to their own codes and ciphers.[4] By 1920, "the total strength of the central office of the German intercept service" fell to twelve people,[5] insufficient to monitor even a small portion of the domestic and foreign frequencies of interest.

Slowly the tide turned. In the two decades following the First World War, German intelligence accomplished a dramatic reversal of fortune. Within a few years Germany had developed ways of evading the Armistice Commission's restrictions. Although all "unauthorized decipherment of foreign cryptographic systems was forbidden by the Inter-allied Military Control Commission,"[6] a disguised signals bureau did intercept and attempt to decipher foreign traffic.

In the early 1930s, Adolf Hitler rose to power with the support of the traditionally conservative German military, support he gained in large part through promises to restore Germany's military strength. Willing to defy the Versailles Treaty openly, the Führer directed Germany's resources to her meager military. Services and departments banned under the Treaty – such as the Luftwaffe and the U-boat division of the Marine – began to flourish. Intelligence benefitted considerably from this expansion.[7] In addition, the Wehrmacht had recreated its Chiffrierabteilung (Cipher Bureau), which had responsibility for translating and distributing "intercepted [foreign] propaganda radio traffic ... [and foreign military] ciphered traffic."[8] By the mid-1930s, the German military branches had all adopted the Enigma machine to secure their main communications nets. They had also begun expanding their signals intelligence and cryptologic operations.

By 1939, Germany had a successful intelligence service. Secretly, cryptanalysts in the Auswärtiges Amt (Foreign Office) could assure Hitler of British and French intentions through reading their diplomatic signals.[9] Like some other Wehrmacht elements, the sigint bureaus had acquired useful practice in the Spanish Civil War. Publicly, German counterintelligence had recently embarrassed the renowned British Secret Service by kidnapping two high-level British officers investigating in the Netherlands. This "Venlo Affair" had shaken Europe's capitals with its demonstration of the reach of Germany's agent network.

At the outbreak of the war, German cryptologic successes equaled or surpassed those of its enemies. In both the cryptanalytic and cryptographic sides of cryptology, the Germans had reason to feel confident. Cryptanalytically, the various intelligence agencies had a good grasp of their enemy's order of battle and frontline communications. Through the late 1930s, the various German intelligence agencies had been reading the codes and ciphers of each of their potential enemies, as well as some of their friends. In particular, the Wehrmacht began the war with several sources of information on British and French positions and intentions. Early in the war, Axis intelligence could decrypt the French-British Inter-Allied cipher.[10] During the war, the Germans stole American diplomatic codes used from Rome, infiltrated the British embassy in Ankara, Turkey, and regularly read even some of the Soviets' relatively sophisticated ciphers.

Cryptographically, German communications experts were certain they had a comprehensive signals network more rapid and secure than any of their enemies had. Expanding on the early radio use of the Great War, Germany's signalers now had a large network for communications between units and back to headquarters. Signals crossed the network under the protection not of vulnerable codebooks but rather of the Enigma machine. With new signals and cipher technologies and a new kind of warfare, Germany's sigint bureaus vowed not to repeat their predecessors' failure. They would make certain their cryptologic operations proved more effective and secure in the next war.

## Separate and Specialized

Effective signals intelligence equaled specialized expertise for these bureaus. Sigint divided and decentralized throughout the three military branches, as well as several civilian departments, each with its own cryptologic section. The Heer, Marine, and Luftwaffe built up their own signals services alongside those of the military and police branches of the Nazi Party (the SS, the SD, and the Gestapo). Although military cryptology was theoretically the Wehrmacht Chiffrierabteilung's [OKW/Chi] responsibility, the three military branches operated almost completely independently. The Wehrmacht's inclination toward tactical intelligence reinforced the compartmentalization of signals intelligence. Each bureau operated autonomously and focused on its own immediate needs. The priorities of its parent organization, whether the Heer's focus on the east or the Marine's worldwide U-boat struggle, shaped the sigint organizations themselves. Each grew and formed to meet the specific needs of its own service branch and, more particularly, the regional units it served.

Perhaps naturally, the three service branches saw their intelligence interests and expertise as largely independent of the others'. Each sigint bureau focused on its counterparts in the enemies' militaries. Ordinarily a bureau would give these multiple enemy targets a priority and assign each one resources and effort according to the target's importance for its own branch. Thus the Marine ranked the British Royal Navy as its greatest threat and the Heer viewed the British army – with reason – as little threat. Marine records have little discussion of Russian targets, whereas the Heer sensibly devoted its greatest attention to the Soviet Union. Moreover, the military sigint agencies did not devote effort to gathering intelligence on any enemy military organizations except their direct counterparts.

The German civilian and Nazi Party organizations had a similar view of their needs. Nearly all of them adopted Enigma for their radio communications (with the notable exception of the Auswärtiges Amt) and nearly all created their own departments to intercept and interpret enemy signals. By the outbreak of war, Germany had a profusion of intercept organizations, even more than the United States:

> With the High Command of the Armed Forces [OKW], with the High Command of the Army [OKH]...the Air Force [OKL]...the Navy [OKM], with the [Luftwaffe's] Forschungsamt, with the Security Service [SD], with the Ministry of the Interior, with the Police, with the Ministry of Propaganda, with the Foreign Office [Auswärtiges Amt] and with a whole string of other agencies and offices.[11]

In all, eight agencies performed cryptanalysis, largely independently of each other. Three departments remained under technically "civilian"

# German Sigint Organization

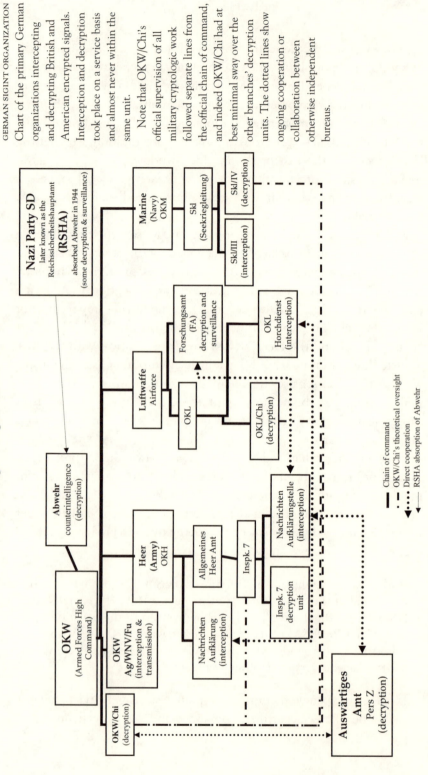

GERMAN SIGINT ORGANIZATION
Chart of the primary German organizations intercepting and decrypting British and American encrypted signals. Interception and decryption took place on a service basis and almost never within the same unit.

Note that OKW/Chi's official supervision of all military cryptologic work followed separate lines from the official chain of command, and indeed OKW/Chi had at best minimal sway over the other branches' decryption units. The dotted lines show ongoing cooperation or collaboration between otherwise independent bureaus.

**Nazi Party SD**
later known as the Reichssicherheitshauptamt **(RSHA)**
absorbed Abwehr in 1944
(some decryption & surveillance)

**Marine** (Navy) OKM
Skl (Seekriegsleitung)
Skl/III (interception)
Skl/IV (decryption)

Forschungsamt (FA) decryption and surveillance

**Luftwaffe** Airforce
OKL
OKL Horchdienst (interception)
OKL/Chi (decryption)

**Abwehr** counterintelligence (decryption)

**OKW** (Armed Forces High Command)
OKW Ag/WNV/Fu (interception & transmission)
OKW/Chi (decryption)

**Heer** (Army) OKH
Allgemeines Heer Amt
Inspk. 7
Inspk. 7 decryption unit
Nachrichten Aufklärung (interception)
Nachrichten Aufklärungstelle (interception)

**Auswärtiges Amt** Pers Z (decryption)

Chain of command
OKW/Chi's theoretical oversight
Direct cooperation
RSHA absorption of Abwehr

*Sources: NARA: RG 457 HCC Box 1327 NR 4003 Organization of GermanCommunications Intelligence Command; Box 1098 NR 3454 Some Details of the German Intercept Service.*

control, the Auswärtiges Amt (AA), the Reichssicherheitshauptamt (RSHA),[12] and Hermann Göring's "personal" Forschungsamt (Research Bureau). The military had five organizations: the OKW/Chi[13] (Chiffrierabteilung [cipher bureau] of the Wehrmacht), the Abwehr, the Heer's Inspektorate 7 (Inspk. 7), the Marine's B-Dienst (Beobachtung or Observation Service), and the OKL's (Air Force High Command's) Chi-Stelle.[14] The RSHA and the Abwehr focused on agents and counterintelligence rather than military signals intelligence and cryptanalysis. The remaining agencies, broadly speaking, targeted their enemy counterparts, focusing their expertise narrowly.

In the civilian arena, the predominant agency for attacking diplomatic enemy systems operated in the Auswärtiges Amt as the "Sonderdienst Pers. Z."[15] Pers Z made the usual division of personnel and work by national language, each group having a leader with technical and statistical assistants. Pers Z would succeed in reading many diplomatic ciphers, including some Japanese, British, and Italian systems.[16] Both during and after the war, members of Pers Z took great pride in the security and sophistication of their own ciphers as well as in their successes against foreign diplomatic systems.[17]

Whereas agents and counterintelligence remained the province of the (more famous) Abwehr, by 1939 OKW/Chi had jurisdiction over the entire military effort attacking enemy codes and ciphers.[18] OKW/Chi had ultimate responsibility for the monitoring of enemy radio communications and the "breaking and evaluation of codes and ciphers."[19] OKW/Chi was, at least in theory, supervising all the service branches' cryptanalytic efforts against all enemy military systems. The OKW/Chi also had responsibility for overseeing the cryptographic development of its own systems. This charge included developing all German military codes and ciphers.

## Decentralization

In practice, neither intelligence nor, more specifically, signals intelligence, had a central home. The German military's emphasis on tactical intelligence reinforced compartmentalization by service arm as well as by geography and similar delineations. The B-Dienst "worked with very few exceptions only on foreign naval messages" and assumed that little in the signals of any other armed forces branch would have relevance to their own branch.[20] The Heer and Luftwaffe likewise concentrated on their counterparts.

The signals intelligence bureaus reinforced their separation geographically.[21] The Marine, claiming it needed to protect its independence, moved its interception and decipherment section, the B-Dienst, from Berlin to its main submarine base in Kiel on the Baltic coast. While OKW/Chi remained in Berlin until the last days of the war, the other services moved more than once. After the Barbarossa invasion of the Soviet Union in June 1941, "the [Luftwaffe's] entire Chiffrier-Stelle ObdL moved its headquarters to East Prussia."[22] Moving closer to the front made sense as the fighting swiftly moved deep into Russia. The Chiffrier-Stelle needed greater proximity to the enemy's airfields to boost interception clarity and to speed decryption.

Decentralization extended down into the separate branch organizations as well. In the Heer, signals intelligence separated into two pieces: "Foreign Armies East" and "Foreign Armies West." The former concentrated on the Soviet Union, while the latter had responsibility for England, France, and the United States, in addition to numerous smaller countries. The two divisions communicated with each other only rarely.[23]

Interception of enemy signals also remained dispersed, although OKW/Chi officially served as "the control point for the entire intercept service of the armed forces." The OKW and OKH theoretically coordinated their interception, but the intercept systems of the Marine and of the Luftwaffe each operated completely independently. The Luftwaffe intercept stations reported to their own main station, called "W-LEIT" on the western front.[24] All the Marine station intercepts went to its own intelligence section, the B-Dienst. The separate receiving stations knew not to intercept signals from the "incorrect" divisions of foreign forces. If OKW/Chi stations "erroneously" intercepted foreign naval signals, the messages were "automatically turned over to 'M' [Marine intelligence] forthwith . . . while 'M' did the same with diplomatic messages."[25] Straying into another service's purview was discouraged.

In the Heer, intercept direction operated around divisional needs rather than centralized strategy. Each Heer division had intercept units assigned to it. These units reported "all messages believed to have any importance"[26] up the chain of command from small intercept units to regional headquarters, which, in turn, passed intelligence to headquarters in Berlin. In western Europe, the regional headquarters was NAAST 5 (Nachrichten Aufklärungs Auswertestelle [Heer Group Intercept Evaluation Unit] 5) in Paris.[27] These and the permanent signals intelligence stations worked independently. Copies of intercepted signals went to both the NAAST and the Berlin office (Inspk. 7/IV), which worked on the encrypted messages simultaneously.[28] The chief intelligence officer could then quickly broadcast the resulting information directly, down to the division level. Such a system clearly serves tactical needs well: all the staff concentrate on producing rapid results from the richest material available and swiftly disseminating everything with potential immediate benefit.

For each of the services, the majority of signals staff employed worked in outposts or in the field rather than in the main office. The Luftwaffe had hundreds of codebreakers, mostly at these outposts, concentrating on rapid reading of low-grade codes.[29] Smaller numbers of staff worked as "evaluators" or analysts and fewer still worked on traffic analysis. Again the bulk of these worked at outstations rather than in Berlin.[30] This structure and distribution of personnel suited the emphasis on tactical decryption and success against field systems that the Wehrmacht favored. Some outposts garnered accolades for their successes. In the North African theater, the head of General Rommel's radio monitoring company, Lt. Seebohm, attacked primarily British systems. He designed streamlined procedures for passing decrypted "intercepts direct to the C-in-C, his operations staff and the troops concerned."[31] Rommel attributed much of his stunning success against the British Eighth Army to the valuable information which this swift, efficient operation brought him.

Like the Heer, the Luftwaffe had a bifurcated intelligence organization. Luftwaffe chief Hermann Göring had under him two intelligence branches: the Forschungsamt (FA) and an OKL (Air Force High Command) Chiffrier-Stelle. Göring had created the Forschungsamt

(Research Bureau), a more political than military agency reporting to him and monitoring domestic communications as well as foreign propaganda. The FA concerned itself with foreign diplomatic codes and ciphers rather than with military ones.[32] It expended considerable resources maintaining various types of surveillance on the "German industrial establishments," as well as on nearly all the high-level Nazi Party members.[33] The FA alone had over fifteen different divisions, responsible for everything from national security (literally internal evaluation) and German economic problems to decryption and intelligence evaluation.[34]

From the beginning, the Luftwaffe High Command "resolved to make itself entirely independent of the army in this field [cryptology]."[35] One Luftwaffe officer explained after the war that OKL Chi-Stelle operated with only limited control from OKW. "OKL had their own special stores and equipment organization. OKW had no control over OKL [communication] circuits."[36] The OKL's Chi even arranged its own independent collaboration with the Finnish and Hungarian signals intelligence agencies.[37]

Internally, the OKL took the Heer model even further and decentralized by geography and division. Much of the decryption work took place at the intercept "outstations" scattered around Europe, particularly on the Eastern Front. "Each outstation also had its subordinate stations . . . manned by [intercept] operators and a few cryptanalysts and evaluators."[38]

OKL divided cryptologic responsibility among its stations by region. On the Eastern Front, each station had an assigned area in which it held responsibility for working on the Soviet air force's associated codes and cryptographic systems. "Only [Soviet] units lying at the intersection of the areas of two outstations were worked by both outstations." None of these stations could see the big picture of all the Eastern Front's cipher nets, although the central Chi-Stelle had responsibility for these stations and served "as the court of final appeal . . . for the entire [OKL] intercept service in the East."[39]

Unlike the Heer and Luftwaffe, the Marine created a smaller, tightly centralized signals intelligence agency. All of its intercept stations reported back directly to its B-Dienst, based originally in Kiel.

Throughout its existence, the Marine's B-Dienst had between one and three "outstations" that tackled low-grade cryptanalysis on the spot. These stations produced both daily and bimonthly reports for headquarters.[40] The remainder of Marine cryptanalysis took place at the main office. By 1939, the B-Dienst was focusing its attention on the Royal (and later the American) Navy. After the war broke out, the Marine centralized its cryptanalysis in X-B-Dienst and separated it from the regular B-Dienst for greater security.[41] This concentration of effort in the Marine signals intelligence would produce several successes against its primary targets throughout the first half of the war.

## Creating Expertise

This decentralization of signals intelligence by service arm and region stemmed in part from the Wehrmacht's emphasis on tactical intelligence. The compartmentalization also arose from each service arm's emphasis on creating expertise in its own area. By limiting its focus to its own service, each bureau could concentrate on evolving an expertise. Further dividing decryption sections along target country lines allowed cryptanalysts to learn the linguistic, military, and cultural patterns of a single organization.[42] Each decryption section could gain a thorough familiarity with his opponent that would both assist in cryptanalysis and broaden intelligence analysis. In these sections, cryptanalysts worked without the distraction of learning the details of other groups' experience with other systems and against other countries. Focusing in depth on one problem, each individual developed a clearly defined specialty. Creating such a collection of specialists stemmed from the principle that the division of labor creates better results through greater efficiency and expertise.

This strong division of specialization has roots in the German bureaucratic tradition beginning with Frederick the Great. Despite its often negative connotations, Frederick's bureaucracy rationalized administrative functions, rewarding prestige from competence rather than from social connections and creating highly skilled functionaries. Within this well-defined hierarchy, everyone ideally had a clearly defined realm of responsibility and worked on his own project without intruding in anyone else's sphere. These specialists produced the tactical results demanded of them, particularly early on.

## Tactical Successes

The Wehrmacht's intelligence successes came primarily in the tactical arena. To find this tactical information, the signals intelligence organizations in Germany turned their attention to working on traffic analysis[43] and their enemies' medium- and low-grade cryptologic systems.

During the mid-1930s, Germany had focused on her immediate neighbors, primarily France. The Marine's B-Dienst watched the French Navy closely during the interwar period, and this continuous attention paid off. By the outbreak of war, four important French tactical codes had been solved almost in their entirety.[44] In one clear example of the rich dividends of continuity, the Germans benefitted from tracking the French Navy's exercises in the mid-1930s. In June 1936, the B-Dienst had deciphered a scant twenty messages sent on a special system during French exercises. When France switched its codes upon declaration of war in 1939, the French Navy turned back to this 1936 system, to the B-Dienst staff's delight.[45]

Naturally, the B-Dienst used decrypts from these signals to follow enemy action against their own forces. From French Admiralty signals, the Marine learned the orders issued to submarines, warships, and merchant marine ships. During the phony war they decrypted French signals reporting a hunt for a German steamer.[46] They noted the apparent good cooperation between French and British "agent networks."[47] They also monitored their targets' actions against other nations, such as the Russian blockade of Finnish shipping.[48] The Marine noted that the French Navy had ordered a French vessel to attack an Italian submarine "even before the official commence of hostilities" (emphasis in original).[49]

The Marine attempted to use this knowledge of French naval codes to sow havoc among the enemy's forces. They sent an encrypted radio signal ordering, in Admiral Darlan's name, the immediate cessation of all hostilities, the return of all French warships to French harbors, and the rejection of English orders. Although the French soon recognized the deception, the Marine seemed satisfied with the results and, perhaps overly confident in their defeat of the French fleet, did not seem concerned that their ruse revealed the compromise of French codes.[50]

Whereas the Marine focused originally on their French and British counterparts, the Luftwaffe turned its attention eastward. Long before the invasion of the Soviet Union and "[i]n spite of the Non-aggression Pact between Germany and the Soviet Union," the OKL's interception service vigorously attacked the Red Air Force systems. Before Barbarossa, "the [Soviet Air Force] code was recovered and the deciphered messages were read almost 100%." In spite of the Soviets' code changes to wartime footing, the OKL's Chiffrierstelle solved the new Air Force codes "thanks to the collection of [pre-invasion] tactical practice messages . . . in a brief time."[51] Luftwaffe intelligence expert Edwin von Lingen estimated after the war that the OKL Chi-Stelle "was able at all times to decipher up to 70% of all intercepted messages of the Russian Air Force," including as much as 90% of some lower-grade systems.

Luftwaffe intelligence officers collected order-of-battle information from decrypted enemy signals. With this material they created a thorough index of enemy military units, call signs, frequencies, and the like.[52] Perhaps most impressive of all, Göring's FA claimed to have broken into the Russian Baudot teletype scrambler by mid-1943. "The break-in was due to a peculiarity of the machine . . . that [produced] compromises [of] seven characters in length. . . ." Once the FA recognized this compromise, they turned to OKW cryptologic specialists Dr. Liebknecht, Dr. Pietsch, and William Döring. These three men decided "the [German teletype machine] SZ 40 [could] easily be reconstructed to receive the Russian" raw intercepts. Ongoing decipherment would require additional "cipher machines," which the FA set out to build but apparently never finished.[53] Nonetheless, "all the intentions and preparations of the enemy down to the last great offensive in the East could be recognized and notice was given promptly on the basis of decrypted traffic."[54] Indeed, the Western Allies, Britain in particular, noted with alarm several times that Russian ciphers provided the Wehrmacht with "a fairly steady stream" of intelligence.[55]

The German records of cryptanalytic attack reveal significant success against many low- and medium-grade ciphers used by the Western

Allies. France yielded secrets to the Wehrmacht's cryptanalysts for the entire period of war. After the Third Republic surrendered, the armistice required Vichy France to hand copies of all its systems to the Germans. By the last year of the war, the British and Americans had become aware that German intelligence could read Free French cryptologic systems. In addition to cracking de Gaullist codes regularly, the Germans attacked the Hagelin B-211 cipher machine used by, among others, the Free French in western Europe.[56]

One section of the Heer's signal corps attacked the American weather cipher, "out of purely technical cryptologic reasons."[57] The reports do not indicate precisely what use the Heer gained from these reports, but western weather information was always valuable for Germany. Because weather moves west to east, from the Atlantic across Europe, the Western Allies had a natural advantage in weather information and prediction. By the time weather got to Germany, it was old news. The Wehrmacht, particularly the Marine, expended considerable effort attempting to gather more weather information directly, sending ships and later U-boats into the Atlantic specifically for weather information. Although one POW reportedly did "not think much of the Allied weather codes and claim[ed] that they are easy to decipher,"[58] Heer officers at the main western station disagreed. These cryptanalysts deemed the cipher "so well thought out" that it guaranteed the traffic's absolute security.[59]

This same Heer station had broken into the British railroads codes by late November 1943 and claimed a 98 percent success rate in reading the two thousand–plus signals produced by twenty-six keys in December 1943.[60] Although not considered vital in peacetime, such intelligence on Britain proved important by providing information on the movement of troops and supplies. The Heer attacked other nonmachine British systems, some of which offered intelligence on "bombing and artillery objectives."[61]

## Successful Attacks on U.S. Systems

The signals intelligence agencies scored successes against American systems as well. In the diplomatic arena, U.S. State Department systems offered valuable information. After the war, SD Sturmbannfuehrer

Dr. Huegel told his American interrogators he had received a daily bulletin from the OKW's cryptologic section.

> He recall[ed] that three or four messages from the American Minister in Berne to Washington were included daily, as well as those of the British Minister there. The American Minister's information on Nazi personalities was highly regarded by the Germans, who considered it better than that obtained by the British Minister.[62]

Far more valuable information emerged from breaking the American military attaché code. As General Erwin Rommel's Afrika Korps chased Britain's Eighth Army across Tunisia and Libya, the general had unwitting help from a U.S. diplomat. Rommel learned Allied dispositions from encrypted Washington-bound telegrams sent from the American consul in Cairo, Colonel Bonner F. Fellers. Beginning in the fall of 1941, Fellers, as the military attaché in Cairo, sent his Washington superiors regular and very detailed reports of British North African operations. As Hitler told Marshal Keitel in late June 1942, with the emotional importance of Alexandria, "it is to be hoped that the US sender in Cairo continues to instruct us so well about the English military plans with his badly enciphered cables."[63] Such successes offered the Wehrmacht concrete tactical information.

In general, German intelligence staff considered U.S. signalers less security conscious and more prone to mistakes than the British. Although "the German Navy had not started a systematical observation and deciphering of U.S. radiograms before America entered the war,"[64] they and other bureaus quickly found rich targets. Both in internal wartime memos and during interrogations by their Allied captors, German cryptologists and interceptors from listening posts chastised the enemy for sloppy security. A Heer signals officer explained to his captors that they should have made their signals more difficult to intercept by changing frequencies more frequently and speeding up transmissions. He told them that numbering their messages had made his job easier because he knew if he had received everything. He offered specific examples, noting

> Military Police traffic control messages betrayed new units, new tactical locations, and numbers of vehicles. Supply nets in the rear areas supplied information also....The arrival of the 9 U.S. Armored

Division in November, together with any details, was betrayed in this way.[65]

After the war, "Radio Representatives" from the OKW explained that low-grade systems, such as supply and liaison signals, had given "everything away – order of battle, intentions, etc."[66] Over and over, Allied signaling mistakes offered German intelligence insight into troop movements and strengths.

Of all the belligerents they faced, the Germans considered British units the most security conscious. They attributed this awareness in part to their own success; years of fighting the superior Germans had taught the British a thing or two. In particular, several German intelligence men noted that the capture of a German intercept unit in North Africa had inspired the British to overhaul their signaling techniques, making their systems "very much more secure."[67] The Americans rarely garnered any such positive comments from German signals or intelligence men. A POW summed up the German opinion of American procedures by noting that "if US troops win the war – which [the POW] does not doubt – it will be in spite of their signal security and not because of it."[68]

As the United States expanded their involvement in the European theater, German intelligence turned to American tactical systems with enthusiasm. Heer cryptanalysts began attacking the American M-209, a hand-held cipher they called a "machine" cipher. The M-209 (code named AM-1 by the Germans) operated mechanically, not electrically. Far more portable than the Enigma, M-209 appeared in all the theaters where Americans fought, carrying tactical-grade information. Well before D-Day, the Heer cryptanalysts exploited two types of weaknesses in the M-209: physical capture of key lists and messages in "depth."[69]

The Germans quickly discovered the vulnerability of the M-209 to depths (more than one message being encrypted at the same or nearly the same setting). Two German cryptanalysts, Herbert Schwartz and Werner Graupe, described the cracking of M-209 signals to their captors in late 1944. They noted that in five days they could locate the set of similar messages and then establish the internal settings of the M-209s that sent them. Since decryption of these messages took about five days, "the value of cracking this code ... lay ... in the order of battle information, casualty figures and personality data which it was valuable

2. The American M-209. Small size and portability made this mechanical cipher ideal for short-term tactical messages. German cryptanalysts broke about 10 percent of M-209 messages sent by U.S. forces liberating Europe. U.S. cryptologists knew the M-209 offered limited security and restricted its use to lower-grade traffic. (Courtesy of the National Security Agency)

to learn even after five days' delay."[70] Consistently they read 10 percent of all M-209 traffic in the European theater.

The Wehrmacht put intelligence from decrypts to good use. In 1942, cryptanalysis helped German troops rebuff the Allied attack on Dieppe. In part through poor British signals security, the Germans learned of this attempt to open a "second front" some five days before the raid.[71] German interception followed the raiders' signals from the first moments of the landing and stayed abreast of the Allied forces' progress through their retreat.

### The Naval Battles

Perhaps the most consistently valuable intelligence came from British naval signals. The surviving Marine documents reveal the wealth of information that the B-Dienst culled from signals intelligence. After capturing code material off a steamer, the B-Dienst read Britain's Merchant Naval Code.[72] Decrypts of these messages shed light on the comings and goings of Britain's essential supplies. From Britain's Royal Air Force reconnaissance reports, the B-Dienst acquired considerable information on Royal Navy movements all through the war.[73] In addition to providing reconnaissance over land and sea, the RAF escorted Allied convoys all over the world to defend them against enemy attackers. These planes' warnings and reconnaissance reports often revealed the presence of Allied supply ships or escort defenses to German bombers and U-boats.

The B-Dienst had begun the war already reading the main British Naval Code and Naval Cypher. These primary systems, based on long subtractor tables, remained in use until August 1940. In early 1940, these vulnerable systems allowed the B-Dienst an important victory when their decrypts revealed British preparations for a landing in Narvik, Norway.[74] With this information in hand, the Marine dashed British hopes of a foothold in Norway.

Marine intelligence reached out to encompass other sources, including open press items, German and international shipping agents, and the observations of their own naval crews.[75] By combining these elements with signals intelligence, the B-Dienst provided the Seekriegsleitung (Marine Command) with good information on the movements of enemy ships on several fronts. With the invasion of the Soviet Union, the Marine stepped up its surveillance in both north and east. In the east, the Marine acquired "very satisfactory intelligence" on Russian naval movements, particularly for the Black Sea area. "Much of this [intelligence] came from the study of Russian communications.... [and] such intelligence was passed immediately to the local naval command..." and put to good use.[76]

In the west, the B-Dienst intercepted valuable traffic from enemy aircraft reconnaissance and between enemy ships and aircraft. From these sources, they provided the Seekriegsleitung (Skl) with rapid tactical information on Allied forces in the Mediterranean, particularly in the first years of the war. In July 1940, a Royal Navy force led by HMS *Hood* set out to escort a vital convoy for Egypt and to threaten the Italian navy. The B-Dienst deciphered and located through direction finding (D/F)[77] sufficient enemy traffic swiftly enough to follow the progress of the fleet.[78] By reading French traffic, which reported almost hourly on the position, course, and speed of Group Hood,[79] the cryptanalysts could tell their own forces precisely where to attack. The episode ended with mixed results for the Germans. Although no decisive battle occurred, neither had the British ships escaped unscathed. Marine command officers considered their "[k]nowledge concerning Allied shipping and convoy routes in the Mediterranean was almost complete."[80]

To supplement the land-based units, the Marine instituted "on board" B-Dienst teams. These special Marine signals intelligence teams served aboard battleships and other surface vessels. Eventually, similar teams showed up on some U-boats to eavesdrop on traffic between enemy convoy vessels and their escorts. These teams intercepted low-grade Allied traffic, decrypting it themselves for immediate tactical use.[81] On board teams could also help locate the origin of (or D/F) nearby enemy signals, revealing the position of enemy vessels. In the midst of battle, having these teams on pursuing U-boats gave their commanders an extra edge.[82]

With Britain forming the base for the western threat, the Marine focused on the island's supply lines. The U-boats' primary task became destroying the ships supplying Britain from its colonies and from the United States. From U-boat Command's point of view, the richest information for these battles came from Allied signals directing their convoys. The Marine command staff had quickly learned the general disposition of the British convoy system, its network of radio stations, its cooperation with the RAF, the meaning of the two-letter cover codes, and other valuable details.[83] The B-Dienst "English section" headed by Oberregierungsrat Wilhelm Tranow constantly read the codes of C-in-C Western Approaches, who reported everything from mine warnings and convoy arrivals to the level of German radio traffic.[84] The signals of the C-in-C Western Approaches provided, among other details, the arrivals and departures of supply convoys crossing the North Atlantic. Even more useful to the Marine, orders for convoys to take evasive action around U-boat patrols often passed through this station. Thus U-boat Command could follow a convoy's "evasive" maneuvers and begin to sense when the convoys knew U-boats threatened them.

Once the Americans entered the war officially, the B-Dienst looked to the western Atlantic. From the codes of the New York Portmaster and from Canada's Halifax, the Marine learned the sailings of convoys heading east with vital supplies. Britain's Convoy Cypher (which the B-Dienst referred to as "Frankfurt") offered rich material to U-boat Command. Between 1940 and 1943, at any one time 40–60 percent of the Allies' North Atlantic convoys were "compromised"; that is, had their position revealed to the B-Dienst through decrypted signals.[85] The Convoy Cypher offered U-boat Command the vital statistics of each convoy. The B-Dienst could learn the anticipated date, time, and location of each convoy's departure, assembly point (for rendezvous with their escorts), and arrival. In addition, the signals repeated the number of ships, their projected route and speed, and even the meeting point for stragglers.[86] With this information, the B-Dienst could give the patrolling U-boats an almost exact point and time where a convoy would cross the waiting wolfpack line.

Reports of signals from individual British and American ships appear in the B-Dienst's weekly summaries.[87] These ships traveling without the well-armed escort proved increasingly worthwhile targets for roaming U-boats. Individual ships would fall prey to U-boats at even higher rates than those in convoys.

One B-Dienst report mentions that "C-in-C Western Approaches' signals giving the situation as of 2000 each day were being read with fair regularity...."[88] In the beginning, the B-Dienst read the enemy's ciphers swiftly. Sometimes B-Dienst cryptanalysts could break vital British systems in about twenty-four hours. The enemy appeared unaware of its vulnerability. Only after nearly a year of war did the British change their main naval codes at midnight 20 August 1940.[89] Even immediately following this change, the B-Dienst gathered important information on the convoys and their escorts from "so-called routine radio messages regarding the departure of escort forces, the starting of escort aircraft, rendezvous reports, messages on where and when convoys dispersed, etc."[90] The B-Dienst had largely conquered this British cipher change by the end of 1941.

When they had difficulties actually breaking Allied convoy traffic, the B-Dienst staff could fall back on their knowledge of convoy "cycles." Having studied the Allies' habits through many months of decrypting convoy routing signals, the B-Dienst knew the general pattern of sailings, their frequency, usual assembly points, and general course. By knowing these cycles, and with the help of current traffic analysis, Ober-regierungsrat Tranow's section could frequently forecast the enemy's movement, such as convoy sailings.[91] Because of this long familiarity with British habits, the B-Dienst could roughly locate convoys, even though the decryption section could not read the Combined Convoy Cipher. German D/F rarely played a role in the tracking of sea vessels. Only one time, according to postwar analyses, did land-based D/F detect a convoy and guide U-boats to intercept it.[92] Nonetheless, the noncryp-tologic skills of signals intelligence gave the B-Dienst shadows to follow in periods of darkness caused by the enemy's cipher changes.

Time and again, the B-Dienst recovered from the blackouts of Royal Navy cipher changes. In the spring of 1943, the B-Dienst reached its zenith of success against the various convoy signals. Marine command officers found signals intelligence "reached a level...that had never been reached before since the outbreak of the war." To the U-boat com-mand's delight, "alterations of [Allied] convoy routes could be radioed within a few hours to operational submarines."[93] Until the introduction of the upgraded Naval Cypher No 5 in June 1943, the B-Dienst reveled in this insight into Allied convoy routes.

## Tactical Victories

Every branch of the Wehrmacht had what it considered significant sig-int victories. The Luftwaffe Chi-Stelle touted its rate of reading the Red Air Force codes. The Heer overcame such varied systems as basic weather codes and even the U.S. mechanical cipher M-209. Anglo-American convoy ciphers betrayed critical supply line routes to the Marine's B-Dienst. Even the Americans' military attaché system helped Rommel learn British strengths and positions in North Africa.

All these successes were tactical successes, providing precisely the type of information that each of the service commands wanted. These military commands considered tactical information vital: order-of-battle identification, troop movements, coming operations. In postwar assessments, the Wehrmacht's efforts in acquiring this tactical level of intelligence garner clear praise.[94] The bureaus collected and indexed this information thoroughly. The Heer kept "an order of Battle [which] included personality lists, regimental numbering, etc.,"[95] and the

Luftwaffe's index proved at least as thorough. B-Dienst successes in locating Anglo-American vessels caused severe losses of Allied supplies and ships.[96]

For these intelligence successes, the command staffs turned to their own service's signals intelligence. These specialized bureaus knew their enemy counterparts best and had no need to consult with the other services. The Marine wanted to know where the convoys were; the Luftwaffe what type and number of fighters they would be facing; the Heer the numbers and strengths of the units facing it. They all saw these needs as distinct and appropriate to their own service branch.

This emphasis on service-specific tactical intelligence increased the service branches' drive for segregation and autonomy. The Red Air Force codes had no obvious connection with the Royal Navy's convoy ciphers or the American military attaché Black Code, so the OKL Chi-Stelle, the B-Dienst, and the OKH Inspk. 7 saw little need for collaboration.

All branches of the Wehrmacht focused on tactical intelligence – thorough information on the enemy's Order of Battle, locations, and capabilities. Wartime officers on both sides considered this tactical signals intelligence successful. Wehrmacht generals and admirals in postwar interrogations and memoirs praised intelligence for its contribution.[97] Indeed, on the Eastern Front these bureaus proved so effective that the Western Allies relied not on the Soviets but on decrypts of *German* intelligence for tactical information throughout the war.

The Anglo-American appreciation for German efforts persisted. After the war, both Britain and the United States sent in TICOM (Target Intelligence Committee) teams to interrogate German intelligence staff and collect every possible scrap of documented information about German work on Soviet cryptologic systems. Captured German general staff and flag officers produced "homework," which serves as the basis for many of the declassified reports on German signals intelligence cited herein. The resulting information remains so sensitive that the British government still refuses to release, or allow the United States to release, a large portion of the captured and interrogative material.

The available documents detail the considerable German success in breaking lower-grade cryptosystems and how these successes led to the location of many an Allied convoy and squadron. German cryptologic experts took full advantage of the enemy's inadequate security procedures in the field and exploited all the mistakes they unearthed. The histories also reiterate how the autonomous German intelligence bureaus targeted the tactical signals of their enemy counterparts separately. Although unified on paper through the OKW/Chi, these sections generally focused on their own specialties and rarely found cause to collaborate with other sections. This division, however, as we shall see in the following chapter, brought disadvantages.

# THREE

# OF NO MUTUAL ASSISTANCE

## Compartmentalization and Competition in German Signals Intelligence

Thus it was – as one can see – a question of personalities if there was to be a collaboration, and not a question of the organization.
  – postwar POW report on the German Intercept Service

"co-operation" took the place of clearly-defined responsibility and . . . led to a waste of effort.
  – General A. Praun, chief of Heer Communications on the Eastern Front

The tactical successes of the prewar and early war years allowed the numerous German signals intelligence bureaus to believe their organizations were adequate and appropriate for their intelligence needs. Their emphasis on short-term tactical success, along with their isolation from each other, meant they did not see the big picture of German communications. Each bureau assumed it was fulfilling its responsibilities to its parent organization adequately and did not need to integrate its work with any of its brother agencies.

However, the decentralization and compartmentalization of the German sigint organizations began to show disadvantages. The sigint bureaus found the flow of information about enemy systems impeded and at times discovered they had made themselves redundant. They apparently failed to recognize that their lack of cooperation meant an uneven implementation of their best security and cryptanalytic practices. Only decades after the war would they realize that decentralizing and working in isolation had kept them from fully exploiting what intelligence they had and providing adequate security for their own communications.

Officially, the Wehrmacht's Chiffrierabteilung (OKW/Chi) had control over an enormous territory, including "all press and broadcasts outside Germany. All radio telegraphy stations outside Germany. [Germany's] own radio traffic."[1] In theory, OKW/Chi centralized control of interception and signals intelligence (meaning TA and cryptanalysis of enemy signals), as well as signal security (monitoring and protection of Germany's signals). Beyond OKW/Chi's control lay the Nazi Party cryptologic sections and the Auswärtiges Amt's Pers Z, which cooperated somewhat through informal ties with OKW/Chi.

Each of these branches not only collected their signals intelligence independently but also handled the dissemination of its results. The emphasis on tactical intelligence made such a decentralized system logical. Sigint tended to follow a generally regional structure, operating according to the needs of the local field command. The sigint customers – frontline commanders – needed tactical intelligence as swiftly as possible, and the bureaus strove for the most efficient dissemination.

With this structure, the independent sigint bureaus had responsibility also for the security of this intelligence. Here again such segregation by service arm made sense from a security perspective. Each service knows what pieces of information are most vital for its survival and can protect them accordingly. Segregating information on a "need-to-know" basis forms one of the most fundamental elements of security. Sharp lines of knowledge will lessen the chance that important cryptologic information might fall into disinterested or even hostile hands.

However, drawing narrow boundaries inevitably excludes some people who could contribute crucial insights on the information. Particularly in the Heer, these information limits meant that even within a service branch, no single commander had a complete picture in intelligence. In the fall of 1944, the Heer created "the position 'General of Signals Intelligence attached to the Chief of Staff of the Army Signal Service in the General Staff of the Army.' "[2] Some members of intelligence considered the creation of this position "a tribute to the steadily increasing importance of communication intelligence in warfare." They believed the general and his staff would coordinate intelligence and make its dissemination more efficient and effective.[3]

Rarely did these need-to-know circles include anyone from other service branches. The cryptologists seldom saw any need to include members of other Wehrmacht branches in their signals intelligence or cryptanalytic operations. OKW/Chi did maintain an attitude of "open collaboration" with the Luftwaffe's Chistelle and the Marine's Skl/III, as one of its chief cryptanalysts has noted.[4] Lt. Col. Nielsen of the Luftwaffe seconded this view. Nielsen told his postwar interrogators that OKW and OKL had collaborated and even that OKW "had some control" over OKL.[5] OKW/Chi had occasionally given Marine intelligence copies of its cryptanalytic reports and Skl/III reciprocated. "A study of the reports showed, however, that they could be of no mutual assistance: the traffic worked on was too different."[6] Although not averse to cooperation, these agencies simply did not see the point.

The various cryptologic services even separated themselves physically, making collaboration on enemy cipher systems and even the exchange of decrypted traffic more difficult. One of the Auswärtiges Amt's cryptanalysts complained about the physical distance between Pers Z and OKW/Chi, although both occupied offices in Berlin. He recognized that the separation of bureaus by even a few miles within the same city made his work more difficult.[7] The separation of hundreds of miles over occupied territory with uncertain communication lines made coordination, let alone true collaboration, nearly impossible.

## Working Together

In a few cases, cryptanalytic bureaus found their interests overlapped. The Forschungsamt, OKW/Chi, and Pers Z all targeted certain diplomatic signals. They agreed to divide cryptanalytic responsibility based on which traffic had military value and which diplomatic or political value.[8] Although Pers Z attempted to coordinate the divided effort, cooperating on these systems proved difficult. Pers Z claimed the military tended to encroach on its diplomatic territory. Similarly the military complained that the Auswärtiges Amt "refused to turn over [foreign] dispatches ... [asserting] that decryption of diplomatic messages did not concern soldiers."[9]

Pers Z found the Forschungsamt (FA) particularly difficult to direct. In turn, the Forschungsamt claimed both the OKW/Chi and Pers Z presented only "a cold shoulder" in response to requests for assistance. The agencies proved unwilling to give up any territory. Formal communication continued along minimal lines, "with each party endeavoring not to let the other gain any insight into its own work."[10] On rare occasions, personnel from the different agencies (particularly OKW/Chi and Pers Z) exchanged information on specific diplomatic systems but generally on an ad hoc and purely personal basis.[11]

The absence of centralized coordination and control meant the Wehrmacht had "in fact, no single [intelligence] plan...but several rival plans."[12] Even with OKW/Chi as the formal head of all Wehrmacht cryptology, the separate agencies in each of the military services remained strong and largely autonomous.[13] The habits and traditions of military culture divided the work and the aims of the different intelligence agencies. Through the war, the Marine followed signals to Allied convoys, the Luftwaffe listened to RAF and Soviet fighters, and the Heer attacked signals directing tank movements in North Africa and the East. This separation and decentralization of intelligence responsibility had long existed in the German military. Each service branch knew what it wanted and took responsibility for its own area.

### Pragmatic Limited Cooperation

Formal connections certainly existed. The Marine war diary notes that their command "kept [the OKW] up to date about the...knowledge revealed from radio intelligence."[14] OKW Field Marshals Keitel and Jodl apparently also received Göring's FA intelligence reports, nicknamed "Brown Sheets." The Heer received some Luftwaffe intelligence and decryption results, at least for the Eastern Front, but connections with the Marine apparently were minimal.[15] The Marine command asked the Luftwaffe for reconnaissance information from its planes flying near and over the seas. The Luftwaffe returned assurances that when its units collected information pertinent to the naval theater, such as convoy sightings, the intelligence would be sent to the Marine. In turn, the Marine's B-Dienst passed intelligence based on decrypts of British signals through its own intelligence stations (Leitstelle) to specific squadrons. The increasing pressures of war, however, soon discouraged any extra effort required to maintain such cooperation.[16]

OKW/Chi's contribution to cooperation included serving as the conduit for Hitler's questions and orders to the various signals intelligence departments. Through the OKW/Chi, Hitler asked, for example, about British cipher traffic and how much of it the various departments could read.[17] In other areas, the sigint bureaus preserved considerable autonomy. The OKH's Inspk. 7, while acknowledging and even drawing on OKW/Chi's expertise, went so far as to take over cryptanalytic responsibilities formally assigned to the OKW bureau.[18] While allowing this change, OKW/Chi continued to claim authority in cryptographic areas, particularly the development of all cryptography, whatever the service branch.[19]

## Personal Connections

Under the pressures of war, compartmentalization could be overcome on the ground. So, in North Africa, General Albert Praun of Heer intelligence claimed that his unit produced high-quality signals intelligence, generating excellent relations with the theater's Heer and Luftwaffe headquarters.[20] Inside the OKL, Edwin von Lingen established a monthly collaboration for all the section cryptanalysts. These few successful collaborations tended to be limited in scope and duration.

When direct collaboration between intelligence agencies did occur, the conduit was often personal connections between the staffs, particularly the section heads. Von Lingen's experience in the OKL offers a vivid example of how a sigint section could build collaboration around individual ties. Von Lingen worked for the OKL Chiffrier-Stelle in East Prussia. This Chi-Stelle had intercepted a series of encrypted messages of the Red Army and recognized them as a potentially rich source of information. Since the Chi-Stelle's own personnel had not been trained to work the five-digit systems of these signals, von Lingen approached the head of OKW/Chi, a personal acquaintance, about cooperation. He pointed out that OKW/Chi had no intercept facilities of its own for this traffic. In spite of not having ready access to ongoing intercepts, the "virtually crippled Cryptanalytic Unit...was well versed in the [Red Army five-digit] enciphered code." Von Lingen's OKW/Chi colleague agreed to collaborate on this code, so long as "the Cryptanalytic Group of OKW should not be subordinated to the Chi-Stelle [OKL] but would merely be assigned to it."[21]

Now the two agencies both had sections attacking the Red Army system. OKL passed intercepts to OKW/Chi in Berlin and received back "from Chi/OKW the documents (code, difference catalogue) for decrypting the messages. . . . " Then German troops captured the code itself. The physical compromise apparently went unnoticed by the Russians, and soon the two agencies had their hands full decrypting the intercept traffic.

Von Lingen then learned "that Chi/OKH [the Heer cipher section] was . . . deciphering the same messages." Recognizing the unnecessary duplication of effort, he approached the "Chief of Chi/OKH," again a personal acquaintance, and "proposed close collaboration of the three cryptanalytic groups." His OKH contact agreed and a "direct line was laid at once." With the reduction in duplication, decryption increased and the cryptanalysts soon read even more material.[22] Indeed, so much Red Army traffic used this system that "the few [OKL and OKW] experts who were able to deal with the code could not possibly decrypt everything." From these decrypts, OKL and OKH acquired valuable tactical information: "the status of the troop units, supply, regroupings of units of all branches, and impending actions."[23]

Von Lingen's story of cooperation remains an exception to the rule of Germany's compartmentalized sigint effort. Central coordination of either interception or decryption of enemy signals proved elusive. Although at various times both Admiral Canaris's Abwehr[24] and the OKW's Chiffrierabteilung had the mandate to oversee intelligence, neither could control the numerous organizations. In this climate of compartmentalization, even the successful collaboration von Lingen created on the Eastern Front did not last. Under pressure from OKW and "higher authorities," von Lingen agreed to pull his OKL group out of the three-way collaboration, believing the OKH's and OKW's attack on the traffic would continue unabated. He was soon disabused of this notion. The intelligence organizations could not overcome their rivalries. Von Lingen later learned "that the Chi-Stelle OKH was . . . only trying to separate the two cryptanalytic groups which were collaborating so well." Having successfully ended OKL collaboration, OKH dropped its interest in working with OKW. Von Lingen attributed these reversals to interservice rivalry.[25]

## Descent into Conflict

This rejection of cooperation would severely damage the effectiveness of each sigint agency. They would fail to benefit from the insights and experiences of other bureaus' staff and would even repeat work already done by another bureau. Their divisiveness led to confusion. After the midwar creation of the Heer's cryptologic division, Inspk. 7, OKW/Chi "was forbidden to continue deciphering systems of foreign armies."[26] Inspk. 7 attacked foreign army systems, although OKW/Chi's Wilhelm Fenner remained in charge of decrypting messages of foreign governments; that is, diplomatic systems. Fenner never learned "the true reasons" for this split of responsibilities but said that thereafter "no sensible rational collaboration" existed between the Heer's intelligence section and that of OKW/Chi.

The strict divisions between the services ran through all forms of intelligence, interception, and cryptanalysis. Naval officers complained that the Marine "had jealously been denied an aerial reconnaissance facility of its own [and so] possessed no long-distance aircraft to survey from above."[27] Yet the Luftwaffe ignored requests from the Marine that it provide planes and pilots for reconnaissance. Großadmiral Dönitz complained that "the U-boat war could be very different, if the U-boats did not have to do the seeking and finding of the enemy on their own" because the Luftwaffe had failed at the task.[28] Had the U-boats had access to airborne scouts, they would have found more convoys faster and been surprised by Allied destroyers less frequently. As late as July 1944, the Marine still hoped to prod the Luftwaffe for intelligence.[29]

As the agencies grew and demands on them expanded, the strain intensified for the staffs in cryptanalysis and evaluation.[30] When the OKL turned its attention to "the so-called additive enciphered code used by the Russians which was employed by the upper echelons and staff of the Red Army," it became apparent that OKL "had no trained personnel of [its] own for this complicated system and...could not...handle all the traffic in [this] 5-digit code."[31] In spite of their internal shortage, the military declined to seek intelligence staff outside military circles and particularly resisted civilian encroachment.[32]

Although the heads of the intelligence bureaus frequently complained of a lack of qualified personnel, they continued to hire from a limited pool. Like the general German military, they emphasized "origin and background, tradition and social standing, qualities which cannot be learned."[33] The military trusted its own and did not want to turn to members of nonmilitary circles. The intelligence analysts, chief POW interrogators, and heads of evaluation centers and signals corps were reserved for commissioned officers.[34] Civilians in intelligence bureaus usually appeared only in clerk, typist, and support positions.

The intelligence agencies did not band together to solve their personnel shortage through consolidation or cooperation. None of the bureaus wanted to believe that any of its brother agencies produced quality – either in personnel or in results. Although OKW/Chi used Heer signals operators to staff its radio intercept stations, its staff was dismissive of the Heer's training: "Radio operators...from the Army [always needed] a period of special training before they could work independently without constant supervision."[35] The Marine considered the Luftwaffe "inadequate," if not incompetent, and blamed it for a range of problems, including the increasing sinkings of German supply convoys in the Mediterranean.[36] This dissension made simply coordinating efforts next to impossible. No one managed to keep track of the many pieces, and the distribution of intelligence remained piecemeal.

### Competition Generates Redundancy

The traditional lines between the military services' responsibilities frequently blurred during the Second World War. Technologic advances meant that armies, air forces, and navies could work together in both defensive and offensive operations. In this setting, operating each signals intelligence bureau as an isolated, separate entity made little sense. Although specialization and decentralization can meet short-term, tactical needs effectively, success in a long, multifront Total War requires a more sustained, strategic effort.

Some men in sigint – OKW's Fenner and OKL's Nielsen, along with von Lingen and several other German intelligence men – saw the

mistake of not combining, or at least coordinating, the military cryptologic agencies. These men would do what they could to rectify the
situation, as when von Lingen created his interservice collaboration.
In the end, the multiplicity of cryptologic agencies bred competition.
The "constant struggle for existence, rivalry and a desire for prestige
between...cipher units...led to a dispersion of the few good cryptanalysts available."[37] The division and duplication of work led to wasted
effort and redundancy.

These flaws cannot be blamed simply on the Nazis. This pattern of
redundancy and duplication did not appear in 1933; it had dogged the
German military for many years before the Machtergreifung. The intelligence services of the three branches of the Wehrmacht thought of
themselves as entirely separate divisions. Their multiple staffs would
breed duplication and fragmentation in all aspects of intelligence.

These increasingly divisive attitudes rarely received censure from
above. In fact, Hitler encouraged antagonism. Discord and redundancy
suited him; the former kept the various organizations from uniting
against him, and the latter meant no one organization acquired such
power or value that he could not replace it. Hitler discouraged any
creation of a central intelligence bureau, civilian or military. Since
no intelligence bureau was unique, each had to remain alert, constantly currying favor with Hitler's circle and amassing more power as
insurance.

Wehrmacht officers recognized this tactic and some even exploited
the competition spawned by this duplication. When the Luftwaffe's
chief interrogator, Hanns Scharff, wanted to be certain an intelligence
report reached the Wehrmacht command, he sent two copies, each one
through a different branch of the military. "By [thus] utilizing a certain
jealousy between two organizations, I assumed myself that each party
would work on the plan quickly and neither would dare to ignore it."
As insurance, he told each recipient that a second copy had gone to
"another organization."[38]

Such turf battles increased as Hitler's party consolidated its power
and looked to turn even intelligence to its own ends. Even after purg-
ing the party's SA and the traditional Heer command, the Nazis could
not seem to leave the military alone. As the war progressed, generals
were constantly reminded that "military tactics must be subordinated to

the requirements of politics and propaganda." Commanders who defied Hitler often lost their rank, if not their lives.[39] Some German officers expressed concern about political constraints taking precedence over military objectives.[40] Most learned to obey anyway: "Any actions not in accordance with orders might be nipped in the bud by the strict control through the Party spy system of which officers of all ranks are afraid."[41] Hitler kept the German intelligence services divided and conquered, no threat to his rule; but their division meant that they also remained less of a threat to the enemy, Allied intelligence.

Cryptanalysis suffered from the strain and the isolationist practices of the separate bureaus. At least one agency unknowingly began work on a problem already solved elsewhere. In 1942, the OKW learned that their staff was struggling to solve "scrambled" telephone conversations that the Reichspost researchers had already unscrambled.[42] (General Praun, chief of the Heer's intelligence troops, would tell the Allies that "the army did not know anything about the Reichspost except insofar as they used the [postal service]."[43]) The sharp divisions between agencies increased the chances of such duplication. The scarce resources of time and expertise needed for an ever-increasing number of enemy systems were consumed by redundant efforts. As the war continued and new enemy systems demanded attention, German cryptanalytic results would suffer increasingly from these divisions between agencies.

### Cryptographic Security

The complete alienation of the intelligence agencies also adversely affected the other side of cryptology: the improvements and protection of their own cipher systems. Although all the military branches had adopted Enigma, they never actually unified their development of the high-grade machine, let alone lower-grade cryptologic systems.

The OKW/Chi was supposed to control the development of all codes and ciphers used by the military services.[44] Assuming this responsibility long after Enigma had been adopted, of course, made OKW/Chi's situation all the more difficult. OKW/Chi attempted to reinforce its supervisory position with numerous directives aimed at concentrating "the common development of all Armed Forces cryptographic systems at Chi OKW."[45] In late 1943, the OKW ordered every branch of the

Wehrmacht to secure OKW/Chi's approval before introducing a new code or cipher system. One year later, OKW/Chi obtained an order from the Führer himself, "stating that the responsibility for the security of all ciphers used within the territory of the Reich lay with OKW/Chi."[46]

These official orders did little to challenge the autonomy of the various cryptologic divisions. Wilhelm Fenner of OKW/Chi complained that each military branch "developed the cryptographic systems it required without any testing or criticism by the other branches."[47] Despite its official mandate, in truth, "OKW (Chi) produced codes and ciphers for the [Heer] only."[48] The Marine and Luftwaffe developed their own codes and, in some cases, their own variations of Enigma. They generally alerted OKW/Chi to their changes but implemented them on their own plan and time schedule. Eventually, the OKH's Inspk. 7 began creating systems independently as well. OKW/Chi developed "a coordinating committee [of Heer, Marine and Luftwaffe,] . . . [which] met every month," presumably to discuss their latest changes and preserve the theory of OKW/Chi oversight.[49]

In spite of these meetings, the military services continued to assert their independence in cryptography just as they did in cryptanalysis. Each branch of the military continued to issue its own orders about how Enigma should be used and protected. They clearly did not coordinate such details as setting indicators or other vital security procedures. For instance, as a sensible, and indeed effective, security precaution, the Heer dropped double encipherment of message indicators early in the war. Yet the Heer participants at these coordinating meetings either did not tell or could not convince their Luftwaffe and Marine counterparts how important dropping double encipherment of indicators was for Enigma's security. Both the Luftwaffe and sections of the Marine continued to use the double encipherment for years.[50] Cryptographers rarely consulted their peers in other services at all. In numerous cases, one branch applied prudent security precautions that other branches adopted only much later, if at all. The official coordination offered by OKW/Chi clearly did not produce benefits on the cryptographic side.

Moreover, cryptography also remained firmly divided from cryptanalysis. Few cryptographers drew on the expertise of their own cryptanalysts. The civilian Pers Z did attempt to integrate cryptography and cryptanalysis, using its experience with breaking other countries' cryptologic systems to test various German cipher systems.[51] OKW/Chi and the Marine's B-Dienst also made "a connection...between deciphering and development."[52] The other bureaus did not. One of OKW/Chi's top cryptanalysts, Dr. Erich Hüttenhain, complained that the Heer would develop enciphering machines "without the aid of cryptology experts [i.e., cryptanalysts]."[53] Nor did the Luftwaffe have collaboration between the development and the cracking sides of cryptology. With such internal separation, cryptographers creating Germany's code and cipher systems did not have the benefit of their own cryptanalysts' experience in attacking similar systems. This handicap could account for some of the dangerous practices outlined earlier, such as reusing old key settings.

Both internal and interagency cryptographic segregation would soon cause problems for Germany's cipher security. The division between the Wehrmacht and the Auswärtiges Amt opened the first information gap. Unlike other German agencies, the Auswärtiges Amt's Pers Z determined early on that Enigma did not meet its security standards.[54] A developer of Enigma attempted to improve the machine to meet Pers Z's requirements and frequently presented the bureau with upgraded models, but the Auswärtiges Amt rejected all of them as inadequate.[55]

After considerable research and testing, Pers Z decided the Auswärtiges Amt could rely on the Siemens-Schlüssel-Fernschreib-maschine T-52. With the T-52 machine, Pers Z believed it had found a secure system and, even in the 1980s, in spite of numerous revelations about Allied wartime cryptanalytic successes, one former Pers Z analyst maintained his system's relative security (albeit only after improvements to the original T-52).[56] Yet Pers Z apparently never informed any other cryptologic division of these conclusions and never warned them of Enigma's security deficiencies.

Had the Pers Z cryptologists demonstrated their methods for proving Enigma's insecurity, the military branches might nonetheless have continued to use the existing Enigma network as the most easily available system. However, they might also have been a bit more skeptical of Enigma's security and taken signs of enemy intrusions more seriously. Pers Z's studies might have helped pop the bubble of absolute certainty in Enigma's protection. However, although Pers Z had proof that some Enigma machine variations did not offer significant security, they could convince themselves that their own systems could not be broken. Years after Germany's wartime cryptologists accepted the compromise of Enigma, Pers Z cryptologists maintained belief in other systems, particularly the Siemens T-52 non-Morse machines. In fact, the most recent Allied declassifications of wartime cryptology demonstrate that even these connections, touted by a former Pers Z cryptologist as late as 1983 as secure, also succumbed to Allied cryptanalysts.[57] Knowledge of the limitations of one system did not, at least in this case, cause German cryptologists to reconsider the security of other machine ciphers.

Long after the war ended, most German cryptologists persisted in their belief that their successes in the tactical intelligence arena were mirrored by their cryptographic success with Enigma. They had no doubt that their men in the field used a cryptologic system far superior to the Allies' error-prone methods. They remained confident in their conviction that their own security procedures did not allow for the mistakes that their opponents made.

## From Separate to Antagonistic

In fact, a shortage of quality sources in, as well as effective exploitation of, intelligence plagued the Wehrmacht. Signals intelligence had fallen victim to German military segregation and lack of cooperation. German intelligence never managed to consolidate either its cryptanalysis of foreign systems or its cryptographic security. Mere coordination of effort or exchange of information and experiences proved ineffective and frequently short-lived. The cryptologists discussed working together, but true cooperation never emerged.

The tension between cooperation and antagonism surfaced over and over in all levels of the Axis intelligence operation. The service branches, to say nothing of the many nonmilitary organizations, saw their needs, skills, and interests as so divergent that they could not see eye-to-eye with their brother cryptologists. Even when they found themselves offered an opportunity to work alongside a colleague, the German signals intelligence bureaus found it difficult to trust – and thus to cooperate with – any of their associates.

For many of the same reasons, the German agencies did not cooperate effectively with their Axis partners. The Wehrmacht intercepted the signals of Germany's most trusted partner, Japan, even the messages sent to Tokyo by Ambassador Baron Oshima. "What Oshima radioed was known. Also what he received by radio."[58] The Marine B-Dienst, at least, had concerns that the Allies might crack Japanese codes.[59] Nonetheless, the Heer allowed Oshima extensive access to sensitive areas, such as their Atlantic "fortress" battlements.[60] In his postwar assessment of "the [OKW's] collaboration with the Japanese cryptanalysis unit," Fenner observed "that despite good will on the part of both partners any real basis for collaboration was entirely wanting."[61]

The Nazi rise to power had only exacerbated these existing rivalries. The NSDAP had its own intelligence agencies and some party members attempted to expand their power by chipping away at existing intelligence agencies. The Wehrmacht had no reason to trust or cooperate with these Nazi organizations. Moreover, Hitler encouraged duplication of effort for his own reasons.

Yet blaming these divisions on the Nazi Party ignores the previous century of history. As in other countries, Germany's military had strong interservice rivalries. The Heer saw the other services – Luftwaffe and Marine – as subordinate, if not inferior. Each of the wartime army's predecessors, the Imperial army and the Prussian army, had considered itself a "state within a state." Its hierarchy answered only to the king, and its status as an honored elite in German society[62] rose with the increasing modernization and expansion in military warfare. The Heer of the Second World War consisted of officers who considered themselves upper class (the list of wartime generals is littered with aristocratic "vons"). The other services could not be considered equals in either experience or skill.

The Marine itself recognized "the inferiority of the German Navy," as its chief Großadmiral Raeder called it.[63] Although Prussian Germany had had a famous army for centuries, its navy was a more recent development. This relative youth undoubtedly contributed to the Marine's inferiority complex, but the greatest cause for friction between the Heer and Marine stemmed from the last days of World War I. In 1918 Marine sailors had mutinied, sparking a short-lived Communist revolution and leading to Germany's surrender. The Heer had not forgiven the Marine for this contribution to its "stab in the back." Undoubtedly, this distrust contributed to the traditional army-navy rivalry.[64]

The Luftwaffe stood apart as the youngest of the three services and originally as a clandestine service. Banned by the Versailles Treaty, the German air force originally went underground as a glider club before training secretly with the Soviet Red Air Force in the 1920s. After 1933, the Luftwaffe became known as a heavily Nazi service branch, partly because its chief, Hermann Göring, moved in Hitler's smallest inner circle. Moreover, Hitler defied the Treaty and openly championed the service.

With this tradition of rivalry, the different branches of the armed forces had long found reasons, only reinforced by the divisions caused by World War I and the Nazi putsch, to mistrust each other. Even the desperation of the second half of the war and the relentless pressure of the enemy could not bring them to work together consistently.

This dissension becomes all the more visible with the widespread use of Enigma. Although numerous German organizations adopted this cipher machine to facilitate cooperation, they failed to recognize that sharing the cryptographic piece of the communications sphere meant sharing the cryptanalytic half. They failed to recognize that by sharing a single cryptologic system, they shared the risk of enemy decryption. German commanders did recognize that the increase in signaling exposed their tanks, planes, and especially their U-boats to Allied direction finding.[65] Yet none of the intelligence agencies of the various services appeared to consider that another branch's profuse or careless signaling could affect their own ciphers' security. Without coordination, settings and signaling procedures for Enigma became a hodgepodge of different theories and requirements. Some nets used excellent security and nearly random message and key settings; others tolerated sloppy signaling habits and predictable settings. The best practices of security procedures emerged here and there but never predominated.

Achieving sufficient security would have required the agencies to cooperate. The belief in their own success and the actual less-than-successful reality stemmed in large part from the isolation in which the many German signals intelligence bureaus operated. By focusing on their narrow tactical needs, they ignored the larger picture of how German communications functioned as a whole. The very versatility of their cipher system meant they needed to share their work on their own communications security, on improving their cryptography, and against the enemy's ciphers. How these organizations cooperated with each other would affect the information they had on their own security and would shape their reactions to security breaches. Their failure to cooperate in each of these areas proved fatal to the security of the German cipher system and to German intelligence as a whole.

# FOUR

# THE WORK OF STATION X

## Centralizing Allied Cryptology at Bletchley Park

All the resources of the Army, Navy, Air Force, and RSS [Radio Security Service] nets can be marshalled as needed...
  – Telford Taylor, the first American loaned to Bletchley Park,
      describing BP's working to U.S. Army generals

Great Britain's signals intelligence entered the war woefully unpre-
pared. Its primary agency, the Government Code and Cypher School
(GC&CS),[1] had a small core of professionals to draw upon and no
professional training organization, only an informal connection with
academia. What cryptanalysis staff it had was small and poorly funded.
And it faced a seemingly insurmountable problem: cracking Enigma,
Germany's "secure" machine cipher system. GC&CS seemed unlikely
to triumph. However, with the outbreak of war, GC&CS centralized its
cryptanalytic effort on the grounds of Bletchley Park and began directing financial and personnel resources into the attack on enemy codes
and ciphers. Within three years, the members of Allied intelligence had
produced a remarkable coup: nearly daily, they were cracking and reading thousands of the German Enigma ciphers.[2]

What made the Bletchley Park cryptanalytic effort so successful? How
did Bletchley overcome the Germans' initial intelligence advantage?

Some historians have suggested that luck played a decisive role in
this extraordinary feat. A serious consideration of the organizations that
cracked the ciphers, however, yields a different conclusion. Luck played
a role, but as is so often the case, the Allies created their own luck. As
with the German example, the places where the Allies put their greatest

## British Sigint Organization

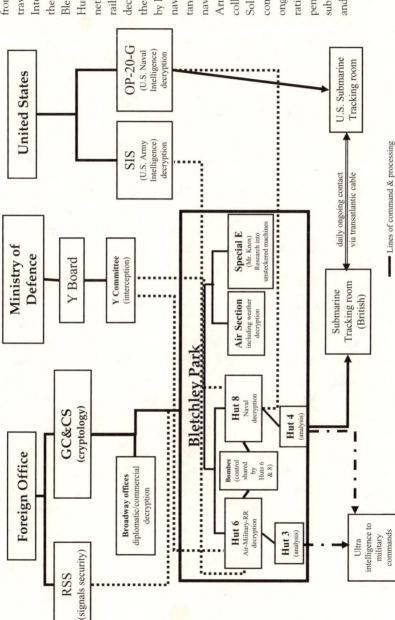

BRITISH SIGINT ORGANIZATION Virtually all signals intercepted from the European theater traveled through Bletchley Park. Interception was directed by the Y Board in cooperation with Bletchley Park, particularly Hut 3. The majority of Enigma networks – Heer, Luftwaffe, railroad, and Naval – were decrypted by Huts 6 and 8 and then analyzed and disseminated by Huts 3 and 4. The American naval OP-20-G worked in tandem with Huts 8 and 4 on naval, material and the U.S. Army's cryptologists in the SIS collaborated with Huts 6 and 3. Solid lines show the chain of command. Dotted lines show ongoing cooperation or collaboration between otherwise independent bureaus. The two submarine tracking rooms (U.S. and British) operated in tandem.

*Sources:* PRO: HW 3/96 Sig Int Org. Jan. 1941; NARA: RG457 HCC Box 808 NR 2336 British Communications Intelligence; Box 1424 NR 4683 US Memos.

effort showed the greatest success. The Allies gave intelligence a high priority, in terms of both financial and human resources and its position in planning and executing the war. They took the long view and put considerable effort into high-grade strategic intelligence. Believing they could succeed, they did.

The Allied sigint success rested on the British development of a centralized signals intelligence organization. The British put a single agency in charge of all cryptology and related signals intelligence, whether Japanese or German, naval or enemy agent, diplomatic or military. This new type of agency streamlined the cryptanalytic effort, encouraged cooperation and cross-pollination between different sections, and in the process fully exploited the weaknesses of the Enigma system.

## Central Intelligence

What would become the model of postwar "central intelligence" took root in Great Britain before the outbreak of World War II. Britain's centralized intelligence owed its configuration to the legacy of World War I intelligence, specifically Room 40. Room 40 decrypted German signals[3] through the Great War, and its work helped to shape the war's outcome.[4] Like the other cryptologic organizations considered in this work, Britain's Room 40 shriveled in the aftermath of peace, but its success during the war earned its survival. Renamed the Government Code and Cypher School in November 1919, the reduced band of cryptanalysts had moved to the Foreign Office by 1922.[5] There GC&CS assumed a predominantly civilian role and attacked primarily diplomatic codes and ciphers. GC&CS's placement under the Foreign Office would entrench the presence of civilians in signals intelligence.[6]

World War I had apparently taught the British that they needed greater signals intelligence coordination. In the interwar period, the government consolidated cryptology under the rubric of GC&CS. Overseeing GC&CS's operations was the Joint Intelligence Committee (JIC) with representatives from the three services and one from the Foreign Office.[7] With this new interservice structure, the new GC&CS

> put an end to the duplicative and inefficient practice of allowing...
> separate departments and services to mount attacks on foreign codes

and ciphers, [instead] concentrating its complete cryptanalytic effort in a single centralized organization...[8]

The idea of centralizing intelligence, specifically cryptologic intelligence, occurred to other countries besides Britain. Although Germans had discussed centralizing, or at least coordinating cryptologic intelligence several times through the 1930s, these discussions stalled.

Polish intelligence, however, began centralizing early. By the late 1920s, the Polish military had given a clear priority to intelligence and specifically cryptology. First, the Polish Cipher Office and the Radio Intelligence Office merged, joining interception, communications, direction finding, and cryptology under the umbrella of the Cipher Bureau. Later the military concentrated radio interception from both east and west, while cryptanalysis and interception consolidated outside Warsaw.[9]

The priority Poland accorded intelligence meant providing the best tools and people for the job. Some of the best people included three young university students. Polish intelligence set out to give them top-notch training, in one case even providing a year's study at, of all places, Göttingen Universität, Germany. The tools for the job came from cooperation with civilian and industrial resources.

This consolidated effort produced considerable cryptanalytic success. In January 1938, Polish intelligence requested a report on the current results against Germany. The report concluded that for a sample two-week period, the small Polish team was reading 75 percent of all Wehrmacht Enigma signals.[10] Unfortunately, on 15 December 1938, the Germans introduced two new Enigma rotors, and the Poles lost their ability to read all Enigma versions except those on the Sicherheitsdienst (SD) net.[11] Worse, Poland had not had the military resources to make full use of the high-grade intelligence that came from decrypting Enigma. Their military would prove unable to hold off the German invasion. However, their signals intelligence work would pass to the French and the British and eventually the Americans, who would exploit it.

Success would reinforce efforts at centralizing intelligence. Such centralization of signals intelligence stems ultimately from the priority that both nation and military place on intelligence. In Britain, support for intelligence, and for cryptanalysis in particular, came from the highest level: the Prime Minister himself. This priority had a long tradition, one recognized by other countries, including Germany. (The Germans believed the British had excelled in the field of intelligence "... by virtue of their tradition, their experience, and certain facets of their national character – unscrupulousness, self-control, cool deliberateness and ruthless action".[12]) Traditionally, militaries on the defense have believed intelligence offers greater rewards than have militaries on the offense. Great Britain's self-image as a nation on the defense in the 1930s, along with Room 40's Great War successes, only reinforced a traditional British emphasis on intelligence.

Once the cryptanalysts began producing results in the Second World War, their high priority solidified. Prime Minister Winston Churchill took an active and personal interest in cryptologic intelligence throughout the war. His patronage of GC&CS, and of Bletchley Park in particular, made certain that finances and personnel poured into cryptanalysis. As cryptanalysts unlocked the dam of Enigma-encrypted signals, Bletchley quickly moved to a twenty-four-hour operation. Shifts, or watches, were organized around the decryption process so that the day began at midnight, the time when German units sent the first signals with a new daily key.

New recruits arrived almost constantly. For "Hut 6 operations alone [the staff increased] to almost 1300," not including the intercept personnel at listening posts collecting "the raw material."[13] Estimates of the total wartime personnel at Bletchley run around seven to ten thousand. The figures are uncertain, as the numbers of both military personnel "on secondment" and the temporary staff remain unspecified.[14] Over roughly the same period, the U.S. [Army] Signal Security Agency jumped from 331 to more than 26,000 employees, for Army sigint alone.[15] In spite of the enormous increases that these numbers represent, the centralization of military and diplomatic signals intelligence took shape relatively smoothly.

## Using Civilians

The Government Code and Cypher School had the advantage of using primarily civilian amateurs. Like their German counterpart, the British military preferred its officers not linger in intelligence posts. Ambitious and talented officers were expected to command on the front lines. A prolonged stay in intelligence could stunt an officer's career.

GC&CS circumvented this problem of military promotion standards. Through GC&CS, the British turned over a large portion of their intelligence work, particularly in the area of cryptology, to civilians and civilians-in-uniform. These civilians did not have traditional interservice rivalries or even much notion of signals intelligence. This large staff of civilians handled intelligence, counterintelligence (including the successful XX Committee), and cryptology. Bletchley Park's entire operation could function using only a limited number of purely military advisers, recipients, and trainers. This melding of civilian and military allowed Bletchley to create experts who stayed in intelligence for the war's duration. Although some chafed for a change of duty,[16] few felt the need for frontline service, the track to military promotion, as a predominant concern.

The road to strong intelligence requires a long view. The British military had recognized that "it is the intelligent putting together of little tid-bits, the sifting of the unimportant from the important that produces operational intelligence...."[17] For this job of sifting tidbits, Britain has long believed gentlemen, or intellectual amateurs, do best. In Elizabethan times, English intelligence drew heavily on amateur agents, including the playwright Christopher Marlowe, who spied overseas for the Privy Council.[18] In the early twentieth century, Boy Scouts founder Lord Baden-Powell drew pictures of butterfly wings that concealed diagrams of Turkish fortresses.[19] In World War I, the successful Oxbridge cryptanalysts of Room 40 solidified the connection between Britain's universities and her Secret Service.[20] Even the eventual location of GC&CS's headquarters at Bletchley Park signaled this connection: halfway between Oxford and Cambridge, in the Oxbridge-London "Golden Triangle."[21]

While many scholars of Ultra (the Allied name for Enigma's decrypts) have mentioned the amateurs of Poland and Bletchley Park, none have explored the pivotal importance of this tradition of amateurism for Ultra's success. In fact, all of the Allied organizations sent out extensive lures to bring in the best talent for their cryptanalytic effort. When British intelligence began laying the ground

3. SIS (the U.S. Army's Signals Intelligence Service) in 1937. Standing, left to right: H. Frank Bearce, Solomon Kullback, Army Captain Harrod Miller, William Friedman, Abraham Sinkov, Coast Guard Lieutenant L. D. Jones, Frank Rowlett. Sitting: Louise Newkirk Nelson. Friedman hired the first cryptanalysts in 1930 – they were Solomon Kullback, Abraham Sinkov, and Frank Rowlett. They cracked the Japanese "Purple" machine without ever seeing it. Note the staff mix: although they are all in civilian dress, they are in fact both civilian and military, from different military services, and even include a woman. The famous "Think" sign demonstrates Friedman's approach to problem solving. (Courtesy of the National Security Agency)

for rapid wartime expansion, its recruiters turned to universities for their potential analysts.[22] Some academics already had ties to signals intelligence from work during the First World War. By the time GC&CS began trawling the universities for potential recruits, many senior dons had already earmarked, "if only mentally, further suitable candidates."[23]

In turning to the universities, GC&CS was seeking "the best brains of Britain" for the Bletchley Park operation.[24] There GC&CS found "a large number of top ranking university people, particularly students of linguistics, mathematicians, historians, physical scientists and others who have done original research." GC&CS also scavenged the business world, turning up gems such as Squadron Leader [later Wing Commander and Sir] Eric M. Jones, formerly "a high executive with a textile firm in Manchester," who became head of Hut 3. His knowledge of management and production would help turn the Air and Army hut into a highly efficient assembly line of intelligence on Germany's Heer and Luftwaffe.[25] This collection of personnel struck Colonel Alfred McCormack, future American Director of Intelligence, as being "of an extraordinary high caliber." After a two-month tour of British intelligence, McCormack summed up the general British attitude toward personnel as "bold and forward-looking."[26]

These former professors and students had acquired the skills important for cryptologic work: critical thinking and problem solving. While ostensibly preparing for such future careers as solicitors, business executives, and scholars, university students learned to give the unknown a context. They continually faced new material that required learning methods to recognize and categorize the unfamiliar. Classical scholars, for example, "had been trained from youth" to translate "at sights," essentially decoding texts they had never seen before. These sights required the student to categorize unknown words and phrases and to guess their meaning.[27] Many university men interviewed informally and were given to believe that if they joined up, they would find themselves picked out of drilling regiments and sent to quieter jobs that would use their academic skills.[28] Volunteers to do this "secret war work" began to increase from a trickle to a flood.

The recruiters' strategies seem puzzling at first glance. Following in Room 40's footsteps, but unlike Polish intelligence hiring, Bletchley Park disdained theoretical mathematicians, even for pure cryptanalytic work. Mathematicians were told "the work did not really need mathematics but mathematicians tended to be good at it."[29] The two most distinguished and eventually most crucial mathematicians, Alan Turing and Gordon Welchman, were recruited "not because of their distinction as mathematicians but because of their skill at chess."[30] Perhaps because chess required thinking in more than one dimension as well as several moves ahead, the recruiters for BP looked for those who excelled at the game. Three quarters of the British chess team worked for Ultra intelligence during the war, along with, oddly enough, part of the national bridge team. Bletchley recruited winners of *The Times*' crossword puzzle contests, and the United States kept an eye (through a "stool pigeon") on suitable members of the American Cryptogram Association.[31] Even less likely specialties appeared at Bletchley: Egyptologists, antiquarian booksellers, and experts on porcelain.[32] All had in common the ability to recognize, categorize, and contextualize unfamiliar material. These skills formed the ideal of critical thinking and problem solving honed by a liberal arts education.

While GC&CS's "old-boy network" clearly did not open the door to everyone,[33] it did embrace some rather unlikely candidates. Bletchley used Germans, Jews, Muslims, naturalized British subjects (technically not even eligible for British diplomatic service), even communists. Sensitive hiring decisions depended on informal inquiries among the "right sort," a practice that seems remarkably casual, even for the pre-McCarthy era. (Indeed, this informality nearly proved British intelligence's undoing during the Cold War when several of these informally recruited men turned out to be working for the Soviets. Although the most famous of these, Kim Philby, along with John Cairncross, who was at BP for a while, passed sensitive information to the Soviets, both while they were Britain's allies and later, no one involved with Ultra appears to have attempted to pass information to their wartime enemy, Germany.)

Indeed, the perception of signals intelligence and cryptanalysis as a pressing need even brought women in for crucial jobs. Having learned how much valuable work women had provided in Europe's first "Total War,"[34] the British moved more decisively in World War II. In 1941, the government organized a general mobilization, and then conscription, of women for war work.[35] Thousands of WRENS (Women's Royal Naval Service), WAAFS, and WAVES (the Air Force and U.S. equivalents) worked on some part of Ultra. Around two thousand women ran the all-important Bombes, waiting for the endless ticking to stop so they could note the rotor settings for the cryptanalysts.[36] The Americans also brought large numbers of women into cryptology. The U.S. Navy discovered early on that women proved generally more efficient at certain tasks, among other things, at wiring rotors for the highly classified Sigaba cipher machines. The average (male) Navy Electrician wired seven rotors per day, while the average (female) WAVES (Women's Appointed Volunteer Emergency Services) wired twice as many rotors in a day. The "high" WAVE wired over three times as many rotors: twenty-two per day. So the navy replaced the male electricians with female WAVES.[37]

Women also provided the vast majority of listening ears that intercepted the German messages from stations all around England. Some did not know precisely how their "work fitted into a bigger picture" but trusted the word that their piece was vital.[38] Some of these intercept operators did receive Ultra-indoctrination and even served overseas. Several served as instructors of male intercept operators heading to the front.[39] At Bletchley Park, women ran the indexing process – about two dozen had charge of the Air Section's "hundreds of thousands of [index] cards,"[40] and, in much fewer numbers, they worked at the very top as translators, intelligence analysts, and even pure cryptanalysts. Miss White, for example, who originally served as secretary to the Naval Section head, William Clarke, was "found to have the makings of a quite passable" cryptanalyst, high praise in these circles, and so she moved into that capacity.[41] Margaret Rock, working with Dilly Knox, not only unraveled cribs (known or guessed plaintext) in weather reports but single-handedly recovered the wiring of an unknown Enigma.[42]

Indeed, several "men of the professor type" were actually women. Joan Clarke (later Murray), a Cambridge mathematician, came to the naval Hut 8 in June 1940. Although as a woman she was listed as a linguist on the civil service lists and did not receive equal pay and rank, she was in fact assigned to work with Alan Turing to break the Naval Enigma.[43] As part of Hut 8, she became a member of the core senior staff, whose number never exceeded sixteen.[44]

By 1942, the Allies had created scores of successful analysts, cryptanalysts, indexers, and translators from people of varied experience, European ethnicities, educational training, and political backgrounds. In Britain, this peculiar conglomeration of amateurs worked together at Bletchley Park without a strict hierarchy or compartmentalization of labor. The Bletchley team provided the military with the fruits of their labor, but technically many of them worked for the (civilian) Foreign Office. Almost exclusively civilian at the war's start, GC&CS rather smoothly integrated an ever-increasing number of military personnel.

## Civilians and Military Together

The numbers and importance of amateurs in cryptanalysis increased under the pressures of World War II, and the presence of so many non-career analysts at Bletchley Park promoted job efficiency over traditional interservice and military-civilian rivalries. Once inside Bletchley Park, the staff found hierarchy at a minimum. When problems arose, the analysts and cryptanalysts turned first to their colleagues for solutions. They determined the priorities for interception and attack as well as for the use of equipment, rarely resorting to rank or superiors for decisions. The success of Ultra arose from this system: without the centralization of cryptology at GC&CS, Ultra would not have happened.

Bletchley Park achieved a balance of military structure and civilian mentality. Even after conscription got under way, the civilian GC&CS maintained its preeminence. When GC&CS personnel received draft notices, their superiors, often civilians themselves, fought hard to keep them at Bletchley, and usually won. Throughout the war, the "Park" had a long arm, even "recruiting officers from the intelligence organizations of the Army, Navy, and Air Force."[45] Prime Minister Churchill's support of signals intelligence no doubt played a significant role in this privilege. With his favor, Bletchley continued to exercise its prerogative for qualified personnel as well as financial resources. Churchill's insistence that "there must be no obstacles to this job"[46] demonstrates the high priority given to intelligence. These civilians had power at least equal to that of the military. Although a civilian organization, GC&CS could pull personnel even from the hard-pressed military. Once at Bletchley, all service personnel came under GC&CS's supervision, although they had to submit to the discipline of their particular service. Unlike the Wehrmacht, the British military services had to accept civilian control in signals intelligence, not just the oversight of the country's leader but of a civilian intelligence organization.

Bletchley Park soon found command officers would listen more readily to a civilian than "'only' a colonel," and so many did not seek military commissions.[47] McCormack, as one of the first Americans at Bletchley, "was especially impressed by how much the British had accomplished by eschewing rigid military formalities and getting 'the best man for the job.'"[48] "Bletchley was notorious for its unhierarchical attitudes."[49] Bletchley's hodgepodge of staff managed to balance civilian and military practices, emphasizing the advantages of one or the other as necessary. Outside Bletchley, military practices proved useful. Military "orders" served as sufficient explanation for the odd activities of lowly lieutenants "hidden among the trees" during the North African campaign[50] or the curious incongruities of young, but obviously powerful, civilians. Military requisitioning offered an efficient mechanism for acquiring personnel and material to work on Ultra and then for disseminating Ultra swiftly and appropriately.[51] Otherwise, ties to outside employers played little role once participants entered the Park. In the words of one participant, the Codebreakers "didn't worry much about more distant relations" outside of BP itself.[52] Ultimately, Bletchley "was an outfit that was nine-tenths civilian ..."; however, many were "thinly disguised" by their uniforms.[53]

Bletchley Park's civilians-in-uniform took their work seriously and personally. Britain's position on the frontier of Nazi-occupied Europe undoubtedly helped spur them to their considerable heights. They also tended to work past their actual shift time, simply because they found their piece of the puzzle interesting. Even on leave and days off, their thoughts drifted back to work. Some even drifted back physically. Alan Turing spent many of his free days working on his own research in Bletchley's huts. When Dilly Knox died in 1943, general BP lore placed the cause of his death squarely in the lap of overwork. Medical rules came down from above requiring that the various analysts take their weekly day off and their seven days' vacation every three months.[54] From the beginning, the BP staff often received memos reminding them, "You must have your rest day – you need it."[55] They bowed to these requests because they had learned the importance of their work.

## Knowing the Big Picture

The heads of GC&CS made certain that BP staff working on Ultra knew how their piece fit into the larger war effort. To boost Bletchley's morale, the heads of intelligence often reported back with tales of successes based on Ultra – successful convoy battles, the destruction of German targets such as the rocket launch site at Penemünde, effective attacks in anticipation of German maneuvers. Cryptanalysts were told which Enigma keys or book codes had provided the most useful information, so that they might continue to attack the most fruitful type of messages rather than spending their energies on unproductive work.

Not only cryptanalysts learned their place in the sigint puzzle. "Ultra-indoctrination," official knowledge of Ultra, spread all the way down to the women supervising the interception of Luftwaffe fighter and bomber traffic at outlying RAF stations. At the other end, the intelligence analysts who digested the translated and decrypted material learned something of how the cryptanalysts were breaking the ciphers, as well as how the interception and tracking of enemy signals worked. Commander Edward Travis, head of Bletchley after 1941, believed both the cryptanalyst and the traffic analyst "needed to have available a sound knowledge of the whole W/T [wireless traffic] organisation before they could begin." With this fusion, the fields of TA and DF[56] could contribute far more about "the enemy's activities and short term intentions."[57]

Personnel at Bletchley used every opportunity to stay abreast of the breadth and scope of activity at the Park. When anticipating a slow period at Bletchley, the Hut 3 head, Squadron Leader E. M. Jones, began "a series of lectures for members of Hut 3 ... to increase members' general knowledge of the work of other sections of the Hut."[58] He took suggestions of topics for the brief lectures and at times requested "All central watch room personnel to attend ... when they are on duty."[59] Topics included the German Secret Service and the Fish cipher system.[60] Through this education, GC&CS made "a conscious effort ... to give every one a broad knowledge, critical understanding and practical appreciation of the whole ... problem."[61] Educating vital intelligence staff took priority over compartmentalization and allowed tremendous cross-service successes.

4. The manor house at Bletchley Park where Government Code and Cypher School (GC&CS) first housed its main cryptologic effort against Enigma and other military cipher systems. GC&CS operations quickly grew too large for the main house and numerous temporary huts and additional buildings sprung up on the Park's extensive grounds. The manor house today looks much as it did during the war and is maintained, along with some of the surviving buildings and grounds, by the Bletchley Park Trust, which provides tours and Enigma-related events to the public. (Courtesy of the National Security Agency)

Such broad education of the intelligence staff could develop because Bletchley Park held virtually the entire cryptanalytic effort in one physical location.[62] Britain coordinated all its cryptology through GC&CS and, in turn, GC&CS placed the bulk of the personnel and equipment for that effort at the Bletchley Park complex. This physical centralization at BP made viewing the entire sigint operation possible. Because virtually all the necessary people, equipment, and knowledge of the intelligence effort accumulated at Bletchley, the people there could learn how their piece fit the puzzle. Both the audience and speakers of weekly information lectures worked within a few hundred yards of each other. Squadron Leader Jones could, without placing too great an onus on staff, detail one senior member of each Watch to attend the lecture on the German teleprinter call signs system, so that "there will be two senior members of each Watch...who will thoroughly understand it."[63]

In addition to educating analysts in problems beyond their own, Bletchley Park developed cross-training. Personnel locating signals through direction finding learned the "language and approach" of the next step in the process, log reading. With this knowledge, they could organize their records along a "log reading orientation," which fostered "the fullest possible trading of points of view between these two departments."[64] "Sixta," the Traffic Analysis Section working primarily on locating and tracking the travels of German land-based troops, developed a comprehensive, well-integrated training program by 1943.[65] Everyone, "regardless of how menial his eventual assignment," would first receive a course in "practical cryptography." Then came a lecture series "on the intelligence which derives from the cryptographic and T.A. enterprise." In other words, the traffic analyst learned what intelligence officers and military commanders want, the ultimate purpose of signals intelligence. Only once these traffic analysts knew why their job mattered did they sit down to do the actual work.

By fitting even TA staff assigned "menial" tasks into the larger puzzle, Bletchley Park boosted its potential and its effectiveness. At first the log readers, who sorted raw traffic looking for similar indicator groups, "in theory" were not "in the know"; that is, not Ultra-indoctrinated.[66] By 1943, however, they regularly received "the latest order of battle discoveries, intelligence evaluations of cipher keys, cryptographic [sic] methods and successes."[67] Aware of the latest information, they now produced more accurate results. Even better, they developed capabilities beyond the menial. They proved quite good at spotting potential cribs, a job usually done by analysts or cryptanalysts. Potential cribs, particularly those relying on routine messages and signatures, emerge "because of the familiarity of a single mind with the habits and idiosyncracies of the commanders and cipher clerks."[68] Once they had some understanding of the cryptanalysts' work, log readers pointed out many such useful leads. They would search the chronological collection of decrypts and raw traffic for possible repeated signals. At times, log readers found a decrypted message and an undecrypted message of the same length traveling on related networks. Such a correlation suggested a crib, the match between a known plaintext and its enciphered signal. Using these cribs, Bletchley's cryptanalysts could break the second net's key.

The British experience soon demonstrated that "with a wider understanding and deeper appreciation of the whole T.A., Cryptography and Intelligence problem," not just the log readers, but even the intelligence analysts produced "a higher quality product."[69] The fusion of the different elements of signals intelligence set the stage for greater efficiency and effectiveness. Because "fully aware" intelligence analysts followed the "cryptographic frontiers," they could direct interception and log reading with an eye to assisting breaks into new ciphers.

In the process of giving intelligence staff this broad knowledge of the whole problem, GC&CS intensified its centralization of signals intelligence. The heads of Bletchley's huts recognized "the interdependency of T.A., Cryptography and Intelligence." The "processes and products" of these elements of signals intelligence are both "interdependent and mutually useful to the ... other two." So GC&CS set out to make these sections "unified at the top and operationally intimate below."[70] One history of the Park, begun as the war wound down, noted, "to achieve integrated operations by means of diffuse authority may seem contradictory and unworkable."[71] In fact, this diffuse authority proved a vital piece of Bletchley's success. With this considerable autonomy, a broad cross section of staff solved a range of problems, both logistical and technical. With the power to propose solutions and make decisions, the young men and women in Bletchley's huts devised countless changes and improvements, as well as a few bold tactics,[72] that extended the Allies' window into German ciphers.

GC&CS needed both Bletchley Park's centralization and diffuse authority to extract the staff's potential and wring every ounce of information from Enigma signals. Cryptanalysts could not track the various Enigma nets, weed the vital traffic from less critical signals, and watch for repeated messages on their own. Fully exploiting cryptology required all the help of W/T.I. (wireless traffic intelligence): traffic analysis, direction finding, and log reading.[73] Through fusing these different elements of signals intelligence (W/T.I. and cryptanalysis), Bletchley's staff pieced together the enemy's entire wireless communications organization.

## Information Fusion

Joining the results of these different forms and sources of information became known at Bletchley as "fusion." By 1942, Hut 3 developed a Fusion Room, a section designed to fuse knowledge of call signs, results of TA and D/F, information from decrypted signals, and "intercipher" information.[74] Intelligence analysts performed this "fusion process." Called the "I staff," these men both absorbed and generated the big picture in the Fusion Room.

The I staff combined wireless intelligence "with identities derived from decodes and with any knowledge obtained from captures."[75] The emended text of every Ultra-decrypted message came into the Fusion Room and went into a chronological file.[76] The fusion staff correlated the call signs with the reported locations of enemy units in these decrypted messages. They traced the routing of messages to learn the "actual working" of enemy networks. Then they entered the information on wall maps and on cards, which went into a central "index."[77] From this collation, the Fusion Room produced daily and weekly reports, as well as a weekly summary of the "significant changes" in enemy radio activity.[78]

Intelligence analysts all had access to the massive index, which cross-referenced call signs, names, and troop movements. Should an analyst find a tantalizing reference in the card index, he could then turn to the chronological file for a copy of the original German message. One section, called the "Intelligence Exchange," received a copy of all intelligence produced at Bletchley, regardless of which enemy service branch originally generated it. Each of the armed services and the various agencies of GC&CS assigned someone to the Exchange to examine this mass of material. Each representative had the responsibility of ensuring "that if there is anything there of interest which has not been routed to his group it will be sent, or to make a protest if it is withheld from the group he represents."[79]

This massive correlation required connecting interception and cryptanalysis. To create this connection, GC&CS acquired the responsibility for directing interception. Although GC&CS had no intercept stations at Bletchley Park, it eventually had considerable control over the activities of the various military interception stations around Britain and the world. From its cryptanalytic center at Bletchley Park, GC&CS directed the outlying interception, changing the requirements according to its cryptanalytic needs. All intercepted Enigma traffic came directly to Bletchley, at first by dispatch rider, later almost exclusively over teleprinters.[80] One officer in the Fusion Room had responsibility for planning the interception coverage. He consulted with analysts and log readers and passed the final program to the outlying intercept stations.[81] Thus GC&CS put interception at the service of cryptanalysis.

With the direction of interception largely controlled by GC&CS at Bletchley Park, Britain had coordinated and centralized the elements of signals intelligence: wireless intelligence, cryptanalysis, and analysis. Bletchley Park's reach soon extended deep into the general military framework. Bletchley trained and indoctrinated the intelligence officers who advised the Prime Minister, the Ministries and military headquarters, and the commanders in the field. Once the United States joined the effort, GC&CS would teach the Americans "the importance of having close union of intelligence and operations from top to bottom."[82] The importance of physical proximity extended to Britain's Joint Intelligence Committee. In London, the JIC arranged its offices so that the planning staff and the intelligence staff had rooms side-by-side, "with a wide door open between them." The JIC made certain Bletchley Park had operational material "freely available at all times"[83] and could coordinate its effort as effectively as possible.

Thus Bletchley Park combined physical centralization of signals intelligence work and the centralization of control over the entire signals intelligence organization from collection (interception) through, as detailed in the next chapter, the final dissemination of results.

## Intelligent Cooperation

Bletchley Park's centralization created strong lines of cooperation. Locating virtually all facets of signals intelligence on the grounds of Bletchley Park made cooperation physically easy. Giving a view of the big picture not just to cryptanalysts but also to log readers and traffic analysts created the institutional mind-set for cooperation. The obvious need to defeat their common enemy convinced everyone at Bletchley that "there was no room for any rivalry at all. . . ."[84] Conflicts, of course, did arise, but Bletchley's personnel never forgot how vitally they fit into the overall war effort. This sense of a common purpose – acquiring the intelligence to defeat the Axis – gave extra impetus to resolving conflicts.[85]

Cooperation began within each Hut. Civilians worked side-by-side with military officers and enlistees. The Watch, responsible for translation and forwarding of decrypts, encouraged collaboration. Members translated their decrypts around a table and frequently consulted each other on challenging difficulties. This encouragement of exchange included the clerical staff. One secretary described the "Soviet" meetings, "where any grievance was aired and any suggestion was examined," whoever the speaker. This collaborative attitude "did away with any underground feeling of discontent."[86]

Collaboration extended to the use of the crucial decryption aides, the Bombes, as well. Through most of the war, all of the cryptanalytic sections working on Enigma ciphers "operated with the same battery of machines, Bombes."[87] "The bombes were considered the common property of Hut 6 and Hut 8," the cryptanalytic sections working on Heer and Luftwaffe Enigma and on Enigma M (naval), respectively. These two groups determined the priorities for the Bombe work after consulting with their respective intelligence sections (Hut 3 and Hut 4).[88] Indeed, a February 1942 log of Bombe time by "colour" (Bletchley nicknames for various Enigma keys) shows that the Bombes allocated roughly the same amount of time for Red (the main Luftwaffe key) as for Naval Enigma.[89] When faced with obstacles, such as the scheduling of Bombe time, the Huts informed each other of their needs and concerns. "Questions of priority about the urgency" of the two sections' Bombe requirements arose at times and were "in practice . . . settled by negotiation between the senior officers of the two huts." A more formal arrangement also developed, periodic meetings where the Huts "la[id] down general lines of policy . . . modified from time to time as circumstances change[d]." The Huts even helped by testing "each other's bombe stops and . . . assisting [each other] in decoding."[90] This cooperation in Bombe time expanded to weekly meetings which included the Americans.[91]

5. The U.S. Navy four-rotor Bombe with the banks of rotors wired to duplicate all the possible Enigma M rotors. These Bombes were enormous, noisy, and kept a team of mechanics busy. The last known Navy Bombe resides in the NSA's National Cryptologic Museum. The others were apparently destroyed sometime after the war, possibly by being dumped at sea. (Courtesy of the National Security Agency)

Although differences between the sections, or Huts, existed, particularly in "intelligence techniques,"[92] "intelligence work at the GC&CS [was] essentially inter-service in nature."[93] The cryptanalysts and analysts at Bletchley recognized the single system that Enigma had created in German communications. Early on they saw that intelligence of value for a particular military branch might come from a variety of avenues, not just from the Enigma signals of the counterpart German service. Perusal of Luftwaffe sources often gleaned information useful to the Allied army and sometimes for the Royal Navy, as in the case of the *Bismarck* sinking.[94]

These many crosscurrents of information connected the cryptanalysis and intelligence Huts in the person of a "crypto liaison officer." This officer kept the cryptanalysts "informed continuously of intelligence priorities as seen from" the analysis Huts.[95] The cryptanalysts recognized when a Bombe began producing clear text, the sign that they had cracked a daily key, but they did not read the signals they had decrypted. They relied on their liaison and the Watch to tell them which cipher keys carried the most valuable information and, hence, should receive priority for daily attack. The Fusion Room officers assisted various cryptanalytic sections, notifying them of relevant intelligence and representing their interests in the Fusion Room.[96] Cryptanalysts, in turn, might suggest attacking a new key that they had noticed carried frequent or very regular signals or might discourage attacking a key that carried amounts of traffic insufficient for simple solution. By exchanging information frequently and exploiting each other's talents, Bletchley's participants streamlined their attack on enemy keys and made the most efficient use of their combined efforts.

Multilevel cooperation extended beyond Bletchley Park's physical boundaries. As Hut 3's Air Advisor, Peter Calvocoressi, notes

> it is impossible to imagine Hut 3 without the scrambler telephone. Its invention meant we could discuss the latest detail or puzzle with colleagues in the Air Ministry in the same way as we discussed these matters among ourselves . . . [97]

Many of the interservice oversight committees established both before and during the war found this air of cooperation at lower levels made their work virtually redundant. "The Radio Security Committee . . . met only twice before the end of the war because the new working level committee proved to be effective in solving most problems that arose."[98]

Intelligence cooperation included technical solutions. For the original reconstructions of Enigma and the first Bombes, the Polish cryptanalysts turned to a technical manufacturing firm, AVA, for the expertise of its engineers. This commercial connection gave Polish intelligence a secure production source for several mechanical and electromechanical cryptanalytic aids.[99] As Polish intelligence trusted its cryptanalytic needs to AVA, the British and Americans also found industrial assistance for their cryptologic machines. British engineers from the Post Office constructed the protocomputer Colossus.[100] In the United States, both of the military services had a commercial connection. The Army drew engineers from IBM, while the Navy used the National Cash Register Company to create the High Speed Navy Bombe to break the U-boat Enigma.[101] The ability of these signals intelligence agencies to draw in commercial expertise and capabilities gave the Allies an edge in cryptologic technology.

In addition to such technical solutions, this connection to the business world yielded dividends by addressing sigint with the methods of industrialization, mechanization, and automation. Just as Henry Ford imposed his assembly-line process to increase airplane production dramatically, Allied sigint adopted assembly-line techniques to handle the masses of signals flowing into its cryptologic center. Any piece of the process that did not need a cryptanalyst's expertise was farmed out to other staff.[102] Over the course of a few years, GC&CS grew from a small artisan-like facility to a bustling community of several thousand operating around the clock seven days a week. Using automation and industrialization, this signals intelligence center absorbed thousands of raw recruits, trained them in their place in a decryption "assembly line," and processed thousands of decrypts every day.

### Beyond Bletchley

Not everyone approved of the increasing concentration and centralization of signals intelligence work at Bletchley Park. Diplomatic traffic left Bletchley for London.[103] The Admiralty resisted centralization to the point of maintaining its separation from the RAF and Army sections (Hut 3). Throughout the war, naval intelligence and naval cryptanalysis of Enigma remained a distinct unit and occurred in separate spaces (Huts 8 and 4, respectively). The Admiralty also won a separate dissemination system for Ultra intelligence – teleprinter lines to the submarine tracking room. Ultra, however, convinced the Admiralty of the effectiveness of centralizing cryptologic work in one physical location, and they never attempted to separate from the Bletchley Park system.[104]

Bletchley Park served as the main cryptologic site, but GC&CS developed a few auxiliary posts. Although the diplomatic and commercial unit moved to Berkeley Street in London, it remained under GC&CS direction. Interception stations within Britain and closer to the fighting around the world did some immediate traffic analysis and direction finding, and even some code work. GC&CS also set up small cryptanalytic sections, such as the Middle East bureau in Cairo (CBME). These sections served as outposts of Bletchley Park, communicating directly with Bletchley's Huts and remaining under Bletchley's control. Through these connections, Bletchley Park embraced the full range of ciphers, all grades and all languages.

This centralization "brought psychological and technical benefits"; in particular, "the consequent concentration of talent was intellectually stimulating."[105] They could streamline their efforts and so afford to expend time and energy on small details and long-term research. For example, long-term issues and use of intelligence came under the rubric of a separate interservice section. This section handled some seemingly mundane topics, such as the meaning of German abbreviations. With access to Bletchley's complete signals intelligence results, the interservice staff undertook special studies: investigations of enemy cover names or technical equipment. Their results went back to the services as "appreciations" for the intelligence analysts.[106] These interservice sections would produce welcome dividends.

### Exploiting Connections

The Enigma system proved particularly vulnerable to attack by a centralized operation such as Bletchley's. Since much of German enciphering used variations of the original military Enigma, the entire network operated as a single system of related variations. As the analysts, log readers, and indexers at Bletchley began correlating information from different Enigma nets, they found connecting patterns.

One useful connection was weather. Weather plays an important role in warfare, and every military branch transmits weather reports. Moreover, weather moves eastward across Europe, giving Britain a geographical advantage. Bletchley consolidated all weather codes under one person, Dr. MacVittie, "to whom all collateral information was available."[107] This centralization allowed an amazing thread of continuity and generated prolific cipher breaks at Bletchley. By 1942, Bletchley analysts claimed they had broken every weather cipher they had encountered: German, Italian, Soviet, and Vichy French.[108] The numerous systems created much repetition of essentially identical plaintext. Knowledge of the weather report from one system produced a possible break into all the other systems carrying the same report. Because Britain experienced the weather before German troops on the Continent, Bletchley could sometimes even guess the plaintext of an enciphered weather report. Weather codes allowed breaks into "F," the Geheimschreiber machines, and also played a vital role in making and maintaining Hut 8's breaks into the Marine Enigma ciphers.[109] After the Marine upgraded their Enigma to a four-rotor machine in February 1942, most of BP's cracking relied on the weather messages sent back to Berlin on the old three-rotor settings.[110]

Bletchley soon recognized how all the different versions of Enigma connected as a single interconnected system. Bletchley Park's analysts and cryptanalysts began treating Enigma as "a single and indivisible problem of increasing complexity." In Hut 6 (Heer and Luftwaffe Enigma cryptanalysis), cryptanalysts faced an intricate net of some sixty Enigma keys, "Fish" traffic, three-letter codes, and weather ciphers, all "so linked together that they constitute one single problem."[111]

At times a low-grade system, such as a weather code, provided a re-encodement, identical plaintext enciphered in two separate ciphers, and hence a crib into a high-grade (Enigma or Fish) cipher. Every cryptanalyst knows this valuable method. Hence, the importance of reenciphering a text with significant paraphrasing ranks at the top of general cipher security lists. Nonetheless, re-encodements happen. Bletchley log readers and analysts kept a keen eye fixed on numerous Enigma keys and found rewarding repetition. In the Mediterranean, for example, the Heer's keys all linked through re-encodements, "any one of [which] might prove to be the best starting point."[112] These re-encodements connected the many Heer keys of the Mediterranean into a single problem. Once one key succumbed to the day's attack, the rest usually followed quickly. Although the Germans periodically issued warnings against reciphering without significant paraphrasing, the re-encodements usually reappeared quickly.

One particularly striking example of this type of security violation came from a security order itself. Oberinspektor Menzer, in charge of vetting ciphers and security procedures, sent word of a procedural upgrade to all of the Abwehr stations throughout Europe. His message provided the perfect re-encodement from Bletchley's point of view, and

**eine Kommandosache!**
...im Flugzeug mitnehmen!

## Heeres-Stabs-Maschinenschlüssel Süd Nr. 70

| Datum | Walzenlage | | | Ringstellung | | | Steckerverbindungen | | | | | | | | | | Kenngruppen | | | |
|---|---|---|---|---|---|---|---|---|---|---|---|---|---|---|---|---|---|---|---|---|
| 31. | III | I | IV | 16 | 03 | 24 | HZ | YR | IF | QT | JN | GC | AP | UX | BD | KS | vfw | wbh | nuf | re |
| 30. | V | IV | I | 26 | 22 | 25 | BL | AN | GC | IY | VE | MX | SW | QZ | PO | UK | fze | fug | rdq | bd |
| 29. | III | IV | V | 14 | 18 | 05 | CV | WK | MS | UP | OJ | DZ | XA | LR | IY | HN | hyy | fao | wka | wt |
| 28. | I | II | V | 11 | 10 | 02 | ZJ | BP | VK | UG | LN | QX | SA | MT | ZD | YH | yor | xef | oxq | oo |
| 27. | V | I | III | 20 | 07 | 15 | KZ | FD | UP | MG | XB | OC | WR | ZB | YL | IA | lwc | aug | fwi | lu |
| 26. | II | V | IV | 01 | 02 | 21 | GS | VG | IL | HR | JN | XO | TQ | BD | PP | EU | cle | myk | ezl | za |
| 25. | I | V | II | 07 | 08 | 19 | BD | WN | CX | TI | KS | MQ | UH | VF | JZ | LG | pkw | nwn | bfw | vb |
| 24. | IV | II | I | 17 | 19 | 08 | GU | OE | XA | CI | MS | NY | JN | PF | KL | ZW | hlo | chv | lgc | lu |
| 23. | II | V | III | 13 | 24 | 07 | XP | VB | ZM | HW | QI | DS | LC | UG | FK | EO | xqu | pcu | gcl | zc |
| 22. | III | II | I | 18 | 16 | 01 | QI | HE | BP | MU | AR | YL | KO | GJ | XV | ZN | tal | tuq | nmj | ra |
| 21. | V | II | IV | 23 | 09 | 26 | VQ | IN | EB | PY | ZX | GJ | HM | RL | CW | SK | jlb | yae | bce | tf |
| 20. | V | I | II | 25 | 25 | 14 | PV | EY | HN | US | KJ | IM | WD | XL | GT | HZ | ehd | kfg | oqd | xx |
| 19. | I | III | II | 06 | 20 | 23 | JZ | FW | XK | GC | PQ | MH | US | DB | OY | VE | tav | may | rmc | en |
| 18. | I | IV | III | 22 | 26 | 22 | XK | ZS | QU | WA | TV | IE | HD | YO | PR | ML | gnb | ouy | zlx | vd |
| 17. | III | I | II | 24 | 21 | 18 | JN | GP | CB | KS | WU | ZL | OI | VR | DF | YH | wkj | yrc | rro | vd |
| 16. | V | IV | II | 19 | 06 | 06 | UQ | BD | EI | MO | HF | GT | WZ | CP | LA | SV | trd | rtp | ptx | t |
| 15. | III | V | IV | 04 | 13 | 13 | XV | KF | YS | PI | UE | LJ | AW | QH | CR | GZ | uye | pjp | elu | gz |
| 14. | I | II | IV | 09 | 11 | 17 | EY | UR | IQ | ZK | CF | WM | LP | ON | HA | VS | uod | bvl | hoo | ak |
| 13. | V | III | II | 05 | 25 | 09 | LY | XU | VN | OM | RC | PD | IA | EZ | GT | KQ | xsg | bsd | rzk | ol |
| 12. | I | V | IV | 03 | 06 | 12 | XW | KB | IZ | UN | DA | MP | LY | HJ | RV | QF | okq | uvf | uvl | ba |
| 11. | V | I | IV | 10 | 02 | 20 | DA | IG | SY | GL | OE | XN | MU | PZ | HQ | TJ | npd | byz | cas | lq |
| 10. | II | IV | V | 08 | 05 | 16 | QT | AZ | UY | JS | DW | CN | OH | IB | KP | GM | vxp | ymy | tmx | kz |
| 9. | IV | II | III | 26 | 09 | 11 | ZU | PD | KR | XT | BM | AO | ES | IL | HO | QG | ajh | tmw | tes | rp |
| 8. | I | V | III | 20 | 10 | 10 | ZD | YQ | AK | IE | RB | VS | CU | FL | WM | NP | lsd | xux | eva | bz |
| 7. | III | IV | I | 01 | 19 | 24 | AH | GM | OV | RP | BF | EJ | XC | SZ | UI | NQ | mcb | cwo | lwv | et |
| 6. | III | II | V | 07 | 14 | 10 | VN | AY | GM | ZG | XU | RT | LP | HS | IF | KQ | mdt | sxf | lxl | bc |
| 5. | II | III | IV | 04 | 12 | 18 | CA | YW | HO | ZB | KP | ID | LT | VN | GZ | XM | yck | fcs | fcr | xx |
| 4. | II | I | V | 14 | 08 | 19 | HD | PY | XM | FU | IG | LK | WZ | JC | EO | RQ | ril | swb | opv | lq |
| 3. | IV | V | II | 25 | 07 | 14 | OM | QS | BT | KJ | FY | VN | RZ | HA | IW | UO | esq | eey | och | us |
| 2. | II | I | III | 06 | 23 | 03 | KV | FA | NT | UW | ZD | OM | JR | LE | XI | PY | bjv | eax | ofr | fc |
| 1. | IV | III | V | 19 | 22 | 17 | GZ | UD | TY | KN | PW | RH | EA | SC | QF | MO | fvm | yrw | vlm | ur |

6. A month's worth of daily settings for the military (three-rotor) Enigma used in southern Europe. The four elements of the setting are clearly divided: Walzenlage, or which three of the five possible rotors to use; Ringstellung, or at which letter to set the turnover rotor (letters being designated by the number corresponding to their position in the alphabet a=01, b=02, etc.); Steckerverbindungen, or the letter pairs for the 10 pairs of plugs allowed (although the machine had 13 pairs of jacks and could handle any number of plug pairings from 0 to 13); and finally the Kenngruppen, or recognition letters for this particular net. Note that the clerk has followed the rules restricting the possibilities for the month. For example, the same rotors do not reappear in the same order. There are ten and only ten Stecker pairings; no adjacent letters are paired. (Courtesy of the National Security Agency)

the cryptanalysts pried their way into "several links hitherto unbroken."[113] Although most re-encodement cribs were less spectacular, they gave Bletchley's cryptanalysts tremendous assistance.

Another form of repetition proved even more helpful to the British: key repeats. Here again Bletchley reaped rich benefits from its massive operation of catalogues and cross-indexing. By 1941, analysts at Bletchley had spotted familiar pieces of daily settings. German cipher officers had gotten lazy and begun to reuse rotor orders, Steckerboard settings, and discriminants from other nets or previous months.[114] Occasionally, all the pieces of one key – rings, rotors, and Steckerboard – reappeared together. In late 1942, one of the three principal Mediterranean air keys (code-named Scorpion II) began using the entire key used by another of the three (Primrose) in the previous month.[115] One month the Enigma net nicknamed Skunk began using settings from the previous month, but in reverse, "i.e. the key of the 31st was used on the 1st, etc. Consequently two days can be read for every one broken."[116] As the war continued, these repeats expanded.

More often only one or two pieces of a month's key repeated. For much of 1942, the Luftwaffe provided systematic key repeats that reduced the cryptanalysts' work by half.

> Instead of making up a new set of keys every month they were made up every other month. In order to provide keys for the second month the four parts of the first month's key were divided into two sections, namely, A = wheel order and ringstellung, and B = stecker and discriminants.[117]

This repetition meant that breaking one month's keys gave the cryptanalysts a second "free" month. One Luftwaffe clerk then compounded this mistake by allocating the pieces of these repeating sections among four networks (nicknamed Mosquito, Leek, Cockroach, and Cabbage). As the repeats rotated, Bletchley cryptanalysts could break into all four networks. Unfortunately, this particular set of repeats stopped at the beginning of 1943.[118] Although tracking these repeats required considerable time and paperwork, the effort had paid off.

By early 1942, Bletchley's analysts and cryptanalysts had realized the importance of keeping up with as many different Enigma keys as possible, "of however little intelligence value." With each key broken the chance of finding a key repeat increased. Such "repetitions have a double value – not only do they enable the repeating key to be broken quickly and regularly, but in so doing they liberate a great deal of bombe time for other keys."[119]

As the Germans upgraded Enigma and their enciphering procedures, Bletchley depended more and more on the repeats of keys and messages. As the number of Enigma keys proliferated, Bletchley's cryptanalysts scrambled to crack into as many as possible. Apparently minor keys, from an intelligence analysis perspective, often contained vital re-encodements and key repeats for primary keys. In July 1942, Bletchley's Bombes broke 183 Luftwaffe daily keys. In the next month, Bletchley cracked 396 Luftwaffe keys, more than double that of the previous month. Many of these breaks, including those into two principal Luftwaffe keys, came from repeats of July keys used in minor nets. These Luftwaffe repeats released Bombes for work on the more difficult Heer keys.[120] Analysts became skilled at spotting the repetitions and connections across nets and at playing one key off another. The champion bridge players at Bletchley compared the cross-cribbing in this round robin of connections to "cross-ruffing" suits in bridge.

Cross-cribbing proved particularly valuable across service lines. Tracing messages from one Wehrmacht branch to another often revealed cribs into otherwise difficult keys. Bletchley's analysts learned how to exploit anything they read, not only the weather ciphers but the vulnerable Luftwaffe Enigma keys. Often the day's initial break into the set of Mediterranean Heer keys came from "Red," the most extensively read Enigma cipher.[121] Because Bletchley broke Red, the main Luftwaffe key, every day from early 1940 through the end of the war, any message circulated on that Luftwaffe net could serve as a crib if it reappeared elsewhere. The Luftwaffe keys also offered breaks into Marine keys. Bletchley cryptanalysts broke a Marine key in the Mediterranean theater, Porpoise, through cribs from Gadfly, the key for Luftwaffenkommando Südost (Balkans).[122] The final, fatal detection of the *Bismarck* appeared in a Red decrypt, informing a Luftwaffe officer of his sailor son's location – aboard the heavy ship.[123]

## Inter-Allied Cooperation

By 1940, GC&CS's centralization had expanded to cover the coordination of cryptologic work done on Enigma by its allies – at various times French, Polish, and American.[124] The coordination began before the war as a loose cooperation begun by the French and then the Poles. In 1939, Polish intelligence passed news of their success and copies of reconstructed Enigma machines to the French and British. This collaboration had hardly begun in earnest when Germany invaded Poland in September 1939. Bletchley Park learned 17 October 1939 that the Polish cryptologists had fled through Romania and Italy and had returned to work in France.[125]

Cooperation between the Allied intelligence organizations prospered through the period of the phony war. British, French, and Polish cryptanalysts exchanged methods, successes, and material on cracking Enigma via teletype line.[126] The two cryptanalytic centers of Bletchley in England and the French-Polish "P. C. Bruno" team in France communicated as well through a liaison, Capt. Kenneth "Pinky" McFarlan. Alan Turing visited his Polish colleagues in France more than once in 1940, although he kept some details of BP's work secret even from them.[127]

Britain by no means had complete control over these other efforts. Although Bletchley Park's chief, Alastair Denniston, and its chief cryptanalyst, Dilly Knox, wanted the Polish mathematicians to visit and perhaps even work at the Park, the French vetoed the plan.[128] Nonetheless, ongoing contacts promoted collaboration and fostered the international attack on more and more Enigma keys.

The multinational teams coordinated their efforts to reduce redundancy. They split the work on German police traffic, for example, by day, with the team in France handling the odd days and Bletchley's section taking the even.[129] After France fell in 1940, the P. C. Bruno team resumed work on Enigma in Vichy until forced once again to flee German occupying forces in November 1942.[130] With this collapse, the British-French-Polish collaboration on Enigma ended for good.[131] However, Britain had learned the value of international cooperation and now turned to another partner.

On the other side of the Atlantic, American intelligence took longer to reach GC&CS's level of efficient cooperation. By 1939, the United States still had no centralized intelligence agency (and would not have one until after 1945).[132] Six major agencies worked on codes and ciphers.[133] These agencies competed for budget allocations and for credit. Viewing each other as rivals, they kept their work secret as much as possible.[134] The Americans did not tackle the problem of their interservice secrecy until after they experienced the effectiveness of Bletchley's system.

Well before Pearl Harbor, Britain and the United States cooperated in signals intelligence. By September 1940, the two nations discussed pooling their resources, albeit with a focus on Japan and the Far East.[135] Britain initially offered the United States a "pretty free interchange," at least for Japanese and Russian systems.[136] In the case of German and Italian material, however, GC&CS insisted that "any progress we have made is of such vital importance to us that we cannot agree at once to hand it over unreservedly."[137]

As roughly equal but complementary players in signals intelligence, the two cryptanalytic organizations found themselves forced into closer cooperation by their very intelligence successes. Secure belief in Ultra's reliability required knowing its source. By early 1941, American intelligence officers were meeting their GC&CS counterparts. Four American officers (two army and two navy) traveled to Britain in February 1941. They saw most of Bletchley Park itself and spent ten weeks discussing cryptanalytic issues, primarily those "related to German, Japanese, Italian and Russian secret systems."[138] The British welcomed the Americans enthusiastically and "suggested definite plans for such cooperation including the possibility of a division of effort in order to avoid duplication." For example,

> The British have a cipher section in Singapore which is getting fairly good results but is handicapped by lack of competent Japanese translators. They would be glad to turn over to us the results of these labors if we did no more than supply the translators.[139]

Several Britons, including Commander Denniston, later visited Canada and the United States in return. Denniston's trip was marked by his explanation that the notorious Herbert Yardley (now working for the Canadians) had to go.[140] The greatest contention between the two powers came when Alan Turing was initially barred from Bell Labs.[141] Overall, cooperation improved steadily and in mid-1941, when Britain and the United States began running the Atlantic convoys, they included pertinent intelligence as a joint operation.

This ongoing project, along with the 1942 North African campaign, ironed out inter-Allied cooperation, leaving only Bomber Command as a coordinated, but not integrated, operation.[142] By mid-1943, most of the British intelligence committees "were in close touch with the Americans and [their planning] corresponded closely with the American system."[143] Working out the details of the cooperation initially caused difficulties at top levels on both sides of the Atlantic. The British worried about lax American security, whereas U.S. Army General Strong wanted to "make certain he was not cheated of any information."[144] At Bletchley and in the field, however, British and American analysts found that the merger "was so smooth that we hardly noticed it."[145] Bletchley remained the focus of cryptanalytic cooperation for the European theater and in April 1943 the first American, Telford Taylor, arrived to work at the Park. From the beginning, GC&CS took the lead in training U.S. personnel "in all phases of signals intelligence."[146] Signals personnel soon crossed the Atlantic frequently for training and general cooperation, as well as to confer on specific sigint activities.[147]

This cooperation led to an Anglo-American Combined Intelligence Committee (CIC), which attempted to minimize redundancy across service and national lines. In general, the United States assumed responsibility for cryptanalysis in the Pacific theater and Britain for cryptanalysis in the European theater. While this division was by no means complete, a rough centralization emerged with most Enigma keys decrypted in England and most Japanese ciphers (particularly the "Red" and "Purple" machine ciphers) attacked in the United States.[148]

Soon the United Kingdom and United States were sharing and coordinating all their Ultra intelligence. All of the U.S. intelligence organizations developed "some liaison or other with the British intelligence agencies; and [were] freer in giving information to the British than to one another."[149] They exchanged material at all levels and "arbitrarily" divided the labor "to avoid duplication of effort."[150] They supplied each other with copies of captured and reconstructed enemy material, including Spanish, French, and Italian codebooks. They traded instructions for finding keys and using indicator and additive tables.[151]

Cryptologists not only exchanged visits, methods, and machinery but frequent, sometimes daily, progress reports and analyses. The U.S. Army's Signals Agency received copies of BP project committee meetings (such as those on the potential introduction of the pluggable Umkehrwalz Dora), Hut 3's weekly reports, memos on various diplomatic ciphers, and "Fish Notes" on various mathematical formulae and mechanical processes for breaking the Baudot machines Sturgeon and Tunny.[152] In turn, the Signals Agency sent GC&CS regular memos about a wide range of issues: progress on specific codes and ciphers, use of machines in decryption, methods of determining cipher elements, and the numbers of personnel and how their work was structured, to name only a few.[153] The two naval sections cooperated directly, discussing the day's keys, submarine reports, the use of Ultra, and intelligence difficulties via teleprinter lines.[154]

Cooperation between the European and Pacific theaters also bore unforeseen fruit. The Japanese diplomatic cipher, Purple, included the messages of the Japanese ambassador in Berlin, Baron Oshima, to Tokyo. These reports provided considerable information of interest to the European theater, most notably details of the "Western Wall" fortifications on the Normandy coast.[155] The joint Allied forces attacking Normandy in June 1944 benefited from U.S. decrypts of these Japanese signals. By war's end, British and American cryptology had become well intertwined, and they remain woven together today.

## Mechanizing and Automating Cryptology

Whereas GC&CS had experience and success with Enigma to offer the American intelligence services, in exchange the United States brought what Britain needed most desperately of all: natural resources and production capability. In nearly every way, the vast resources and production of the United States would far outstrip those of any other belligerent, even the Soviet Union.[156] Those resources included staff and machines for cryptanalysis as well as the most modern production techniques and just in time. By the end of 1941, Allied intelligence already faced an information onslaught and desperately needed to automate as much of its processing as possible.

Early in the war, staff at Bletchley Park had instituted a process that would industrialize and rationalize sigint production as never before. Within months of the war's start, Gordon Welchman and Edward Travis laid out a plan to build up Bletchley's organization and capabilities rapidly. They turned to an assortment of experts to refine this enormous undertaking. For Bletchley Park's physical security, a former Scotland Yard employee developed "a system of guards, gates, and passes."[157] Welchman designed a production line with "five closely coordinated departments" to move each decrypt from arrival as a raw intercept through traffic analysis, decryption, emendation and translation, to analysis and distribution as special intelligence.[158] Inside both the cryptanalytic and the analysis Huts, the staff streamlined the work, finding ways to make tasks routine and easily teachable so they could be passed on to new recruits. Indeed, the typists tended to be young women with minimal, if any, German, but they learned to process the enormous number of Enigma decrypts quickly. This swiftly designed system worked very successfully. William Friedman noted that "provided that the Watch do not make the mistake of breaking all their keys at the same moment, ... a complete day's traffic can be disposed of in an hour or less." He called the resulting deluge of information for Hut 3 analysts "rather like saturation bombing."[159]

With thousands of signals arriving every day, the Park's personnel risked overlooking the most critical tidbits of information among the heaps of routine messages. The Air Index alone contained "over 15,000 [enemy] names ... going down as far as NCO's [providing] practically the data of his whole career, including promotions, leaves, illnesses, trips, etc."[160] Only a vigilant, cooperative staff using modern assembly-line techniques could efficiently and effectively sort out the vital intelligence and then decrypt and disseminate it in time for operational use. Bletchley's staff melded individual familiarity with the enemy's operations with the principle of automating wherever possible. They made creative use of simple techniques such as color coding to provide an instant overview of intercepted traffic.

Allied sigint not only used the techniques of the business world but also commandeered staff and facilities. Britain asked for help from the British Tabulating Machine Company and the Post Office's engineers in developing machines for cryptanalysis. American sigint took over much of National Cash Register's (NCR) Dayton plant for building cryptologic machines, sending NCR its military recruits – both regular Navy and WAVES. Access to such modern facilities proved useful in such cases as the emergency rewiring of Sigaba rotors in early 1945. This sigint-industry collaboration performed its most crucial role in the battle to stay ahead of German upgrades to Enigma. Within two months of the U.S. entry into the war, German U-boats went over to a four-rotor Enigma, making the old Bombes obsolete. Britain had already designed four-rotor Bombes but none had come through production. The U.S. Navy agreed to produce four-rotor Bombes to attack the U-boat ciphers, eventually creating the highly successful Navy High-Speed Bombe.[161] Where the British asked what could be automated and what machines could do for cryptanalysis, the Americans asked how a machine could do it. American engineers, in cooperation with their British counterparts, would design numerous machines to cope with German cipher upgrades, including Madame X, Duenna, and the Auto- and Super-Scritchers.[162]

GC&CS coordinated the work done by the machines on both sides of the Atlantic so "the British and the American work on naval Enigma settings was carried out according to a single programme."[163] The two navies linked their Tracking Rooms via teleprinter, exchanging analysis, locations of U-boats, and cryptanalytic results, including the daily setting for Marine keys as soon as they were recovered.[164] "This unique network of information . . . no doubt had a synergistic effect and probably made Ultra information far more valuable than it otherwise might have been."[165]

This unprecedented cooperation had limits. The Americans made an exception of Sigaba, their highest-grade cipher machine. They refused for quite some time to allow the British even a look at the machine. When the agreement for cryptologic cooperation with the British was drawn up, the Army noted in its own policy:

> Specifically no information of any kind shall be transmitted to them [i.e., the British] with respect to the converter type M-134-A, B or C [CSP-888 = ECM = Sigaba] nor should the existence or general principles of these machines be disclosed.[166]

Even though the British displayed Typex, their own electromechanical cipher machine, the Sigaba "prohibition was rigidly adhered to by the members of the mission sent to England."[167]

With Sigaba off-limits (and Typex disqualified), the U.S. Signals Intelligence Service "turned down the proposal of using the Type X and/or M-134-C [for joint U.S.-British communications]" because of "the desire of both countries to maintain physical control of their own equipment."[168] Agreeing on a new cryptographic system for joint communications took time. Soon the two Allies had "good reasons to believe that the failure to provide secure cryptographic systems for the purpose resulted in considerable losses in matériel and personnel, by submarine action."[169] Only after this squabbling cost many lives did cryptanalysts and policy makers find a solution: the CCM [Combined Cipher Machine]. CCM actually did not exist on its own, but rather emerged as an adapted version of the Navy Sigaba (ECM), the British Typex, or a partially gutted Sigaba.[170]

In the end, the British and the Americans recognized the need for cooperation in cryptography as well as in cryptanalysis. They began the war as the underdogs, with little success against important enemy systems and disastrous leaks in their own codes and ciphers. Their emphasis on and centralization of signals intelligence, however, would allow them to overcome these deficiencies. Ultimately, history would prove them successful in both these halves of cryptology: the successful and extensive cryptanalysis of their enemy's systems, and, as we shall see in the next chapter, secure cryptography of their own.

# FIVE

# PROTECTING BONIFACE

## Allied Security, Disguise, and Dissemination of Ultra

The value of the information is extremely high; therefore the security
of its sources cannot be too carefully maintained.
— Allied wartime report on Enigma decryption

Any action based upon Ultra must be so camouflaged that the action
itself cannot lead the enemy to the conclusion that it is based on Ultra.
Momentary tactical advantage is not sufficient ground for taking any
risk of compromising the source. No action may be taken against specific sea or land targets revealed by Ultra unless appropriate air or land
reconnaissance or other suitable camouflage measures have also been
undertaken.
— Regulations for Maintaining the Security of Special
Intelligence (1944)

The whole structure rests on a slender base and could easily be toppled
by breaches of security.
— Colonel McCormack, reporting on his trip to Bletchley Park
in 1943

Enigma's decrypts lay wrapped for thirty years under a heavy veil of
secrecy, which hints and unauthorized allusions could not part. The
miracle of Ultra, particularly in the cynical eyes of the computer age,
lies not so much in Enigma's cracking as in the nearly perfect security which surrounded the deciphering effort. This secrecy allowed the
machine's users to retain full confidence in their system, not just during
the war but for decades thereafter. Unlike their German counterparts,
the Allies made a concerted effort at disguise and protection. They kept

the enemy from learning about the Ultra decrypts, Allied personnel with knowledge of Ultra's existence, and high-grade ciphers, which carried Ultra intelligence and Allied command decisions.

Roughly ten thousand people worked at Bletchley, and they all kept their involvement with Ultra a secret – generally even from their families – for more than thirty years. While the Allied intelligence system, exemplified by Bletchley Park, made possible the actual cracking of the German Enigma ciphers, Allied security allowed that cracking to continue.

## Central Control of Security

This remarkable security, as well as the success it protected, rested on the centralization embodied by Bletchley Park. Here within the confines of the Park, the Allies' cipher experts cracked the enemy's systems and governed their own cryptologic security. Specifically, Bletchley Park coordinated the handling of Special Intelligence. This highest grade of intelligence passed only through Special Liaison Units (SLUs) or direct lines to the Admiralty and the submarine tracking rooms.

The centralization at Bletchley Park rested on the premise that all the elements of signals intelligence "are part and parcel of each other."[1] Ultra's success required fusing all grades of intelligence and all the sigint elements – interception, traffic analysis, direction finding, and cryptanalysis. The parts of the organization needed a clear view of where they fit into the whole to create both the most efficient cryptanalysis and the most effective security. Creating a functional view of security removed the potentially damaging blinders of restricted knowledge. The traffic analyst could point out potential cribs to the cryptanalyst. Faced with a code he had never seen before, a cryptanalyst could talk to a colleague who had seen something similar and cracked it. They could do so because Bletchley had abandoned traditional rigid security in favor of a more fluid system.

Although not all ten thousand people working in the Park knew exactly what was going on, there was "no 'security blindness' in their processes."[2] From the directors on down, Bletchley's staff applied the "need to know" restriction neither rigidly nor narrowly. Instead, they used a "broadly construed" definition that considered how a job fit into the larger interception-cryptanalysis-evaluation process. Personnel were included under "need to know" when greater knowledge of Ultra would allow them to anticipate and assist the cryptanalysts' needs. Thus a WAAF intercepting German fighter traffic would be Ultra-indoctrinated to direct Enigma interception more effectively. One indoctrinated interceptor, Aileen Clayton, also assisted the scientific and technical departments tracing new Luftwaffe developments.[3] At Bletchley, the Fusion Room head requested that dozens of log readers sorting Enigma traffic "be put 'in the know'" so that they could direct their own efforts most efficiently.[4]

All of these WRENS, WAAFs, "professor types," and enlisted men had sworn themselves to secrecy before they knew what they would be working on. Some never knew. Thousands of WRENS, WAAFs, and American WAVES worked on the mechanical aspects of breaking Enigma, running the Bombes, wiring rotors, and recording and transcribing seemingly meaningless messages. Many of them only realized the role they had played after the 1974 publication of Winterbotham's *Ultra Secret*. But they had kept their oath of secrecy.

Those "indoctrinated" into the Ultra secret bound themselves not just to secrecy but to certain conduct. Indoctrination meant agreeing to the "Ultra regulations," which included restrictions such as who handled Ultra and how. Knowing the Ultra Secret meant accepting sometimes severe limitations on one's freedom, even where one could receive mail.[5] Under a military intelligence agreement, those who had cryptanalytic experience with Ultra could not transfer out of Bletchley Park.[6] One did not speak of Enigma or Ultra outside of BP,[7] and even inside the Park one did not mention Ultra's source outside of the "huts," so as not to mention Ultra inadvertently to someone not fully indoctrinated. Needless to say, one did not speak of Enigma, Ultra, or cipher work to outsiders, no matter how trustworthy or closely related. When the head of Bletchley Park, Edward Travis, received a knighthood for his war service, his wife asked "What for?"[8] The women working on the Bombes' wirings knew only that if they mentioned their work, they "would be shot."[9] None were, but many remember the dramatic announcement.

Such ultimate enforcement of Ultra's security proved unnecessary. In general, GC&CS tended to rely on more informal means for enforcing security, even when legal methods existed. To minimize newspaper leaks, the government had established the "D" (Defense) Notice, a censorship review and penalty system. In theory, the government could issue a formal D Notice legally binding British newspapers to silence on a cited topic. In practice, the government almost never issued formal D Notices during the war. Instead, the newspaper editors were approached informally. When the topic in question, for instance, stemmed from Ultra, the contact would explain to the editor that publishing it would damage national security. Without divulging the details of why (Ultra's existence), he would indicate that the government could invoke the D Notice but would prefer the editor simply not publish the information. Invariably, the editor agreed.[10]

For those already indoctrinated, informal reasoning for security appeared more effective than threats of jail or a firing squad. Learning the big picture meant the men and women of Bletchley knew the rich content of Ultra and its obvious benefits for the war effort. Once aware, they watched their own tongues far better than anyone else could have done for them. They knew just how vital a contribution Ultra was making to the Allied war effort. Telling them the truth made them realize the tremendous damage that a security lapse could cause.[11] Such awareness and self-policing increased security by lessening the sort of lapses that arise from unintentional slips. Even appeals from the highest quarters went unanswered. When King George VI asked a young woman working on the Bombes how she was contributing to the war effort, she replied with a security-conscious "I can't tell you sir."[12]

Even today, former Ultra recipients and BP analysts find themselves instinctively disinclined to speak of the secret war work. Some say that, after the war, they rarely thought of Ultra. They simply trained themselves to forget the secret. The secrecy rules operated so effectively that even in various secret histories of the war, written for internal consumption only, Ultra is never mentioned directly. Instead the researcher discovers a thick sprinkling of references to "Intelligence" or "Special Intelligence."[13]

In the end, the British had found an extremely effective security system. By sketching in the recipient's position on Ultra's big picture, the heads of Allied intelligence let the recipient know just how damaging a slip could be. Aware of the terrible consequences, the members of

Bletchley Park's team became their own policemen, watching their own words as well as those of their colleagues.

For Ultra recipients outside BP, the restrictions increased. Unlike any other security level, Ultra indoctrination meant one could never again be on the front lines in danger of capture. This rule held for everyone, even the top generals and admirals, including Admiral Godfrey, who had been promised in 1938 that he could go back to sea at the end of his three-year term as Director of Naval Intelligence (DNI).[14] General Patton stopped his indoctrination at this warning and delayed learning about Ultra because he could not endure the sidelines. Ultra material and "materials founded on Ultra" stayed back with indoctrinated personnel far from the front. In North Africa, even as late as February 1943 with the enemy essentially routed, Eisenhower's chief intelligence officer, Brigadier E. R. Mockler-Ferryman, continued to reassure Churchill that "Ultra messages are not permitted to leave Headquarters [and] arrangements exist for destruction at short notice."[15] Ultra could not appear near the front lines.

Security for Ultra garnered support from the very highest level. Churchill himself developed a personal obsession for keeping Ultra secret. Originally he had expressed impatience with the rigid handling requirements and the limited access. By late 1941, he began delivering his personal admonitions for the protection of his "golden eggs." He asked that only absolutely necessary information from this special intelligence go to field commands and that even such signals should appear "as statements on your authority with no trace of origin and not too close a coincidence...." Churchill did not hesitate to issue sharp rebukes to his generals and admirals when he suspected them of carelessly handling the golden eggs.[16] GC&CS could also be expected to react swiftly when they suspected someone, regardless of rank, of not taking the proper precautions for using Ultra.[17]

## Monitoring Friends

Britain and the United States did not trust their other allies' security. Decrypts of Enigma signals often reinforced their concerns. In particular, France posed a difficult problem in the eyes of both British and American cryptanalysts. The Germans had read numerous French cryptosystems before France's surrender in 1940. Under the terms of the 1940 armistice, Vichy France was required to give German intelligence copies of its codes and ciphers.[18] Yet Britain had maintained contact with pro-Allied French military and intelligence groups. After the armistice, France's General Gustave Bertrand and the team of mathematicians who had escaped from Poland had continued to work in Vichy, secretly intercepting and attacking German signals. Bletchley Park, however, grew increasingly nervous about the pressure that the Vichy regime might place on this team. Although GC&CS maintained contact with Bertrand and the Polish team at "PC Cadix" until November 1942, cooperation never returned to pre-armistice levels. BP's cryptanalysts feared the Germans would find these men and force them to reveal Allied secrets. (None of them did.)

Bletchley soon found General de Gaulle's army also presented severe security problems. Even though his Free French forces were all outside occupied territory and vehemently anti-German, they carried the taint of being "leaky." In North Africa, and after D-Day in Europe as well, the Free French reused the already compromised French ciphers of 1939. Then General Giraud gave Bletchley Park a scare when he announced to a crowd in 1943 that he had seen an intercepted German message from General Kesselring. Giraud's comment appeared in the *Times*, prompting Churchill to launch an investigation at Bletchley Park. Hut 3, responsible for German army decrypts, fortunately could not find "any message from Kesselring which fits the one quoted by General Giraud."[19] Although in this case the Frenchman's claim would not give the Germans definitive proof that their Enigma ciphers had been read, his actions reinforced the analysts' position. Bletchley would never pass the French identifiable Ultra.

The close cryptologic cooperation that evolved between the British and Americans explicitly excluded the French. Even when U.S. analysts advocated "close technical co-operation between U.S. and French Sigint organisations," they stressed that "ULTRA, of course, will be taboo."[20] Anglo-American cryptanalysts considered French signaling and cipher security inadequate. Bletchley's cipher experts discovered significant insecurities in the main Free French enciphering machine, the B-211, and the cryptanalysts breaking Enigma believed the Germans could read its ciphers. They drew up strict security instructions for the French and limited their access to signals intelligence. Finally they insisted that any

> messages containing or discussing Signals Intelligence from U.S. sources ... must ... be enciphered in the special U.S. cipher supplied to you for the enciphering of messages containing or discussing Signals Intelligence.[21]

Even mere hints of Ultra could not be exposed to the dangers of traveling on any but the most secure cryptosystems, even if this restriction offended other allies.

In the East, Stalinist Russia remained a riddle. Notorious for his paranoia, Stalin revealed so little about his own intentions that his Western Allies garnered their information on the Red Army through German appreciations appearing in Ultra decrypts. GC&CS's chief had long worried about Soviet security, and Ultra exposed the deficiencies of many Soviet ciphers. So GC&CS refused to reveal Ultra's existence to Soviet intelligence and resisted passing Ultra-derived information to Stalin.[22] Even after the USSR formally joined the Allies, Bletchley made certain Ultra information passed to the Soviets had a thorough disguise.

## Cover Stories

Ultra required close and constant cover at all times. Germany would expect British intelligence to be gathering whatever information it could, and the British government could not completely hide the existence of a codebreaking organization. For one thing, evidence of budget appropriations for GC&CS appeared in unclassified annual government publications. These appropriations contained such information as the "new grades such as punch card operators and tabulating staff...."[23] Their presence would certainly suggest to enemy intelligence that Britain was putting considerable resources into machines that could greatly assist in cryptanalysis.

What work went on and where received greater protection. Even in secure settings, analysts tended to call Ultra intelligence by one of its cover names.[24] In general, these names arose from one of the cover stories GC&CS was using to disguise Ultra.[25] Early on, Bletchley suggested hinting at contacts "with a secret German left-wing organisation."[26] The Foreign Office developed the habit of referring to intercepts and decrypts as "most secret and reliable indications."[27] These "indications" came from "Station X," Bletchley Park's pseudonym in all transactions with intercept stations, government offices, and Ultra recipients. These latter may have thus remained unaware of BP's location, but the Bletchley town locals were not deceived; they knew secret intelligence work went on in Bletchley's manor, but they, too, held their tongues.[28]

The analysts and cryptanalysts working inside the Park recognized the unremitting threat of exposure. If the enemy developed the slightest suspicion of Enigma's vulnerability, the entire Ultra secret could disappear. The analysts saw reports of German suspicions about leaks in the Ultra decrypts themselves. They warned that if German suspicions continued to "be awakened," the enemy "must by a process of elimination reach the truth that his cypher is insecure."[29] During the Blitz of 1941, they worried in particular about air raid countermeasures. Ordering the Air Raid Precautions (ARP) for the correct target well before the Luftwaffe bombers appeared in the sky would reveal foreknowledge of the bombing raid and jeopardize the intelligence source. The Hut 3 analysts directed all ARP orders be postponed until the Germans began their raid preparations and turned on their radio guidance beams. These beams led the Luftwaffe planes to their targets and had no connection to Enigma. In addition, the analysts suggested that ARP measures be ordered not only for the target revealed by Ultra but "in [other towns] also, preferably situated along the line of the . . . beam."[30] Then, if the Germans heard about the ARP measures, they would assume the British had been warned by the beams rather than by Enigma messages.

In those cases when information from Enigma messages could be used, the source of the decrypts required a disguise. Early Ultra decrypts carried the code name "Boniface," suggesting that the paraphrased information had come from an agent so named, highly placed in the German command. The thought of a notional German agent depositing daily tidbits seems to have caught Churchill's fancy and soon he took to referring to "Boniface" even in his notes to the GC&CS head, "C."

Although Bletchley dropped this facade sometime around the Torch landings,[31] "Boniface" continued to appear as a cryptic reference to Ultra.

The fiction of a highly placed turncoat continued at least through the end of 1942, if not through the end of the war.[32] This notional source proved a convenient way of explaining the importance and high level of the intelligence as well as dealing with the gaps left by garbled transmissions. GC&CS might claim their source had seen a telegram from the Fliegerführer Africa or Feldmarschall Rommel, perhaps in a correspondence file, thus indicating that the information therein was neither speculation nor from a low-level, presumably less-informed, source.[33] The "agent" explained gaps by reporting having seen "a badly tattered copy of a report" or "part of an order."[34] This vivid, yet essentially simple, image of an agent finding scraps of valuable documents in trash bins proved effective in conveying the context and content of Ultra. Although such tales sound fantastic, especially to our postwar ears, they made a kind of sense among the swirling rumors of wartime Europe. They fed the hopes of a teletype operator or cleaning woman that someone on their side was working behind the lines for Allied victory. As one U.S. intelligence officer reported home, "there is no limit to what people will believe about the Secret Service and...even high officials read spy stories."[35]

## Ultra as Guiding Light

Such sources did raise other difficulties. Many commanders distrusted agents in general and so gave Ultra short shrift when weighing differing intelligence reports. GC&CS countered this problem by developing an intelligence rating system: A–D indicated the quality level and 1–4 the reliability of the source. Information from Ultra would appear as "Special Intelligence" with an A-1 rating – "A" being the highest level of quality and "1" being highest reliability. Such a rating indicated a virtually unimpeachable high-level source, which a field commander should consider invaluable.

Intelligence messages going to field commanders began referring to Ultra as "the usual source." This term worried some Bletchley analysts. Bletchley's Assistant Director, Nigel de Grey,[36] noted that if the term came to German attention, it would "clearly indicate" the sensitive intelligence source. Worse, frequent reiteration of the term in signals created an excellent crib for enemy cryptanalysts. Finally, "why in days of congested traffic use three words when one would do?"[37] Ultra, however, required a cover, and the "source" in one form or another persisted throughout the war.

In wars as long and all-encompassing as World War II, the opposing sides suffer less from a dearth than from a surfeit of information. The difficulty then becomes evaluating all the various sources correctly and dismissing those elements that might be planted "disinformation," deception, or simply the source's wishful thinking. Ultra helped remove this difficulty.

Ultra's great value was its reliability. Ultra served as a guide for the Allies, telling them exactly what the German commanders were telling each other. With Ultra's pronouncement in hand, Bletchley could disregard less reliable, contradictory intelligence and confidently present the tidbits of information corroborating the position that the Ultra decrypts outlined.

In disseminating this intelligence, BP's analysts wanted to make certain the Germans could not trace any single piece of Allied information back to only an Enigma signal and nowhere else. They wanted the Germans always to find some other possible explanation. So military commanders basing an action on Ultra information had to have another source as cover. They often found low-grade intelligence proved a convenient and ready reason for operations. Such sources included D/F,[38] radar, sonar, and aircraft reconnaissance, and they did in fact provide considerable information about German movements. At times the second source was simple and immediate: the radio beams guiding Luftwaffe bombers pointed to their target. A reconnaissance aircraft on its daily sweep would locate an expected U-boat and radio back its coordinates. Other times, however, intelligence officers had to delve more deeply for their ostensible intelligence.

In this quest, Ultra helped. The intelligence officer used Ultra to sort through the huge mass of often contradictory snippets coming from sources such as agents, reconnaissance, POW interrogations, captured material, and low-grade ciphers. Ultra also allowed intelligence officers to arrange for confirming low-grade intelligence. When, for example,

Ultra gave the sailing date and route of a vital convoy heading to Rommel in North Africa, the Allied command could schedule several days of routine air reconnaissance sweeps over the route.[39] When the convoy finally appeared, the reconnaissance planes would be in the correct position for a sighting. This physical sighting of the convoy would trigger an attack, which the Axis would attribute to routine reconnaissance, not decrypts of Enigma signals. Thus, through judicious use and disguise of Ultra, a secondary source (reconnaissance aircraft) could both exploit the information (the convoy's position) and provide Ultra's cover story.

## Cryptologic Security

Ultra required more than cover stories for protection, however. Enigma decrypts needed secure lines of transmission from interception through their final dissemination. The masses of raw intercept gathered on British soil traveled over secure land lines to Bletchley Park. Getting Ultra out of Bletchley Park and into the hands of commanders need-ing the information proved more of a problem. Indeed, some decrypted information never made it to the field because of concerns for its security.

Cryptographic security for Ultra developed slowly. Originally, Ultra went from Bletchley to the three service ministries, who then decided what to forward to the frontline commands. This system led to the possibility that "the same information [might] be sent in 3 different cyphers."[40] With such a repetition, if the enemy broke into one cipher, he could, as Bletchley was doing itself, break into the others. That sys-tem put not only the ciphers of all three services at risk of compromise but the Ultra secret itself. So Bletchley focused on tightening crypto-logic security.

The cryptographic safeguards for Ultra began in the intelligence Huts 3 and 4 at Bletchley. When a Hut's Advisor found a decrypt worth pass-ing on to the Prime Minister and the Military Commands, he ordered the "Special Messages" typed onto one of the "Most Secret" (later "Ultra Secret") forms that carried the warning "...to be kept under lock and key and never to be removed from the office."[41] Milder warnings included: "Particular attention is drawn to the <u>MOST SECRET</u> nature of this. It is requested that <u>it be handled with special care.</u>"[42] Most crucial of all, the addresses of sender and recipient never appeared at the message's start, but lay buried in the main body of the text.[43] This precaution eliminated potential cribs from the stereotyped addresses and signatures all militaries use.

The heading on cipher telegrams reminded their recipients of the first rule of cryptographic security: "This message will not be distributed outside British or U.S. government departments or Headquarters or retransmitted even in cipher without being paraphrased."[44] The original text could not travel outside Britain or over the airwaves verbatim "even in translation." A paraphrase might, for a brief signal, be as simple as repeating the text in indirect speech. For longer messages, Bletchley frequently used their notional agent as the inspiration for the paraphrasing, creating the illusion of a man going through enemy files: "Source saw a telegram . . . to the effect that communications between his signals station and Rome and Naples had to cease at once."[45] In this example, only a few common words ("station," "Rome," "Naples") and one phrase ("cease at once") could possibly provide a direct match with the original message.

Such basic rewording of decrypted messages was essential for two reasons. First and foremost, paraphrasing counters the threat of exact repeats providing the enemy a break from one cipher into another. Second and equally vital for Ultra, verbatim transmission of a message offers the enemy the chance to discover his own cipher's compromise. Should he crack your cipher – and only "one-time pads" are theoretically unbreakable – the precise wording of a message will allow him to compare your information directly to his own signals. As discussed in the following chapter, Bletchley's often simple rephrasing proved remarkably effective.

The rules for Ultra allowed only two exceptions to the paraphrasing requirement: decrypts sent by secure teleprinter lines or by true one-time-pad ciphers. The former originally defined only teleprinter lines inside Great Britain, specifically those from the intercept stations around the country and Bletchley Park and those from Bletchley to Whitehall and the Prime Minister. Later teleprinter lines sprang up in the Allied occupied areas of North Africa, Italy, and finally western Europe. Messages sent by teleprinter carried the stern reminder: "<u>NO</u> repetition either in cipher or plain text."[46] Even the raw signals intercepted overseas had to have their "meaningless German texts . . . re-encoded in a British cypher."[47] The Allies preferred the Germans not notice that their enemy was repeating Enigma messages. Any such sign of active interest on the Allied side could only fan the flames of German apprehension for their cipher system.

## Physical Security

The possibility of Ultra's physical compromise worried the Allies constantly. Inside Allied territory, Ultra traveled over teleprinter lines and only to a limited circle of indoctrinated recipients. Ultra information sent to Churchill and other authorized recipients inside Britain went by hand or on teleprinter lines directly from Bletchley. Hut 4 sent its Ultra information straight to the Admiralty via teleprinter lines. Once in Room 39, the home of the DNI, decrypts went to the personal secretariat who made certain they circulated in a special folder, often marked "Eyes Only," only to those on the indoctrinated list. Original intercepts of Enigma traffic and the later decrypted and translated Ultra transcripts remained at Bletchley Park.

In the field, ground battles and naval clashes risked both Ultra material and the Allies' own ciphers. Early in the war, both Churchill and GC&CS recognized the dangerous probability of losing revealing documents to enemy capture.[48] Bletchley quickly developed strict regulations for the physical protection of any original decrypts of Enigma messages or unaltered Ultra leaving the Park's premises.

Every mention of Ultra intelligence destined to go beyond Bletchley Park had to pass through several steps: (1) the original text was paraphrased to disguise its origin, (2) the information traveled under a cover name, (3) it left Bletchley classified as the highest grade of secrecy, (4) it traveled on a separate network independent from other military signals and only after being encrypted by the top grade of cipher system (one-time pad or Typex or Sigaba), and, finally, (5) it was further camouflaged by a cover story before being used in actual operation. Outside Britain,

Ultra's security became largely the responsibility of a special network eventually known as the Special Liaison Units, or SLUs.

## Special Liaison Units

For Ultra to be useful operationally, commanders in the field needed rapid access to the intelligence. How could they send this highly secret information with as little risk of exposure as possible? The answer came in the form of the SLU network. Ultra intelligence would travel to the field only through these Ultra-indoctrinated stations.

Under Wing Captain (later Group Captain) F. W. Winterbotham, GC&CS created the SLU network to protect Ultra physically, militarily, and cryptographically. The SLU signals would concern Ultra and only Ultra, isolating this precious source of intelligence from all others. SLUs would operate under the direct control of GC&CS and their signals would use only the Allies' highest grade of encryption. Through this isolation and priority, the SLUs would keep Ultra safe from enemy capture and suspicions.

The SLUs began as "Special Signals Units" (SSUs) responsible for signaling GC&CS Secret material throughout the field commands. GC&CS soon decided to change the SSU name, however, because the unindoctrinated community assumed the initials stood for "Secret Service Unit."[49] This entire organization became known as the Special Liaison Units (SLU), although they actually consisted of two parts – signaling and intelligence. The "SLU (Special Liaison Unit) carr[ied] the cypher, delivery and security functions, and SCU [Special Communications Unit], the signalling function.... Normally ... the two [units] moved hand in hand...."[50]

The first of these Special Liaison Units set up shop (as an SSU) in Cairo in the spring of 1941. This first unit foreshadowed "an organisation, which grew to control at the height of the Battle of Europe over 40 separate units in Europe and the Middle East."[51] Each SLU had at least one fully Ultra-indoctrinated intelligence officer who supervised several cipher sergeants and signalers (the latter were not necessarily indoctrinated). To deflect any curiosity about their activities, the unit remained small and isolated. Although they served in combat areas, they remained a significant distance behind the lines to avoid capture.[52]

Each SLU received regular transmissions of Ultra from Bletchley. Wherever possible, the SLUs used secure teleprinter lines. Where distance made wireless necessary, the SLUs used ciphers of only two types: one-time pad or Typex.[53] These two systems offered the greatest security available to Britain at the time. One-time pads, as the only theoretically unbreakable cipher system, provided very high security at the price of ease and speed.[54] Typex, an Enigma-style electromechanical cipher machine, offered reasonable security for the time. Although during the war both the British and Americans had concerns about Typex's security, in fact the Germans never broke into it at all.[55] As added security, Winterbotham forbade signalling any SLU traffic further on, even if paraphrased.[56] The SLUs made certain Ultra stayed under their control.

The staff for the SLUs came from all three services and eventually even from the United States. The units served primarily RAF and Army commands, regardless of their own service affiliation. The SLU providing intelligence for the invasion of southern France served both the nearby Army command and the Air "officer [who] used to drive over to Army HQ to read his intelligence" nearly every day.[57] Interservice conflict did crop up at times, as in early 1943, when the Navy and the RAF on Malta both believed the SLUs were not giving them all the necessary intelligence nor quickly enough.[58] On the whole, however, the SLUs managed to overcome service rivalries in their concern for protecting the "Most Secret Source."

The often junior officers and the isolated networks of the SLUs had complete responsibility for receiving and disseminating Ultra. The SLUs both received Ultra-grade intelligence and provided a specialized cipher unit trained in using the Allied one-time pads and top-grade cipher machines.[59] Only they had the authority to decipher the messages sent from Bletchley.[60] Once the cipher sergeants had deciphered the material, the intelligence officer personally delivered it to the designated recipient. The recipient officers soon viewed these SLU officers "as experts in all the aspects of Ultra," including its protection and its interpretation. SLU commanders often found themselves advising generals on future operations.[61] After the day's intelligence discussion

7. The British Typex machine, converted for compatibility with the U.S. ECM, used for joint high-grade naval communications. The Typex operated on the same general principle as the Enigma, but used seven reversible rotors (two of which remained stationary) and a more irregular stepping pattern. (Courtesy of the National Security Agency)

ended, the SLU officer took back the Ultra documents. Then he burned them.

The SLUs attached to the field headquarters lived and worked in isolation from ordinary troops. Their tents often sat on the edge of the local encampment, hidden among the trees – to help disguise their radio antennae. They did not come under the local military authority, "although their members had to submit to the discipline of the particular Service to which each belonged...."[62] The commanding officer of each SL Unit reported not to the local air or army general but "direct to A.I.1(c) in London, representing 'C' and the Director of Intelligence."[63] Winterbotham had responsibility for all "of the SLU H. Q.s in the various theaters of war."[64] He served as the direct connection between Bletchley Park and the front lines. This chain of command emphasized that the SLU's primary responsibility was not the goals or operations of local command but the security of Ultra intelligence.

## Benefits of Independence

The independence that the SLUs had from local control gave them greater autonomy. While the Ultra material "was under his control, [the SLU commanding officer's] responsibility was absolute." The information itself became the responsibility of the recipient once he learned it and he had the "chief liability for conforming with the Security Regulations." The SLU officer would intervene, however, "if any dangerous practice or possible breach [of Ultra security regulations] came to his notice." Any breach "of the rules had to be reported back to England."[65] If necessary, the SLU officer could override top-ranking commanders in the field to protect the Most Secret Source. Such cases could "become most delicate"[66] when a lowly junior SLU officer had to correct a high ranking officer's handling of Ultra. Nonetheless, the SLU staff soon learned that Ultra's security made reporting any irregularities vitally important. They could not shrink from speaking up when it was the SLUs that bore the burden of responsibility for Ultra's security.[67]

In the European and North African theaters, no one else, whether British or American, however high ranking, not even the Prime Minister, received Ultra directly.[68] Only the SLUs received Bletchley's golden eggs. Special Liaison Units also served the Prime Minister and top generals as a route for discussing Ultra. They provided an entirely independent network through which Ultra-indoctrinated personnel could communicate about Ultra with other indoctrinated staff and with the home base at Bletchley Park. These Ultra discussions and intelligence traveled only via the SLUs.[69]

The SLU network provided both speed and security. As an independent network, it need not ever compete with other types of signals for priority. More important, its users did not have to explain or defend the signals' security procedures or urgency. Only indoctrinated personnel used the network's services and all indoctrinated personnel knew the absolute secrecy required to keep Ultra secure.[70]

The development of the SLU network demonstrated that the British had learned from the case of Enigma. Enigma carried both the highest grade of traffic alongside more routine, often stereotyped messages about supplies or fuel consumption, even the regular U-boat announcements of crossing into "home" waters. Through such repetitive signals, Bletchley cryptanalysts broke into more and more and higher and higher-grade Enigma traffic. Finally, decrypted Enigma signals revealed that the Germans could read various Allied codes and ciphers. Thus Germany's widespread use of a single system of ciphers not only compromised the various ciphers themselves but exposed the successes of German cryptanalysis. The Allies became determined never to subject their own successes to the same dangers. Ultra would run on communication lines parallel to those used for other intelligence but completely separate from them.

By its very separateness, the SLU network offered extra protection both in general cryptologic terms and for the Ultra secret in particular. As a completely high-grade system, the SLUs lowered their own risk of compromise. Without routine or even medium-grade messages, enemy cryptanalysts would have had a hard time finding cribs with which to break into the high-grade cipher. Cryptanalytic triumph and cryptographic security united in the SLUs.

As the amount and quality of Ultra increased, the number of SLUs proliferated. The SLUs followed the Allied fighting, providing the military commands constant contact with Bletchley's intelligence from Enigma decrypts. Having "proved its value," the SLU serving the Eighth Army and its air associate followed to "Sicily and Italy, finally ending up in May 1945 at Udine in Northern Italy...."[71] Once the fighting in North Africa died down in late 1942 and early 1943, the Cairo station scaled back and its staff went back to Bletchley or into new SLUs.[72] The SLUs would spread to headquarters from North Africa to New Delhi and the South Pacific. As the Americans entered the fighting, they, too, acquired SLUs. General Patton had an SLU when he landed at Sicily.[73] SLUs went ashore in Normandy and then in southern France, and finally marched into Germany itself.

The SLUs proved flexible and responsive to the changing needs of mobile warfare. Two SLUs serving neighboring headquarters could provide uninterrupted service even during rapid advances and retreats by "leapfrogging." While one unit stayed behind, the other would establish the new station in preparation for the move. Eventually, the SLUs formed extra "flying squads," mobile SCUs (communications) which could quickly move to any SLU falling behind in the time-consuming signaling work.[74] Mobile, self-contained, and secure, the SLUs delivered the vital intelligence safe from the prying eyes of German intelligence organizations.

## Red Herrings

Bletchley's analysts continued to break into the last Enigma puzzles as well as Germany's teleprinter cipher, the Siemens T-52c. Yet they continued to worry that their German counterpart would "by a process of elimination reach the truth that his cypher is insecure."[75] Through tight security and low-grade cover stories, Bletchley's experts worked to keep the Germans from suspecting this compromise. They set out to offer their counterpart the most appealing red herrings imaginable.

Here Ultra helped again. Reading Enigma messages meant knowing the Germans' expectations. This knowledge allowed Allied intelligence to confirm and exploit those German beliefs which directed attention away from Enigma. As Bletchley learned the Germans' predilections, they fed them. Ultra revealed German fears that telephone conversations leaked vital information on Marine and merchant convoy sailings.[76] They feared agents spying for the enemy from inside the territories the Reich occupied. They readily believed even their associates, particularly the Italians, would betray everything to the Allies when given the chance. Playing on this German distrust, Bletchley at times attributed Ultra intelligence to Italian agents and prisoners of war instead. Many commanders in North Africa, such as General Montgomery, used Italian POWs' statements as camouflage for Ultra intercepts, including for their expectation of the Alam el Halfa attack.[77]

Axis POWs became an ever more valuable source once Anglo-American forces stepped on European soil. Even German POWs served as camouflage for Ultra. In fact, the Allies found many POWs – German as well as those from Italy and the Greater Reich – willing, even eager, to talk. The information from even enlisted men often confirmed Ultra and, particularly in land battles, could fill in gaps when Ultra decrypts were not available for one reason or another.[78] If a POW had information, say a date for an offensive, German security could trace the leak back to the POW, as well as to Enigma. So captured Germans themselves provided protection against the compromise of Ultra.

Meanwhile, the Allies worked to reinforce German assumptions of Allied superiority in reconnaissance, radar, and D/F. Allied air forces provided camouflage through increasing reconnaissance flights and by photo reconnaissance. Bletchley's analysts reminded the RAF commands to make these reconnaissance sweeps appear repetitive and routine, never guided by precise knowledge. The cover story had to hold not just for the Germans located by the planes but for the Allied pilots who might succumb to capture and interrogation about their orders.[79] Knowing the valuable cover offered by reconnaissance, the Allies pushed their aircraft development and production to extremes, increasing both the number and the range of their winged eyes and ears. As the war went on, they had ever more planes on the lookout for German attackers. Gradually, the Germans accepted that they could hide almost nothing from Allied flying eyes.

To extend their sight further, the Royal Navy, and later the U.S. Navy as well, poured financial and personnel resources into their radar and sonar programs.[80] They built a vast land-based network of radar stations around the globe, of which the Germans could not help but be informed. They weighted down their ships, submarines, and aircraft with increasingly sophisticated radar systems. They introduced centimetric radar while German experts were still insisting that such shortwave radar was impossible.

The Admiralty's long dearth of Marine intelligence, ironically, gave the Allied navies an excellent system for disguising Ultra when they did receive it regularly. Months and months of intercepting unintelligible Enigma messages had provided ample opportunity for perfecting operators' skills at locating a signal's origin through D/F. Here GC&CS worked with the scientific community, and the cooperation paid dividends to both. A D/F fix could immediately locate a U-boat with an error margin of 10–15 miles or less.[81]

In addition, the Admiralty had hired scientists to study, among other things, U-boat fuel capacities. When the scientists' knowledge was coupled with D/F results of a boat's general location, the Admiralty and U.S. Navy submarine trackers could "estimate the extent of its future operations and . . . plot a rough course." These rough estimates filled the gaps created by blackout periods when Bletchley's Hut 8 could not crack Marine signals.[82] Later, as a familiar source, they served well as camouflage for Ultra, at least internally. Moreover, if Allied POWs betrayed this source to their German captors, they were unlikely to endanger Ultra.

Allied security exploited these other sources – POWs, air reconnaissance, radar, D/F – as convenient cover stories for Ultra intelligence. Whenever possible, references to information would mention one of these methods. While these various alternative sources did not always "lull German suspicions,"[83] neither did they fuel them.

Even as Allied penetration of Enigma expanded to cover nearly every network, German experts never seriously considered the compromise of their own high-grade systems. Neither German historians nor military veterans would believe Enigma breakable until Britain's official admission of 1974.

SIX

# THE ILLUSION OF SECURITY

## The German Explanations for Allied Successes

Confidential material has been destroyed. Cipher security is guaranteed.
> – Communications Officer of torpedoed U-boat to Marine HQ,
> 11 Sept 1944, as decrypted by Allied sigint[1]

Even though in the course of the war, the enemy found not only the cipher machine, but also the cipher drums and other documents ... he was still not in the position to decipher generally the radio signals. Even the enemy incursion into the Naval cipher M was not complete ...
> – Herbert Dammert, a Heer Signals Officer, who used
> Enigma, in 1985[2]

Throughout the war, the German military had numerous signs that the Allies had information about Wehrmacht intentions and operations. On several occasions, the Germans recognized that their enemy somehow could locate U-boats, bomb the most vital supplies bound for North Africa, and otherwise demonstrate that it knew the Germans' situation and intentions. Clearly, the Allies had intelligence sources that Germany needed to silence at all costs.

Through the course of the war, numerous setbacks prompted repeated investigations into the origins of the enemy's knowledge. As part of these investigations, nearly every branch of the German military, including the OKW's Chiffrierabteilung (cipher service), apparently probed Enigma as the present or future possible source of Allied information.[3] In particular, the Marine continued to investigate the cipher machine's security and possible compromise throughout the war. Archival documents reveal several explanations given by the Marine for the enemy's knowledge, for example, about the location of U-boats in the Atlantic. None of the explanations include enemy success cracking Enigma. Members of the German command maintained unyielding confidence in their cipher system and could not bring themselves to believe Enigma to be the source of so many of their problems.

Much of this Allied knowledge did in fact come from the decrypts of hundreds of thousands of signals enciphered by the Enigma cipher machine. The Germans did not acknowledge this overwhelming compromise of their cipher system until after the publication, and public acknowledgment, of Winterbotham's book. Since 1974, many have claimed that the Germans "never suspected" the Allies might be reading German ciphers. On the contrary! They took obvious and repeated steps to guard the security of the cipher machines. Neither did they ignore completely the possibility of the enemy acquiring information through decipherment.

How then did the German internal investigations always fail to perceive that the Allies had actually broken their codes?

From the beginning, German cipher experts recognized the limits of the commercial Enigma and sought to improve the military Enigma's security. Early versions of the machine had not passed their tests. The Wehrmacht declared the unsteckered version of Enigma, used in the late 1920s, possible to crack.[4] Even the Italians believed there was "some possibility of decryption when one has a machine and the discs [rotors] that go with it, provided one has the plain text corresponding to a secret text." They considered this possibility unlikely, however.[5] With the adoption of the Steckerboard and then additional rotors, however, the Wehrmacht cipher experts were satisfied.

The Heer, the Marine, and the Luftwaffe all worried at some point during the war that the enemy could read Enigma-encrypted signals. When important operations went awry, when the enemy had a string of successes, when the Wehrmacht found itself attacked at its weak points, military commanders asked why. Sometimes these requests and concerns traveled as Enigma signals. In some cases, we have the investigations and reports that these episodes sparked.

## The Marine Case

From surviving documents, we know that several times during the war, Admiral Dönitz, Commander of U-boats and later Chief of the Marine, considered the possibility of the Enigma cipher system's compromise. In particular, he and his officers requested two substantial investigations into the source of enemy information: the first in the fall of 1941 and the second in the spring of 1943.

The Marine realized the Allies had information, sometimes very precise information, about U-boat positions and the times and locations of attacks. Much of this information could have come from a variety of sources: agents, POW interrogations, undecrypted radio messages pinpointed by D/F. In both 1941 and 1943, however, the Allies working at Bletchley Park were in fact cracking and reading many of the Marine's Enigma ciphers, including, in 1943, the newer U-boat Enigma variation. Why did the investigators not realize this?

Examining the Marine security investigations makes clear that the Germans held two central assumptions. First, they assumed Enigma would be vulnerable only through a physical compromise of the machines and books of key settings. They did not believe their enemy could crack the cipher without such tangible aids. Their second assumption arose from this first one: enemy sources of information must come either through spies, possession of Enigma cipher components (given them by traitors or capture), or some advance in Allied technology, such as infrared or radar. Their investigations first focus on countering the possibilities of physical compromise and then attempt to eliminate the possibility of Enigma's responsibility.

These German investigations into Allied information sources were triggered by "unexplained losses," declines in sightings and sinkings of Allied convoys, or the appearance of German intentions and positions in deciphered Allied messages. Here the Wehrmacht paid a heavy price for not centralizing or even coordinating its intelligence or counterintelligence: each branch investigated its own suspicious circumstances. And there were suspicions.

By the very first week of the war, the Germans believed a complete cipher system could have fallen into enemy hands. The U-boat U-26

hit a mine in shallow waters off the English coast, leading the Marine
to believe the English could have salvaged her equipment, including
the Enigma machine, rotors, directions, and daily key settings.[6] But in
spite of this and other cases of cipher material falling into Allied hands,
the Germans remained confident.

Nonetheless, Admiral Dönitz took immediate steps to restrict the
high-level Marine cipher, Enigma M. He decreed that U-boats patrol-
ing off British shores, and therefore most likely to fall into enemy hands,
carry only lesser Marine ciphers, not Enigma M. Thereafter Dönitz continued to raise concerns about the security of his ciphers. After the loss
of a surface vessel, Ship 26, in early May 1940 and of another U-boat,
U-13, the next month, then-Konteradmiral Dönitz asked for and
received assurances of Enigma M's security.[7]

## Success Breeds Complacency

Dönitz himself relied heavily on decryption in the deployment of his
U-boats. In the first half of the war, the cryptanalysts in the Marine
X-B-Dienst could read many British naval ciphers, including those used
by convoys.[8] With this information, Dönitz knew where his U-boat
patrols would most likely intercept Allied ships.

Ironically, these very codebreaking successes led to a fatal error.
Throughout their investigations, the Germans maintained that so long
as they could read Allied codes and ciphers, they would learn the origins
of the enemy's information, particularly if that source were decipherment of German signals. The reality was seldom so simple. With so
much information available to all sides in World War II, especially in
the Western theaters, determining the precise source of the enemy's
knowledge proved daunting for both sides. Tracking the source of a single detail of information rarely resulted in a clear answer. The truth
revealed itself less in details than in larger patterns. The Germans consistently ignored the patterns of the big picture.

Throughout the war, Marine intelligence maintained a sense of superiority toward its enemy counterpart and was not quick to raise alarm
at Admiralty signaling reforms. For example, when the Royal Navy
introduced new codes on 20 August 1940, Marine intelligence did not
see this change as an indication either that the Allies were reading

Enigma or that they had captured documents which revealed their convoy ciphers' weaknesses. Rather, the Germans had expected that the Allies would eventually upgrade their weak ciphers and only found it "remarkable that [a change] had not been done before now – after almost a year of war."[9] They regarded this long-expected loss of easy decryption as the explanation for the subsequent decline in successful sightings and sinkings of convoys. By March and April of 1941, the X-B-Dienst had once more begun deciphering some of the British convoy ciphers and so generally knew the convoys' approximate locations. When several Vorposten ships and U-boats nonetheless failed to locate one of these expected convoys, Admiral Dönitz suspected that somehow the Allies were learning the range of at least one U-boat patrol area.

In April 1941, he ordered that the need-to-know list for access to Enigma M be "made as small as possible."[10] Particularly concerned about his U-boats, Dönitz also restricted the number of radio relay and sending stations transmitting U-boat messages and warned all of them of his suspicions of information leaks. In addition, he asked the Marine Command for a special, separate U-boat Enigma key.[11] Then he had an additional code for position coordinates introduced.[12]

## The *Bismarck* Sinking

Then the prize of the Marine, the *Schlachtschiff Bismarck* went to sea on her maiden voyage and was sunk. The *Bismarck's* destruction during the Rheinübung (Rhein operation) heightened the Flottenkommando's (Fleet command's) concerns about how the enemy was tracking German vessels. The Marine intelligence division produced a report on the security of the operation. In their report to the Flottenkommando they noted the appearance during the operation of "the most senior soldiers of the [English] intelligence service."[13] They also admitted the possibility that the enemy had acquired Enigma M hardware. Nonetheless, they determined that even if the enemy had perhaps managed a "partial capture of supporting material in another region, reading [Enigma was] not possible." The report concluded that, in any case, a complete capture of the vital supporting material was by no means to be presumed.[14]

With this report the Marine intelligence section renewed their position that the enemy could not read Enigma. As would be their usual pattern, they blamed agents and betrayals, some unintentional. They noted that the wife of an officer at sea had informed other civilians in Berlin, within a day or so of the fleet's departure, that the *Bismarck* had once more put to sea.[15] Moreover, from material captured in now-occupied France, they concluded that the intelligence agencies of the "Western powers" were well informed of what went on in German ports. The OKW had determined that in the western regions of occupied Europe, particularly in Norway, the enemy had agents reporting by radio on German movements. Non-Germans worked in Marine communications, and those communications themselves ran through occupied territory. The physical tapping of these lines by "English" agents was considered "very probable." Thus traitors and agents working for the enemy could explain how British ships had found the *Bismarck* and her escorts.

Such betrayals would constantly worry the Wehrmacht. In his report on the security surrounding the *Bismarck* sinking, Sonderführer Dr. Fricke of the OKW/Chi expressed concern that the men entrusted with Enigma's settings be the oldest, the most reliable, and appropriately trained. With this concern about betrayal in mind, Fricke recommended that the circle of staff working on secret material [geheime Kommandosache] be reduced.[16] As others would decree throughout the war, Fricke concluded that security remained a point of concern and the Marine needed continuing "protective measures."[17]

The Wehrmacht would return to this episode in the next year. "After a renewed, very comprehensive examination," the Marine again determined that the enemy could not be reading Enigma. The signal experts of the OKW had uncovered "a tenacious and skillful" agent radio organization communicating with London from points in Norway and in France.[18] So the Marine made several security recommendations: shrink the need-to-know circle within the Marine and make sure the codebooks of settings are on soluble paper and written in soluble ink for rapid destruction in case of capture. They would also keep an eye on the enemy's encrypted signals for any sign that he could read Marine signals, however unlikely that scenario might seem.

## A Major Investigation

By September 1941, with U-boat sightings of convoys still seeming more accidental than planned, Dönitz again tightened the need-to-know circle for U-boat operations signals, eliminating even the Marine Nachrichten Offizier (Naval Intelligence Officer).[19] In these actions, Dönitz mirrored the moves of other German security experts. Various departments of the Wehrmacht had also begun to shrink access to Enigmas on land and tighten security procedures. In the fall of 1941, the OKW had the Abwehr begin surprise inspections of departments using secret material, especially Enigma ciphers. These inspections targeted offices from Norway to Rome, and they focused on ensuring correct compliance with procedures for secret documents.[20]

The suspicions were not allayed. By October 1941, the enemy had captured another U-boat (U-570) and the supply ship *Gedania* had gone missing.

According to the record of these investigations, these incidents prompted a full investigation of the Marine Enigma's security.[21] The investigation team analyzed a series of Admiralty messages decrypted by the X-B-Dienst and found one striking case. A decrypted British report correctly described a group of U-boats in the southern sector. The investigators found this particularly striking because according to the BdU (Commander of U-boats) reports, these U-boats had not signaled at all after their departure, and the Germans themselves had received no information about their performance once they had headed south. Moreover, the Admiralty's signals had contained "no cross bearing" and "no direction finding," so British D/F did not appear to be the source of the information locating the U-boats.[22]

Although Marine headquarters did not know of any signals from the U-boats in question, the investigators discovered that another U-boat, not in the group, had signaled. Since every "trace of a Uboat proved itself to be necessary to the Admiralty," the British must have noticed it and included its presence in the situation report. Thus, the report deduced, "it is unambiguously clear that that U-boat would have been announced with the one which signaled at 1209 on 2 September (U-83)."[23] This explanation allowed the investigators to decide British

D/F did after all explain this disquieting case. Their belief in the superiority of British location technology, particularly in the area of radar-type detection, would emerge time and again in the Marine's evaluations of its security.

The investigators then found two additional scenarios that could tie the Admiralty's information to D/F. These prospects lay in the possible actions of the U-boats themselves.

> ... it is very possible that the U-boats ... either had developed traffic among themselves or had attempted, at an inopportune time, to signal the base, without this attempt being noticed, whereas clearly the English D/F service had succeeded nonetheless in an approximate tactical location [of the U-boats].[24]

With this belief that the U-boats had signaled unbeknownst to headquarters, the Marine could settle for the explanation of the excellent British D/F, radar, and other locating devices. They developed a hypothetical and completely unsubstantiated scenario to explain away an unsettling incident. This flimsy explanation appeased the Marine command.

Although the investigators concluded that the British source of information was locating devices, they did go on to consider the possible capture – intact – of all the "secret material" from another U-boat, U-570. The Commander of the Marine Nachrichtendienst, Konteradmiral Maertens, admitted that U-570's papers included all the supporting documentation for the Enigma M ciphers. Because of their long voyages, U-boats routinely carried two to three months' worth of daily key settings, so in theory, the enemy could have used U-570's material to read enciphered messages until November 1941. If these documents had all fallen into enemy hands intact, the result, Maertens conceded, would be "without a doubt a weakening of the security of our cipher."[25]

However, the investigators concluded that even with U-570's papers and machines, the enemy had not broken Enigma.[26] German experts maintained that Enigma would withstand enemy cryptanalytic attack, even if a complete machine fell into Allied hands. This investigation, like all the others, mentions the near impossibility of reading Enigma without every single element of the cipher materials. The investigators insisted that by the time anyone lacking just one of these elements could decrypt an Enigma message, the information would be worthless. They repeatedly emphasized the uselessness of delayed information, even though other nonnaval sections of German intelligence (such as the Luftwaffe interrogation centers) made excellent use of Allied information even years old.

These Marine investigators based their certainty on the (false) assumption that the Allied cryptanalysts could only break Enigma using pure statistical methods. None of the German cipher experts or military commanders appears to have imagined that their enemies might use electromechanical assistance or an analytical, rather than merely statistical, approach in their assault on the ciphers. They insisted that even the possession of both Enigma hardware *and* a month's worth of daily key settings would allow the Allies to decipher no more than that month's Enigma signals. After the month ended, the cryptanalysts would have no further advantage. Thus any capture like that of U-570 could offer the Allies only a short-term ability to read Enigma and not a permanent solution to the cipher machine.

(In this belief Maertens and his team proved largely correct, if for the wrong reasons. Few captures enabled Bletchley Park to break previously insurmountable codes. Rather, captured material confirmed previous analytical reconstructions of coordinate codebooks or Enigma rotor wirings, and temporarily reduced the time Bombes spent finding the daily settings.[27])

For this particular case of the material possibly captured with U-570, Maertens did not believe the British capable of reading Enigma for any significant period because the method for creating the key of the initial daily setting had since been changed.[28] Without just one of these operational documents or of the interchangeable parts of the machine (a rotor or plugboard cable, for example), Maertens insisted the British could only decipher messages by trial and error. The change in the daily key setting had surely offset whatever advantage U-570's documents had given the enemy.

If, however, this loss of the cipher machine and all the cipher documentation were combined with a betrayal by some German POW of the new method for changing the daily key – or if the British had in some other way (several being listed) learned how the settings changed, then the Marine would have to reckon with continuing decipherment by the enemy. For Maertens, this was all very improbable. He intimated that sensitive material had not fallen into British hands anyway. The last signal from U-570, he said, had probably been the attempt to notify the BdU that the crucial cipher documents had been destroyed. Given these numerous possibilities, successful decryption held "little probability" and Marine intelligence was not concerned. They could attribute all the suspicious losses of the autumn to the capabilities of British D/F.[29]

Admiral Dönitz accepted these hypothetical scenarios and subsequent comfortable explanations. He received additional reassurance in December from a coded letter from a U-570 POW reporting proper destruction of all secret material.[30] The planned introduction of the U-boat Enigma key and the February 1942 upgrade of Enigma (to a four-rotor machine) proceeded, but produced no apparent sudden or significant improvement in German fortunes, so concerns of a cipher compromise died down.[31]

### Renewed Losses Cause Concern

In the summer and fall of 1942, German sinkings of Allied convoys increased, peaking in December 1942 at 109 convoy and independent ships sunk, with the loss of only nine U-boats to the enemy.[32] But January 1943 began the trend's reversal. This shift against the U-boats showed up in the Marine monthly statistics and triggered a series of security investigations and reports which continued throughout the spring and summer of 1943.[33] Each one of these investigations exonerated Enigma.

As with the 1941 inquiry, this series of reports produced in 1943 never laid out all the sources that the investigators were using nor did they supply the criteria used for deciding why certain messages suggested compromise and others did not. They merely announced that the investigators had eliminated 94 percent of the Admiralty messages and had decided only 6 percent (or ten messages) "were disquieting."[34] Then the reports' authors explicitly compared the precise numbers and position coordinates radioed in their own messages (and enciphered with Enigma) with those numbers and coordinates in deciphered Admiralty reports. In their emphasis on exact, correct numbers of U-boats and exact locations in the weekly Admiralty situation reports, they seem to have overlooked the convoy routing messages as harmless. They did not analyze how well the convoys were being routed *around* wolfpacks, even if the details of U-boat positioning lacked complete accuracy.

They focused on details rather than the overall picture of their U-boat losses and declines in sinkage tons: in accounting for the trees, they missed the forest.

In the first 1943 report, the investigators focused on a series of Admiralty signals about four wolfpacks that came uncomfortably close to reporting the actual U-boat deployment situation. They determined Enigma's current security by comparing the ten unsettling messages with the relevant U-boat messages sent in January.[35] At first glance, the decrypted British signals appeared to be accurately tracking the four groups: Jaguar, Delphin, Falke, and Habicht.

The Marine report established that the disposition orders for each of the four had used the special U-boat Enigma cipher (called "Triton" by the Germans, "Shark" by the British). All of the signals containing sensitive X-B-Dienst intelligence from the decrypted text of Admiralty messages had been sent in the "officer-only" cipher.[36] Could the Admiralty be learning the wolfpacks' locations by reading Enigma? The report said no.

## The Allied Reality

In fact, the Allies had again been reading the Marine's Enigma since December 1942.[37] The month of January 1943 proved irregular for Bletchley Park's decryption. At times the break into a day's setting took several days or a week and then two or three days would break at almost the same time. The U-boat Enigma keys for 16 January broke within two days, while 13–15 January keys came out 21 January. The general U-boat Enigma keys for 22, 24–28 January were read by 1 February and even the Offizier (top grade) Enigma keys for this period had all been broken by 10 February.[38] Most of the specific days that the German investigators considered were good ones for the Allied cryptanalysts.

Indeed, the Allies apparently read all of the signals that the Germans considered possibly compromised, although they appear to have had difficulties with the coordinate codes.

### The Report's Explanation

The investigators blamed the Admiralty's excellent estimates partially on the U-boat groups themselves because they had "stood in the same formation and in the same regions of the ocean with practically no appreciable change of position throughout several days and nights."[39] This lack of movement coupled with their periodic signals back to base made them vulnerable to the enemy's powerful D/F. The U-boats had made themselves "visible" to the enemy by signaling.

The signals, then, were assumed to be the source of the Admiralty's information, not the information in the text enciphered by Enigma. The investigators verified Enigma's security by comparing the actual U-boat messages sent with the ten disquieting Admiralty messages.

One disquietingly precise Admiralty signal was easily explained: they simply blamed compromised Italian ciphers.[40] For most of the others, the Marine team noted that the numbers of U-boats were nearly always incorrect and the range of U-boat positions was articulated as an inexact estimate rather than as specific coordinates.[41] Such inaccuracy, the Marine investigation concluded, proved the Admiralty had not read the specific messages that the Marine considered possibly vulnerable. Ergo the Admiralty had not cracked Enigma. Enigma had not been compromised.

### A Flawed Method

There are several fundamental flaws in this approach. The investigators not create transparent, verifiable reports with explanations for why they could eliminate huge numbers of enemy signals as unimportant. Nor do they provide evidence for their hypothetical scenarios. An interested recipient would have had a difficult, if not impossible, task confirming a report's evidence and conclusion.

The investigators clearly set out to prove only what could not have been the leak, Enigma. They did not set out to prove what was the source and they did not produce a scenario that explained the Admiralty's information. Indeed, the Marine investigations appear designed less to discover the enemy's source of information than to reinforce the sense of Enigma's invulnerability. They spend considerable space identifying which information in enemy signals proved incorrect, however slightly, and when important maneuvers succeeded without Allied detection (such as tanker U-boats completing a supply rendezvous).[42]

These reports demonstrate a crucial underlying premise: German intelligence assumed the enemy would either be able to read the ciphers completely or not at all – and within a three-to-five-day time period. Such speed and consistency would presumably be the case if the enemy were reading Enigma simply through captured codebooks. Having to reconstruct the key every day (or even every eight hours), however, meant at times Bletchley would miss the entire day's traffic, deciphering it only sometime later or, when particularly inundated, not at all. The Marine officers apparently were not concerned about a more delayed reading of the ciphers. They appear not to have considered a partial reading important[43] nor to have accounted for the "half-knowledge," which, at times, was all Bletchley could verify.[44] In the end, their explanation for any example of Admiralty accuracy seems to have been simply that the "anglo-saxons" used "clever adding."[45]

In their rush to identify the Admiralty's errors, German investigators overlooked patterns in the mistakes. When discussing the British signals concerning the two U-boat patrol groups – Falke and Habicht – they note with scorn that on 15 January 1943, the Admiralty reported the correct number of U-boats in the patrol group Falke (17), but on the following day, 16 January, had "forgotten" three. This mistake, they declare, demonstrated that the Admiralty was not reading Enigma because

> on our own side no appreciable change in the position of the U-boats was introduced between the 15th and 16th. A decrease in U-boat numbers was not introduced; on the contrary, group Habicht was increased from 6 to 9.[46]

No notice is taken of the fact that the forgotten U-boats number the same as the U-boats actually added to the second patrol group. This coincidence could be explained by a partial or corrupted decryption leading the British to assume the additional U-boats in Habicht were coming from the Falke group. If the British were reading the signals partially or incorrectly, they might have seen the three U-boats as being moved from one group to another rather than added from elsewhere – explaining the parallel drop from the original group.

Locating U-boats from decrypted signals presented the enemy with an added problem ignored by the investigators. The coordinates (longitude and latitude) used in Marine signals were always encoded before being enciphered on Enigma. These coordinate codes used a system unrelated to Enigma. An enemy cryptanalyst could be reading Enigma but still find the coordinates gibberish. Recovering the specific coordinates required not just cracking Enigma but also breaking (or reconstructing) the special coordinate code. Although the investigators mentioned this extra code, the report did not note that the enemy's often vague estimates of U-boat positions generally included the correct region. Such imprecise accuracy did not suggest to them Enigma's compromise, although the coordinates' very precision relied on the extra code. On the contrary, they saw this imprecision as proof of Enigma's strength. "Why is the Admiralty here so modest and why report for the German U-boats' position such a large inclusive sea region, if they have deciphered [our signals]?"[47] Greater precision would have required cracking both Enigma and the coordinate code. The Allies did partially reconstruct the coordinate code, and finally captured a coordinate codebook intact,[48] but for much of the war, they were reading Enigma without knowing the actual coordinates of the U-boats' locations.

In their dissection of enemy information, German intelligence failed to consider the possibility that the Allies were adding together information on U-boats from Enigma with that from D/F, air reconnaissance, and other sightings, thus ending up with some duplication. The Allies did not always correctly calculate the number of U-boats in a particular section of the Atlantic. At times the Allies knew of a U-boat's presence through Enigma and at the same time had a report of a U-boat sighting by a convoy or reconnaissance plane, or a location of a U-boat through the D/F of its signal, in a slightly different area. The Allies, to be on the safe side, would have counted these two sightings as two U-boats until they had definite reason to believe both Enigma and the convoy, plane, or D/F were revealing the very same U-boat. This practice would lead to the Allies overestimating the number of U-boats on patrol at any one time.[49]

## The Allied Reality II

In fact, U.S. naval intelligence documents suggest that the "forgotten" three U-boats of 16 January never did disappear from Allied estimates, at least not in U.S. daily reports.

British and American cryptanalysts remained in close contact throughout this period. They cabled recovered Enigma keys and message settings to each other, while the two submarine tracking rooms exchanged – in addition to Ultra intelligence – D/Fs, sightings, and other reports of U-boats. Hence, the U.S. Daily Submarine Situation Reports would have held precisely the same estimates of numbers and positions which the Admiralty had.

These American U-boat estimates do not make the erroneous drop in Falke's numbers from 17 to 14. The daily report from 16 January reads virtually identical to that of 15 January, including "Seventeen [U-boats] estimated patrolling general area 52 to 59[° North] 28 to 33[° West]."[50] If the Admiralty's estimate did mention the lower number of U-boats, the error must have been clerical; somewhere between Bletchley Park and the B-Dienst reception of the Admiralty's signal, "14" replaced "17." (Note that *vierzehn* and *siebzehn* sound and look much more alike than fourteen and seventeen.) The security investigators decided to emphasize this single numerical error; yet, that error was merely introduced on one day and did not appear in both daily estimates, only in the Admiralty's. A check of the U.S. daily report would have shown, once again, that the Allies had the correct number of U-boats for the Falke group.

Indeed, the Marine investigators could have compared the two Allies' daily estimates for Falke. The B-Dienst's weekly X-B-Berichte for this period reveal that the B-Dienst could read Halifax L's traffic at this time. Throughout early 1943, Halifax L received the COMINCH's U-boat report Part 3, which covered the North Atlantic (specifically the "Atlantic North of 40 degrees N. and West of 26 degrees W. less Eastern Sea Frontier") and "when necessary" Part 4 (covering the

"Atlantic between 40 degrees North and 25 degrees North and West of 26 degrees W. less Sea Frontiers").[51] We can presume that the B-Dienst acquired these U.S. submarine estimates for the North Atlantic, which Halifax L received. The "forgotten" three U-boats were not so clearly missing after all.

In several other cases, Allied signals projected numbers of U-boats that did not agree with the true German figures. The investigators failed to note that the Allies nearly always overestimated the number of U-boats, rather than underestimated them.[52] The general absence of underestimation alone should have concerned the Germans – the greatest advantage of the U-boat is its general invisibility. If the Allies never undercounted the German U-boats, clearly this trait of invisibility had disappeared, lessening the menace of the wolfpacks.

## A Farfetched Explanation

One British signal did suggest U-boats were being tracked when no signals could have provided coordinates. In late January 1943, the BdU signaled two U-boats in the North Atlantic that they were to circle ("schwabbern") in "Quadrat DF 50" (grid coordinates for $31°$ north and $39°$ west) and await supplies. The supply boat, however, proved too slow and so the BdU signaled new coordinates for the resupply point. Then the Marine X-B-Dienst decrypted a British Admiralty signal of 29 January giving estimated positions for two U-boats. These coordinates corresponded exactly with those designated as the spot where the two (now redirected) U-boats were to have waited to be resupplied.

How could the British have known there were going to be U-boats in this precise region? Had there actually been U-boats there, the British might have located them through a D/F of a signal back to base, or a reconnaissance plane might have spotted the boats. Both U-boats, however, had never arrived at the designated meeting place, and apparently no other U-boats had coincidentally crossed that region. Thus there had been no U-boats there for British radar, reconnaissance, or D/F to find. There appeared to be only two logical explanations for the British report: sheer coincidence or decryption of the Enigma-enciphered signal.[53]

The Marine investigators produced a six-page report on this incident. They outlined the seven relevant signals sent by the BdU between 22 January and 28 January 1943 and the movements of the two U-boats involved. They then analyzed how the Admiralty could have come to its conclusion.

The Marine Nachrichtendienst determined that the British had not read the BdU's signals by the afternoon of 24 January.[54] True, the Admiralty had signaled the same coordinates which the BdU had used. However, they had not said the U-boats were circling ("Schwabbern") there but rather were on their voyage home ("Rückmarsch"). This "false characterization" of the two U-boats demonstrated, the German investigators said, that the enemy had not read the signal.[55] Had they read the signal well enough to know there were two U-boats at those exact coordinates, they would never have made the mistake of describing them as "returning" rather than waiting.

Moreover, the report insisted that by 29 January the enemy clearly had still not read the signals of 25 January redirecting the tardy U-boats because they then would not have used those coordinates at all, since the meeting location had been changed.[56]

The Marine then considered as an explanation whether the enemy had been "partially reading" the ciphers. This possibility, however, could "hardly serve as the explanation for this coincidence" because the coordinates used for both the original meeting place and the reassigned one had been disguised with the code system.[57] (They did not remind their superiors that this same coordinate code system had been in place since November 1941. Hence there had been considerable opportunity for the Allies to reconstruct the code.[58]) Once again, the culprit could not have been Enigma.

## Expecting Conspicuous Signs

Both of these 1943 reports merely examined the question of whether the enemy could be receiving its information from Marine signals. They did not attempt to tackle the security of Enigma itself, although the Germans had long been aware that the Allies were attempting to crack Enigma. After the fall of France in 1940, as the former head of the Marine intelligence, Captain Heinz Bonatz, noted, German intelligence had discovered documents

> in the French Naval Ministry, from which emerged unassailably, that up to this point in time it was possible for neither the French nor the British decipherment positions to solve the German naval radio signals. The French had even let English deciphering experts from London come to support them in their work. But these experts also failed.[59]

Again, long after the Second World War, Captain Bonatz pursued the question of Allied attempts at cracking Enigma. Conversations with his counterparts in Allied intelligence never produced any hints that the Allies had read Enigma M. After early hints of Enigma's compromise were emerging, Bonatz still insisted the Allies had not cracked the ciphers. He noted in 1970:

> The Americans have asserted that they had seized a cipher machine...out of a captured Uboat; this is unquestionably true, perhaps even for several cases (also for the English). But they mention nothing about whether with this machine they could continuously solve the German radio signals. There is little chance of that, as otherwise they would not have let these facts go unmentioned, besides this would have been visible in their own Sigint.[60]

He just could not envision a nation refusing even to hint at its cryptanalytic success – not during the war when signaling its officers nor for three decades after victory – simply for reasons of security.

Other members of German intelligence also assumed that the enemy would reveal any successful decryption of German ciphers in its signals. The Marine, in its own signals to U-boats, included intelligence from decrypted Allied ciphers, complete with routing details, as well as the actual names of the Allied ships and submarines. This procedure led Germans to believe that so long as they could read some of the Allied ciphers, any information the Allies might have gleaned from deciphering Enigma would eventually emerge, since references would show up in the decrypted ciphers.

In other words, German intelligence failed to imagine the lengths to which the Allies would go to protect their source. The Germans did not expect that the Allies would disguise their source of information in their own signals. Bletchley Park, however, insisted all intelligence from Ultra always carry a "cover story" from a corroborating source, and this requirement proved successful at pivotal points. The Marine trusted the cover stories implied by rephrased and slightly altered Ultra in Allied signals. They reported that the enemy, "by its own declaration," located U-boat positions primarily through D/F and occasionally through sightings.[61]

The investigators clearly assumed the information did not come from Enigma if the signal was not a word-for-word translation of the German message. They noted that

> it could be objected that the enemy uses his deciphering results so cleverly that this remains concealed in our deciphering results of his signal traffic. This is not correct.[62]

The enemy made too many mistakes and the Admiralty reports of U-boat positions contained too many minor errors for the Germans to believe that their information came from the texts of U-boat signals.

Finally, the Germans believed if the British could read Enigma, they would have long since improved their own code and cipher systems, which the Marine X-B-Dienst had been reading on and off for most of the war. "The measures so far taken there would not be satisfactory given an English discovery of German decipherment."[63] Because they had not made such improvements, they could not be reading Enigma. Nor did the Royal Navy's various upgrades alter this belief – not even the June 1943 introduction of Naval Cypher No 5, which effectively defeated Marine decryption for the rest of the war.[64]

Nonetheless, as a precaution, the Marine decided to check their cipher machine's security themselves. They began a "Hundert-Tagearbeit" (hundred-day project) of attacking enciphered messages in an attempt to crack the Enigma M. This test used old traffic, originally sent on the three-rotor Enigma M during the Norwegian campaign. A second attempt also made use of "a document cover and pieces of signaled messages" – again old, not live, traffic.[65] A third study requested by the OKW/Chi used the letter frequency method without coming any closer to a solution.[66] Each time, the investigations concluded that Enigma could not be broken.

These conclusions appear to have reassured the Marine general staff and intelligence commanders. Whether they satisfied the U-boat commanders, who found themselves under increasingly frequent Allied attack, is another matter. One prominent expert on U-boat captains has concluded that the commanders' increasing reluctance to signal headquarters except in emergencies indicates that they believed Enigma had been compromised.[67] Marine intelligence, however, did not report such concerns, although it did eventually admit to a general "unrest" about security in the U-boat service.[68] Although Dönitz met with each of the U-boat commanders when they returned from a voyage, this meeting served as a debriefing rather than the launchpad for a general discussion. The U-boat commanders did not meet together formally to compare their experiences, which might have revealed a pattern of Allied sightings or movements exposing Ultra. No forum existed for the commanders to voice their concerns collectively. Instead meetings occurred informally, in Paris cafés or by chance. What uneasiness they must have had about Enigma did not receive attention in the Marine's reports.

## Other Technical Explanations

Instead, the investigations turned their attention to another possible cause for the increase in U-boat losses: a new Allied radar. The Germans had long credited the Allies – and particularly the British – with "undisputed leadership"[69] in the field of detection through radar. While this concept had justifiable grounds, the Marine proceeded to take this belief to extremes.

By December 1942, the Germans had fitted virtually all U-boats with a radar detector, Metox, which would give the U-boat crew warning of a radar sweep.[70] In early March 1943, Dönitz ordered his subs to submerge for one half hour after a Metox radar warning,[71] with the expectation that a sustained dive would allow the sub to escape the detection of Allied aircraft. This tactic succeeded: U-boats warned by Metox alarms generally survived the encounter.

Nevertheless, Allied aircraft continued to surprise U-boats, and the U-boat Command (BdU) noted the increasing sightings and attacks with alarm.[72] This increase suggested to the Germans that the Allies had developed a new radar outside the reception range of the

Metox.[73] Soon a technician aboard U-382 confirmed their deduction. He reported that he had, in a quiet hour, patched a Metox receiver to a visible tuner that received wavelengths beyond the usual range. The visual frequency of this jerry-rigged receiver had sounded a warning of a radar sweep that had not triggered the ordinary Metox alarm.[74] This incident confirmed Command's suspicions of a new radar. The Marine swiftly copied the technician's device, naming it "Magic Eye," and installed one in each returning U-boat.

Still the surprise attacks and U-boat losses mounted. Clearly, the enemy had an "excellent" device for locating U-boats,[75] and the Marine suspected the culprit came from their own ranks. Not Enigma, but rather the Metox radar detector, was betraying them. The Metox, experts had determined, emitted radiation.[76] Given the long-acknowledged British superiority in the field of radar, the explanation for the increasing Allied detection of U-boats must be an Allied device which homed in on these emissions: in effect, an antiradar detector.

The Marine had had its radar specialists attempt to locate the Metox emissions from airplanes. Their report indicated the possibility of detecting emissions from 500 to 2,000 meters.[77] The timing seemed to fit as well. The U-boats had begun carrying the Metox receivers in December 1942, and their losses had begun climbing in January 1943.

Then a decisive corroboration of the Marine's hypothesis appeared. In interrogation, an English pilot

had stated that the English aircraft now hardly ever used their ASV [Anti-Surface Vessel radar] for anti-sub hunts because the U-boats themselves emitted sufficient radiation on which the aircraft was able to make a target run-in. ASV sets were only switched on for short periods to check the range. This radiation from U-boats could be detected at ranges up to 90 miles....[78]

The Marine Command, now under Großadmiral Dönitz, swallowed the explanation. It confirmed all their suspicions. To foil this antiradar detector, Dönitz ordered the Metox receivers shut off. With that, the U-boat crews lost the only early warning they might have had.

In fact, no such antiradar detector existed. Nor did U-boat logs of actual surprise attacks suggest its existence. Frequently, the attacks happened when U-boats had *not* had their Metox switched on. What the

Germans did not know was that December 1942 was also when Bletchley Park had finally cracked the nine-month-old four-rotor Enigma M. (The Allies then read the Marine ciphers, albeit with some delays, through the end of the war.)

## Irrespective of the Evidence

The results of the security investigations suggest that the Marine was too complacent and that the investigators did not thoroughly examine Enigma's culpability but rather went to great lengths in their search to absolve their ciphers. Other than the *Bismarck* incident, the investigations concerned only signals sent to U-boats. At no point apparently did the investigators broaden their inquiry to ask other sections of the Marine or other arms of the military[79] whether any of their signals contained pertinent information. They focused on specific incidents of U-boats, tankers, and large ships being surprised by Allied planes and ships. They considered whether a signal had been sent to or from that vessel, revealing its position either literally in its decrypted text or as a source for D/F. Then they analyzed the British Admiralty's coded signals, which the X-B-Dienst had deciphered, and compared the specific information in the British messages with the signals sent to the Marine's vessels.

German military cryptologic experts continued to explain away even striking warnings that Enigma was the source of Allied information. In its August 1943 log, the BdU noted that word had come through Switzerland from a Swiss man working as a secretary in the U.S. Navy that the Americans were reading the Enigma ciphers concerning U-boats.[80] German counterintelligence had done its job and discovered the biggest secret of the war: Enigma's compromise. Just this sort of leak was what the Allies most feared. Surely direct disclosure of Allied cryptanalysis would cause the Germans to alter Enigma dramatically, if not replace the machines entirely. All of the elaborate security measures surrounding Ultra were designed to prevent just such an incident. Somehow Allied security precautions had failed and a German agent had seen Ultra material.

Yet the agent's straightforward words do not appear to have aroused a high level of alarm. Indeed, the Marine response suggests considerable skepticism. The announcement merely prompted a request to the Abwehr for verification and produced yet another consideration of the possibility that the Allies were reading Enigma.

Yet the events of summer 1943 had added some urgency to uncovering the source of enemy information. The Western Allies had taken the offensive in naval battles, and the U-boats were suffering badly. Gradually at first, American aircraft had begun attacking tanker U-boats as they met the U-boats waiting for resupply. The BdU noted in his log of 15 August 1943 that between mid-June and 1 August 1943, of twenty-one rendezvous between U-boats and their resupply tankers, thirteen meetings went undisturbed.[81] What interruptions occurred in the other eight BdU could easily consider as due to normal Allied air reconnaissance, either from regular sweeps or nearby convoys.

From the beginning of August, however, the situation changed. BdU ordered ten rendezvous between 3 and 11 August, and all of them came under attack by Allied aircraft. Even a rendezvous that the tanker did not reach appeared compromised. Clearly, the enemy had information about resupply orders, and Enigma seemed the most likely source. BdU decided that "it would seem reasonable to assume" the enemy had "read currently the order for Uboat rendezvous." Not that the enemy could break Enigma. Rather, BdU assumed, "the enemy got possession of the keys" for August 1943 – how, his log does not speculate. He does note, however, that three U-boats entered the Bay of Biscay "unmolested," a surprising oversight if indeed the Allies could read Enigma messages of early August.

The explanation, according to the log, lay in the enemy's ineptitude. The Allies could not figure out how to use "the keys captured in one area for reading the traffic in another area." Evidence for this assumption lay in the fact that "all the rendezvous, which were interrupted during the critical period, are in the American area," whereas the orders to the unmolested U-boats had traveled on other networks. (In fact, the Americans had decided upon an aggressive campaign, which the British disapproved on security grounds, of targeting the tankers. By taking out this fleet of resupply boats, the U.S. Navy hoped to curtail the range of U-boat patrols.)

In spite of these alarming activities, the Marine's documented discussion of cipher security produced on this occasion comes no closer to the truth than previous reports. The report considers the breaking of Enigma through depths impossible because the U-boats had not sent enough "genuine" traffic. In making their calculations, the investigators placed considerable reliance on the high statistical security of the variables of the Enigma daily key. Testing these many variables would cost the enemy "a very considerable expenditure of time and labour." So the investigators conclude, "there is no question of current reading."[82]

Having dismissed the possibility of actual decipherment, the Marine turned to the likelihood that the Allies had captured a machine and the settings for the month intact. Such a physical capture seemed entirely probable under the circumstances. Many U-boats had sunk or gone missing in the disastrous preceding months. Their vital cryptologic components might have escaped destruction and fallen into enemy hands. With the correct machine and month of daily settings in hand, the enemy could read Enigma currently, explaining their source of information.

However, this disaster had already been adequately addressed, according to the BdU log. The BdU stated it had negated such a capture by sending the signal, "Andromeda," for U-boats to change to the new Enigma key settings. Faced with new settings, the enemy would lose its window into the U-boat Enigma ciphers.

The underlying assumption that Enigma could only be compromised physically meant the Marine commanders believed their routine change could and had blocked any temporary deciphering ability the U.S. Navy had had. In what they considered an added measure of security, the newly signaled method of setting Enigma's daily key was known only to U-boat officers. Moreover, the officers carried the method of change in their heads, not on paper, so there was nothing for the enemy to capture.[83] Once again the experts reassured the senior officers that without even one component of Enigma's daily setup, the enemy could not read the machine's ciphers.

The Luftwaffe apparently held a similar belief. Its machines fell into enemy hands more frequently as the Allies advanced on the ground and overran airfields and Luftwaffe command posts. At times, the Luftwaffe declared a month's cipher setting compromised, presumably because machines and documents had been lost. The usual practice for the nets then was to drop the rest of the month's daily settings and use instead those for the following month. Once the month was up and a new batch of daily settings had arrived, the net returned to normal.[84] Clearly, Luftwaffe cryptologists did not believe that such an individual compromise – or indeed several as eventually occurred during the war – gave the enemy any long-term break into Enigma. Although Bletchley Park read the main Luftwaffe cipher, nicknamed Red, for virtually the entire war, Luftwaffe intelligence, like the Marine B-Dienst, apparently found other explanations for the enemy's information.

In 1944, when the U-boat arm again raised concerns about the Allied ability to find the U-boats, German intelligence could point the finger at numerous sources other than Enigma. They did note in a July 1944 report that Heer cryptographers had admitted that their three-rotor Enigma had "certain weak points." These weaknesses in fact meant that this Enigma could be broken under certain conditions, although they considered such an occurrence unlikely. A break required a long message (at least 300 elements) and "a particularly complicated cryptographic requirement" (which the Enigma M did not have). Moreover, the enemy would need to "indulge" in an "extraordinary mechanical outlay" to take advantage of these flaws. Lt. R. Hans-Joachim Frowein of the B-Dienst believed that such mechanical assistance could be in fact quite effective. However, the B-Dienst considered such an indulgence unlikely, given the expense and difficulty.[85] Instead, the Marine investigators again focused quickly on spies reporting on naval movements through the telephone and postal traffic in increasingly hostile occupied France. Allied cryptanalytic success no longer figured as a possibility.

## Human Explanations

The Germans turned repeatedly to two other types of possibilities: human betrayal and Allied mechanical superiority. The former theory obsessed Hitler and, especially after the 20 July 1944 assassination plot, the theme of a high-level spy frequently appeared. Yet, for individual cases, the Wehrmacht considered treason by their own officers unlikely.[86] Surprise inspections in 1941 and 1942 had exposed few irregularities, and none of the security investigations uncovered any suspicions of disloyalty among officers using Enigma. So the military ascribed the betrayal to the enlisted soldier and crewman, whose carelessness and lack of discipline unwittingly leaked information to the enemy.[87]

The Germans preferred to suspect human fallibility before that of the machine. In North Africa, the Heer began to suspect the enemy was "to some extent exploiting W/T traffic." The signals director announced that since "the deciphering of Enigma seems out of the question,"[88] the problem had to be with the people using the machine. He asked whether the Enigma operators were following proper procedures, whether any documents might have been captured, and whether the Italians were using Enigma. Even if Enigma-encrypted signals could be giving the enemy information, the machine was not at fault. Enigma could only betray German military secrets if its human operators did not follow procedures. The very form the director's questions took suggests he was seeking some non-Enigma source for the enemy's intelligence, even if that source was Italian cryptology or German mistakes.[89]

German officers also accorded enemy agents considerable blame for information leaks, although in fact the Nazi government's Gestapo and the Wehrmacht's constant distrust managed to conceal most high-level material from agents' eyes.[90] German intelligence feared agents working in neutral countries, partisans in occupied territories working alone or with the Allies, and Allied agents (generally, British) infiltrating into German territory. The various branches of German intelligence had had considerable success using spies themselves. Their agents had, for example, successfully stolen crucial documents from the Allies in Turkey[91] and codes from Allied embassies.[92] Naturally, they suspected their enemy of similar behavior.[93] Long before the war the Germans had been concerned about spies, and the blitzkrieg conquests only offered greater room for worry. In 1941, the Marine Nachrichtendienst (MND) focused on the "unhindered" activities of British agents in Norway. In June 1941, the MND noted that agents in southern Norway sent several telegrams, their text apparently unknown, to London just as the battleship *Bismarck* left its Norwegian berth for the open sea. In October 1941, the Marine felt again betrayed by agents, this time from Bordeaux.[94]

The Marine made certain that its listening service (the B-Dienst) watched radio traffic not just in foreign waters but across occupied Europe. The notorious Gestapo had primary responsibility for tracking and silencing illegal radios throughout Nazi Europe,[95] but the B-Dienst also tracked "English radio agents" and charted the illegal traffic's rise just prior to important Axis operations. They followed both direct traffic to enemy territory and the more convoluted transmissions sent via neutrals – generally Sweden.[96] At least some of Germany's otherwise unexplained losses were attributed to these spies. In December 1941, the Marine Command "assumed certain" that agents had passed vital departure information for supply ships out of western France. The Command concluded that this information, along with enemy TA and D/F – but not decryption – of radio messages explained both the loss of at least two German ships and why the enemy had established new patrol routes.[97]

Germans captured by the Allies often cited agents as sources for the enemy's information. In conversations overheard by his Allied captors, one pilot speculated that information came from military officers still loyal to Kaiser Wilhelm.[98] Another German POW considered agents and factory spies a logical intelligence source because such avenues had proved useful for the Germans.[99]

Long after the war and even after the official British acknowledgments of Ultra, German military men continued to blame agents for German losses. One retired military man claimed as late as 1976 that attributing the Allied victory to Ultra was "nonsense." He argued that information the Allies had garnered came from a network of agents, called RCA, left behind in France and operating to the end of the war.[100] Others, including Chief of Intelligence (Fremde Heer Ost) Richard Gehlen, believed Hitler's own right-hand man, the mysterious Martin Bormann, had betrayed Germany's highest secrets.[101]

Hitler's own distrust of his fellow Germans is well documented.[102] At first he raged primarily about incompetence. He and the Wehrmacht Command blamed the failures of the highly touted Tiger tank on insufficiently trained Panzer crews.[103] In the case of inaccurate U-boat torpedoes, he insisted that U-boat crews were misfiring the weapons until Admiral Dönitz arranged for a demonstration of the torpedo's tendency toward premature detonation.[104] Anyone who defied, or even questioned, the Führer's genius earned his wrath. By 1944, commanders who "allowed" anything less than complete victory (let alone permitted retreat) had committed treason: in the famous cases of Generals von Kluge and Rommel, earlier victories gave them the privilege of choosing suicide first. After the 20 July 1944 hapless assassination attempt, Hitler's paranoia grew without bounds. By 1945 he was convinced that planes which had not returned from bombing missions had flown over to the enemy.[105]

This obsession filtered down to the military commands as well. The Marine suggested, for instance, that "U-570" fell into enemy hands because the Captain's collapse from gas poisoning left the less-competent Oberleutnant zur See in charge of the sub during the enemy attack.[106] Decades after the war, even former signals intelligence officers insisted "British intelligence got a major portion of its information from radio agents, since through these it had available the services of confidential agents (men or women) in the very highest offices in Germany."[107] Most Germans believed someone like the notional agent Boniface not only survived inside Germany's police state but thrived.

In spite of this considerable paranoia, the cryptologists apparently paid little attention to one potentially damaging leak: POWs. Oddly, they apparently did not consider just how much POWs could say about Enigma. Of course, all German recruits were admonished to remember the Geneva Convention when captured and to say no more than name, rank, and serial number. At the same time, German sailors and soldiers had heard horror stories of how the Allies treated German POWs: deprivation, starvation, torture. When they fell into enemy hands and found their treatment decent, many of them readily spilled all they knew and even "security conscious Nazi POW's" readily talked among themselves without concern for possible hidden microphones.[108] While pilots talked of new planes and improved flak, radio operators explained, often voluntarily, antiradar measures and everything they knew about operating Enigma machines. At least by 1943,[109] POWs had described the inner workings of Enigma, complete with sketches, and had voiced the general opinion of Enigma's security:

> If you have no basis to work on, you can't do anything with it. Such a coding device has, I believe, 15 million possibilities. And by the time you have made 15 million tries, a year has passed. So it is very difficult to break. . . . If they [our own people] make a real mistake, even we can't decode it. When they make slight errors, then one sits down and works it out, but generally that can't be done either. I've tried it already, but generally it can't be done.[110]

After the war moved back into western Europe in June 1944, some Germans in intelligence, for example, the intelligence interpreter, Obergefreiter Karl Exner, even began pilfering official documents and crossing the front lines to surrender themselves and their information.[111] Such possible crucial security leaks by POWs do not seem to have overly concerned the German commands. Apparently, they viewed the radio operators as recruits acceptable for operating the machine but not capable of grasping or explaining the analytical and conceptual elements of the cipher system. The leaders concentrated rather on the physical security of the key settings and of the machine itself.[112]

## Faulty Assumptions

These erroneous conclusions owe their existence in large part to conditions in place before the investigations began. Intelligence investigators refused to begin with the assumption that Enigma *could* be solved. When they did set personnel the task of testing the Enigma machine, they adhered to statistical attacks and apparently did not attempt any of the less straightforward methods employed by the Allies. The investigations appeased the higher echelons, at least until the next rise in losses, and the concerns of frontline commanders received little consideration.

The investigations themselves reveal no more interservice cooperation or exchange of information than any other aspect of the German war effort. By dividing their intelligence resources between the various branches of the military and the government, the Germans ensured that their investigations were flawed from the start. Their lack of cooperation made them all the more unlikely to recognize just how widespread and thorough Allied sources of information had become. Yet the Marine correctly instigated investigations at points when the Allies *were* reading Enigma and not at those times when Bletchley Park had been blacked out. Their instincts were correct; but they failed to accept the evidence, instead believing their experts, who insisted Enigma remained secure.

The Germans trusted their own intelligence personnel so thoroughly that they apparently never felt the need to challenge these experts' assumptions. They did criticize their own commanders, industrialists, and rank-and-file radio operators as inadequate, incompetent, or undisciplined. They never seem to have turned a similarly judging eye on their more intellectual personnel. Specifically, no one challenged the belief that the enemy would only approach Enigma statistically or that other cryptanalysts could not develop and use machines equal to Enigma in their attack.

The Wehrmacht had put its trust in security experts who could not bring themselves to imagine that the Allies could actually crack Germany's cipher machine. Yet the Germans believed strongly in Allied production and mechanical superiority, and these convictions had justification. After the successive entries into the war of the Soviet Union and the United States, the Allies had a clear preeminence in personnel, material, and production capacity. Allied production outstripped the Germans' highest estimates by 1942–1943. New and modified Allied aircraft, including the very long range (VLR) *Liberator* aircraft, closed the "Atlantic" or "Greenland Gap" in the mid-North Atlantic, where U-boats had roamed largely unseen and unmolested until they attacked a convoy.[113] Aircraft outfitted with "Leigh lights" (essentially spotlights) made U-boats easy targets at night, and planes alerted the even more deadly escort ships to the U-boats' precise location. The Allies developed an increasing barrage of weapons – bombs, mines, torpedoes, and depth charges – to destroy the detected enemy ships. Allied locating devices and jamming methods could find and destroy German targets faster and more effectively while disguising and protecting their own positions increasingly thoroughly.

In addition, the Allies had some advantage in radar and direction finding, a strength which the Wehrmacht willingly, almost obsequiously, admitted.[114] To the Germans, D/F, radar, and TA represented mechanical and production capabilities, capabilities they had no hesitation attributing to their enemy. Even when they had little evidence, they envisioned the Allies constructing an entirely new radar device that could defeat the Metox. Why then did they ignore the potential role of such technical and mechanical superiority in cryptanalysis?

Their writings and interrogations reveal that German officers and cryptologic experts considered cryptology and ciphers an intellectual invention rather than a mechanical one. The Germans had endowed the Allies, specifically the British, with almost mythical abilities in the fields of radar and D/F, but failed to credit them with any ingenuity in

8. Großadmiral Karl Dönitz, (center) as the new leader of Germany, surrendering unconditionally to the Allies. After Hermann Göring infuriated Adolf Hitler, the Führer unexpectedly bequeathed his position to the Marine's Dönitz and then committed suicide. (Courtesy of the National Security Agency)

the area of cryptology. This juxtaposition suggests the German military distorted their investigations and conclusion with a fundamental assumption: German intellectual superiority. While they were willing to admit the Allies could outman them, outgun them, and even overpower them, they could not imagine their enemy could outthink them. Germany might lose the physical war, but never the mental one.

Confident of their own intellectual superiority, they never expanded on their own experience cracking Allied codes and ciphers and imagined themselves in their enemy's shoes. Although the Marine command was using decrypts to find its targets, they could not believe that the enemy was doing the same. The security investigations reflect this assumption. The goal of the Marine investigations should have been to discover the source of the enemy's information, whatever it might be. Instead, the investigators clearly set out to prove Enigma was *not* the source, virtually predetermining their results. They did not want to find Enigma capable of being compromised, let alone the source of the enemy's information. They tied themselves in knots explaining how the leak could not be Enigma, but they failed to present another scenario that could explain the enemy's increasing success. By eliminating each episode separately, one by one, the Marine investigators refused to broaden their inquiry to develop a single pattern that explained the trend of events as more than simply a series of coincidences.

Most important, the security investigations neglected the fundamental problem. By 1943, if not before, the enemy had clearly found a way to locate U-boats and sink them in ever larger numbers. In the end of May 1943, Dönitz withdrew his U-boats from the Atlantic, halting attacks on convoys between the United States and the United Kingdom. With this decision, he "practically cancelled" the war against Allied convoys in the Atlantic.[115] Whatever the cause of the enemy's increasing success, the Marine would have to reverse this trend to survive.

Yet the situation from the German point of view only worsened. In June 1943, the Allies again changed their ciphers and the B-Dienst was again in the dark, this time for good. The offensive in the Battle of the Atlantic went to the Allies.[116] They continued to use Ultra information to route convoys around patrols, but now they used Enigma "offensively" to locate U-boat rendezvous and tanker U-boat (Milchkühe) routes.[117] But Ultra's camouflage continued to deceive convincingly. Before Dönitz could safely launch his U-boats again in the North Atlantic in wolfpack raids on convoys, the war ended.

After numerous investigations into probable sources of enemy information, after many tests of their own cipher machines, after losing their grip on enemy system after enemy system, with oil tankers sunk and U-boats lost in ever-increasing numbers, the German cipher experts always came to the same conclusion:

> solution of a military Enigma (with a Steckerboard) is indeed theoretically possible, but practically speaking is hardly feasible.[118]

# SEVEN

# A LONG-STANDING ANXIETY

## Allied Communications Security

The entire [U.S.] Machine Analysis Group has been pressed into service in preparing material for the solution of [our own] Navy problem [Combined Cipher Machine]. The initial alignment of the fifth wheel was determined last week and the process of isolating the third and fourth wheels has been begun.

– Cryptanalytic efforts against *own* equipment, June 1944

Allied cipher security could not claim to be perfect. Like the Germans, the British learned from the Great War that their "own methods of ciphering were far from perfect," and a post–World War I commission had recommended "sweeping reforms."[1] In World War II, they reacted by planning for the worst. Allied cryptologists had reason to fear their German intelligence counterparts. They expected the enemy would crack their codes; it was only a matter of time, as they had learned in the First World War. Their own successes had shown them how far ingenuity, a little luck, and some basic training could go toward breaking most ciphers. Bletchley Park's success against Enigma and that of the Poles before them made the Allies ever more aware of the limits of their own cryptosystems.

The compromise of Germany's highest grade of ciphers forced Allied cryptographers to face the fact that they could not consider any of their cipher systems, however complex, completely secure. They planned accordingly. They sharply segregated their high-grade traffic from routine messages and invested in cipher machines more advanced than Enigma. Both the British and Americans instituted ongoing, active monitoring of their own signals systems, and they searched for signs of weaknesses in their ciphers and their procedures. They expected to find leaks in their systems and they did. Postmortems and analyses of failures led to changes in procedures and to cipher upgrades. Because they planned for periodic failures, cryptographers could correct them before the entire system succumbed.

## Connecting Cryptography and Cryptanalysis

GC&CS's experience attacking German ciphers clearly shaped the procedures the Allies developed for ciphers and signals. Analysts at Bletchley saw the connection between the cryptanalysis of the enemy's systems and the protection of their own cryptology as obvious. Here they had tradition to support them. After the cryptologic experiences of the Great War, Britain had emphasized the interdependence of cryptography and cryptanalysis. When naval officers, for example, attended prewar lectures on cryptology, the speakers gave these "end users" of cryptanalysis concrete proof of how security lapses allowed the enemy to crack their own ciphers. Although the lectures stopped for fear of sensitive "leaks,"[2] the policy of such "full indoctrination" developed later for Ultra continued the practice of connecting cryptology's halves.

This connection between cryptanalysis and cryptography benefitted from the physical and administrative centralization of GC&CS. The cryptographic half moved to Bletchley Park along with cryptanalysis. GC&CS had responsibility for both developing and protecting British ciphers. The "Construction of Ciphers" and the security of ciphers appear on GC&CS organizational charts of the Park.[3] The minutes of a December 1942 meeting reiterate GC&CS's responsibility for "All questions regarding Allied ciphers." More specifically, GC&CS developed a position that would handle the "technical aspects of British ciphers, including...maintaining their technical security."[4] Unfortunately for the historian, many exchanges between cryptanalysts and those responsible for Allied cipher development and security apparently took place verbally without leaving a written record.[5] What records do exist show that Bletchley Park's analysts gave Allied signal security important lessons.[6]

From the start, the British accepted the vulnerability of their ciphers. GC&CS had admitted that, with British diplomatic ciphers for example, they must expect "that the cyphered text may be available to foreign gov[ernmen]ts."[7] They recognized the probability of both physical and cryptanalytic compromise. Indeed, every Allied cryptographic system would suffer a physical compromise during the war.[8] In early 1940, the British Admiralty believed the Germans had acquired cipher material from both a submarine sunk in shallow waters and the HMS *Hardy* in Norway. These losses were only the first. Such examples of the ciphers' physical vulnerability convinced the Admiralty to separate their ciphers: vessels in "dangerous waters" received special tables. In mid-1941, a further split sealed off the Atlantic Allied convoys from all other operations when the three navies adopted Naval Cypher No 3 exclusively for convoy routing signals. Independently routed ships each acquired a separate code table, so that the capture of one ship's codes would not endanger the entire fleet.[9]

Lowering the risks of purely physical compromise was not the only way this division of code traffic improved cipher security. With each new network, the amount of traffic sent in a single code or cipher decreases. The enemy now has less material for finding mistakes, depths, and cribs. True, the likelihood rises that a message (for instance, a weather warning) will be repeated in more than one cipher and thereby expose a hitherto unbroken cipher to easy attack. Yet overall the cost to the enemy increases.[10] The multiplication of different systems forces the enemy's cryptanalysts to work on a greater number of ciphers and compels them to divide their attention and their effort among many possibilities rather than focusing on a few.

Like the Germans, Allied security experts reiterated the importance of security procedures. Indeed, they viewed as part of their duty pointing out any hint that Allied systems suffered weaknesses or compromise. As the Germans did, they reprimanded lapses, changed heavily used superencipherment codes (such as coordinates codes), and upgraded ciphers. Then they went further.

At Bletchley Park, analysts identified the damage the enemy could do through long-term accumulation of apparently low-grade, insignificant material. With this threat in mind, Bletchley's security experts went to considerable effort to avoid giving the enemy any crib texts, even inadvertently. Before allowing any nonsecret information to be passed to the Press, they insisted on a complete rewording of "the literal text of a signal, for example of congratulations from Admiralty to ship."[11] They insisted "stereotyped beginnings and preamble be buried" in the middle of a signal's text and directed that "no addresses (to or from) [be] entered on the cryptogram" itself.[12] These rules reflect Bletchley's own use of German addresses for breaking into Enigma.

Bletchley's analysts clearly cared more for cipher security than for proper comportment. They issued directives on a range of signal security issues. Hut 3 analysts following the Luftwaffe's signals noted flaws in British procedures and complained that RAF fighters regularly compromised their own movements through routine takeoff acknowledgments. "Saying 'now airborne' seems to me to be equivalent to sending a wire to Goering to say that you are coming!" one wrote in fury.[13] They rapped out such reprimands bluntly when necessary. In July 1941, Naval Section analysts explained "that the need for withholding information from the enemy is greater than usual." They laid out several examples of sloppy British cipher security during the operations against the German heavy ships *Bismarck* and *Luetzow*. Valuable information had passed to the enemy far too easily. They insisted that "the security of aircraft signals and of tactical signals from ships could be increased without prejudice to speed and efficiency." Furious, they snapped,

> if our own authorities cannot think out an alternative, we should be pleased to show them [Germany's] code...for overwater aircraft, which is practically unbreakable.[14]

Such outbursts played a significant role in the Allied sigint victory. The "long-standing anxiety on the part of the signals security authorities...about the cryptographic security of their cyphers"[15] kept them on the lookout for evidence of leaks and for ways of improving security.

Like most institutions and like the Wehrmacht, the Allied militaries resisted accepting that their security had been compromised. Often they demanded proof of compromise (which fortunately the Germans provided at crucial moments) and appeared slow to adopt changes. Yet they did finally accept the arguments of their signals intelligence staff and the young civilians in cryptology. They agreed to security monitoring units, to investigations into potential cipher leaks, and to plugging those leaks when they emerged. Most important, the military accepted the possibility of mistakes and failure in cryptology. They allowed both military and civilian staff to point out problems. They agreed to necessary changes and upgrades in codes and machines. They expended considerable resources for all aspects of the cryptologic effort and gave cryptology a significant priority.

Britain and the United States developed teams whose job was to observe, test, and attack Allied signal and cipher security. The British began the practice first with a police watch from Britain and then with a worldwide organization of monitoring teams.[16] These teams observed Allied transmissions to make sure that signalers followed security procedures and they chided their own side for sloppy signaling security. These teams monitored everything from voice signals sent in the clear to procedures for using the top-grade cipher machines.[17]

The Americans admired these units and developed their own parallel organization, which they named SIAM (Signal Information and Monitoring). SIAM radio operators monitored Allied transmissions twenty-four hours a day. The SIAM platoon commander searched for violations of signaling procedures and of cipher security procedures.[18] He then delivered a weekly security report on the frontline units under his observation. One such report noted that after monitoring 53 nets over 878 hours, the security teams had recorded 67 violations (50 by American units and 17 by French units).[19] Violations ranged from signaling in plain language instead of code to misuse of ciphers. The Signal Officer, 88th Infantry Division, for example, received a reprimand because his operators were "not using padding at the beginning and ending of their [cipher] messages."[20] These monitors kept a keen eye on Allied signal security.

The Allies expected some of their own cryptosystems would succumb to enemy attack, a few quite swiftly. GC&CS accepted evidence early on that German intelligence could read naval tactical signals at times and decipher some "British aircraft traffic immediately on receipt."[21] Bletchley's analysts recognized that battle conditions often demanded speed of communication above security, and they strove to create codes and ciphers that would meet both those needs. Emergencies were not sufficient excuse for sending plain-language signals. GC&CS insisted on use of even very low-level codes because "the process of breaking…absorbs manpower and takes time." Therefore, the more codes the enemy faced, the more effort he had to expend, "which he can ill afford."[22] Keeping the Germans busy attacking frontline codes for map references and bomb lines would detract him from higher-grade systems. The high-grade systems were the central treasure the Allies sought to protect.

## Testing Allied Machines

The Allies analyzed the security risks of their own systems with an unforgiving eye. They actively and repeatedly tested the security of their own cipher machines. The Polish cryptanalytic team performed a full formal assault on their own cipher machine, Lacida. They concluded their ciphers did not provide adequate security against attack.[23] The British and Americans carefully graded each cipher system according to the amount and the level (Unclassified, Confidential, Secret, Most Secret, etc.) of traffic it could carry. Signals intelligence, particularly intelligence derived from Ultra, could only travel on the most secure systems: one-time pads, Typex (British), Sigaba (United States), or the CCM (a Typex-Sigaba hybrid). The Allies were never complacent about their most complex high-grade electromechanical cipher systems, nor did they relax their vigilance over lower-grade systems.

The U.S. Signal Security Service conducted a "cryptographic security survey of other government departments," including the State Department.[24] They also had units to attack the security of all military systems. One unit, headed by Margaret Evans Lerche, took on the popular M-209 (a medium-grade nonelectric rotor cipher).[25] The unit broke this widely used machine numerous times in several different ways. The first SIS attack on the M-209 in 1942 found several possible methods of acquiring material sufficient for an initial break. When they studied "live" traffic from the battles in Europe, the team reconstructed key and read several days' signals. They urged better security training for operators and noted that the forces using M-209s in North Africa had demonstrated improved security.[26] With this proof of M-209's weaknesses, the Americans did not remove the system completely but rather limited its use to information of only short-term value to the enemy.

Other U.S. cipher systems also endured ongoing assaults conducted by the Machine Analysis Group. The head of the Machine Analysis

9. An American preparing to use M-209 in the field. He appears to be taking dictation of the message before enciphering it. Note the very small size of M-209, making it ideal for use on the frontlines. Enigma, both larger and far heavier, was not normally carried by hand. (Courtesy of the National Security Agency)

Group, first P. R. Reimers and then 2nd Lt. Frank C. Austin, filed weekly reports on the staff's methods and successes. They used existing and newly developed mechanical aids to attack medium-grade and high-grade systems, often successfully.[27] These studies produced a variety of changes. They made recommendations for various cipher machines such as increasing the frequency of rotor turnovers and having multiple fast-turning rotors. The results of another study declared one cipher device lacked adequate security; it was ordered destroyed.[28]

Through the last two years of the war, the Machine Analysis Unit devoted considerable attention to the two highest-grade American systems: M-134-C (known as Sigaba or "The Big Machine") and CCM, a Sigaba variant used to communicate with the British. The American Sigaba has been labeled "the most secure cipher machine of the Second World War."[29] As with Enigma, these multirotor American machines had ever-changing settings that relied on key lists. Cracking

Sigaba would require more than possessing the machine and even "all wiring diagrams of the machine and the rotors."[30]

To test these high-grade machines, the Machine Analysis Unit simulated both best-case and worst-case conditions from the enemy's point of view. Some scenarios assumed the cryptanalyst had the machine's rotors in hand; others limited knowledge to only the order of the rotors (not their wiring). At times, these manufactured scenarios meant the analysts worked "under more difficult conditions than would be the case with enemy cryptanalysts."[31]

In addition to these scenarios designed specifically for tests, cryptanalysts studied "live" traffic. They examined such traffic for the human errors which provide cryptanalysts with valuable breaks, such as "special characteristics of the operators."[32] They attacked indicator settings and messages in depth. These attacks searched for any and all cases of circumstances that might render Sigaba vulnerable. When they tried scenarios that violated the rules for operating the Sigaba, they had some success. By January 1945, the team had reconstructed "six complete rotors and two partial rotors of a set of ten" from a simulation using nonrandom indicators. After issuing a stern reminder to use only random indicators, they immediately began another attack using yet another approach.[33]

The U.S. attacks on Sigaba – the Allies' highest-grade machine – and on other Allied systems were ongoing. The team attacking them outlined their progressive breaks into the machine as triumphs, perhaps savoring the difficulty they faced. They did not stop with statistical or strictly mathematical attacks. They went further, focusing on real traffic sent under real wartime stresses and exploiting all the human operating mistakes they could find. They appear to have attacked the Sigaba and other cipher systems as eagerly as if they were attacking enemy systems to help the war effort. They would stop at nothing to uncover every flaw they could find in the Allied machines and their operation. Indeed, their attacks on Allied ciphers could offer as much to the war effort as breaking enemy systems. If they could find a flaw before the enemy did, they could fix it before the enemy took advantage of it. Security of their own systems did mean as much to the war effort as the insecurity of the enemy's systems.

These security investigations, as well as the Allied high-grade systems themselves, owe much to the Allied experience breaking Enigma. The investigators took note of Enigma's weak points and examined their own systems for similar flaws. They included the possibility that the enemy had access to machine and operational documents, to the machine itself, or to portions of the machine, particularly the internal wiring of the rotors. They presupposed the enemy's long-term scrutiny of machines, actual signals, and operating procedures.

The teams paid particular attention to those points of human error that offered such rich possibilities to the Allies. Their reports have frequent discussions of how lazy operators and nonrandom indicator systems simplified their work. They also attacked the weak points of the machine's cycle length and message depths. In short, they focused on all of the conditions that the Polish team and the Bletchley Park cryptanalysts had used to such great effect. One study examined more than fifty thousand indicator groups produced in live traffic over a period of four months. The team concluded that serious violations of indicator rules could allow the reconstruction of rotors.[34]

Once they found a way in, even if its exploitation appeared to require too many man-hours to produce current reading, they continued to modify their tactics, in case a refined approach would reduce the time to a manageable amount. They also sought mechanical aids, like "a high-speed method for identification of rotors,"[35] just as their fellow cryptanalysts used machines in attacking German and Japanese cipher systems.

On the cryptographic side, Britain and the United States also used what they had learned from their cryptanalysis of enemy systems. Both nations' cryptographers had examined Enigma before building their high-grade cipher machines. The high-grade Allied systems themselves show how Anglo-American cryptographers learned from Enigma's mistakes. The British Typex machine was a generation beyond Enigma, using five of a possible ten rotors rather than three or four of eight. Its electromechanical stepping also appears more sophisticated than Enigma's because not all five rotors stepped evenly. Typex proved secure throughout the war. Yet the Americans considered Typex inadequate, snidely calling it "nothing but a glorified German Enigma, with 5 rotors instead of 3 and with arrangements for printing."[36]

The CCM received higher praise from American cryptanalysts. They declared this hybrid Sigaba-Typex "theoretically secure enough for the communications safeguarded by it."[37] At the same time, their emphasis on excellent theoretical – not operational – security demonstrates that they recognized the limits human use created. They knew the machines' human operators would open a gap between the system's tremendous theoretical security and its lesser degree of practical security.

American cryptologists designed the Sigaba to eliminate many of Enigma's weaknesses. Sigaba not only used more rotors than either Enigma or Typex, its rotors worked in either direction. Sigaba's most revolutionary element abolished simple mechanical rotor stepping. Instead, a second set of electrically wired rotors controlled the progression of the cipher alphabet rotors.[38] This electrically driven rotor stepping meant the enemy cryptanalyst would struggle first with an enciphering system for the rotor movement before attacking the cipher rotors themselves.

Even with this innovative stepping complication, the Americans remained obsessive about security, particularly physical security: even long after the war, decommissioned Sigaba rotors had their wires cut or completely removed.[39] American cryptologists constantly planned for compromise. Early in the war, Leo Rosen, one of the first Americans to see Bletchley Park's work against Enigma, developed an emergency pluggable rotor for the Sigaba. Named SIGHEK, this rotor was designed to counter a physical compromise. SIGHEK would temporarily replace one of the compromised rotors to foil the enemy until a complete set of new rotors arrived.[40] Such a pluggable rotor for Enigma would nearly defeat Bletchley Park in 1944. Only its piecemeal and ultimately incomplete introduction saved Bletchley from a major blackout in decryption. Knowing their own successes with decryption, the Allies remained alert for signs of any comparable enemy success.

## Finding and Plugging Leaks

Throughout the war, the Bletchley staff kept a close eye on Enigma decrypts for signs that the enemy was breaking Allied codes and ciphers, not just currently but over the long haul.[41] The German investigations into Enigma's security had each focused on an individual episode of possible compromise and ignored the probability of ongoing imperfect decryption. Allied investigators took the opposite approach. Several intelligence analysis sections within the huts at Bletchley studied "the state of enemy intelligence" and watched "over the security of Allied ciphers."[42] They reported suspicious items swiftly and included decryption of Allied signals as a potential source for enemy information. "Investigation usually established that the source had been plain language or low-grade code signals...."[43] GC&CS did not, however, become complacent.

From early on, Germany's B-Dienst gave Bletchley analysts considerable concern. Once Hut 8 cracked the first Marine Enigma ciphers, the analysts focused on decrypts of reports about British maritime movements. They speculated "whether the [B-Dienst] reports [were] forecasts based on incomplete information (e.g. d/f, reconnaissance, non-current special intelligence), or ... current special intelligence." The reference to noncurrent special intelligence shows that they grasped how long-term scrutiny of a cipher system can offer tremendous advantages. Old decrypts could give the Germans enough information to make reasonably accurate forecasts without reading current messages. By including noncurrent and imperfect sigint, the investigators avoided the trap of requiring that a leak be traced to the exact wording of a currently compromised signal. Their investigations do not attempt to rule out a system's compromise but rather to search for the source of the enemy's information.

The Germans, as the investigators noted, attributed this intelligence as "according to B report" and "the B Service [was] that part of German Naval Intelligence which deals with the interception and deciphering of enemy traffic." The British investigators concluded that enemy decrypts of Admiralty signals "would appear [the] more probable [explanation] owing to the (in some cases) very precise details given."[44] Bletchley Park's analysts could have presented only the rather more palatable explanation of low-grade intelligence compromise through D/F and reconnaissance. They did not hesitate, however, to draw the more undesirable conclusion that British cryptologic systems had been penetrated.

Having decided the Germans had cracked one cipher, the Allies continued to check for signs of more compromises. The knowledge of the

German organization and the enemy's casual references to its own crypt-analytic services alerted BP to a serious leak from an unexpected quarter. For nine months in 1941 and 1942, General Rommel had appeared unstoppable in North Africa. Seeming to possess a second sense about British strengths and intentions, he raced his tanks across Libya and crossed into Egypt itself. Then, "just before Montgomery [went over] to the offensive" in North Africa, the Allies stumbled on the source of Rommel's omnipotence. Their cryptanalysts produced a decrypt of an Italian signal "which stated that Rommel's successes had been in good measure due to his reading of the American military attaché cypher" from Cairo.[45] By early June 1942, "C" told Prime Minister Churchill he was certain "the American cyphers in Cairo are compromised. I am taking action."[46]

The Americans traced the leakage back to their own Colonel Fellers. As military attaché he sent detailed reports of British positions in weekly signals to Washington. His ciphers had either been stolen or cracked (disagreement on this detail continues),[47] and German intelligence had been reading his messages for nine months. An investigation of Fellers cleared him personally of traitorous activities, and the United States swiftly realized the weakness of the military attaché code he had employed. (Fellers, needless to say, was not Ultra-indoctrinated and so his compromised messages did not prompt the Axis powers to check their own ciphers.) Once they located the blown cipher, the Americans swiftly replaced it, sealing off another puncture by German intelligence.

Rommel continued to furnish security scares for the Allies. Not only did he have excellent intelligence sources himself, but he personally provoked a potentially damaging Ultra leak. His illness and hospitalization in the winter of 1942–43 appeared in Ultra decrypts[48] and somehow leaked out to become gossip in London's social circles. Bletchley suspected some Ultra recipient at Whitehall had found the knowledge of the Desert Fox's tendency for fainting attacks too tantalizing to keep quiet. This incident led GC&CS to tighten Ultra's security further; specifically, the rules around tidbits of gossip tightened, restricting how and to whom these tales traveled.[49] With these more stringent rules, leaks of juicy rumors ceased.

Allied signal security was far from perfect. Not just human error but weak ciphers provided the enemy with low-hanging fruit. For some time, British Naval Intelligence relied on periodic changes to protect its "long subtractor system" ciphers. Moreover, the Royal Navy believed cipher material had fallen into enemy hands, and its signal security staff took swift steps. When a submarine went missing in the Mediterranean, the Admiralty imposed radio silence on the cipher that sub had carried. Normal radio traffic resumed "six weeks later, after couriers had been able to deliver new codes throughout this far-flung theater [Mediterranean] of operations."[50]

After the swift German invasion trapped the HMS *Hardy* in Norway, the Admiralty ordered the split in cipher traffic for vessels in "dangerous waters." This episode also undoubtedly contributed to the 20 August 1940 change of Naval Cyphers from No 1 to the reserve book, No 2. This new cipher book put the B-Dienst in the dark temporarily. Nonetheless, Britain's navy continued to provide the Marine's cryptanalysis service with a substantial harvest for several years.

British signal security staff continued to argue for changes. They worried in particular about "the heavily used 'convoy cipher'." With GC&CS's assistance, the Royal Navy began planning as early as April 1941 for the introduction of more secure cyphers. In addition, they prepared a number of more immediate changes to improve the security of existing ciphers.[51] Like the Germans, they would periodically alter their indicator procedures for daily cipher settings as a stopgap measure.

The Royal Navy next upgraded their main Cypher No 2 in September 1941, although this change did not prove entirely effective. In January 1942, British ships made their second complete cipher book change; this time Cypher No 2 was replaced by Cypher No 4. (Throughout this period, the convoy cipher, Naval Cypher No 3, had suffered persistent German breaks.) This change largely foiled German assault for some nine months. An additional indicator upgrade of December 1942 threw the B-Dienst into a two-month blackout.[52] By combining upgrades with periodic cipher book changes, the Admiralty partially achieved its goal of security.

The Royal Navy had developed an entirely new reciphering system – more than just an upgrade – by late 1941, and over the next year naval intelligence ran the new system through field trials. They planned to complete production and distribution of the new system by the end of 1943. But the end of 1942 brought hints of German breaks into Naval Cypher No 3 on a broader scale than expected.

In January 1943, the Allies warned their naval officers that the B-Dienst was reading the combined convoy cipher (Naval Cypher No 3) and urged reduced signaling and the use of one-time pads for all vital transmissions. Bletchley's analysts did not wait for absolute confirmation of compromise but urged an immediate change to the new system. Apparently, the Admiralty remained unconvinced. Devastating U-boat attacks in May on Convoy HX 237 (a westbound convoy) again drove GC&CS to argue forcefully that the convoy ciphers had been compromised.[53]

Finally, the analysts gained access to all of their own navies' dispatched signals:

> The examination of the convoy files showed that German cryptanalysis had a good depth with which to work, for the diversion of the convoys, complicated by a bad fog off of Newfoundland Banks, had led to frequent exchanges of dispatches between shore authorities and the escorts – all in Naval Cipher #3, table "S." On 7 May, for example, there were at least 6 transmissions from escorts ... While there was no way of determining how many dispatches the Germans had read, the first [suspect message examined] could be traced without question to [dispatches in Cypher No 3 table "S"].

The analysts could not pinpoint each of the convoy signals that had been decrypted by the Germans and had caused U-boat Command to reroute the U-boats. In fact, they concluded that the Marine's cryptanalysts "had apparently failed to make a complete recovery [of the cipher] and [so the B-Dienst] remained in ignorance of the southerly diversion [of the convoy] until the evening of 8 May."[54] In those cases when Allied and German reports of convoy coordinates or routes did not precisely agree, Bletchley's staff (unlike their German counterparts) refused to consider this difference grounds for doubting the compromise of their ciphers. Instead they suggested that this discrepancy could be explained "by a garbled German intercept copy or by partial recovery [of the Allied cipher tables]."[55] After all, they themselves had used such garbled or partial decrypts to great effect. "Even though there was no definite proof of compromise," the analysts were convinced.

Bletchley presented these suspicions of the cipher's vulnerability to the "appropriate authorities."[56] Finally, the Admiralty admitted the likelihood that Naval Cypher No 3 had been compromised. The presentation persuaded the Allied navies to order the changeover to the new cipher system (Naval Cypher No 5) moved up to 10 June 1943.[57]

This new cipher proved largely resistant to German attack, and the Admiralty continued its periodic upgrades both to Cypher No 5 and to the Merchant Marine code. Bletchley's analysts remained sensitive to Ultra messages carrying convoy information. Another "expected convoy" signal in September 1943 triggered the "reopening of [the] compromise question," and investigations continued into January 1945.[58] By 1943, the Royal Navy finally agreed to adopt the cipher machine Typex for shore-based communications and the CCM (Combined Cypher Machine) for general inter-Allied signals.[59]

With the Royal Navy's change to Typex and Cypher No 5, Germany's cryptanalysts were essentially shut out of all Allied naval signals, although a few lapses occurred elsewhere. In November 1944, "4 mailbags containing 8 boxes of Typex secret cypher equipment in transit" across liberated Italy disappeared from an unguarded vehicle and were apparently never recovered.[60] Fortunately, such mistakes proved too late, as well as too little, to cost the Allies their sigint victory.

In the end, the Allies recognized the fundamental problem of cipher insecurity: absolute security remains a myth. Any system operated by humans will have mistakes. Security depends on catching and rectifying these mistakes before the enemy can exploit them for a long-term break. The Allies had used such mistakes to their profit, and they vowed the enemy would not do the same to them. They took note of where they were able to break into Enigma nets and tried to make certain that the enemy would not gain the same advantage. For example, Bletchley Park had broken into vital Enigma nets, such as the Marine four-rotor U-boat machines, through vital, yet routine weather reports.[61] So BP's analysts watched German weather reports for signs that the enemy was gaining information by reading British weather ciphers.[62] They used their success against enemy ciphers to improve their own systems.

In addition to these general security precautions, Allied intelligence analysts conducted specific postmortems of signals intelligence failures throughout the war. A few concise reports survive, including analyses of sigint failures in several famous conflicts. During the *Bismarck* operation in 1941, Allied security was poor and the enemy gathered vital information through Allied signals. Indeed, the Germans read the British naval and air force ciphers so quickly that Admiral Dönitz announced he could keep "in touch with "Bismarck's" position by the receipt of enemy shadowing reports."[63] The investigators were able to turn to Enigma decrypts and the enemy's own declaration that he knew what the British forces shadowing the *Bismarck* were reporting home.

A discussion of the campaign in Italy called attention to damage caused by seemingly minor security transgressions. Announcing coordinates in the clear could compromise map coordinate codes, saving the enemy valuable time and resources in tactical decryption. The report's authors also noted that they decided to "amend the rule which previously allowed enemy locations to be sent in clear" because thus the enemy, confused by the battle's rapid progress, had learned his own situation too easily.[64]

The postmortem of the December 1944 Ardennes offensive took a different form. Here the analysts investigated a failure of interpretation rather than one of communication security. Their postmortem provides the texts of Enigma signals that, in hindsight, seem to hint at the coming offensive. They lay out Bletchley analysts' (mis)interpretation at the time and an idea of the signals' true relevance to the offensive. They warn against "a risk of relying too much on Source." They also noted that lax security on the Allied side gave the Wehrmacht important Order of Battle information. The report concludes with a warning about low-level security lapses, warning that "leakage is continuing as badly as ever." Although Bletchley analysts already had confidence in Allied high-grade sigint superiority, they knew even these low-grade leaks jeopardized nearly as much and had to stop.[65]

Allied studies on communications security and cryptology continued through the end of the war and beyond. In the archives, researchers can find a history of SIAM as well as one of the Special Liaison Units and accounts of work done in Bletchley Park's Huts. Clearly, both the British and the Americans took a long-term view of cryptology and communication security. They considered the ramifications of ongoing enemy scrutiny of their ciphers along with the useful lifetime of cipher components, even when not physically compromised.

Allied cryptologists also recognized that electricity and electronics were revolutionizing both cryptography and cryptanalysis. Almost as soon as the United States entered the war, the chief of U.S. Army cryptology, William Friedman, began requesting a research unit "freed from responsibilities connected with active operations." This unit would ignore the practical needs of wartime and instead "'dream' up new things for the future."[66] This future in cryptology appeared very close to the Allied cryptologists who were facing, as well as developing themselves, new developments in ciphers and machines. The continuing struggle to stay ahead of the enemy compelled British and American cryptologists to recognize cryptologic security as a constant process of vigilance and improvement.

## The Sigaba Compromise

The most serious compromise in American eyes came in the last months of the war and threatened the Big Machine – Sigaba. In early 1945, a division in the town of Colmar, France, reported a "possible serious compromise of cryptographic systems." The signal company had lost a truck loaded with cipher materials. The drivers had parked the signal company's truck one February night in an unguarded area not far from the front lines. The next morning the truck was gone. The truck contained at least one complete Sigaba cipher machine, a complete set of the worldwide Combined Cipher Machine rotors used by both the British and Americans, and the corresponding key lists and codebooks. In short, the truck held all the elements necessary for reading Sigaba-enciphered messages.

The Allied response is instructive. Naturally, the compromise immediately sparked complaints of "inadequate protection of documents in the field."[67] (The signals officers responsible for the machine's security were subsequently court-martialed.) Plans to impose a complete long-term ban on use of the Sigaba appeared untenable. The Americans admitted that "without a Combined Cipher Machine system, communications would be severely crippled, so it was decided to resume the use of the rotors and the current key lists, with certain restrictions."[68] As the Germans had a "Stichwortbefehl" for cases of suspected compromise

10. Sigaba machine – the U.S. Big Machine and "the most secure cipher machine of the Second World War" according to the NSA. The machine's signature index rotors are under the cover. The five visible rotors are the cipher or alphabet rotors, which operate roughly as Enigma's do, except that they move both forward and backward. The index rotors create a more random step progression for the alphabet rotors than Enigma's odometer-like advance. Note that the machine also has a tape for printing the outgoing text, whether cipher or plaintext. (Courtesy of the National Security Agency)

of Enigma M, the Allies had instituted similar emergency measures for Sigaba.

American security experts considered these restrictions merely a temporary patch. Quickly they established "a vigorous emergency wiring program" for all five Anglo-American services. The wiring program aimed to wire and distribute an entirely new set of rotors for all the CCMs (Combined Cipher Machines) around the world: 8,500 machines. In six months, the U.S. Army wired 17,840 replacement rotors.[69]

Meanwhile, the Allies in the field conducted a search for the missing truck. On 12 March 1945, just over a month after the truck disappeared, the cipher materials "reappeared in the bottom of a river." Still concerned that the enemy had examined the top-secret machine in the intervening month, Allied security experts documented the recovery and detailed the condition of the machine and material. They noted that the safes did not show signs of having been forced open, although one had been damaged, perhaps by the submersion, and had to be cut open. To the security experts' almost audible relief, all the rotors still lay in the correct positions for the settings of 5 February 1945, the day of disappearance. Although no one could say for certain, "general appearances indicate[d] that neither the field safe nor the [rotors] had been examined by any unauthorized personnel." The dreaded physical compromise had not happened.[70]

Nonetheless, the rotor rewiring program continued unabated. U.S. cipher security experts felt that the time had come to change all Sigaba rotors anyway, since the rotors had seen considerable service. The rotors had been in use eighteen months.[71] (In 1945, in contrast, the original three Enigma rotors had seen nearly eighteen *years* of service.)

### Dominating the Sigint War

Having begun the war well behind the Germans in signals intelligence, the Allies soon began to turn the tide their way. Some have argued the turning point came in 1941 with the capture of the German U-boat U-110, its top secret material intact.[72] Others see 1942 as the pivotal year: Rommel's intelligence suffered the double blow of losing Bonner Fellers' reports and the Afrika Korps' own signal company; the Americans had begun reading the most crucial Japanese systems consistently; and Bletchley Park finally broke the four-rotor Enigma machine.

Certainly, by 1943 Allied intelligence began to soar unfettered. The Americans had plugged their attaché code leak, and the British replaced the tattered Naval Cyphers No 3 and No 4 with the more secure No 5. In the summer of 1943, all Allied services adopted a new superenciphering system, both "novel and secure," while all Allied high-level signals now used machine ciphers a generation beyond Enigma.[73] These machines remained secure throughout the war. Although the Germans learned the British Typex's general principles early on, they "abandoned work on it" before 1942.[74] The American Sigaba (or the Big Machine) likewise defied both German and Japanese scrutiny.

Thus Allied cryptanalytic success worked to improve Allied cryptographic security. The Allies' double-sided rise on the cryptologic seesaw began long before their landings in Europe. Its seeds were sown by the successful British cryptanalysis of the First World War and the consequent revelations of Britain's "far from perfect" enciphering.[75] The early germination of interwar cipher reforms was further fertilized by the British "tendency to attribute to Germany in every respect [a] sort of Machiavellian super-intelligence."[76] The ripening began after the war's outbreak. By early 1941, signal security experts introduced "stop-gap measures" of changes and upgrades while developing new, more secure ciphers.[77] Incidents of lapses coupled with Bletchley's success tackling Enigma only highlighted the parallel of Allied vulnerability. The Germans' fatal mistake of mentioning their own successful decryption proved the final catalyst for the Allied signals intelligence victory.

In the end, the Allies' cryptanalytic success combined with their "long-standing anxiety" to increase their own systems' security. Like the Germans, the Allies upgraded their various codes and ciphers periodically. Unlike the Germans, they went further than upgrading ciphers – they replaced them. Moreover, they were prepared to admit to their own ciphers' imperfections.

Any lingering belief British cryptologists might have had about machine ciphers offering complete security crumbled with the Polish break into Enigma. Knowing Enigma had been and was being successfully attacked and read surely caused a reevaluation of any remaining belief in the security provided by cipher machines. In particular, the Typex used the same principles as Enigma and could not dazzle British cryptanalysts who had conquered Enigma. Indeed, the Americans did not hesitate to voice their contempt for the limits of the Typex machine and to revoke its use for some of the highest-level signals. Britain's cryptologists also voiced dissatisfaction as early as 1940 with the practical security of the Typex. The British military then asked the civilian cryptologic experts for a more complete analysis of the wartime use of Typex and appear to have acted on their recommended changes.[78]

Certainly, the Allies were not always willing to concede their own failings swiftly; however, they usually acknowledged security problems and information leaks before too long. Their structure and their diversity of personnel ensured dissenting opinions could surface. The Allied governments and militaries remained willing to allow, even insist, that their signals intelligence staffs question assumptions and expose mistakes, even by commanders at the highest levels. They could challenge both methodology and procedures as well as propose new tactics – from "pinching" weather ships for cipher documents to indoctrinating traffic analysts so they could help find cribs. Cryptologists and analysts could, and did, use diverse approaches and opinions in their long search for success.

Only after the end of the war would the Allies know the extent of their success. As the enemy surrendered, the British and Americans sent out TICOM (Target Intelligence Committee) teams, specially trained units that captured enemy cryptologic material and located and interrogated enemy intelligence personnel. As these teams put together the complete picture of German (and Japanese) cryptography and cryptanalysis, they began to realize the results of Allied secrecy. All of their high-grade systems had successfully resisted enemy attack.

# EIGHT

# DETERMINED ANSWERS

## Structural Problems in German Signals Intelligence

In conclusion, the success of these [Enigma] cyphers has been further
assured and confirmed by all existing proofs and by the precautions
taken to secure our own main systems against being broken by enemy
cryptographic analysis. To contradict this view there have been and
are only suspicions and circumstantial deductions which it has always
been possible to refute....

— 1944 Marine report on cyphers and W/T[1]

The idea of overwhelming, continuous Allied success decrypting
Enigma never arose in the numerous wartime security investigations
in Germany. Yet the foregoing close examination of these investigative reports has shown that the Germans did consider the possibility
of the machine's cryptanalytic compromise – at least in theory. Several
agencies – OKH's Inspk. 7, Pers Z – determined the un-Steckered three-
rotor Enigma vulnerable but still considered the Steckered and four-
rotor versions secure. Still, they did have suspicions. They did conduct
investigations. They did not find the leaks. Although only the Marine's
investigations have survived largely intact, we know that no branch was
entirely complacent about these ciphers' security. As the German intelligence agencies considered possible sources of Allied information, they
at least formally included Enigma, albeit not at the top of their list. They
all explicitly considered and examined the possibility of Enigma's compromise. Why then did they all fail to recognize their enemy's valuable
source?

Examining these security investigations, particularly with hindsight,
has revealed patterns, odd coincidences, and even outright Allied

mistakes that pointed to Enigma's compromise. The reports did in fact suggest Enigma as the enemy's intelligence source. However, the larger system and culture in the Wehrmacht of the 1940s made any straightforward admission of Enigma's limitations virtually impossible.

These system pressures stemmed from the history and culture of the Wehrmacht, not from peculiarities of the Third Reich. As discussed in earlier chapters, when Wehrmacht commanders demanded intelligence, they sought tactical intelligence. The nature of tactical intelligence prompted each service to build its own autonomous intelligence bureau. These bureaus did not see much point in cooperating with their brother agencies: not only did they have a history of interservice rivalry, but more importantly, they did not believe their fellow services had much to offer them in their hunt for tactical intelligence. This combination of indifference and distrust led them to establish redundant and frequently competing intelligence and cryptologic agencies.

Certainly, this tendency toward competition and redundancy increased under National Socialism and the polyocracy of the Third Reich. The offensive nature and pressing conditions of Hitler's war meant that the Wehrmacht did not put a high priority on signals intelligence. Indeed, signals intelligence would lose resources, both financial and human, through the course of the war. Moreover, the "aryanization" of Germany under the Reich exacerbated the lack of diversity among signals intelligence personnel and inhibited access to civilian resources that might have helped meet the military's cryptologic needs. The repressive culture shrouding Nazi Germany solidified the rigidity of Wehrmacht investigations and increasingly skewed the questions, and hence the solutions, German cryptologists faced. These myriad restrictions led to an inability to produce the creative and critical thinking necessary for success in this age of changing technology in cryptology.

## Tactical Intelligence and Cryptology

According to postwar American thinking, no military "turns to low-level by preference."[2] One American postwar analysis argues that success "in tackling high-level material" drives the centralization of a military's intelligence. Thus form (centralization) follows success at the strategic level. This argument establishes the tightly centralized

intelligence organization as the ideal, in part because centralization sig-
nifies success with high-grade, strategic intelligence.

The Wehrmacht clearly did not agree. As we have seen, the Wehrmacht never centralized signals intelligence. Since the Versailles Treaty
had made German cryptanalysis illegal, cryptologic and signals intelligence sections needed to remain hidden in the 1920s and early 1930s.
For better cover, these sections lay scattered among the different services. The traditional separation of the military services contributed to
this splintering. Each service arm saw its needs and abilities as distinct
from those of the other branches. Thus each created its own, to some
degree decentralized, intelligence organizations.

These bureaus clearly had numerous excellent reasons for decentralizing sigint – reasons still put forward with success today. These sigint
divisions provided rapid, focused tactical intelligence for commanders
in the field. They established critical expertise and specialists vital for a
rapidly changing worldwide conflict. The bureaus offered efficiency and
reasonably tight security. They also all emphasized tactical intelligence
over strategic, high-grade, long-term intelligence.

In the best of all possible worlds, any intelligence organization would
prefer to have endless resources and to tackle all grades of the enemy's
signals. Given the necessary limits on any intelligence organization,
each must choose the points of emphasis and it may be logical to
emphasize low-grade and tactical sigint. Germany's problem, however,
stemmed from a general lack of importance placed on intelligence. Only
low-level, tactical intelligence really mattered. Cryptanalysis received
less attention than other elements of signals intelligence; high-grade
cryptanalysis appears to have had the lowest priority of all. "The Chief
of the Air Force Signal Service" in the words of one of his subordinates, "understandably enough had no particular knowledge in the field
of cryptanalysis."[3] Important signals intelligence was "unit identifications, front locations, and identifications of higher headquarters"; that
is, tactical, short-term information.[4] The quest for high-grade intelligence received little support from Germany's highest levels.

This lack of support could be laid at several doors. Hitler's sense of
his own genius, of course, made strategic intelligence less important
than his intuition. When Hitler had determined a course of action, he
would ask for intelligence to assist the execution of the plan. He was

determined to set the strategy, however, rather than in any way react to the enemy's strategy.[5] The Wehrmacht as well appears to have expressed interest in tactical intelligence on the enemy's strengths and deployment to the virtual exclusion of long-term strategic intelligence.

Clearly, the Wehrmacht's emphasis was offensive. Consequently, in their demands for intelligence, officers wanted enemy order of battle information, so as to know where the stronger and weaker lines were, and the strength of the enemy's numbers and matériel. Possibly they perceived intelligence, particularly strategic intelligence, as a defensive weapon rather than an offensive tool. The Wehrmacht (as well as Hitler) traditionally ranked intelligence as a low priority in their own planning. With numerous demands for resources on all sides, intelligence surely appeared as one area which could go by the wayside without too much damage (unlike, say, weapons production, pilot training, and U-boat construction).

Low priority for long-term intelligence in particular also stemmed from these many demands for personnel and matériel on numerous fronts. After 1941, the Germans opposed two of the most resource-rich and productive countries in the world.[6] The Wehrmacht quickly had problems of supply, production, a multifront war, and weak or absent allies, along with a host of lesser obstacles. Clearly, the Wehrmacht appears to have considered funding signals intelligence, particularly cryptology, less vital than training pilots, seamen, reconnaissance patrols, and tank drivers. This ranking makes sense. On the Eastern Front, Heer units suffered losses at appalling, and then unsustainable, rates.[7] On the Western Front, the Battle of Britain proved more costly for Germany than her enemy in terms of planes and, more vitally, pilots.[8] The Marine and particularly Admiral Dönitz struggled on many fronts with problems far more pressing than intelligence: lack of experienced personnel, the need for U-boat construction and repair, and inadequate air escort and reconnaissance, to name just a few. The Marine command (Skl) saw the difficult choices as attacking supply convoys in the Atlantic or attacking enemy supplies in the Mediterranean or guarding the coast of Norway and western Europe.[9] Men and equipment for these missions remained at a premium throughout the war. When faced with such shortages, the Marine command placed intelligence low on their list.

The Marine did attempt to cover high-level intelligence as well as low-level, albeit ultimately failing on the former. Even its "more centralized" B-Dienst focused on "the sort of intelligence which can be had practically for the listening...plain language and self-evident codes."[10] Much of this low-grade work took place at outstations. The B-Dienst's headquarters staff could be said to have developed strategic intelligence by following convoy decrypts over time and learning the patterns of convoy movements. When lacking current sigint, this staff used that expertise in convoy patterns to direct their U-boats. They proved successful enough that Admiral Dönitz found "the absence of current special intelligence was quite tolerable as long as convoys might be expected to act as they were known to have acted in the past."[11] Yet even the U-boat successes against convoys do not suggest the Marine valued strategic intelligence, particularly when there was tactical information to be had. If a U-boat patrol failed to sight an expected convoy, rather than "bothering to inquire what went wrong," BdU moved the patrol toward another potential target. The BdU considered the most important task locating the next target, not figuring out why the enemy was not there. They focused their efforts on the tactical details rather than on the question of the enemy's strategies.

The B-Dienst's attempts to work on high-level traffic succeeded only because the Royal Navy (and earlier the French Navy) sent high-grade traffic over outdated cryptosystems. Once the Royal Navy (and the U.S. Navy) upgraded their additive systems and introduced high-grade electromechanical systems, the B-Dienst practically threw up its collective hands in defeat.

As the Allies closed the leaks in their cipher systems, the Marine's cryptology atrophied. Rather than stepping up efforts to break into new systems or regain old ones, "it was proposed that more and more attention be paid to D/F and traffic analysis." This low-level, albeit valuable, work would all happen at the outstations. The B-Dienst headquarters would abandon its cryptanalysis and be reduced to "merely overseeing the work of the net."[12]

Most telling of all is the Marine intelligence record on Allied invasions. The B-Dienst did not predict any of the Allied amphibious invasions. All achieved complete surprise: the Torch invasion in North Africa, the assaults on Sicily and Italy, the landings in southern France, and most important for Britain and the United States, the Normandy landings.

In the case of the November 1942 landings in North Africa, the B-Dienst had no inkling of Allied intentions and saw no portents in the preceding week's radio silence. The B-Dienst learned the enemy's movements only when "the [North African Vichy] French announced the attack early on the morning of 8 November."[13] In the wake of the Normandy landings, the usual weekly report first mentions history's largest amphibious assault by saying, "On 6 June the invasion began." Again signal traffic in the week before the landings had been minimal. As with the Torch invasion, the enemy maintained radio silence until landing. Given this silence, the weekly report asserted that "the B-Dienst could gain no knowledge" of the coming assault until the attack forces' first signals at 6:55 a.m.[14]

The B-Dienst scarcely bothered to apologize for these surprises. Their reports in the weeks following the successful Torch landings noted simply that the "USA landing operation against French North Africa did not make itself evident through radio traffic." Since the assault ships had maintained "complete radio silence," only the first signals from the landing sites gave the B-Dienst anything to report.[15] In other words, their duty was to decipher signals, not to interpret the implications of silence.

The surviving X-B-Berichte (decryption reports) do indicate that the B-Dienst spotted activities which could have alerted them to the impending invasions. Important signs before Torch included the appearance of heavy naval units in the Gibraltar area. Moreover, the strength of escorts for Atlantic convoys decreased at the same time transports in the Gibraltar area increased.[16] However, the B-Dienst and its Berichte remained preoccupied with the present and the immediate past. What investigation they may have made of the enemy's future intentions remains uncertain. At least in the Berichte, the B-Dienst analysts clearly do not predict future operations.

Even when the Allies themselves tried to warn the Germans, the landings achieved complete surprise. For purposes of a larger deception, the Allies agreed to allow the double agent Garbo to warn the Wehrmacht's Abwehr of the Normandy landings.[17] So just before D-Day, Garbo informed his Abwehr handler that he would have important information shortly after midnight, 6 June 1944. But when he attempted to report the massive Normandy invasion a few hours before the landings began, no one in Germany answered his hail. Released from the burden of being the first warning of D-Day's arrival, Garbo could smugly berate his control. Chagrined, the Germans apologized and told him "to report anything suspicious: 'until further notice we shall be listening here everyday' said his control; adding, a little surprisingly, 'except on Sundays'."[18] Even with the enemy on the continent's soil, traditional peacetime schedules outweighed intelligence needs.

German command staff appear neither to have demanded nor to have provided for high-grade signals intelligence. The effort required to read the highest grade of Allied ciphers seemed exorbitant and unnecessary. Commanders remained content with tactical intelligence. Even late in the war, the various signals intelligence agencies found plenty of tactical material to tackle. Often obvious entries presented themselves, such as the depths which quickly emerged in U.S. Army M-209 signals.

Generally, the German attacks on all these systems seem to have been statistical and straightforward, albeit (given those conditions) thorough. When faced with a system that seemed statistically unbreakable in a reasonable period of time, they simply gave up. Even in the case of Enigma's security, the Marine command took the easy way out and decided to believe the experts when they declared the system secure. Figuring out if Enigma was being read appeared an even lower priority than high-grade intelligence.

Even after the war, the remnants of the German military saw intelligence and cryptology as primarily useful for tactical information. In a postwar plea for the continued existence of a German intercept and cryptanalysis service, a group of Marine officers said such a service would obtain vital information on the enemy: "his organization, his disposition, his activities at sea, the significance of his bases, etc."[19] Even at this late date, they did not turn their intelligence efforts toward the enemy's intentions, long-term goals, or future strategies.

## Compartmentalization and Compartmentation, not Cooperation

This constant emphasis on tactical intelligence only escalated the sigint agencies' existing reluctance to cooperate. Because they were looking after the immediate tactical needs of their own service arm, the various bureaus saw little, if any, reason to collaborate with each other. The individual Wehrmacht branches disliked each other only slightly less than they distrusted their civilian and Nazi Party counterparts. Several agencies, including the Forschungsamt and the RSHA (Reichsicherheit HauptAmt), wasted additional energy on surveillance of other German intelligence organizations and personnel. This hostile, suspicious outlook foiled any moves to streamline intelligence and conserve precious wartime resources.

The damage caused by this cryptanalytic dissension increased with the de facto cryptographic connection created by Enigma. Because numerous military and civilian organizations, even other Axis units, used Enigma ciphers for their signals, the need for cryptologic cooperation intensified. An enemy break into any one of these Enigma variations could lead to breaks into all the others. Even the Marine's most secure four-rotor Enigma communicated with other nets as a de facto three-rotor machine, opening a door to compromise. Because many nets and variations used the same original three rotors, the enemy conserved time and resources it might have spent reconstructing rotor wirings. Far worse damage arose from the indiscriminate widespread use of Enigma for low-level, routine, and cross-service messages, such as weather reports. The enemy frequently found similar or identical messages traveling different circuits and used the repetition to break into hitherto impenetrable nets.[20] None of the German sigint bureaus recognized the lurking disaster of pairing cryptographic cooperation via Enigma with compartmentalization in cryptanalysis and security.

Moreover, the Marine experts compartmentalized the enemy as thoroughly as they did themselves. An investigation of suspicious British naval movements need consider only Admiralty signals – not those from other British services, such as the Royal Air Force, and not those from U.S. sources. Yet they knew from documents captured in occupied France and other sources that British intelligence, specifically cryptology, had cooperated with friendly intelligence agencies. They consistently ignored the implications of this cooperation in their own investigations. Although they had access to North American signals, they did not incorporate these elements in their investigations of British Admiralty information. Some of these sources, such as the Halifax L traffic, could have disproved at least one claim that Enigma was secure.[21] An investigation of British information sources, however, apparently did not require consideration of American or even Canadian intelligence.

Although they knew the two countries ran convoys and other operations jointly, the Germans did not consider British and American collaboration significant for signals intelligence and decryption. They no more recognized the enemy as an interdependent problem than they realized the inherent cooperation that their interconnected cipher system imposed upon their own organizations.

German cryptology further compromised itself when its experts conducted isolated and independent security investigations. When a service branch investigated the security of its own Enigma variation, it rarely passed the results to any other branch of the Wehrmacht[22], let alone to any section of the Nazi Party (some of which also used Enigmas). Before and during the war, when the Marine's B-Dienst had concerns about Enigma, it investigated the security of only its own Schlüssel M, not that of Enigma in general. The B-Dienst apparently did not consult its counterparts in these investigations nor report its findings to them. The B-Dienst officers appear never to have considered times when other services' Enigma messages gave the enemy clues, as in the *Bismarck* incident. The cryptographic cooperation forced by Enigma's very flexibility cried out for close cryptanalytic cooperation, but no German heard the call.

Even within service branches, tight circles of information limited effective use of intelligence. As one captured Heer officer complained, "the high ranking officers are never in a position [to] see the whole picture. Secret orders reach only the person whom they affect."[23] In the Forschungsamt, intelligence employees were not allowed to share their work with anyone, not even other FA colleagues.[24] Evaluators in the OKL supposedly received "complete cipher materials," including a survey of "current work in cryptanalysis." The evaluators, however, could "not be initiated into the work of cryptanalysis and the cryptanalysts never got any exact information regarding the results of evaluation."[25] With this rigid division, those officers working on the ciphers did not know the outcome of their decryption work, whereas the evaluators could not contribute their knowledge of the enemy's habits to help in breaking the enemy's signals. This dearth of cooperation inside and between Germany's numerous intelligence divisions would exacerbate the lack of resources available for signals intelligence.

## Sigint Resources

Given intelligence's low priority, funding sigint remained a problem for nearly two decades. In peacetime, intelligence often merited neither its own full-time personnel nor its own offices. At first one officer directed all the Marine's signal communications and organizations in addition to having responsibility "in a sort of a sub-office" for all signals intelligence. For several years, interception and cipher personnel worked in the Torpedo and Mining Inspectorate in Kiel. According to the German Marine command, the reason for this odd amalgamation "was the saving of the additional allowance granted for Berlin."[26]

Once war broke out and increased intercepted traffic, the demands on cryptologic personnel escalated. In the various signals intelligence bureaus, "the Heads of the Cryptologic Sections were always beating their brains out trying to...handle all this traffic with the few available specialists." Having too few skilled cryptanalysts meant overworking them. They remained on call "at all times," so that, according to one intelligence officer, their work deteriorated as the war continued.[27] Even physical space became a problem. OKW/Chi requested additional room as having more than two decipherers to one table had proved intolerable. (However, statisticians did not require as much space.)[28]

When these intelligence divisions petitioned for more staff and equipment, they usually found the requests refused. Two years after the occupation of Norway, the Marine intelligence division was still complaining that it did not have an intercept station capable of eavesdropping on Allied radio traffic off the northwestern Norwegian coast. With the huge base for the British fleet located in Scapa Flow across the Norwegian sea, such an intercept station seems hardly a luxury.

At the same time that Bletchley Park cryptanalysts were writing to Churchill for increased allocations, the head of the German Marine (English) decipherment section was making similar complaints. Faced with both an upgrade in the British naval cipher and captured documents demonstrating the Typex machine's sophistication, Oberregierungsrat Tranow applied up the chain of command for more staff.

Tranow declared "without an increase of personnel, exploitation of these materials is pointless."[29] Tranow never got the resources he felt necessary and he continued to complain bitterly, not surprisingly, about the denial of his requests long after the war. When promises of intelligence staff increases did come from Marine Command, they did not include personnel for the central deciphering section.[30] This constant "lack of personnel" would ultimately make breaking into the enemy's machine ciphers an impossibility.[31]

Such staffing problems were by no means confined to one service. Personnel for the Heer's interception posts remained at a premium along the Eastern Front.[32] The Luftwaffe's FA had insufficient numbers of qualified personnel to staff their intercept stations in the occupied territories, probably in part because of their reluctance to use non-Germans.[33] Retaining trained and productive staff proved increasingly difficult. One of the OKH Inspk. 7's top cryptanalysts and a section leader, Major (later Lt. Col.) Mettig, was transferred to the infantry [Feldheer] in mid-June 1943.[34] As the situation on the home front worsened, even the minimal existing resources for intelligence diminished. Intelligence employees had to put down their work to harvest the local crop of potatoes. Eventually, all male intelligence employees not already transferred to the front found themselves in the Volkssturm, the last-ditch defense forces.[35] Some of this redirection of labor would have occurred in any army facing total destruction, but the transfer of an entire intelligence division to potato harvesting in 1944 suggests the low level of priority given intelligence.

The personnel and resource shortages need not have been so severe. Not so much quantity but quality and efficiency created the resource deficit. Centralization might have ameliorated the effects of the low priority given cryptology. One German officer estimated after the war that centralizing the Heer and Luftwaffe efforts "would have saved about half the personnel [and] the quality would have been raised some 20 to 25 percent."[36]

Alternatively, gaps in personnel could have been filled from various civilian sources, which the Wehrmacht ignored and the Nazi regime's laws and policies eventually excluded completely. Women served in some clerical positions but do not appear on the rolls of decrypt translators or analysts, let alone cryptologists. Virtually no non-Germans served in intelligence at all, and none emerged in the subfield of cryptology. The Nazi racial laws of 1934 and 1935 drove many Germans, including well-known intellectuals and technical experts, into exile.[37] Jews and Mischlinge (those of mixed Jewish and "Aryan" descent), as well as socialists, intellectuals, and other dissidents, left before 1939: famous names like Edward Teller and Albert Einstein, as well as numerous professors, mathematicians, engineers, and more anonymous Germans. The Wehrmacht further exacerbated the problem by tightening the racial restrictions as German men rose through the military hierarchy. Eventually, even decorated World War I Jewish veterans had to fight "eastern resettlement" – commissions in the Wehrmacht were far beyond their grasp. Many of these "undesirables" proved quite desirable to the Allies and added strong muscle to the fight against the Axis powers.[38] The Wehrmacht hampered its results by not capitalizing on these resources and assuming an "all-out" effort.

Germany suffered from a general reluctance to move to total war footing that also aggravated the signals intelligence crisis.[39] Shortages and disappointing results would persist so long as Germany clung to peacetime assumptions about work. Long after the British had set up twenty-four-hour watches, seven days a week, for signals interception and decryption, much of German intelligence remained on a peacetime six-day-week schedule with few, if any, late-night shifts.[40] The Marine first mentions night shifts for deciphering in December 1942.[41] This aversion to broadening coverage meant the Germans missed several key warnings of Allied action. As late as 1943, during the final Allied assaults in North Africa, "the French messages which might have given warning had not been monitored."[42] Dropping peacetime work schedules might have offset some resource shortages and forestalled some Allied surprises.

Even had these deficiencies and shortages been alleviated, the Wehrmacht still had difficulty retaining staff with the vital skills and talents for signals intelligence and cryptanalysis. Even the basic need for translators skilled in enemy languages proved challenging. POWs described how Western Front intercept companies had few officers who knew English.[43] Finding speakers fluent in French proved a problem for the Luftwaffe. Their Forschungsamt's French bureau's expert was a Hungarian who had trouble with the names of French generals.[44]

Men who had the requisite language skills by birth or years of living outside Germany rarely appear on the intelligence rolls. The

Wehrmacht did not go looking for this resource and indeed appears often to have considered such men suspect. (Women, of course, did not appeal to the Wehrmacht for intelligence assignments, whatever their skills.) Hanns Scharff, for example, became the Luftwaffe's "master interrogator" accidentally. Although years in South Africa made Scharff bilingual, he would have landed on the Eastern Front had his wife not obtained for him a last-minute transfer to translator.[45]

This dearth of language skills could have been corrected through immersion and crash courses. Such courses patched the holes in British and American resources in Japanese and other languages. (The Americans also used *nisei* and third-generation Japanese Americans, sometimes out of the relocation camps, for some translation needs, but not for high-grade cryptologic work.) Yet the Wehrmacht did not set up similar rapid training programs. The omission of such crash courses in languages of the Allies, combined with the neglect of their resource of foreign-language speakers, created problems in intelligence translations. Forschungsamt translations from English were often simply wrong. Translators confused "petrol" with "patrol" and translated ships as people.[46] Such "erroneous translations and interpretation" naturally led to confusion for intelligence.[47] By war's end, the military turned in desperation, particularly in the East, to enemy deserters for much of their intelligence translation.[48]

Popular opinion has often dismissed such problems, and the subsequent German defeat, as the result of destructive Nazi policies. Certainly Nazism, as well as Hitler's mishandling of the war effort, contributed to the German loss in the intelligence war. Yet German intelligence had long limited its resources for intelligence personnel through its own rigid hiring practices, which emphasized military loyalty, racial and social heritage, seniority, and class, rather than aptitude, skill, and a proven track record. The Heer remained, even under National Socialism, a class-bound system, drawing its officers largely from the ranks of the nobility, as it had done in the nineteenth century.[49] Germany's intelligence and communications departments consisted almost exclusively of military personnel, not civilians. Their experts, whether scientific or technical, were usually also military officers, subject to the demands of a military career and locked into the military command structure. Only reluctantly did any of the services employ such non-military categories of people as women and academics, even those with analytical and cryptanalytical skills. Again, many of these deficiencies could have been overcome by other means – such as greater cooperation and coordination between bureaus.

The lack of resources – financial, human, and technological – created a vicious circle. Fewer resources meant diminished intelligence results, which lowered the standing of the intelligence departments and staff. When the staff did manage to break into a major system, they would be inundated with material needing decryption and translation. None of the agencies had the resources or foresight to prepare for these massive influxes of information. When, for example, the multiservice collaboration under von Lingen broke into the Red Army system, the cryptanalysts soon found themselves overwhelmed. The agencies could not fully exploit their entry into the valuable system for lack of trained clerical and production staff. No one had developed a production system to break the deciphering process into parts, which could then be processed by specially trained clerks or, perhaps, by machines.[50] Instead the entire decryption process lay in the hands of the cryptanalysts. They had to look up the codegroups one by one, as a cipher clerk would, performing what Heinz Bonatz (head of Marine B-Dienst) called "entschlüsseln" (dekeying), the almost mechanical process of deciphering a system already compromised.[51] With inadequate resources, the results were restricted. Without impressive results, the various signals intelligence agencies could not raise their low prestige or obtain the resources they needed.

Moreover, intelligence's lack of prestige meant the Oberkommando (High Command) listened less thoughtfully to the results presented by intelligence personnel. In the FA, for instance, "one had the impression that the top leadership of the Reich, it is true, took notice of the agreeable intelligence, but let the negative intelligence lie completely unconsidered."[52] General Jodl also "showed a lack of confidence in communication intelligence, especially if the reports were unfavorable."[53] Favorable reports were given different treatment from unfavorable ones "as early as the time of the Salerno landing" (1943). The high-level source and expert evaluation mattered less than how the intelligence fit the receiving officer's presumptions.

In the end, the greatest limitation on Germany's military signals intelligence was its perceived lack of importance. Intelligence's needs always came after the demands of other elements of the military.

Battlefront command was served before intelligence and indeed the High Command seemed determined to rid intelligence of its experienced high-level staff. At least two intelligence chiefs were transferred to the front lines during the war: Lt. Col. Andrae of the Heer in 1939 and the Forschungsamt chief in mid-1943.[54] Clearly, that these men thus carried with them to the front lines (and their possible death or capture) not only their own intelligence skills but also highly sensitive information about intelligence successes against the enemy mattered little to the German High Command.

## Orders Over Initiative

The staff that remained in the signals intelligence bureaus received tasks with precise limitations. Units monitoring enemy transmissions operated under strict regulations. Such constant control by the sigint headquarters negated some of the potential advantages of decentralization. Marine outstations sent all their traffic back to intelligence headquarters to be checked, which surely slowed the work at both places.[55] On the Eastern Front, each Luftwaffe Chiffrier-Stelle outstation had a specific range to observe. Regardless of what movements the enemy made, the outstation "was not permitted to go" outside this preset limit.[56] By enforcing these kinds of rigid restrictions, the Wehrmacht did not encourage initiative among its intelligence staff.

At times, initiative in cryptology appears to have been actively discouraged. Historically, the military censured staff assuming cryptologic duties beyond the scope of their authority. Captain Bonatz, wartime head of Marine intelligence, offers an example from the First World War, when

> a radio officer aboard one of the units of the German High Seas Fleet succeeded in breaking an own staff cipher during a quiet watch ... out of amusement. His report on this subject, however, did not result in a change of the cipher system, but only in a reprimand to himself because he had searched into reports which were intended only for high level staffs. The cipher system was continued in use.[57]

Of course, this nonexpert's work foreshadowed what the Marine would learn between the wars: their ciphers had been insecure throughout the

Great War. The embarrassment over the ciphers' compromise would lead to the Marine's adoption of the far more secure Enigma system. Bonatz and his World War II colleagues, then, knew this radio officer's work could have limited the security leaks of the Great War. Nonetheless, their own attitude during the next war mirrored that of their predecessors: neither amateur nor unofficial initiative in sigint and cryptology received approval.[58]

Even authorized outposts ran into such walls. The "most prominent" of the Marine outstations, MP Abteilung Flanders (Naval D/F Detachment Flanders), found its aspirations rebuffed. The Flanders staff had undertaken special cryptanalytic tasks "and generally solved them satisfactorily." Yet when they asked to make these tasks permanent, their Marine superiors refused. Flanders received various explanations for the decision: the traffic was not properly a naval matter, or it could only be broken at headquarters, or not enough material was available at the outstation to break it continuously.[59]

Postwar accounts have suggested this refusal to expand outstation responsibility actually stemmed from jealousy. "The [Marine] cryptanalytic sections and above all Tranow, the chief cryptanalyst, appear to have strenuously resisted subsidiary organizations taking over any very significant part of [higher-grade cryptanalysis]."[60] Whatever the reason, all the service headquarters did not encourage, indeed some clearly discouraged, outstation personnel from expanding their cryptanalytic activities. Some of this staff had developed considerable experience with enemy systems and shown talent for the work. They might have offered their superiors significant support had their initiative been encouraged.

## Lost Among the Trees

The limiting factor of restricted initiative made itself felt in the central bureaus as well, particularly in their investigations of Enigma's security. In addition to isolating their examinations of information leaks, the investigators employed a flawed methodology. As detailed in Chapter 6, the experts did not create transparent reports that other analysts in their own or another bureau could verify. Anyone wanting to corroborate their evidence and conclusions would find retracing the investigators' steps difficult at best. He would have had simply to accept both the research and interpretation of the investigators without any independent corroboration. The surviving reports do not provide the full transcript of either the Allied or German signals used as evidence. Nor do they refer to any log or database of such documents. Only such a collection could confirm that no additional or misinterpreted signals suggested a different conclusion for the source of the enemy's information.

Moreover, without such references, the reader has no way of verifying the original messages' wording or timing. Yet the reports frequently base their conclusions on just such precise wording or timing of both German and enemy (that is, English-language) signals. Errors, even minor ones of numbers or imprecise wording, they claimed, proved the enemy could not read Enigma signals at all. This focus on finding exact and explicit wording from Enigma-encrypted messages in enemy signals ignores both issues of translation and the possibility of the enemy using the standard practice of paraphrasing. Even minimal paraphrasing would reduce, if not eliminate, the chance that the decrypted signals would carry the original messages' precise language. Insisting on absolute matches in terminology and timing also assumes the enemy could read everything and read it all promptly. Under these parameters, simple mistakes or delays on the part of enemy cryptanalysts could, and did, give the illusion that the enemy could not read Enigma-encrypted signals at all.

All this painstaking work did not further the investigation's ostensible goal: uncovering the source of the enemy's information. Their fastidious emphasis on detail kept the reports' authors and recipients from seeing the real forest. They ignored the big picture: enemy vessels and supplies were escaping attack by German units while the enemy located and destroyed Germany's U-boats, supply tankers, and other units in increasing numbers. These reverses demanded an explanation, demanded that the investigations consider all possible sources for the enemy's information. For all the careful detailing of enemy errors, no report ever provided a consistent, non-Enigma-based explanation for the enemy's information. Yet German experts continued to exclude Enigma from the list of likely sources and to dismiss signs of Enigma's vulnerability as either indeterminate or temporary.

For these cases when they did consider Enigma vulnerable temporarily, German experts focused less on potential cryptanalysis than on possibilities of loss and betrayal. They assumed the presence of countless Allied agents and, erroneously, the virtual omnipresence of the enemy (meaning the British) Secret Service. They maintained a vigilant eye on their own people, particularly officers and Enigma operators. Although they found no proof of treason, they preferred to find fault with their own troops rather than admit the weaknesses of their cipher system. Their machinery, in this case Enigma, could not serve as the source of defeats. Even as evidence to the contrary mounted, they continued to declare their cryptography invulnerable.

German intelligence experts began with the premise that neither they nor their enemy could effectively break Enigma ciphers. As the war continued, they refused to believe the possibility that Enigma could have been compromised. Perhaps some of these experts considered replacing Enigma impossible in any case, so exposing its compromise would do nothing but damage morale. Yet new rotors could have completely replaced old ones, key setting methods could have been completely redesigned, and each net could have divided into several smaller ones, producing far more daily keys for the British to crack. Any of these actions would have made Bletchley Park's life far more difficult.[61]

Isolation and low priority combined to limit the capability of sigint and cryptology. With cooperation seen as unnecessary and production resources nearly nonexistent, Wehrmacht cryptologists could neither recognize their own vulnerability nor fully exploit the enemy's weaknesses. As their initiatives were rebuffed and their intelligence ignored, cryptologists also limited – consciously or not – their imagination. The leap that brought Enigma machines into the German military would never be matched by the development or design of machines for cryptanalysis. The automation, let alone the early electronics, of Bletchley Park could not emerge in these compartmentalized organizations pressured to produce only immediate tactical results.

# NINE

# ENTER THE MACHINES

## The Role of Science and Machines in the Cryptologic War

> Hollerith machines were first used in deciphering work in 1943. The work of these machines...was employed essentially in the statistical screening of the incoming enemy signals....The prospect of creating and exploiting of an electronic deciphering machine for decipherment purposes, an "electric brain", could unfortunately not be accomplished during the war.
> – Captain Heinz Bonatz of the Marine B-Dienst[1]

Throughout the war, low prestige and limited resources meant the field of German cryptologic science had little chance to develop. Nor did Germany draw in and capitalize on the specialists which the more successful Bletchley would find so vital: academic mathematicians and scientists. Why concern ourselves with the Wehrmacht's use of science and scientists? Because in the 1930s and 1940s cryptology had begun to change dramatically. Not only had cryptography become highly mechanized after the First World War, but cryptanalysis was developing as its own science and simultaneously sparking a new field.

The work done to break the electromechanical ciphers of the Second World War would help create the new field of computer science. Enigma and the Geheimschreiber machines would lead to the invention of the Bombes and Colossus. It is no accident that the first computers in cryptology emerged in Britain and the United States rather than in Germany. They sprang from the imaginative, sometimes desperate, often improvised innovations of the Anglo-American war effort against German machine ciphers. This war effort took considerable advantage of scientists, including social scientists, and mathematicians from both applied and theoretical fields. These men (and women) often had volunteered to fight the "Nazi menace," and the Allied cryptologic war benefited greatly from their energy and dedication.

In contrast, German scientists who applied their skills directly to the war effort seem to have participated only reluctantly. This reluctance did not stem from opposition to the war itself. Rather they believed that "academic scientists must confine their attention solely to principles and must have nothing to do with applications," such as those the war effort needed.[2] German academics themselves traditionally distrusted "practical" applications of their work. They disliked having their ideas or their students moving into the business arena or the military.[3]

The Wehrmacht reciprocated this separation of theoretical science and military application, particularly in intelligence. In complete contrast to the methods and expectations of German academia, German military intelligence rarely, if ever, had room for research as an end in itself.[4] The service branches demanded results, with an emphasis on short-term tactical success. The Wehrmacht saw the scientific community as tools to improve technical weapons and methods – not as a piece of overall strategy. This attitude no doubt gained strength with the addition of the Nazi ambivalence toward science and technology. The twelve years of the Reich were, in the words of OKW cryptologist Wilhelm Fenner, "restless times ... not favorable for scientific cryptanalysis."[5] For the Reich's Wehrmacht, scientists held limited appeal.

Hence, as the Wehrmacht prepared for war, it did not draw on many civilian scientists. Unlike in the Allied countries, in Germany scientists neither joined service committees nor conducted research with any "definite war application." (One exception to this rule came in the area of rockets, jet propulsion, jet fuels, and the V-1 and V-2 rockets. Indeed, the United States would employ several of these German rocket scientists after the war.)[6] Few scientists had any prewar contact with the military at all.[7] Such lack of ties to civilians throughout the interwar period meant that few civilians experts, even those interested in assisting the military, knew where their skills would be appreciated.

Those who did know where they would be best employed could rarely ensure that they would receive the appropriate assignment. Once war began, scientists received draft notices and postings to the front line as cannon fodder with no consideration for their potential behind the lines.[8] Late in the war, the Wehrmacht started assembling scientists and exploring their potential. The effort proved too little, too late. The Marine began collecting scientists to create a staff for "operational experience and technical research, following the example of the British."[9] The scientists, however, had so little awareness of the war effort, "they scarcely knew what a U-boat was."[10] When some of the scientists approached did suggest solutions to the problems, the Marine rejected them.

When the service branches worked with the scientific community, they confined their cooperation to specific problems with German equipment and to constructing countermeasures to Allied weapons and locating devices. In these areas, the Wehrmacht employed scientists not for abstract problem-solving skills but for "technical" expertise. Professor Küpfmüller, for example, became head of Scientific Operations in the Marine,

> to make good our technical inferiority and restore the fighting capability of the U-boat which the enemy has taken from us, not by superior tactics or strategy, but through his superiority in the technical field.[11]

With this emphasis on asking and answering limited technical questions, these scientists were never encouraged to fully exploit their talents. Scientists, and even engineers in war industries, found only limited problems handed to them. In the view of Allied interrogators, Wehrmacht officers had a "lack of appreciation of their [scientists'] possibilities."[12] With few exceptions, when military commands, or even industry, consulted scientists, they would ask narrowly circumscribed questions, perhaps only a request for a specific measurement. "The idea was that the fighting Services would state their problems and these would be distributed to the appropriate persons."[13] When the services made requests, they gave each scientist only an isolated piece of the problem without revealing the broader issues or long-term goal of the inquiry.[14] This slicing up of the task meant scientists had little grasp of the larger problems and so could not offer the full benefit of their training.

German scientists themselves clearly did not fully exploit their own expertise. When Professor Küpfmüller participated in Dönitz' postmission debriefings of U-boat commanders, his presence appears to have been limited to questions about the performance of weapons and to determining whether problems resulted from the machines' functioning or from human error. Perhaps understandably, he does not appear to have tried to acquire an overall grasp of a U-boat's operation.[15] Far more amazing was that war work for many of these scientists remained a moonlighting job. Through 1944 they continued or even increased their usual schedules of teaching, lectures, and colloquia.[16]

Signals intelligence and cryptology was no exception to this pattern of neglecting scientific potential. Declassified records do not suggest any of the sigint bureaus tried recruiting academics or other scientists for cryptology. Just as they rarely consulted their peers in other service branches, German cryptanalysts apparently did not turn to anyone further afield for ideas. At least officially, sigint staff did not consider consulting with outside experts in science, mathematics, or related fields on Allied codes or ciphers. Without this expert help, they toiled under a sizable handicap as cryptology advanced.

## The Age of Machine Cryptology

With their initial adoption of Enigma, the Wehrmacht had outstripped other powers in protecting wireless communications and creating beneficial cryptographic conditions for the thorough exploitation of wireless communications. However, after this great leap forward, Wehrmacht cryptography stood still while the enemy's cryptography sped ahead. Other nations began adopting similar cryptographic machines for military and diplomatic secrets. These machines, however, were at least a half generation more advanced than Enigma. They incorporated more secure and often more advanced operations – 5 rotors and a different stepping pattern in the Typex, 10 rotors and a "cascade" stepping mechanism for the Sigaba. By 1940, the high level of cryptologic security offered by Enigma had depreciated.

Throughout this shift, the Germans maintained a stubborn belief in the possibility of real security through machine ciphers. Although they recognized that cipher machines could be cracked theoretically, they persisted in the belief that few machine ciphers could be read in time to be of any practical use. This belief proved a self-fulfilling prophecy. They did read some enemy cipher machines but generally through enemy mistakes that created short-term openings. The breaks into M-209, perhaps the most widely used and most insecure mechanical U.S. system, came almost exclusively from depths. These depths into the "American Hagelin," as the Germans called it, all stemmed from errors such as sloppily repeated messages, reuse of identical indicators, and similar security violations. None of the Wehrmacht's cryptanalysts seems to have expanded these lucky breaks into a more systematic compromise of the system. In spite of having known the general weaknesses of Hagelin machines for years, even the OKW/Chi's experts considered "common and regular solution impossible."[17]

This assumption of ongoing, practical security for machine ciphers became only stronger for Enigma and the Anglo-American machines. German cryptanalysts knew the general principles of the British Typex machine. The Marine reported having captured material describing the Typex as well as the actual machines, albeit without a set of rotors.[18] With these bits of information, more than one cryptanalytic section proposed attacks on Typex. The B-Dienst team under Oberregierungsrat Wilhelm Tranow gave up on the British Typex cipher machine after six weeks.[19] Tranow considered further work on the Typex impossible without expenditures of time and personnel, which his superiors refused.

No section made an all-out attempt to break Typex. As one cryptologic expert reasoned:

> We [Germans] have the enigma which is similar to the Typex, and as we believe that the enigma can not be solved no great effort was made to solve Typex. Typex has seven wheels and we therefore believe it to be more secure than our enigma.[20]

Of the American Sigaba and ECM machines, these cryptanalysts knew far less. With only some rumors and some intercepts, which they suspected were machine ciphers, the Germans made no attempt against the Big Machine.

Here lies the crux of the German cryptanalysts' conceptions of cipher machines and cipher security. Enigma was secure. If Enigma could not be broken, there was little sense in attempting to crack the British and American machines built on similar, but more complex, lines.

Consider, for a moment, the situation even early in the war. Believing their own system virtually impossible to break, Wehrmacht cryptanalysts knew breaking into the enemy's machine systems would require considerable time, effort, and manpower. At the same time, large amounts of tactical and medium-grade traffic, particularly naval traffic, could be intercepted and attacked. So long as these tactical systems continued to offer rich targets, the various commands believed the effort needed to read the highest grade of Allied ciphers was not worthwhile. By the time they realized they could read fewer and fewer tactical systems, they had lost valuable time in the cryptanalytic race. The enemy had adopted more and more secure operating practices, an improvement German officers attributed to their own military's superiority. Now German experts could glean little insight into Allied systems. The probability that they could make a break into high-grade enemy machines had fallen from remote to virtual impossibility. This inability to break enemy machines came directly out of their belief in Enigma's security. Had they believed Enigma breakable, they might have attacked Typex and Sigaba earlier and with greater vigor.

## Relying on Statistics

The Germans' belief in their cipher system rested on statistical calculations. They claimed Enigma was secure because it presented cryptanalysts with an astronomical number of possible combinations for each encipherment. German cryptologists believed this theoretical statistical security of Enigma gave the machine such strength that it would remain invulnerable, even with over a decade of use. None of them seem to have realized the true decrease in Enigma's statistical probabilities under real conditions, particularly those reductions arising from operational procedures and human error.[21] Theoretical statistical considerations formed the center of both the security investigations of their own systems and their attacks on enemy systems.

German security tests of Enigma focused almost exclusively on statistical considerations. In his postwar interrogation, cryptanalyst Erich Hüttenhain suggested Enigma "might be broken if a vast Hollerith [punch card machine] complex is used but this is only slightly possible." To break Enigma, he insisted, one needed to know the rotors' internal wirings, and he could offer no method for recovering the wiring. Once the rotor wiring was known, he posited, "large catalogues must be built up by encoding the letter E in all positions of the machine (unsteck-ered)." Once again, statistics, in this case letter frequency, would serve as "the basis for solution."[22]

Although Enigma's statistical security would remain one of the system's greatest strengths, emphasizing the machine's statistical might ignores other design flaws. These flaws, along with the openings created by human error, gave the enemy its continued breaks into Enigma. Throughout the war, the Allies did not use a statistical test of every single possible combination. Instead they attacked Enigma's limitations – especially the principle that Enigma never enciphered a letter as itself. They also traced the loops and mathematical periods created by Enigma's rotor wiring to shorten their searches.[23] To even greater effect, they exploited the Wehrmacht's rigid use of the machine.

Of their many methods of attack against Enigma, by far the most revolutionary approach the Allies developed was the use of electricity and the machine's own elements to defeat itself. They realized that the speed of electricity would allow the machine to check for possible solutions far faster than any person or set of punch cards could. Beginning in the 1930s, Allied cryptologists developed several mechanical and electro-mechanical aids. Early on, the Polish team designed two electro-mechanical devices that mimicked Enigma's wiring – the Bombe and Jerzy Rozycki's cyclometer. These two devices signaled a revolutionary trend.

Machine-assisted decipherment was not unheard of in the 1930s. Both the Germans and the Americans were using IBM punch card machines, for example.[24] However, the Polish cyclometer and the Bombes were a step beyond the more common mechanical, usually punch card, sorting machines. The Poles actually replicated the Enigma's own processes, working electromechanically. They duplicated Enigma's own rotors, set them in banks, and sent electricity through them to check numerous possible settings one after another at lightning speed. Thus these machines were more sophisticated than mechanical sorters, both technically and conceptually. These machines did not just check the millions of possibilities produced by Enigma signals, one after the other; they specifically targeted and exploited Enigma's design. In the case of the cyclometer, the machine targeted the "loops" or "series" of letters produced by Enigma and tested the entire group at once by linking the rotor wires on a single circuit to find the correct rotor sequence.[25]

The cryptologic Bombes, first designed in 1938, replicated Enigma more precisely and assisted

> largely in the automation and acceleration of the process of reconstructing the daily keys. Each cryptological bombe (six were built in Warsaw for the Cipher Bureau before September 1939) essentially constituted an electrically powered aggregate of six Enigmas. It took the place of about one hundred workers and shortened the time for obtaining a key to about two hours.[26]

These machines proved the most effective of the Polish methods against Enigma. The Polish design soon yielded to the more complex Turing-Welchman Bombes, which eventually helped crack even the troublesome four-wheel Marine Enigma.

The production of these various cryptanalytic aids connected cryptologists with the engineering industry. Each of the Allied intelligence bureaus turned to engineering firms for assistance. Polish intelligence had the AVA Company.[27] In Britain, GC&CS developed a close relationship with the British Post Office and the British Tabulating Machine company. On the other side of the Atlantic, the U.S. Navy used a special division of the National Cash Register Company to build their top-secret cryptanalytic machines, while the Army employed IBM.[28] These collaborations launched a new era of machine-assisted decryption and of the integration of industry with cryptology. These resulting developments saved the cryptanalysts valuable time, allowing them to devote their talents, and their assistants' efforts, to cracking ever more ciphers and codes.

The British and Americans expanded the idea of electromechanical cryptanalysis during the war. Their successful use of machine decryption for Enigma signals inspired more challenging and sophisticated cryptanalytic attempts as the war progressed. When the British realized that the Germans had introduced the ten-rotor *Geheimschreiber* (the T-52c) and the Lorenz SZ 40/42, both of which used Baudot or non-Morse ciphers, GC&CS recruited automation specialists T. G. Flowers and Jack Good

11. The Lorenz SZ 40/42 machine, code-named "Tunny" by the British. Both this German high-grade cipher machine and the Siemens Geheimschreiber T-52 series (code-named "Sturgeon") used the non-Morse Baudot system and were lumped together by the British as the "Fish" problem. (Courtesy of the National Security Agency)

to their development team. Working from the theoretical principles of Alan Turing and J. von Neumann, they produced Colossus, the first vacuum-tube computer, in December 1943.[29] This cross-pollination of science and intelligence launched the next twenty years of computer development and has only recently been acknowledged as the foundation of the modern computer.

## German Mechanization

In contrast, German cryptanalysts never fully exploited technology, especially mechanical aids for decryption. They did explicitly acknowledge the importance of mechanical decryption,[30] and they certainly used mechanical aids in their cryptanalysis. They brought in basic mechanical tools well before the war. In the 1930s, they had developed equipment to assist them in routine testing of possible combinations and letter frequency calculations in enemy systems. The codebreakers quickly "transferred many of the repetitive processes of cryptanalysis to IBM tabulators using punched Hollerith cards."[31]

Eventually, all the intelligence bureaus used punch card machines to reduce what the Auswärtiges Amt's Pers Z called "the hitherto statistical manual work" in decryption.[32] Like the other German cryptologic agencies, Pers Z turned to Hollerith or punch card machines primarily for statistical work. Pers Z used their Holleriths to mechanize their attack on the U.S. State Department's strip cipher, albeit with minimal results.[33]

In spite of this early adoption, German use of technological assistance remained limited. The earliest machines tended to incorporate punch card techniques, although some examples moved beyond the basics of punch card sorting into other statistical calculations. As early as the 1920s, Pers Z built a "difference" machine,[34] apparently for uncovering additives. OKW/Chi also had one by about 1943, using teletypewriter tapes to flag differences in a depth of enciphered code groups.[35] The Heer did attempt to develop an apparatus that combined a teleprinter and a punch card machine. This device apparently was to assist in the interception and transcription of enemy signals – the Allies also developed such machines – and probably had no role in cryptanalysis itself.[36]

The OKW/Chi constructed "Special-Deciphering" machines for particular cipher systems (Spezial-Entzifferungsmaschinen für konkrete Chiffrierverfahren), designed specifically to attack one particular problem. These suffered the usual troubles of any prototype.[37] In the last months of the war, OKW/Chi had ordered a "Repeat Finder" that used photographic film to search for repeats of five letters or more. It was not finished before the war ended.[38]

Some of these devices, particularly those using the photographic method, moved swiftly and could speed up routine testing considerably. This equipment searched for possible depths, assisted with the routine testing of possible additives, and sorted out possible combinations for simpler ciphers, such as the strip ciphers used by the American diplomatic corps.[39]

Clearly, machines had become an accepted and visible part of every German cryptanalytic section well before the war ended, and of some sections long before the war began. However, none of these machines paralleled the Bombes or similar Allied cryptanalytic machines in terms of exploiting the speed or capabilities of electricity and mechanics. The German machines assisted in sorting without addressing the specific design of a cipher or cipher machine. Again, German development focused on statistical possibilities and not the weaknesses of their enemies' cipher designs.

Oddly, in spite of their considerable use of machines, many Germans in cryptology do not appear to have considered the use of mechanical aids either important or worthy of distinction. Several postwar reports and interrogations emphasize the amount of cryptanalytic work done *without* mechanical assistance. Frequently, when experts discuss their use of mechanical aids, their memories of when the machines emerged actually postdate the mention of machines in captured wartime documents. Wilhelm Fenner, head of Group B in the OKW/Chi, told his Allied interrogators that before the war, "All problems occurring up to that point [1939] had been worked on or solved without mechanical aids."[40] According to Heinz Bonatz, head of the Marine B-Dienst, "Hollerith machines were first used in the work of deciphering in 1943."[41] Given the examples above, both these statements sound peculiarly late.

Why would these department heads – Bonatz and Fenner – report such late dates for the appearance of machines? We could speculate that Fenner hoped to throw off his captors, that he did not want the Allies to realize the extent of his division's success, perhaps in hopes of some future reestablishment of German cryptanalysis. Yet, Fenner, after some twenty-five years in cryptanalysis, clearly faced the end of his career, and so we would expect him rather to flaunt his personal and divisional successes, not to diminish them. Bonatz's claim appeared in the 1970s, when declassified wartime documentation already disproved him. We can only conclude that either these men did not remember correctly or did not know the chronology of mechanization in their own divisions.

Nor did these intelligence men understand the mechanization of cryptanalysis. Clearly, although they headed cryptanalytic divisions, they did not do mechanical decryption themselves, let alone devise mechanical methods for attacking cryptologic systems. Note that even when they recognize the machines developed in their own departments, the machines' purpose and their workings remain fuzzy to them. Fenner of OKW/Chi describes the "Röllchengeräte" as a device "for computing differences when a fairly long series of digits had been used for reencipherment." However, he couldn't tell his interrogators how it worked. In the sort of phrase which I have heard other German officers use in discussing their war service, Fenner explained, "The men working under me were satisfied with the gadget."[42] That was enough for him.

Rather more startling is Fenner's remark that he could not describe the device to his interrogators, "*since I never have seen the device in use.*"[43] In other words, Fenner – no mere manager, but a cryptanalyst in his own right – neither used mechanical aids nor interacted directly with the mechanical section. He himself had little interest in exploring the potential of machine-assisted cryptanalysis. Although he headed the decipherment section, he not only did not know how the cryptanalytic mechanical aids worked, he never saw them in action!

In at least some cases, the lack of knowledge about cryptanalytic mechanization stemmed from a lack of belief in its importance. Fenner clearly believed technology's assistance to cryptanalysis could be only minimal. He explained that "experimentation had shown clearly that only the academically trained modern communications engineer would be equal to such a task [as cryptanalysis]."[44] In other words, machines do not do cryptanalysis, people do. These words and those of other intelligence experts suggest these men valued human expertise far more highly than mechanical development. They had no aversion to adapting machines to replace humans for mundane and routine tasks, such as searching for repeats or for encryption itself. At the same time, they did not devote significant effort to developing new mechanical techniques and technology. They had not, after all, invented Enigma themselves. They merely adopted and upgraded an existing system. For them, the application of machines mattered in only the limited arena of routine tasks.

Given this lack of familiarity with mechanized cryptanalysis, Fenner concluded, not surprisingly, that these devices rarely proved useful. He noted in his postwar reflections that, "any mechanical scanning of perforated tapes was always much too slow. ..." Other German intelligence divisions apparently would have agreed with Fenner's assessment. In the middle of the war, the Marine and Heer concluded that their Hollerith machines could not even help with statistical calculations.[45] This frustration, however, does not appear to have propelled the analysts to explore new applications or to develop new technology. Fenner did suggest that "the future belongs to…photo-electric scanning,"[46] but the Germans did not develop such technology during the war.

Although German cryptologists had machines that used more sophisticated methods than punch card sorters, mechanical assistance remained restricted to the statistical. Throughout the war, "the basic idea of every mechanical cryptanalytic aid was to replace the speed of fingers in statistical operations."[47] From the captured documents now available, we see that no one devised a way of exploiting the mechanical abilities of machines to do something different from what fingers do. German cryptologists did not consider how machines could be used beyond statistical counting and sorting. They did not experiment with such innovative approaches as the Poles' method of coupling several Enigmas together, in what they called the Bombe, to check possible settings at the speed of electricity. Although the Germans readily used Hollerith, or punch card machines, as cryptanalytic aids, they neglected mechanically or electromechanically assisted approaches. No mention surfaces of devices comparable to Gordon Welchman's vision of the diagonal board or Alan Turing's use of machines to search for combinations which could *not* work. German cryptologists appear to have had little curiosity about the range of potential that electromechanical technology might offer cryptanalysis. They certainly developed nothing along the lines of a computer.

Now we come to the question of cause or effect. Did the Germans fail to develop technology for cryptanalysis because they believed machines had only limited capabilities – and predominately statistical ones at that?

Or did they ignore the great potential that machines held for cryptanalysis because they restricted their own thinking to statistical approaches?

They awarded mechanical development little prestige in part because they saw so little benefit from it. Yet the benefit they received from mechanical assistance remained limited in large part because they did not give the potential either prestige or priority. In German eyes after all, true cryptanalysis fell into the domain they called *die geistige Arbeit*, or mental work, something outside the realm of machines.

Clearly, mechanical ability and ingenuity held less interest and prestige for these men than mental ability or *geistige Arbeit*. This tenet runs through all the sources here, from Bonatz's proud description of his nation's *geistige Arbeit* in World War I to the academic scientists who believed practical application beneath them.

In other realms, of course, Germans then, as now, held great respect for technological expertise. Indeed, the military put considerable effort and resources into areas of technology such as jet engines, synthetic fuels, and rocketry. Rockets, of course, held a fascination for Hitler, who described the V-2s as the miracle weapon which would destroy the enemy even as forces marched in to occupy Germany itself. Perhaps the Luftwaffe's powerful Nazi leader, Hermann Göring, was able to overcome both the academics' and the military's traditional aversion to the practical application of academic science. In any case, rocketry was one area where the military supported electromechanical and protocomputer efforts. In 1941, an enterprising German engineer, Konrad Züse, built an electromechanical "program-controlled computer," using 35 mm film and numerous relays, which became known as the Z3. Although the Z3 was destroyed by bombing, the military had it rebuilt for the V-1 and V-2 projects.[48] The Wehrmacht used Züse's rapid calculator for trajectory calculations as the Americans used something similar for flight calculations. Züse apparently suggested that an electron-tube-based computer could operate some 1,000 times faster than the relay-based computer and could assist in decoding radio messages. However, "Nothing came of this."[49] Although such technological effort might be expended on other weapons of war, it did not extend to cryptanalysis.

The reason for this lack of technology in cryptology rests at the doors of both cryptologic experts and the military command. Not only did cryptologists reject using the mechanical in their work, but the military viewed intelligence generally, and cryptanalysis specifically, as merely supplementary to field efforts. High-ranking command officers did not involve themselves in cryptology – either offensive or defensive. They certainly saw no reason to pass their technologic achievements, such as the Z3, to the intelligence divisions nor to expend energy promoting the mechanization of cryptanalysis.

Within the German intelligence community, mechanized deciphering remained only a remote possibility, "even though the fancy of some

12. The Colossus being prepared for another run in the effort to crack Tunny. One technician adjusts the tapes, which were notoriously fragile at Colossus' high speeds and frequently broke midrun. Note the vacuum tubes in the center and switches to the left; Colossus I used 1,500 valves, far exceeding the number in any previous electronic device. Volunteers at the Bletchley Park Trust are recreating this machine, which fills the space of a small room. Arguments continue about whether Colossus constitutes the first computer. (Courtesy of the National Security Agency)

analysts had been occupied with this idea [mechanized deciphering]."[50] Intelligence personnel were neither provided, nor encouraged to create, the level of mechanical devices they would have needed to crack ciphers of such sophistication as their own Enigma or the British Typex, let alone the American Sigaba. They did look to the future when they could develop a machine similar to the human brain, and they did believe such an "electric brain" could aid human cryptanalysts. In the end, the "exploitation, for decipherment purposes, of an electronic deciphering machine, an "electric brain," could unfortunately not be accomplished during the war."[51]

This pessimistic attitude toward mechanizing cryptanalysis produces the great paradox of German cryptologists: they mechanized cryptography early on, while allowing mechanization of cryptanalysis to languish. In cryptography, they used electromechanical ciphers from a very early stage – the late 1920s. They used Enigma and other electromechanical systems for a wide range of communications (routine to high-grade). Yet they never applied the same level of electromechanics to cryptanalysis.

Germany's technology fell far behind its enemies' in cryptanalysis. In the postwar list that compares Allied and German rapid analytic machinery in cryptanalysis, numerous Allied machines have no German equivalent. Not only did the Allies build and exploit arguably the first digital computer, Colossus, they constructed numerous other electromechanical or electronic devices to advance decryption of enemy signals. These devices ranged from the "standard" Bombes – which by midwar consisted of sixteen banks of Enigma rotors and derived daily settings for either three-wheel or four-wheel Enigmas – to Scritchers, which could test the pluggable reflector rotor Uncle D.[52]

In spite of German advances in other areas, German experts allowed their technologic development in signals intelligence and cryptology to stagnate and eventually collapse. They had neither the resources nor the inclination to produce the next wave of cryptologic machines. German cryptologists simply could not imagine the future that machines offered their field.

CONCLUSION

# RECOGNIZING THE END OF SECURITY

Technology can't save you...
    – Bruce Schneier, founder, Counterpane Internet Security[1]

This story of World War II's cryptologic battles offers twenty-first-century business and science vital lessons. Like those wartime agencies, we grapple today with revolutions in communications and cryptology. As radio gave militaries worldwide signal capabilities, today computer and satellite networks have broadened the reach of information and communications around the globe. Just as World War II radio signals ran the risk of interception by the enemy, modern Internet connections bring the danger of sensitive messages falling into the wrong hands. In both cases, we have turned for security to cryptology. Dramatic advances in cryptology, both then and now, have promised strong, "user friendly" protection against unauthorized reading of signals. Senders rely on sophisticated mathematics to hold the enemy at bay. Yet neither the statistics of 1940s electromechanical ciphers nor the algorithms of today's computer ciphers can offer protection by themselves. The Allied success against Enigma (and other wartime systems) demonstrates the limitations of relying solely on a cipher's complexity for security.

Initially Germany's Enigma outclassed the code and cipher systems of other countries. With such strong cryptology, as well as considerable success in cryptanalysis, the Germans launched the signals intelligence war understandably confident. Yet they frittered away this valuable advantage. Undetected, the enemy penetrated deeper and deeper into military, diplomatic, railroad, police, SS, and even Abwehr systems. As the war progressed and the Germans found themselves on the

214

defensive, their own sources of intelligence dried up. They discovered increasing numbers of enemy signals acquired greater protection from upgraded systems, and at all levels the enemy's security procedures substantially tightened. The enemy appeared to learn more and more about German positions, strengths, and even intentions – even as German intelligence lost their sources for all but the most immediate tactical information.

Indeed, the Allies eventually penetrated every major code and cipher system their enemies used – not just on the European front, as outlined here, but also in the Pacific theater against Japan.[2] Simultaneously they learned from their early mistakes. As the war progressed, they gradually closed all the leaks in their own major systems. Most important of all, neither Britain nor the United States (nor, apparently, the Soviet Union) suffered the devastating disaster of compromising their highest-grade, hence their most sensitive, systems. They triumphed in both the cryptographic and the cryptanalytic halves of the signals intelligence war.

What explains this dramatic seesaw in the war's intelligence battles? The answer lies in the different, virtually diametrically opposed approaches, organizations, and attitudes of the two sides. The Germans gave intelligence, particularly long-term, strategic intelligence, and cryptanalysis, a low priority reflected by limited resources and fractured intelligence organizations. They approached both cryptanalysis and their own cryptography as a collection of unrelated problems. They confronted a cryptologic issue only once it had become a problem. Rather than seeking future crises, they used their limited resources on immediate problems, tackling them as they arose and seeing little, if any, connection to other cryptologic concerns. Unable to see the larger picture, Germany's cryptologic experts relied heavily on the mathematical security of their machine ciphers. They failed to recognize that this very technology represented a new era for signals intelligence and cryptology.

In contrast, the Allied side made high-grade signals intelligence and cryptology a matter of the highest priority. To meet that need, Allied governments and militaries agreed to expend considerable talent and resources and to emphasize the end goal over the means by which their organizations achieved that result. This goal-oriented approach placed concerns about their own and the enemy's cryptologic capabilities at the center of every cryptologic discussion. Allied cryptologists saw Germany's codes and ciphers as an interlocking system and Enigma as a single cryptanalytic problem. They recognized the beginning of a new cryptologic era and created the conditions for exploiting the emerging technology.

Looking back over more than half a century, we can see that the Germans failed at both the offensive and defensive portions of signals intelligence. Their very successes at the tactical level concealed a parallel dearth of strategic success. Although they could track RAF fighters and crack field codes on both the Eastern and Western fronts, they consistently failed to predict any of the major Allied offensives: the Torch landings in North Africa, the invasion of Sardinia, the major Soviet offensives on the Eastern Front, or the massive Overlord invasion in Normandy. German intelligence divisions did not apologize for these omissions, nor did they make any apparent effort to correct this blindness.

German signals intelligence lacked any impetus to search for strategic information. Signals intelligence in general received no encouragement from the military's top echelons. When Hitler took direct control of the war, he, of course, relied on his genius and intuition, neither of which intelligence could influence. No other individual commander coordinated Wehrmacht efforts across theaters and services, necessitating strategic information. No Winston Churchill figure stepped forward to emphasize the importance of having strategic intelligence, of learning the enemy's strategy, future plans, and future goals.

Without a demand for knowing more than the enemy's strength and position, the military understandably viewed strategic intelligence generally, and cryptanalysis specifically, as less than essential. This low priority gives us a partial explanation for German signals intelligence's apparent paradox. The military willingly invested in a sophisticated cipher machine system because Enigma offered vital communications flexibility and security at a reasonable cost. Clearly, only with the assistance of all the means that 1940s technology possessed could cryptanalysts hope to crack machine ciphers. For the Wehrmacht, however, attacking machine ciphers seemed an improbable benefit at a great expense.

Nonetheless, German intelligence and command officers themselves generally maintained that their bureaus succeeded in their mission. In their view, the service commands asked for specific intelligence and the bureaus responded with it. The commands did not demand either a complete penetration of the Allies' high-grade strategic systems or the consideration of the worst-case scenario for the enemy's information: Enigma's compromise. Nor did they receive them.

However, from the perspective of postwar analysis, the German signals intelligence operation did not meet the definition of success. German cryptography could not keep enemy cryptanalysis at bay, and Enigma soon lost the advantage it had in 1939. Nor could German experts deliver the signals intelligence that revealed Allied intentions and strategy. These failures, as this work has detailed, stem from the structure and operation of Germany's intelligence organizations. The structure of these organizations influenced which problems German cryptologists addressed and how. These experts internalized these limits so thoroughly that they did not recognize the overwhelming evidence of disaster facing them. The structure had virtually eliminated the possibility that any German organization would realize the Allied compromise of Enigma.

## Resources

As it emphasized tactical over strategic intelligence, the German structure also limited the resources, scope, and power available to cryptologists and intelligence experts. The lack of human resources emerged, in the eyes of postwar Allied experts, as a vital component of the Wehrmacht failure in signals intelligence. A postwar U.S. analysis explained that the enemy's "limitations were largely due to insufficient specialists and inadequate training."[3] By late in the war, human resources were stretched extremely thin, but when Germany began its military buildup, considerable human capital existed. Germany entered the 1930s with at least the number and quality of geniuses available to Britain. Germany had produced numerous Nobel Prize winners and was to generate several inventions (such as jet engines and rockets) used by the Allies after the war. In the field of cryptology, however, Germany proved unable to succeed and, in fact, lost ground. These insufficiencies and inadequacies have frequently been laid at the door of Nazism, but the attitudes and practices that created them existed in the military before 1933. The military neglected to maintain channels of communication to civilians through the interwar period and so lost the opportunity to recruit talented, trained minds for cryptanalysis. Nazi rigidity on racial matters may have eliminated a few exceptional hires of "undesirables," particularly in the case of Jews, but the military's restrictive hiring practices existed well before Hitler's racial policies became law. Hitler's distrust of intellectualism, and of academics in particular, did not encourage reliance on civilian specialists. Indeed, an estimated 33 percent of German professors lost their positions under the Third Reich's reign, but the German military and academia had stood in opposition at least as far back as the Revolution of 1848.[4]

Yet these academics and other "outsiders" offered a solution to many of the Wehrmacht's staffing shortages. Moreover, with their outsider perspective, they would have increased the possibility that more or different questions and solutions could have emerged. Numerous Allied outsiders gave the military ingenious solutions, from Harry Hinsley's "pinches" of weather ships to famous engineering feats such as Liberty ships and Mulberry harbors. Like physicist Erwin Schrödinger's theoretical cat, who could walk through walls because he did not know that he could not, many Allied endeavors succeeded because their proponents believed they could.

The refusal to grant material resources helped stifle Germany's cryptologic effort. During and after the war, German cryptology experts complained bitterly that they could not get the finances or equipment, let alone staff, simply to process decryptable material. The military refused even to develop a training program in languages or cryptology for its own men. No one in Germany foresaw the need and use of a production system to handle the mechanical process of decrypting masses of enemy material once a cryptanalyst broke into a system. In many cases, valuable and already overloaded cryptanalysts themselves performed the tedious process of recovering enemy messages letter by letter.[5] Yet this dekeying (or *entschlüsseln*) could, as at Bletchley Park, have been performed by technicians, or even clerical workers, speeding the decryption process. In turn, such processing would have freed highly skilled cryptanalysts for attacks on other enemy systems. Without a significant investment in human resources, attacks on new systems or even the speed of decryption and dissemination could not be expected to increase.

Tackling as-yet-unbroken enemy signals received even less support. Without either the resources or priority for strategic intelligence, the various German intelligence divisions had little impetus to research difficult unbroken enemy systems. Nor did they automate the various steps of the deciphering process so that some could then be handled by specially trained clerks or, perhaps, by machines. This omission meant that they had no chance of successfully attacking higher-grade systems, such as electromechanical ciphers. Worse, they began losing their window into previously accessible tactical systems.

On the security side, limited resources undoubtedly played as important a role. Lack of funding may have stopped the Wehrmacht from replacing rotors, let alone the Enigma machine itself. The sheer number of Enigma machines in use meant a significant change in the system became nearly prohibitively expensive.

Rewiring nets of Enigma rotors certainly would have proved a formidable task – financially and logistically. Although the United States did rewire Sigaba rotors in 1945, at other times even they responded to potential compromise less dramatically. In the case of the tactical cipher machine M-209, the Americans had postwar confirmation that the machine had been read. Yet, the U.S. military continued to include the M-209 in its cryptographic inventory through the Korean War. Only early in the Vietnam War, when a speech ciphony system known as the KY-8 became available, did the United States retire M-209. One reason for the long wait for M-209's replacement may very well have been the considerable costs involved. The World War II production of the M-209 cost just under $150.00 apiece, or nearly $21 million (about $210 million in 2003 dollars) in total. These figures do not include the necessary support elements: training of operators and clerks as well as repair personnel, along with spare parts, operating manuals, keying material, and shipping.[6] If a wealthy, postwar superpower balked at replacing such a system known to be compromised, no wonder wartime Germany, with its desperate financial situation, resisted replacing Enigma. Exchanging cipher machines for each of the thousands and thousands of military and civilian units would have required vital financial and logistical resources desperately needed elsewhere.

With such meager resources and low priority, sigint and cryptanalysis faced significant obstacles to success. Their chances only declined further when Germany's numerous intelligence divisions refused to cooperate even under wartime pressures. Resisting cooperative communication, they unwittingly duplicated each other's work and created inefficient redundancies. One division might spend years attempting to break a system currently being read by another organization. They laid out areas of responsibility by service branch, ignoring similarities of cipher type, and rarely collaborated on cryptanalytic methods. The separation of OKW/Chi from the services' cryptologic bureaus meant the supposedly supervisory agency and its subordinates actually had little contact, coordination, or communication. The British and American cryptologic entities, although separated by national loyalties and thousands of miles of ocean, worked together more closely than the various German cryptologic units, even when housed in the same city.

## Censoring

In addition to the lack of interservice cooperation, Wehrmacht signals intelligence struggled under the weight of a censored, often self-censored, society. Neither the Wehrmacht nor the Third Reich encouraged critiques of existing equipment or procedures. Delivering bad news in the Third Reich, particularly as the war worsened, often proved a career killer, if not an actual death sentence. Rumors abounded, for example, that General Oberst Ernst Udet committed suicide 17 November 1941 over the repeated failures of the Luftwaffe's plane designs.[7] Admitting one had failed did not go over well in military circles and particularly not in Germany under Hitler.

Nazi policies only exacerbated problems already apparent in the German military's bureaucratic culture. In the decades since the war, numerous books have presented the Wehrmacht as the opposition, even a "Resistance," to the Nazi regime. Yet, in large part, the military followed, and even lauded, Nazi intentions and operations. Moreover, long before the war, the Nazi Party had amassed so much power that opposition had become virtually impossible. Where the military disagreed with Nazi orders, they learned to keep quiet.[8]

Military officers found they paid a penalty for even discontent with the Nazi Party. Wilhelm Flicke, for instance, had worked in signals intelligence for the Heer during World War I, but in 1939, "after apparently getting into hot water with his opposition to the Nazi Party," he was sidelined. Throughout the war, he was moved to increasingly remote intercept stations as "technical director," although he had been trained in the more advanced skill of evaluator.[9]

By the last year of the war, the Nazi Party had isolated or ousted much of the traditional military. In the wake of the 20 July 1944 attempt to assassinate Hitler, numerous high-ranking military men, including several pivotal for intelligence, were arrested and later hung for treason. The head of the Abwehr, Admiral Wilhelm Canaris, and his second-in-command, Oster, were imprisoned in September 1944 and executed in April 1945. General Fellgiebel, head of signals communications (which encompassed cryptanalysis) suffered a similar fate. This purge was the culmination of an ever-present clash between military and Nazi Party.

Such widespread constraints and deterrents led to a pervasive culture of self-censorship in Nazi Germany. Studies of even the language of the Third Reich have demonstrated how far ordinary Germans went to avoid unpleasant truths. Such self-censorship emerged among military Germans as well. One Marine staff officer was warned by a colleague at the BdU headquarters about "the atmosphere here." Indeed, the officer discovered that a "lot of people didn't say what they really thought."[10] The temptation for such personnel to provide their superiors with what they wanted to hear rather than what was most objective must have been overwhelming.

In this atmosphere, few would consider suggesting so horrific a disaster as an ongoing compromise of the Reich's main cryptographic system. Most men, whether officers or civilians, must have found admitting a problem of that magnitude beyond their capabilities. Some officers told Allied interrogators after the war that they had not believed Enigma completely secure. One claimed that the Director-General of Signals for the Luftwaffe had at one point refused to radio operational orders at all because he so distrusted Enigma's security.[11] Even these fears appear to have been of short-term security breaches rather than complete compromise. In most cases during the war, the men censored their concerns even from themselves.

Clearly, Germany's cryptologists were not exempt from this self-censorship. None of them could admit the possibility of Enigma's compromise. Their investigative methods and objectives imply a general unwillingness to admit setbacks in intelligence and cryptology unless absolutely necessary. This unwillingness smacks of groupthink, a term coined in the early 1970s by sociologist Irving Janis to describe the group pressure and self-censoring that can cause otherwise intelligent and astute people to make gross miscalculations.[12] Germany's cryptologists exhibit several attributes of groupthink, including an apparent homogeneity of background and outlook, the refusal to consult outside experts, and an isolation of the staff from both their peers in similar organizations and outside specialists. Although the documentation is not complete enough for us to be certain, these characteristics suggest groupthink may have complicated decisionmaking in cryptology. Certainly, the surviving investigations and war diaries demonstrate swift dismissals, if not outright censoring, of concerns about Enigma's vulnerability.

Some of this self-censorship may also have stemmed from the German intelligence community's knowledge of the financial and logistical implications of changing Enigma. Why discuss the weakness of decade-old rotor wirings if replacing those rotors remains virtually impossible? Traditional political considerations may also have perpetrated the silence. One German naval expert posits that the Marine's perceived culpability in the military collapse of 1918 contributed to self-censorship. Moreover, the wartime Marine had already suffered through at least one technical investigation, in this case of malfunctioning torpedoes, where the experts had been proven wrong. These results had only deepened the gulf between the frontline men and the theoretical experts back at headquarters. Whatever its commanders' concerns over Enigma's weakness, the Marine was determined not to be the one to uncover a failure so devastating to morale as Enigma's compromise.[13]

Indeed, the culture of all the signals intelligence agencies appears to have been ideally designed not to test belief in Enigma's security but to reinforce it. In the face of strong evidence, no one working with

Enigma or signals intelligence gave serious consideration to the worst-case scenario of their cipher system's compromise. Time and again, German security investigators developed hypothetical and completely unsubstantiated scenarios to explain away any unsettling incident. They went to great lengths to avoid the truth. They grasped at straws such as imprecise wording in enemy signals, "possible" signals from destroyed vessels, and mysterious technological advances on the enemy's part. The reluctance of the high commands to acknowledge mistakes, particularly the possible mistake of relying too heavily on Enigma, made censorship of the cipher's possible compromise nearly inevitable. They preferred any explanation, however farfetched, that left Enigma's myth of security undamaged.

Not surprisingly, the security investigations did not address the comprehensive issues of the cipher system. These reports needed to consider all the possible ways Enigma could be compromised and what the enemy could glean from even partially decrypted traffic. When investigating the origin of enemy knowledge, they needed to consider all the possible sources for this information and how to close off these sources wherever possible. Instead they separated the problem into isolated, discrete sections. They segregated attacks by service branch, pooling information only minimally, and limiting test attacks on their own systems to artificial environments. Even their upgrades did not solve such long-term flaws in Enigma as the service age of rotors. Nor did they ever glimpse the danger that cross-service use of Enigma brought to individual nets. From Enigma's adoption to the very end, Germany's intelligence and cryptologic experts consistently defined their security and cryptanalytic problems too narrowly.

## Narrow Definitions

This limited vision on the part of German signals intelligence made Enigma's vulnerability persistent: the Germans did not take a long-term, all-encompassing view of cipher security. German cryptologists insisted Enigma solved the compromise problems of Germany's past. The Enigma system could be deployed worldwide and easily operated. Moreover, the machine had promised enough complexity that the information it enciphered could not be used operationally; that is, a break into a cipher system after one year, or five, of war would probably not help the enemy for any practical purpose. These claims ignored the implications of the machine's full life span. If the essential parts of the machine will be used for a decade or two, then long-term security becomes critical. The enemy will get his hands on parts of or complete machines and may be making ongoing attacks from different angles. Security, then, requires more than countering the possibility that the enemy captured material last month. It also means addressing the probability that the enemy has gathered information on the system from its first day of operation. Indeed, the Wehrmacht knew the Poles had successfully broken Enigma as late as 1938. Nonetheless the sigint bureaus consistently investigated Enigma's security as a short-term problem rather than a sigint war beginning with Enigma's pre-Nazi era adoption.

These bureaus failed to consider that the enemy could cobble together information from varied sources and devote years to tracking and chipping away at Enigma-encrypted signals. Security investigations focused on the numbers and almost never even acknowledged the vast difference between theoretical use and live traffic. Although they admonished their operators to follow vital security procedures, cryptologists did not monitor actual use to determine whether lapses could provide enemy cryptanalysts with a significant foothold. Nor did German security experts look for subtle signs that information from Enigma signals was passing to enemy units. Even when explicit claims of the enemy reading Enigma arrived – as in the August 1943 report[14] – German intelligence officers continued to maintain that ongoing breaking of the machine was impossible. They still clung to the literal text of enemy signals and the promise of safety in astronomical numbers.

The history of Enigma suggests a chink in the myth of German technical prowess. In other areas of technology – particularly jet engines, synthetic fuels, and rocketry – the military invested considerable effort and resources. However, once Enigma was in place, cryptology, particularly cryptanalysis, suffered from technologic stagnation. Considered advanced for the time of its initial adoption in the late 1920s, Enigma was far from cutting-edge technology by the 1940s. Numerous other countries, including Italy and Switzerland, used their own variations of Enigmas. Although now associated with the German military, Enigma was not a German government- or military-sponsored innovation.[15] Throughout the war, German cryptologists did make significant modifications to Enigma. None of their developments, however, revolutionized cipher security or produced advances equivalent to the American Sigaba machines.

Enigma reveals the disarray of Germany's national technical effort, at least in cryptology. Technological development for cryptography as well as cryptanalysis foundered under the weight of bureaucratic battles among competing fiefdoms. Even the vaunted German systematic approach collapsed. Enigma's failure reveals that German scientists and cryptologists lacked a strategy for review and improvement. German cryptologists did not revolutionize cryptography, and their record in technology for cryptanalysis shows little ingenuity.

Worse, their understanding of the most vital security factors in cryptology left much to be desired. German experts continued to believe machine ciphers with enormous combinatorial challenges offered tremendous security, and they consistently ignored nonstatistical cryptologic approaches. The statistics of cryptology remained the central focus in reports on the security of Enigma and other ciphers, including enemy systems. German experts' security investigations and cryptanalytic reports examined either the possibility of physical compromise or of statistical methods for breaking a system. Among the surviving wartime documents, no reports deal with the more subtle ways around and into a cryptologic problem.

German cryptologists clearly believed they were being reasonably thorough. The various branches of the German military had cryptanalysts attack their own machines and investigate several Allied cipher machines as well. Investigators conducted statistical attacks on Enigma-enciphered traffic, both with and without the help of "captured" documentation. These attacks also clung to statistical and straightforward approaches. Some did admit to statistical limitations in Enigma's design. At least two German cryptologic bureaus found methods to crack some versions of Enigma.[16] However, they apparently never tackled live traffic and instead stuck to brute-force methods performed under artificial conditions. Needless to say, all of these examinations concluded that the machine would defeat enemy cryptanalysts. Throughout these investigations, German cryptologists seem to have never realized the true reduction of Enigma's statistical possibilities under real conditions, particularly those reductions arising from operational procedures and human error.

German cryptanalysts trusted Enigma and believed it could not be broken. They failed to reexamine this assumption in the face of evidence suggesting the contrary.[17] Since Enigma proved unbreakable, top German cryptanalysts concluded the more complex seven-rotor Typex would be even more impervious to attack.[18] They never saw the American Sigaba but assumed it also could not be broken and not even punch card machines could help the enemy. With this unshakable belief, they did not expend much effort on the assault. Hence, they had no luck breaking British and American high-grade cipher machines. Their very lack of success only reinforced their belief in Enigma's strength and vice versa. Faced with a system that they calculated as statistically unbreakable in a reasonable period of time, they simply gave up.

Clearly, none of these men recognized the emergence of the new technology of electronics. So they failed to develop equipment that could exploit this evolution. Since German cryptologists did not themselves develop and employ a new class of electrical cryptanalytic machines, they did not believe the enemy would. They recognized that, in theory, machines could be designed to break Enigma effectively, but they did not explore such futuristic ideas. Even after the war, German scientists and cryptologists only dreamed of electronic brains and enormous calculators. No one in signals intelligence tried exploiting machines beyond sorters for attacks on Enigma. No one thought the enemy would either. They all considered such projects overly expensive and impractical. In short, these Germans refused to believe the enemy would or could do something they themselves could not, or simply did not, do.

However, to succeed in a previously unknown endeavor, one must start with belief in the possibility of success. Even after the war, the Germans believed in a statistical security that took neither operational reality nor their opponents' years of attention and attack into account. Relying too heavily on such theoretical statistics made the Germans vulnerable. Even their best cryptologic experts could not believe Enigma compromised until faced with the British government's admission of Ultra in 1974.[19] Because of their persistent assumption of Enigma's strength, they did not advocate simple changes that could have hindered, if not completely defeated, their enemies. Had the Wehrmacht, for example, completely replaced Enigma's rotors even once, rather than just adding to the existing set, they might have halted the Allies' success in its tracks.

## In Contrast, Successful Centralized Cooperation

Unlike the Germans, the Allies ended the war with an intelligence system brimming with successes unimaginable in 1939. Initially small, poorly funded prewar Allied sigint organizations had received priority and funding early in the war that allowed them to expand and improve both their staff and scope rapidly. This priority and sense of urgency, even desperation, prompted a spirit of cooperation between intelligence agencies. In most cases, the British and American organizations worked together to further the greater good, not just an individual agency. This wartime system has become the model for today's central intelligence ideal.

The Allies' successful attack on Enigma owes much to the centralization of all elements of signals intelligence that Britain's GC&CS created at Bletchley Park. Here, GC&CS physically concentrated Allied cryptologic resources and cooperated across the traditional lines of military and civilian segregation. This centralization allowed Bletchley Park's team to exploit the cryptographic cooperation that Enigma had created for the Germans. Whereas German cryptologic bureaus compartmentalized their work and their results, the Allied signals intelligence staff eschewed isolation.

Cryptanalysis flourished in Britain because the government, and eventually the military, recognized the importance of signals intelligence. Like Poland before her, Britain made intelligence, particularly cryptanalysis, a priority. With this priority clear, the government and military provided personnel and resources adequate to the task. GC&CS enlisted military and nonmilitary personnel, civil servants, academics, and technical personnel. The composition of the staff as civilians-in-uniform offset the military tradition of interservice rivalry and made centralizing the intelligence effort easier. As Bletchley's cryptanalysts began producing results, the military and the Ministries tolerated their unusual, even eccentric, work styles and lack of traditional hierarchy.

This use of talent from various disciplines exemplifies another leap which Allied wartime intelligence organizations made. Before the war, most laymen and experts did not consider either intelligence or cryptology the work of mathematicians. Intelligence services of the First World War had employed scholars, particularly philologists, who applied their linguistic knowledge to codebreaking. The men in Polish intelligence, as cryptology historian David Kahn has noted, first recognized that electromechanical ciphers would require less philological expertise than mathematical cryptanalysis.[20] Now we take for granted the use of mathematicians and, by extension, computer scientists in cryptology.

Bletchley Park demonstrates the need for both mathematical scientific skills and the approach of nonscientists. Naturally, modern computer-based cryptology requires mathematicians and similar experts to tackle the cryptography of machine ciphers. Like the cryptanalysts tackling Enigma's electromechanics, they make the initial breaks, uncover address changes, and conquer periodic upgrades. For ongoing reading of a system, however, intelligence organizations need a broader combination of talents. Allied intelligence needed scholars familiar with German and military diction to spot cribs. To reconstruct the Wehrmacht's Order of Battle, Bletchley used a historian of ancient Rome. Experts with business and operational experience automated decryption for rapid processing of the mountain of information easy wireless communications produced.

This multifaceted combination offered Bletchley Park an additional benefit. The group's diversity of approaches and perspectives increased creativity and innovation. Combining analysts and log readers from both the sciences and the humanities sparked innovative ideas. These often theoretical innovations passed to business and engineering experts, who turned them into practical applications. The results ranged from streamlined decryption assembly lines to revolutionary machines such as the family of Scritcher machines and the famous Colossus.

For the particular case of the enormous interconnected Enigma network, Bletchley's centralization proved particularly effective. The German interservice, multigrade use of Enigma created links between many different keys and networks. Bletchley's staff quickly saw the importance of these connections and all of the Huts focused on exploiting every cross-reference, every key and setting repeat, and every message re-encipherment. Once cryptanalysts cracked one key, they worked to widen that breach to include every related network.

Although this centralized cryptologic effort had limits, its conspicuous success proved convincing. With few exceptions, Bletchley's cracking of Enigma merely expanded through the course of the war. Even the often-fractious U.S. military admitted Bletchley demonstrated "that centralized control is the more efficient form of organization for such activities."[21] The cross-fertilization and efficiency of centralized intelligence helped tip the seesaw in the Allies' favor.

### Illuminating the Big Picture

The very organizational structure and culture of GC&CS increased the probability of Allied success. The insistence that analysts see the big picture fostered cooperation and collaboration. Section heads encouraged the flow of information across service lines, organizing informational briefings and creating formal liaison positions as well as central information storage points. More informally, they offered staff a view of how their own work fitted into the big picture and even solicited suggestions for improvements. When the Americans joined the intelligence effort, they too became a part of Ultra and Bletchley's centralized, cooperative mode of operation.

Along with knowing one's position in the big picture came considerable autonomy. Although their financial allocations and external operations did require official approval, the collection of scholars and businessmen pursued their attack on enemy systems as they saw fit. They coordinated interception of enemy traffic, built electromechanical devices to automate cryptanalysis, and even directed military operations designed to collect cryptologic information.[22] British intelligence defined cryptologic problems broadly and gave its personnel considerable leeway in their attempts at solutions. As had Polish intelligence before them, the British put few restrictions on the approaches or methods used. The Ultra operation began almost haphazardly: new recruits were put in the picture and then asked for ideas on approaching a solution. When someone saw a need, he filled it. Gordon Welchman, for example, foresaw the masses of decrypted material that successful decryption would produce and began assembling a handling process for the future flood of messages. Although administration and logistics for the growing complex gave Bletchley a visible, but still malleable, structure, rigid hierarchy never overpowered the Park's adaptive flexibility.

A remarkable amount of autonomy filtered down to the lower ranks in GC&CS's sigint organization. The compartments of rank, service, and seniority proved flimsy under the weight of Bletchley's mandate. Bletchley's superiors put the reading of enemy ciphers above hierarchical and personal concerns. They encouraged everyone from intercept personnel to the top cryptanalysts to collaborate and brainstorm ideas for improvements. Initiative was assumed. The diffusion of autonomy and information produced powerful results. Not just cryptanalysts but log readers and others in traffic analysis learned to search numerous nets for cross-cribs and key repeats. Young recruits produced remarkable solutions quickly, and innovations came sometimes from unexpected quarters.

In the end, the Allied cryptanalysts broke not only the various versions of Enigma but also the far more complex Lorenz, the Purple machines, the Hagelin C-38, countless hand ciphers, and even several of their own cryptosystems. This success would ultimately shape the goals and structure of future British and American signals intelligence. Bletchley Park and the successes of World War II have become ideals and models for today's cryptologic agencies. Although true centralization and consolidation of effort has not occurred since in the United States, the ideal remains.

### Maintaining the Defensive

This Allied offensive triumph, however, only succeeded because of its parallel defensive operation. Reading the enemy's cipher systems has value only if one can both transmit the information to troops who can use it and prevent the enemy from realizing that this information comes from his own compromised systems. Bletchley succeeded at both timely dissemination and near total security. The motley collection at Bletchley successfully protected the valuable Ultra system from lax Allied tongues and suspicious German eyes.

Bletchley Park managed this security success by insisting on three components: general recognition of Ultra's overriding importance; the highest level of protection for Ultra, without exception; and finally, never overestimating security or underestimating the enemy. First and foremost, they drilled the importance of Ultra's success into everyone handling the decrypts. They lessened the risk of exposure from lax procedures or inadvertent slips by giving every Ultra-indoctrinated person a complete view of Ultra's importance. Everyone from Bletchley's log readers to Allied Forces generals was told how Ultra could win battles and how security breaches could cost lives. The explanation of how their job, however routine, aided the war effort kept thousands of lips sealed decades after war's end.

Putting handlers and recipients in the picture also made Ultra's constant protection easier to swallow. Ultra could not travel outside Bletchley Park except via secure teleprinter, one-time pad, or the highest-grade cipher (e.g., Typex or Sigaba). Nor could anyone make operational use of Ultra information without a separate, lower-grade cover explanation. Although the Americans chafed at the restrictions,[23] Bletchley granted no exceptions to these protection requirements, regardless of rank or circumstance. Churchill himself had to adhere to them. Lives were sacrificed to provide cover stories for Ultra information.[24] Ultra's protection remained paramount.

This hierarchy of priority stems from several factors, including a democratic tradition and an integration of civilian and military society. However, one factor stands out clearly: entering the war on the defensive. The Allies, particularly the Polish and the British, faced an enemy on the offensive, superior in armaments and numbers. Being on the defense meant the Allies put a higher priority on intelligence. Intelligence could provide tremendous assistance by preparing the defensive militaries for the enemy's attacks, giving them warning of what forces would attack where and in what numbers. This foreknowledge allowed them to use their slender forces most efficiently. In contrast, a military on the offense, like the Wehrmacht of 1939–1941, has less need for intelligence since it plans to pick the time and place of the action. When the seesaw began to tilt the other way, Germany had already become entwined in the offensive, low-priority-for-intelligence mind-set, whereas Allied signals intelligence had already proved sigint's worth. Thus both sides ended the war with the belief in intelligence that they had held at the war's start.

Presupposing the power of intelligence, Allied intelligence personnel made a point never to assume they were outperforming their counterparts. They always insisted the enemy could put two and two together and realize the source of Allied information. This assumption engendered a vigilant attitude toward the security of their own signaling systems. They knew their own side would make mistakes and they were right. The Germans found British and, particularly, American signaling procedures sloppy – at first. But the Allies learned from their mistakes. Even the Germans agreed that Allied security procedures improved as the war progressed. The Allies did not allow themselves to slip into complacency about their own security. They constantly segregated signals containing Ultra information from lower-grade intelligence as well as from operational signals of all grades. At Bletchley Park, the team continued to search for – and at times found – hints in Ultra that the Germans could read Allied signals. They also continued attacking their own systems vigorously and in real time through the war's end.

Moreover, they continued to assume that whatever they could do, the enemy could do. If they could break an electromechanical system after long-term analysis, so could the enemy. Thus Allied cryptologists needed to innovate and improve constantly. They devoted considerable effort and resources to speeding up and automating every aspect of both cryptography and decryption. The Allies took the long view in cryptanalysis. They devoted study to unbroken Enigma ciphers for not just weeks or months but years. They expected changes in the future and they prepared for them – by earmarking staff, developing training, and devoting resources to the development of new machines and new methods of cryptanalysis. (Cryptanalysis was only one example of this farsighted approach. Another was operations research, which often dovetailed with sigint, for example, in convoy operations.)[25] They invested energy in experimental research and machinery, leading to the development of revolutionary mechanical and electronic cryptanalytic devices.

Herein lies the most crucial factor for the Allied success: these cryptologists always knew security could be no more than a moving target, never an absolute. This attitude shaped every facet of their signals intelligence operation. The Allies maintained the basic assumption that even the most sophisticated systems would succumb to attack given enough time, resources, and ingenuity. They believed that, eventually, the enemy would crack their systems.

They put this belief into practice. For the high-grade machine Sigaba, they calculated that the life of its original rotor set should run no more than fifteen to eighteen months – roughly one-tenth the life of Enigma's original rotors. Recognizing the fallibility of humans, they never gave up on finding entry into even the most secure system. Time and again, this vigilance produced success – even against a one-time-pad system.[26] They determined that they would evolve to meet the latest challenge. In the process, they changed cryptology, security, and technology forever.

## Facing Our Own Emerging Technologies

The Allied work during World War II transformed cryptology: modern cryptology has become increasingly mechanized and automated. The electrical currents and moving rotors of World War II's Enigmas and Sigabas have yielded to computers, which base their encipherment on mathematical algorithms. Electronics has expanded on the possibilities of machines such as Bombes and Scritchers. Now computers swiftly execute the once slow, labor-intensive work of crib searches and brute-force attacks. With the introduction of computers, cryptology has gradually become accepted and even expected by the larger public. We have broadened our use of cryptography. With cell phones and the Internet, we frequently use some form of cryptology for daily, routine information as well as for high-grade government and military messages.

As we enter this era of widespread public use of computer-generated ciphers, we face many of the same issues German cryptologists confronted. We rely on increasingly sophisticated computer processors and software. We have put our trust in the sheer mathematical strength of computer-based cryptologic technology and ignored the human factor.

Yet, like the systems of World War II, our systems fail in their practical application. Many people use the same password on all of their accounts – whether at work, at school, or at home. Like Enigma's operators, others create passwords from easily uncovered elements, such as famous names, family initials, and birth dates. Using their knowledge of human regularity and common business practices, hackers find weaknesses and loopholes in operating systems, e-mail operations, and Internet browsers. Academics and amateur enthusiasts have defeated security protection for copyrighted material on devices such as compact disks and DVD players. Anyone who accesses the Internet, the Web, or e-mail remains dependent on the weakest link in a now global security chain.

As we grapple with the powers and threats of emerging technologies in the twenty-first century, we have much to learn from the successes and mistakes of the last century. Although the Allied victory may appear indisputable to us today, at the war's outset, intelligence had no clear winner. Indeed, at first glance, Germany had the upper hand with better resources and a good view into the Allies' systems.

During the war, both sides made efforts to improve and innovate. However, one side used its human resources more effectively and thoroughly. One side believed in offensive as well as defensive innovation, pouring energy and resources into personnel, interception, and technology. The other side limited resources and neglected development. Moreover, the two combatants took opposing approaches to the emerging technologies of the time. Germany viewed modern mathematics and cryptology in isolation, using statistical computations, narrow interpretations, and brute-force attacks to calculate security. Meanwhile, the Allies – the ultimate victors – recognized the large role that humans play in developing and defeating new technologies.

Many people and institutions still cling to the illusion that technology provides security. Even the most sophisticated technology cannot prevent human errors. Internationally linked databases cannot stop potential terrorists not yet listed on some watch list. Cutting-edge biometry cannot lock out criminals if the door gets propped open. The tightest cryptology will not secure sensitive memos left waiting in the office printer. Governments like that of the United States continue to claim that computer monitoring and national restrictions on higher-grade cryptography will increase security, although the Web ignores national borders. If we of the twenty-first century rely on the sheer mathematical capabilities of computers for protection, we will be repeating the Germans' blindness.

Absolute security was a myth in 1939 and remains a myth in the twenty-first century. Like the Allies, today's users of computers, cell phones, and compact disks must recognize that no security can be guaranteed. We can only assume reasonable security – a system which protects information for a limited time. Reasonable security requires a system that can fail without a complete collapse that compromises everything – what one security expert called a smart failure.[27] Smart failures mean each component's crash leaves "the whole as unaffected as possible." Smart systems recognize compromise will come eventually. Security is simply staying one step ahead of the competition.

To stay ahead of the competition, we need people who are trained not in specific technical expertise but in problem solving. These people must offer two more characteristics: diversity and a belief in the possible. These generalists must represent and accept diversity in opinions and approach. Their diversity will encourage multiple creative approaches to problems and foster ingenuity. They need the autonomy to put forward their ideas and pursue their innovations. Then they can fulfill the belief that anything, particularly their own success, is possible.

The Allies' success confirms the axiom that organizational structures determine how problems are handled. The organizations set the parameters for framing questions and, hence, their answers. Those working to exploit technologies effectively need to work in a cooperative, collaborative atmosphere where they can focus on the larger problem rather than on divisive rivalries. Creating expertise and specialization through decentralization and compartmentalization has its advantages. What can go wrong, as not only the Germans of the 1940s but also the Americans of the twenty-first century have learned, is that information fails to get to the right person. Inevitably, many people hold vital pieces of the puzzle; they need to work in a structure that ensures (or tries to ensure) that all those pieces get put together in one place and so reveal the true underlying picture.

Narrowly focused organizations may completely miss the big picture. Recognizing the overall problem helps direct efforts to the heart of the dilemma and fosters the necessary innovation. The organizations must also recognize that mistakes will be made and must allow for their recognition and correction. These lessons learned often help prompt the successful solutions of the future. Truly innovative organizations will only emerge in a society that fosters the values of cooperation and problem solving and encourages flexibility, diversity, and innovation. Only with all of these elements can we consider ourselves adequately prepared to face the swiftly changing future of emerging technologies.

The story of Ultra's triumph reiterates the fact that security systems eventually fail. Interdependent systems are always the most vulnerable: when one Enigma net failed, its links to other nets brought them down as well. Such a linked collapse can happen, and indeed has happened, on the Internet and other sets of connected computers. We must prepare for similar failures. Yet we cannot become experts in emerging technologies in time to counter them. We can only watch for the sudden shifts and large leaps that characterize new technologies and prepare for the mad scramble they will engender. Success will come to those who keep changing and adapting to new advances. Technology cannot solve our problems. Human brains do.

# NOTES

1. Cryptology, the study of codes and ciphers, consists of cryptography, the creation of codes and ciphers, and cryptanalysis, the breaking of same. Whereas codes substitute a symbol or word for a word or a phrase, ciphers substitute a symbol or letter for a letter. This work primarily focuses on ciphers.

2. See, for example, Ralph Bennett, *Ultra and Mediterranean Strategy* (London: H. Hamilton, 1989) and *Ultra in the West: The Normandy Campaign: 1944–1945* (London: Hutchinson, 1979); Günter Hessler, *Uboat War in the Atlantic* (London: HMSO, 1989); David Kahn, *Seizing the Enigma* (Boston: Houghton Mifflin Company, 1991); Ronald Lewin, *The American Magic* (New York: Farrar Straus Giroux, 1982); John Winton, *ULTRA at Sea* (New York: Morrow, 1988).

3. Koch died soon after, nearly penniless. Kahn, *Seizing the Enigma*, p. 31; Józef Garlinski, *The Enigma War* (New York: Scribner & Sons, 1979), p. 9.

4. Because this work describes the three different militaries, I refer to the German services by their wartime German names (Heer [army], Marine [navy], Luftwaffe [air force], etc.). The Marine was formally known as the Reichsmarine and Kriegsmarine. For simplicity, only Marine appears here. Wehrmacht refers to the entire armed forces. Each service's Oberkommando (High Command) had an acronym (OKW [Oberkommando der Wehrmacht], OKH [Oberkommando des Heeres], OKM [Oberkommando ...], OKL), and I frequently use these for brevity. The Marine frequently referred to the British Royal Navy as the Admiralty, and both names are used here.

5. See Ralph Erskine and Michael Smith, eds., *Action This Day* (London: Bantam Press, 2001), chap. 4.

6. The Wehrmacht had other high-grade cipher systems, particularly the non-Baudot machines, Siemens Geheimschreiber T-52 series, and Lorenz SZ 40/42. Nicknamed "Fish" by the British, these systems were not in such widespread use as Enigma and proved far more difficult to crack, although the Allies had some success against them nonetheless. See discussions of Fish and the Colossus built

to break it in Erskine and Smith's *Action This Day* and F. Hinsley and Alan Stripp, *Codebreakers* (Oxford: Oxford University Press, 1993).

7. Gordon F. Welchman, *The Hut 6 Story: Breaking the Enigma Code* (New York: McGraw-Hill, 1982), p. 36.

8. Three young Polish mathematicians, Marian Rejewski, Jerzy Rozycki, and Henryk Zygalski, had shown promise in a Poznan University cryptology course and agreed to work for Polish intelligence. Rejewski made the initial break into Enigma. See Gilbert Bloch's *Enigma avant Ultra* (Paris: n.p., 1985), Garlinski's *The Enigma War*, Wladyslaw Kozaczuk's *Enigma* (Frederick, MD: University Publications of America, 1984), and Richard Woytak's *On the Border of War and Peace* (New York: Columbia University Press, 1979).

9. Bradley Smith, *The Ultra Magic Deals* (Novato, CA: Presidio, 1993), p. 28.

10. For descriptions of attacks on various Enigma systems, see M. Rejewski's descriptions in Wladyslaw Kozaczuk's *Enigma*; David J. Crawford and Philip E. Fox, eds., "The Autoscritcher and the Superscritcher," *IEEE Annals of the History of Computing* 14, no. 3 (1992): 9–22; articles by Cipher A. Deavours and Ralph Erskine in *Cryptologia*; and Andrew Hodges, *Alan Turing* (New York: Simon & Schuster, Inc., 1983), among others. Enigmas are also on the Web: http://frode.home.cern.ch/frode/crypto/CSG/csginfo.html or http://www.xat.nl/enigma/.

11. "Cribs" referred to likely solutions for a coded message, usually from past experience with a particular operator or net.

12. Air forces seem generally to signal more frequently and less securely than other services. One interceptor put this propensity down to the loneliness of pilots (Clayton). Indeed, Allied analysts complained about insecure Royal Air Force (RAF) signaling. PRO: ADM 223/2 ZIP/ZG/25.

13. F. H. Hinsley et al., *British Intelligence in World War II*, 5 vols. (London: HMSO, 1979–1990), 1:109.

14. Threats to this continuity worried cryptanalysts greatly, e.g., NARA: RG 457 HCC Box 880 NR 2612 – Capt. Walter J. Fried Reports, Hut 6 weekly report 14 October 44, p. 5.

15. Hinsley et al., *British Intellligence in World War II*, 1:338.

16. Ibid., Vol. 2, Appendix 4, pp. 658–668.

17. NARA: RG 457 HCC Box 880 NR 2612 – Capt. Walter J. Fried Reports/SSA Liaison with GCCS, Nov. 1944 table, p. 12; 16 March 1944, p. 1.

18. Wladyslaw Kozaczuk, *Bitwa o tajemnice* (Warszawa: Verlag Ksiazka i Wiedza, 1967). The two reviews appeared in the periodicals *Die Nachhut* and *Ost-deutscher Literatur Anzeiger*; "wishful thinking" from interview with Jürgen Rohwer.

19. Heinz Bonatz, *Die deutsche Marine Funkaufklärung* (Darmstadt: Wehr & Wissen, 1970). All translations are my own.

20. Ralph Bennett, *Behind the Battle* (London: Sinclair-Stevenson, 1994), p. 21.

21. Bonatz, *Marine Funkaufklärung*, p. 87.

22. Bonatz, *Marine Funkaufklärung*, pp. 87–89. Dr. Prof. Jürgen Rohwer had also had postwar conversations that appeared to confirm that the Allies had not cracked Enigma. Interview with Dr. Prof. Rohwer.

23. The tale of the struggle to crack the Enigma is the stuff of thrillers, starting with the delightful, albeit unreliable *The Ultra Secret* (1974) that broke the silence. See also S. Budiansky's *Battle of Wits* (2000), Peter Calvocoressi's *Top Secret ULTRA* (1980), R. V. Jones's *The Wizard War* (1978), D. Kahn's *Seizing the Enigma* (1991), Wladyslaw Kozaczuk's *Enigma* (1984), and Gordon Welchman's *The Hut 6 Story* (1982). On the first U.S. admissions, see Roberta Wohlstetter, *Pearl Harbor: Warning and Decision* (Stanford, CA: Stanford University Press, 1962).

## 1. ENIGMA

1. Because this book refers to Allied and German militaries, I refer to the German military services and bureaus by their German names (Heer, Marine, Luftwaffe, etc.). The Marine was formally known as the Reichsmarine and Kriegsmarine. For brevity and simplicity, only Marine appears here. Wehrmacht refers to the entire Armed Forces. Each service's Oberkommando (High Command) had an acronym (OKW [Oberkommando der Wehrmacht], OKH, OKM, OKL), and I frequently use these for brevity. The Marine often referred to the Royal Navy as the Admiralty, and both names are found here.

2. NARA: Microfilm T 1022, roll 2675 PG 38660 "Anlageheft 4 zu 'Kriegsspiel Winter 38/39'" Korvettenkaptän Teubner, p. 2.

3. Heinz Bonatz, *Die Deutsche Marine Funkaufklärung* (Darmstadt: Wehr & Wissen, 1970) and NARA: RG 457 HCC Box 604 NR 1571 – History of the German Naval Radio Intelligence Service, written by Bonatz ca. 1950.

4. NARA: RG 457 HCC Box 604 NR 1571 – History of the German Naval Radio Intelligence Service, p. 5. Note that this theme of treachery would reemerge in the Second World War.

5. NARA: RG 457 HCC Box 604 NR 1571 – History of the German Naval Radio Intelligence Service, p. 6. Bonatz would have a similar mind-set through World War II and into the 1970s.

6. See Frank Rowlett's memoir *The Story of Magic* (Laguna Hills, CA: Aegean Park Press, 1998).

7. Correlli Barnett, ed., *Hitler's Generals* (New York: Grove Weidenfeld, 1989), p. 270.

8. See below, as well as Ratcliff, "How Statistics Led the Germans to Believe Enigma Secure..." in *Cryptologia* 27, no. 3 (April 2003): 119–131; and Ray Miller, "The Cryptographic Mathematics of Enigma" (Fort Meade, MD: NSA, n.d.), passim.

9. The mechanics of the Enigma are too complex to detail here, but an excellent description can be found in Andrew Hodges, *Alan Turing: The Enigma* (New York: Simon & Schuster, Inc., 1983), pp. 160–185. The National Cryptologic Museum, Fort Meade, MD, has various Enigmas on display and at least one working model

for the public to try. Although the reflector rotor could be removed from the machine as the other rotors were, in practice most machines held the same rotor all the time.

10. The British altered the commercial Enigma to hold five rotors and changed the rotors' movement and progression. The RAF would call this cipher machine Type X. See Ralph Erskine's "The Development of the Typex" (manuscript) and the U.S. dismissal of the British machine as "nothing but a glorified German Enigma" (NARA: RG 457 HCC Box 804 NR 2323 – M-228 Converter, p. 3). Although OKW/Chi and the Auswärtiges Amt Pers Z considered the Enigma Model K insecure, see Heer's Inspk. 7/VI report on the security of this basic three-rotor model (Box 1098 NR 3448).

11. NSA: DF 187 (Fenner), p. 9.

12. Gilbert Bloch, *Enigma avant Ultra* (Paris, n.p., 1985), p. A1. The Marine had adopted Enigma two years earlier.

13. F. H. Hinsley et al., *British Intelligence in World War II*, Vol. 3, part 2:948. Note the official history also claims (p. 946) the Luftwaffe adopted Enigma in 1935. Hinsley does not explain the discrepancy.

14. See, for example, descriptions in weekly Hut 6 reports in NARA: RG 457 HCC Box 880 NR 2612 – Capt. Walter J. Fried Reports/SSA Liaison with GCCS.

15. The process of enciphering a message twice, either with an additional code or a second run through the original cipher.

16. Each network had two names, one German and one British; thus the special U-boat key in the North Atlantic was known as "Triton" to the Germans and "Shark" to Bletchley Park. The Marine tended to use rather straightforward names, all starting with Enigma M for Marine: Enigma M general, officer, staff, battleship (Schlachtschiff), and so on (NARA: Microcopy T-1022 (German Navy records 1850–1945) Roll 2310, PG 34534, p. 8). BP grouped code names in categories: main Luftwaffe codes were colors (Red, Blue, etc.); weather codes were vegetables, such as Leek, Garlic; Heer codes were birds (Sparrow, Falcon), the SS fruit (Orange, Quince), and the Baudot ciphers were known as "Fish" (Tunny and Sturgeon). See a list of these "rather whimsical, somewhat illogical" names (as a disapproving William Friedman called them) in NARA: RG 457 HCC Box 1009 NR 3175 – Cryptanalytic Report on Yellow Machine, p. 10. For Friedman's opinion, see Box 1126 NR 3620 – E Operations of the GC & CS at Bletchley Park, p. 41.

17. Hinsley, Vol. 3, part 2:957.

18. Miller, "Cryptographic Mathematics," p. 11.

19. As will be discussed later, the Allies largely took a different approach (see chapters 4, 7, and 9, as well as Rejewski's appendix in Józef Garlinski's *The Enigma War* (New York: Scribner & Sons, 1979).

20. BA/MA: RMD 4/949, pp. 17–18.

21. BA/MA: RW4/v. 910, Anlage 5 "übersicht über die Schlüsselverteilung," p. 14. However, someone got tired of always coming up with new daily settings month

after month and began repeating them, as BP soon noticed. For example, in NARA: RG 457 HCC Box 1126 NR 3620 – E Operations, p. 40. See also below.

22. NARA: RG 457 HCC Box 880 NR 2612 – 13 July 1944 report.

23. See Bletchley Park cryptanalysts' discussion in NARA: RG 457 HCC Box 1424 NR 4685 – History of Hut Eight 1939–1945, pp. 49–50.

24. NARA: Microcopy T-1022 (German Navy records 1850–1945), Roll 2310, PG 34534, Flottenkommando 1941, Akte Gkdos 31 "Taktik, Mob. Angl.," p. 8.

25. Ray Miller calculates that the four-rotor Enigma put in place in 1942 for U-boat communications had a theoretical number of possible combinations as high as 2 × $10^{145}$. "Cryptographic Mathematics," p. 12.

26. For example, see interrogations of Erich Hüttenhain, KTB of May 1943, and internal investigations analyzed below; also Wilhelm Flicke, *War Secrets in the Ether*. 2 vols. (Laguna Hills, CA: Aegean Park Press, 1977), pp. 24–26. Fenner apparently had a more sophisticated approach, e.g., NSA: DF 187 (Fenner), p. 9.

27. A Dutch Army evaluator giving his "expert's opinion" on the early Enigma in 1928 or so agreed with this last opinion. A U.S. Army G-2 expert disagreed, believing it possible to crack Enigma without the message settings. William Friedman's team tested the early Enigma in the late 1920s and declared it insecure. See also Herbert Dammert and Franz Kurowski, *Adler Ruft Führerhauptquartier: Führungsfunk an allen Fronten: 1939–1945* (Leoni am Starnberger See: Druffel, 1985).

28. Both British and Germans referred to Marine Enigmas generally as Enigma M and more specifically when necessary M-3 or M-4 to indicate the number of rotors the machine could accommodate at one time. The fourth rotor was smaller than the others and so could not be interchanged with them. See Ralph Erskine, "Naval Enigma: M4 and Its Rotors." *Cryptologia* 11, no. 4 (October 1987): 235–244.

29. NARA: RG 457 HCC Box 579 NR 1414 Project Monogram, memo, pp. 2–3; Box 1098 NR 3448 – Solution [by Germans] of Enigma Type K; Box 880 NR 2612 Appendix to report on Uhr; Miller, "Cryptographic Mathematics," p. 15 on Umkehrwalz Dora.

30. However, these changes never completely foiled decryption. See Hinsley et al., *British Intelligence in World War II*, 4:182.

31. NARA: RG 457 HCC Box 880 NR 2612 – Capt. Walter J. Fried Reports, Hut 6 weekly report, 14 October 1944, p. 2.

32. Miller, "Cryptographic Mathematics," p. 12.

33. Stephen J. Kelley, "Big Machines: The Relative Cryptographic Security of the German Enigma, the Japanese PURPLE, and the U.S. SIGABA/ECM cipher machines in World War II," unpublished manuscript. See also "How Statistics Led the Germans to Believe Enigma Secure."

34. NARA: RG 457 HCC Box 1407 NR 4541 – Codes and Ciphers: Germany – "Aktennotiz 6 zum Chiffrierverfahren mit der Enigmamaschine," p. 4 and "Aktennotiz 5," passim. Oddly, 11 would seem a better choice; see Miller's calculations in "Cryptographic Mathematics."

35. Bletchley Park cryptanalysts soon realized this rule and created an attachment to the bombes, the CSKO [Consecutive Stecker Knock Out], which threw out "stops," including consecutive Stecker pairings. NARA: RG 457 HCC Box 1009 NR 3175 – Cryptanalytic Report on the Yellow Machine, pp. 39–40.
36. Miller, "Cryptographic Mathematics," p. 13.
37. BA/MA: RM7/108, pp. 10–11. This form of organization stood "in stark opposition to improvisation."
38. This indiscriminant use would compromise the high level of Enigma's security. See later chapters for discussion.
39. On this last, see Richard Breitman, *Official Secrets: What the Nazis Planned. What the British and Americans Knew* (New York: Hill and Wang, 1998); and Robert J. Hanyok, *Eavesdropping on Hell: Historical Guide to Western Communications Intelligence and the Holocaust, 1939–1945* (Fort Meade, MD: Center for Cryptologic History, 2005).
40. The traitorous signals in these examples, however, were generally plaintext, important more as sources for enemy D/F than for cryptanalysis. BA/MA: RHD 7:29/1 (24 June 1944), a vivid example. See also later chapters.
41. The Marine expressed admiration for the Allied reaction of complete radio silence after the disappearance of one of their submarines (see chapter 7 and note 50); yet, they did not do likewise. Compare this episode with the loss of U-570 when the Marine believed cipher materials captured but did not change its signaling significantly. NARA: T-1022/1724 (microfilm), p. 205.
42. For more on the double encipherment issue, see Ralph Erskine, with Gilbert Bloch, "Enigma: The Dropping of the Double Encipherment" in *Cryptologia* (July 1986): 97–118; and in Erskine and Michael Smith, eds., *Action This Day*.
43. Sometimes called psillies or psychological cillies. NARA: RG 457 HCC Box 1126 NR 3620 – E Operations of the GC & CS at Bletchley Park 12 August 1943, p. 36. For an excellent discussion of cillies, see Ralph Erskine's appendix to *Action This Day*, with Michael Smith.
44. NARA: RG 457 HCC Box 1424 NR 4685 – History of Hut Eight 1939–1945, pp. 30–31, for example.
45. PRO: HW 14/17, p. 3, for example.
46. NARA: RG 457 HCC Box 1126 NR 3620 – E Operations of the GC & CS at Bletchley Park, p. 40. See also the 1941 recognition of repeats from as much as a year earlier in PRO: HW 14/17, p. 3.
47. NARA: RG 457 HCC Box 880 NR 2612 – Capt. Walter J. Fried Reports/SSA Liaison with GCCS – 14 October 44, p. 2. See also NARA: RG 457 HCC Box 807 NR 2334 – German Cryptographic Memoranda – 1943–1945, Nr. 103 demanding addresses head messages.
48. NARA: RG 457 HCC Box 1126 NR 3620 – E Operations of the GC & CS at Bletchley Park 12 August 1943, p. 39.

49. The Germans appear not to have greatly trusted the Italians: they passed them only "type D" Enigma, not more advanced versions. See BA/MA: RM7/103, p. 91. The National Cryptologic Museum has an Enigma used by the Japanese.

50. NARA: RG 457 HCC Box 880 NR 2612 – Capt. Walter J. Fried Reports/SSA Liaison with GCCS, 13 July 1944.

51. NARA: RG 457 HCC Box 880 NR 2612 – Capt. Walter J. Fried Reports, Hut 6 weekly report, 14 October 1944, p. 6.

52. On the numerous threats to Allied cryptanalytic success, see Erskine and Smith, eds., *Action This Day*; NARA: RG 457 HCC Box 880 NR 2612 – Capt. Walter J. Fried Reports; and Box 1424 NR 4685 – History of Hut Eight, especially 11:19 and conclusion.

53. See NARA: RG 457 HCC Box 880 NR 2612 – Capt. Walter J. Fried Reports/SSA Liaison with GCCS – 15 July 1944, p. 3 and the appendix to the report on Enigma Uhr noting that the Uhr proved an exception to this rule by being "sprung on us with no warning whatever." Other upgrades had always come after "prior notice ... though on several occasions the warnings have been either fragmentary or highly ambiguous."

54. NARA: RG 457 HCC Box 880 NR 2612 – Capt. Walter J. Fried Reports, 19 October 1944, p. 1.

55. Britain's Inter-Departmental Cypher Committee bickered over suitable machines in the 1930s, but the RAF funded O. G. W. Lywood, Wing Commander Signals Division, to develop an improved Enigma. The first two models of his machine Type X debuted by early 1937. Ralph Erskine, "The Development of Typex" (n.p.), pp. 2–3.

## 2. EARLY TRIUMPH

1. Bonatz, *Marine Funkaufklärung*, pp. 86–87 (see Introduction, n. 18).

2. NARA: RG 457 HCC Box 625 NR 1695 – German Naval Communications Intelligence, p. 67.

3. NARA: RG 457 HCCSRH 355, p. 22.

4. Heer and Marine "retained substantial signals departments" presumably for internal communication. J. M. W. Chapman, "No Final Solution," in *Codebreaking and Signals Intelligence*. C. Andrew, ed. (London: Frank Cass, 1986), p. 15.

5. Flicke, *War Secrets*, 1:89.

6. Ibid. See also F. H. Hinsley et al., *British Intelligence in World War II*, 4:296; Chapman, "No Final Solution," p. 26.

7. Hinsley et al., *British Intelligence in World War II*, 4:295; Kahn, *Seizing the Enigma*, p. 73 (see Introduction, n. 3).

8. NARA: RG 165 Box 666. Alex Eysoldt Interrogation 17 April 1945.

9. AA: Adolf Paschke. "Das Chiffrier- und Fernmeldewesen im Auswärtigen Amt." Aktengruppe VS Band 6025, p. 89.

10. NARA: RG 457 HCC Box 145 NR 607 – Account of Recovery of Keys of French-British Interallied Cipher.

11. Flicke, *War Secrets*, 1:115.

12. The RSHA served as the central Reich security, an office under both the NSDAP (Nazi Party) and the Ministry of the Interior. After Admiral Canaris's fall from grace in 1944, the RSHA, under Walter Schellenberg, absorbed the Abwehr as Amt VI. See Schellenberg's memoirs *Aufzeichnungen des letzten Geheimdienstchefs unter Hitler* (London: André Deutsch, Ltd., 1956).

13. "The full title…is the OBERKOMMANDO DER WEHRMACHT/ AMTSGRUPPE WEHRMACHTNACHRICHTENVERBINDUNGSWESEN/ CHIFFRIERABTEILUNG or more conveniently expressed OKW/AG WNV/Abt. CHI or more briefly OKW/CHI or even CHI." NARA: RG 457 HCC Box 880 NR 2612 – "The German Central Cryptographic Organisation (OKW/CHI)," p. 1.

14. Papers of Erich Hüttenhain, p. 2. By 1945, six agencies (Auswärtiges Amt, OKW/Chi, Heer in its Waffenamt (Weapons Office), Marine, Luftwaffe, and Abwehr) developed codes and ciphers. They, too, worked independently.

15. Or "E-Stelle" (for Entzifferungsdienst). Dr. Horst Hauthal, "Beitrag zur Geschichte des Chiffrierwesens im Auswärtigen Amt – 1939–1945," Politisches Archiv, Auswärtiges Amt, Bonn: Aktengruppe VS, Band 6025, p. 2. Pers Z appears in this work only on the peripheries.

16. Paschke, "Das Chiffrier- und Fernmeldewesen," pp. 71–72, 89.

17. Documents released in the 1980s and 1990s revealed the Allies had broken the AA's machine ciphers as well, although they were more sophisticated than Enigma. Since the AA did not use Enigma, it plays only a minor role in this work.

18. The OKW/Chi had its headquarters in Berlin and thus lost most of its records in the Allied bombings of the capital.

19. NARA: RG 457 HCC Box 1112 NR 3555 Report of OKW Code and Ciphers Official, p. 1.

20. NSA: DF 187C (Fenner) p. 1. Note that decentralizing intelligence, particularly cryptanalysis, was more the norm than otherwise in the 1940s. The United States as well as other major belligerents had multiple sigint organizations, although Germany's compartmentalization would reach impressive heights. Britain's centralization, as detailed in later chapters, was unusual.

21. BA/MA: RM7/100, p. 251b; interview with Jürgen Rohwer.

22. NARA: RG 457 HCC Box 1400 NR 4644 – The Cryptologic Service in World War II, p. 37. Like the Heer, the Luftwaffe focused primarily on the Soviets after June 1941, considering the Western theaters and enemies of secondary importance.

23. NARA: RG 457 HCC Box 594 NR 1515 – German Operational Intelligence, p. 10. Division 12, Fremde Heer Ost, was established 10 Nov. 1938. See David Kahn, *Hitler's Spies* (New York: Macmillan Publishing Co., Inc., 1978), p. 52; Fremde Heer West was Division 3.

24. "W-LEIT" would later have its headquarters in Paris. NARA: RG 457 HCC Box 1316 NR 3948 – Interrogation Reports on Ten German/Italian PW's (including Luftwaffe interceptors), p. 5. Heer signals intelligence also directed their interception through two centers, east and west (Leitstelle Ost, Leitstelle West). NARA: RG 457 HCC Box 594 NR 1515 – German Operational Intelligence, p. 12.

25. NSA: DF 187C (Fenner), pp. 1–2. This strict division appears to have faded later in the war, as General Praun mentions the Heer intercepting Allied air force signals. "German Radio Intelligence," in John J. Mendelsohn, *Intelligence, Counterintelligence and Military Deception During the World War II Era* (New York: Garland Publishing, Inc., 1989), p. 71.

26. NARA: RG 457 HCC Box 180 NR 842 – POW Report/German, p. 1.

27. NARA: RG 457 HCC Box 1316 NR 3948 – Interrogation Reports, p. 2.

28. NARA: RG 457 HCC Box 1327 NR 4003 – Organization of German Communication Intelligence Command, p. 6.

29. According to von Lingen, of these 550–650 male cryptanalysts, 10 percent were "really good." NARA: RG 457 HCC Box 1400 NR 4644 – Cryptologic Service in World War II, p. 41.

30. NARA: RG 457 HCC Box 1400 NR 4644 – The Cryptologic Service in World War II, p. 40. Note that Britain's effort at Bletchley Park had a reversed pyramid with far fewer pure cryptanalysts in relation to log readers, intelligence officers, and translators. See below.

31. Hans-Otto Behrendt, *Rommel's Intelligence in the Desert Campaign* (London: William Kimber, 1985; German edition by Rombach, 1980), p. 52.

32. Günther Gellermann, *…und lauschten für Hitler: Geheime Reichssache: Die Abhörzentralen des Dritten Reiches* (Stuttgart: Bernard & Graefe Verlag, 1991), pp. 18–19. The Forschungsamt was created in early 1933 as a civilian department and originally financed by the Prussian state budget.

33. The section tapping Party members' phones earned the nickname "Giftküche" (poison kitchen). NARA: RG 331, Box 3, Lothar Guenthar interrogation, October 1944.

34. Gellermann, *…und lauscht*, p. 63.

35. NARA: RG 457 HCC Box 1400 NR 4644 – The Cryptologic Service in World War II, p. 9.

36. NARA: RG 457 HCC Box 1112 NR 3554 – Interrogation of Lt. Col. Nielsen – 20 May 1945, p. 2.

37. NARA: RG 457 HCC Box 1400 NR 4644 – The Cryptologic Service in World War II, p. 45. The details of German cryptanalytic cooperation with other nations lie beyond the scope of this work and would make an excellent study. In general, contact with other sigint bureaus, such as those in Japan and Italy, occurred along service lines rather than in a coordinated, centralized fashion.

38. NARA: RG 457 HCC Box 1400 NR 4644 – The Cryptologic Service in World War II, pp. 40–41. See also NSA Museum Library: DF 187 (Fenner), p. 12.

39. NARA: RG 457 HCC Box 1400 NR 4644 – The Cryptologic Service in World War II, pp. 40–41, 44.

40. NARA: RG 457 HCC Box 625 NR 1695 – German Naval Communications Intelligence, p. 68. The daily reports apparently did not survive the war, and the bimonthly reports are "anything but complete." In 1944, there were four intercept detachments – Flanders, Brittany, Wilhelmshaven, and Pomeranian, p. 60.

41. Mentioned as early as 29 March 1941, the units separated 26 September 1941. BA/MA: RM7/104, p. 129.

42. BA/MA: RM7/104 1 Okt 1941, p. 132.

43. Traffic analysis (TA) requires tracking signals, usually undecrypted, by origin, length, and number, and comparing this information with past experience to project bombing raids, offensives, or retreats.

44. Code de Service Tactic; Tous Batiments Militaire (rated most important by German officers), Batiments de Guerre (French Navy cipher) and Rayon Diplomatique. NARA: RG 457 HCC Box 743 NR 1860 – Radio Intercept and Cryptanalysis (German), p. 28.

45. NARA: RG 457 HCC Box 743 NR 1860 – Radio Intercept and Cryptanalysis (German), p. 20. Note that this postwar self-assessment of Marine intelligence leans toward a rosy, rather uncritical, depiction of the service.

46. NARA: RG 457 Entry 9003 B and X-B Berichte; B-Bericht 6/40 11.2.40, indicates that these were decrypted intercepts.

47. NARA: RG 457 Entry 9003 Bericht 7/40 18.2.40, pp. 13–14.

48. NARA: RG 457 Entry 9003 Bericht 6/40 11.2.40, p. 16.

49. NARA: RG 457 Entry 9003 Box 2, vol. 2, p. 23.

50. NARA: RG 457 Entry 9003 Bericht 25/40 23.6.40, p. 22.

51. NARA: RG 457 HCC Box 1400 NR 4644 – The Cryptologic Service in World War II, pp. 16, 18, 30.

52. NARA: RG 457 HCC Box 1400 NR 4644 – The Cryptologic Service in World War II, p. 24, and mention of extensive card file compiled by "Content Evaluation" section, p. 27.

53. No evidence has emerged that in fact FA did construct these cipher machines. See NARA: RG 457 HCC Box 1394 NR 4459 – Russian Baudot Teletype Scrambler, p. 2. The three cryptologists were from Wa Prüf 7. The full story of German successes against Soviet codes and ciphers lies beyond the scope of this work.

54. NARA: RG 457 HCC Box 1400 NR 4644 – The Cryptologic Service in World War II, pp. 30, 50–51. The author Edwin von Lingen notes that this cryptanalytic success did not necessarily translate into operational successes because the Luftwaffe "did not have means for carrying out countermeasures." Nonetheless, OKL "continued to enter [the information] very carefully in the situation charts, but generally this entry was the end of the story," pp. 50–51.

55. PRO: HW 14/60 memo to C.S.S. 2 December 1942.

56. NARA: RG 457 HCC Box 1277 NR 3732 – Liaison with French on Signals Intelligence Matters; Boxes 1405–1409 NR 4541 – Codes and Ciphers:

Germany folder 11. The Wehrmacht acquired Vichy French codes under the 1940 Armistice and also broke Giraudist signals.

57. NARA: RG 457 HCC Box 22 NR 188 "Deciphering Reports-German" E-Bericht 1/44 der NAASt. 5, p. 16 (emphasis in original).
58. NARA: RG 165 (WD General Staff) Box 382, Vol. I, p. 20.
59. NARA: RG 457 HCC Box 22 NR 188 – "Deciphering Reports-German," p. 17.
60. NARA: RG 457 HCC Box 22 NR 188 – "Deciphering Reports-German," p. 6; also Box 625 NR 1695 – German Naval Communications Intelligence, p. 66.
61. Particularly the Slidex and Codex codes. NARA: RG 457 HCC Box 769 NR 1995 – Reports on Interrogations of Werner Graupe and Herbert Schwartz 9 December 1944, p. 10. The Heer also had some luck late in the war against British coordinates encrypted by MAPLAY superencipherment, see NARA: RG 457 HCC Box 22 NR 188 – "Deciphering Reports-German," p. 9.
62. NARA: RG 457 HCC Box 192 NR 899 – Intelligence Summaries (Blue) #1–53. 19 June 1945 summary, p. 3. The American interrogators loved to add such tidbits of praise in their reports. They added that "it was known at the time that the radio reports from the U.S. Legation in Berne were being read by the Germans, but it was not possible to mend matters because the diplomatic bag going to Berne was also not secure."
63. Henry Picker, *Hitler's Tischgespräche im Führerhauptquartier* (Stuttgart: Seewald Verlag, 1976).
64. NARA: RG 457 HCC Box 743 NR 1860 – Radio Intercept and Cryptanalysis (German), p. 31.
65. NARA: RG 457 HCC Box 1277 NR 3737 – German Sigint Activities, undated "cross reference sheet."
66. Ibid. "Report of a Meeting with OKW Radio Representatives at Supreme HQ AEF" (underlining in original).
67. NARA: RG 457 HCC Box 1316 NR 3948 – Interrogation Reports, p. 6.
68. NARA: RG 457 HCC Box 1277 NR 3737 – German Sigint Activities Intelligence Bulletin No. 2/51.
69. NARA: RG 457 HCC Box 1367 NR 4263 – Reports on Enemy Successes Against U.S. Crypto Systems, 17 May 1945, pp. 4–5.
70. NARA: RG 457 HCC Box 769 NR 1995 – Reports on Interrogation of Werner Graupe and Herbert Schwartz, 9 December 1944, p. 10.
71. NARA: RG 457 HCC Box 1316 NR 3948 – Interrogation Reports, p. 6.
72. NARA: RG 457 HCC BOX 743 NR 1860 – Radio Intercept and Cryptanalysis (German), p. 14. Indeed, the B-Dienst often made good use of captured material, ordering that even material "floating in the water, which have become very illegible as a result of oil and other influence, and…seem worthless, are to be picked up nevertheless…." NARA: RG 38 (Crane material) 630A 5/2/6, Box 26 3222/24 "German SIGINT Organization."

73. See NARA: RG 457 Entry 9003 Bericht 17/40, p. 13, as well as the X-B-Berichte in Box 10 (24 April 1944–20 August 1944), which show they still rely on RAF reconnaissance signals.

74. Mentioned in NARA: RG 457 HCC Box 743 NR 1860 – Radio Intercept and Cryptanalysis (German), p. 23.

75. See NARA: RG 457 HCC Box 743 NR 1860 – Radio Intercept and Cryptanalysis (German), pp. 11–12.

76. NARA: RG 457 HCC Box 625 NR 1695 – German Naval Communications Intelligence, p. 65.

77. Direction Finding (D/F; with later British versions called HF/DF or Huff Duff, High Frequency Direction Finding) traces a signal back to its point of origin and reveals the position of its sender, whether submarine, bomber squadron, field command, or headquarters.

78. NARA: RG 457 Entry 9003 "Spezial-Nachricht Nr. 2. vom 25.7.1940," p. 6. D/F uses triangulation to locate the origin of a signal.

79. NARA: RG 457 Entry 9003 "Spezial-Nachricht Nr. 2. vom 25.7.1940," p. 9.

80. NARA: RG 457 HCC Box 743 NR 1860 – Radio Intercept and Cryptanalysis (German), p. 10.

81. See description of these teams in NARA: RG 457 HCC Box 743 NR 1860 – Radio Intercept and Cryptanalysis (German), p. 14.

82. By midwar the Allies also developed on-board intercept teams, starting in the Mediterranean with "Y Parties afloat"; see Aileen Clayton's *The Enemy Is Listening* (New York: Ballantine, 1980), pp. 250–251. The history of on-board intercept teams, whether German or Allied, remains unwritten.

83. NARA: RG 457 HCC Box 743 NR 1860 – Radio Intercept and Cryptanalysis (German) – report by German ex-Flag Officers dated 18 September 1950, pp. 3–4.

84. NARA: RG 457 Entry 9003 Bericht 24/40 16.6.40, p. 21; HCC Box 73 NR 330 – Names and Addresses of former B-Dienst personnel.

85. NARA: RG 457 SRH 368. This situation continued until Naval Cypher No 5 took effect in June 1943. B-Dienst read nothing June–September 1943, read something on 4 out of 87 convoys September 1943–March 1944. See chart in NSA: European Axis Signals Intelligence in World War II as Revealed by TICOM Investigations and by other Prisoner of War Interrogations and Captured Material.

86. See the list in NARA: RG 457 HCC Box 23 NR 192 "Convoy Radio Communications of the Allies in World War II/German," p. 4 and in Box 743 NR 1860 – Radio Intercept and Cryptanalysis (German) – report dated 18 September 1950, p. 9.

87. See, for example, NARA: RG 457 Entry 9003 B-Berichte 25/40 23.6.1940, p. 20. Allied restrictions on information going to Halifax suggest they suspected that leak. See memos in RG 38 (Crane files) Box 49 File: 3840/20 – COMINCH U-BOAT SUMMARIES January–March 1943. For Admiral Western Approaches

leaks: RG 457 HCC Box 743 NR 1860 – Radio Intercept and Cryptanalysis (German), p. 14.

88. NARA: RG 457 HCC Box 743 NR 1862 – German Navy's Use of Special Intelligence (using penciled page numbers at bottom), p. 5. (re: July 1940). Also, pp. 18, 24.

89. See RG 457 Entry 9003 Bericht 34/40 25.8.1940, p. 1.

90. NARA: RG 457 HCC Box 743 NR 1860 – Radio Intercept and Cryptanalysis (German) – report dated 18 September 1950, p. 6.

91. See, for example, X-B-Bericht 2/42 (5.1.–11.1.1942) in NARA: RG 457 Entry 9003.

92. The postwar Naval Historical Team stated "that for various reasons German D/F was not satisfactory. It was only within home waters that any practical benefits were derived therefrom." NARA: RG 457 HCC Box 743 NR 1860 – Radio Intercept and Cryptanalysis (German), pp. 15–16. See also Box 23, "Convoy Radio Communications of the Allies in World War II/German," p. 2.

93. NARA: RG 457 HCC Box 743 NR 1860 – Radio Intercept and Cryptanalysis (German) – report dated 18 September 1950, p. 8.

94. See, for example, NARA: RG 457 HCC Box 594 NR 1515 – German Operational Intelligence, p. 15, on the OKH tactical intelligence organization. Postwar German analyses concur, including the German Naval Historical Team's and Edwin von Lingen's histories (both in the HCC).

95. NARA: RG 457 HCC Box 769 NR 1995 – Reports on Interrogations of Werner Graupe and Herbert Schwartz, 9 December 1944, p. 13.

96. NARA: RG 457 HCC Box 743 NR 1862 – German Navy's Use of Special Intelligence, p. 78; "German success against convoy SC 107, representative of their long success in reading the Combined Cypher, stands in remarkable contrast to their failure to anticipate the Allied invasion of North Africa on 8 November."

97. For example, in their postwar report Marine flag officers describe the radio intercept service as "an important factor…more than only for the submarine war." NARA: RG 457 HCC Box 743 NR 1860 – Radio Intercept and Cryptanalysis (German), p. 15.

3. OF NO MUTUAL ASSISTANCE

1. NARA: RG 457 HCC Box 1112 NR 3555 – Report of OKW Code and Ciphers Official, p. 1.

2. Flicke, *War Secrets in the Ether*, 2:300.

3. General A. Praun in *German Radio Intelligence and the Soldatensender*, introduction by John Mendelsohn (New York: Garland, 1989). (NA: RG 338, Mans. P-038, General A. Praun), p. 177. Heer sigint did not have time to change before the war ended.

4. NSA: DF 187C (Fenner), p. 4.

5. NARA: RG 457 HCC Box 1112 NR 3554 – Interrogation of Lt. Col. Nielsen, p. 2. He did not support this statement, however.

6. NSA: DF 187C (Fenner), p. 1.

7. AA/PA: Adolf Paschke, "Das Chiffrier- und Fernmeldewesen, pp. 66–68.

8. This plan has similarities to U.S. agreements between bureaus of the same era. See Robert Benson, *A History of U.S. Communications Intelligence during World War II: Policy and Administration* (Fort Meade, MD: National Security Agency, 1997).

9. NSA: DF 187 (Fenner), p. 6.

10. Flicke, *War Secrets*, 1:106.

11. AA: Paschke, "Das Chiffrier- und Fernmeldewesen," pp. 77–78.

12. Bennett, *Behind the Battle*, p. 122. He, a former Allied intelligence officer, noted that "the Axis never remedied [this problem]; the Allies did – in the nick of time."

13. NARA: RG 457 HCC Box 1382 NR 4369 – Military HQs and Installations in Germany (Feb 1945).

14. KTB/Skl [Marine war diaries] 10 March 1940, vol. 7, p. 64.

15. Gellermann, *...und lauschten für Hitler*, pp. 104, 106. Arrangements for some type of Luftwaffe/Marine cooperation were made, however. NARA: RG 457 HCC Box 622 NR 1678 – Joint Communications Regulations for Luftwaffe and Navy in Collaboration.

16. BA/MA: RM7/104, 24 September 1941. The B-Dienst informed the squadron (Luftflotte 3) that except in special cases, intelligence from decrypts would not be passed on, RM7/105, 21 December 1942.

17. BA/MA: RM7/108, 6 May 1944, p. 109. By this time the Marine B-Dienst had been unable to read Britain's two main ciphers since June 1943 and June 1944. They could read only some minor traffic and a convoy cipher for stragglers.

18. NARA: RG 457 HCC Boxes 1405–1409 NR 4541 – Codes and Ciphers: Germany, German Cryptanalytic Documents.

19. NARA: RG 457 HCC Box 1112 NR 3555 – Report of OKW Code and Ciphers Official, p. 1; see chapter 2.

20. Praun, in *German Radio Intelligence*, p. 63.

21. These three paragraphs draw on NARA: RG 457 HCC Box 1400 NR 4644 – The Cryptologic Service in World War II, pp. 37–40, 42.

22. NARA: RG 457 HCC Box 1400 NR 4644 – The Cryptologic Service in World War II, p. 42.

23. See the full description of this collaboration in NARA: RG 457 HCC Box 1400 NR 4644 – The Cryptologic Service in World War II, pp. 37–42.

24. For an overview of Canaris, the Abwehr, and the RSHA, see such sources as André Brissaud, *Canaris* (New York: Grosset & Dunlap, 1974); Gert Buchheit, *Der deutsche Geheimdienst: Geschichte der militärischen Abwehr* (München: List, 1966); H. Hohne, *The General Was a Spy* (New York: Coward, McCann &

Geoghegan, Inc., 1971); and Walter Schellenberg, *Aufzeichnungen des letzten Geheimdienst-chefs unter Hitler* (London: André Deutsch, Ltd., 1956).

25. NARA: RG 457 HCC Box 1400 NR 4644 – The Cryptologic Service in World War II, p. 49. (All quotes in this paragraph.)

26. NSA: DF 187C (Fenner), p. 4. Although Fenner continued such deciphering "because to my mind the Army cryptanalytic section could not successfully handle certain problems alone."

27. Peter Cremer, *U-Boat Commander*, trans. Lawrence Wilson (Annapolis, MD: Naval Institute Press, 1984), p. 34. The Marine requested its own reconnaissance planes because the Luftwaffe would not provide them. "The attempts at direct collaboration with the Luftwaffe have been disappointing. In no case have they succeeded in directing U-boats to the enemy." NARA: Microcopy T-1022/4063 PG 30288, 6 May 1941.

28. NARA: Microcopy T-1022 roll 4063 PG 30315, 11 January 1943.

29. BA/MA: RM7/100 p. 255b, 31 July 1944. Although the Marine and Luftwaffe discussed closer cooperation in early 1941, just getting them to use the same radio frequency for joint operations took until February 1942. KTB/Skl 26 Feb 1940, VI, p. 156; 16 Feb 1942, XXX, p. 162; RM7/104 "Ruckblick . . . im ersten halbjahr 1941," p. 100.

30. NARA: RG 457 HCC Box 1400 NR 4644 – The Cryptologic Service in World War II, p. 40.

31. NARA: RG 457 HCC Box 1400 NR 4644 – The Cryptologic Service in World War II, p. 37.

32. Gordon Craig, *The Germans* (New York: Putnam, 1982), p. 250. See also Craig's discussion of the Kaiserreich's struggle to provide civilian control of the Prussian Army in *The Politics of the Prussian Army* (Oxford: Oxford University Press, 1955).

33. Raymond Toliver and Hanns J. Scharff, *The Interrogator: The Story of Hanns Scharff* (Fallbrook, CA: Aero, 1978), p. 305. See AA: Paschke, "Das Chiffrier- und Fernmeldewesen," pp. 43, 49, on the AA's hiring and search for the rare "universal-cryptologists" such as Dr. Josef Seifert.

34. Flicke, *War Secrets*, 1:115. Many World War I officers were recalled for "administrative" work after 1934. Often these officers' major qualification was military service in World War I. NSA: DF 187A (Fenner), p. 22.

35. NSA: DF 187A (Fenner), p. 14.

36. KTB/Skl 15 Dec 1941, XXVIII, p. 153; 25 July 1940, XI, p. 201.

37. NARA: RG 457 HCC Box 1400 NR 4644 – The Cryptologic Service in World War II, p. 21.

38. Toliver and Scharff, *The Interrogator*, p. 309.

39. Flicke, *War Secrets*, p. 154. After Stalingrad, twenty-five generals were relieved of duty. Those suspected in the 20 July 1944 plot were executed.

40. KTB/Skl – 16 September 1939, I, p. 70. Note that until 1944 the traditional apolitical restrictions on the military meant that armed forces personnel were

not to be active members of political parties (including the Nazi Party), see Kahn, *Hitler's Spies*, p. 43.

41. NARA: RG 165 Box 666 – Lt. Gen Schimpf's interrogation 20 March 1945. See also the arguments about the internalization of Nazi thinking set forth in Omar Bartov's *Hitler's Army* (Oxford: Oxford University Press, 1991).

42. Gellermann, *...und lauschten*, p. 169.

43. NARA: RG 457 HCC Box 1112 NR 3560 – Meetings between German Military Mission to Supreme HQ, AEF.

44. Around May 1943, "an order plac[ed] the governance of ciphers in use with the Abwehr entirely in the hands of OKW/CHI" NARA: RG 457 HCC Box 808 NR 2612 – Fried Report, p. 1.

45. NSA: DF 187A (Fenner), p. 26.

46. Papers of Erich Hüttenhain, p. 3–4.

47. NSA: DF 187A (Fenner), p. 26.

48. NARA: RG 457 HCC Box 1112 NR 3555 – Report of OKW Code and Ciphers Official, p. 1.

49. Ibid., p. 1.

50. NARA: RG 457 HCC Box 1424 NR 4685 – History of Hut 8 Chapter XI, pp. 1–2, on Porpoise's 1944 use of double encipherment, although the net had moved to four-rotor machines.

51. AA/PA: Paschke, "Das Chiffrier- und Fernmeldewesen," pp. 66–68.

52. Hüttenhain papers, p. 3.

53. Ibid.

54. Nor did the Kryha cipher machine. AA: Hauthal, "Beitrag zur Geschichte des Chiffrierwesens im Auswärtigen Amt – 1939–1945," p. 51.

55. AA/PA: Paschke, "Das Chiffrier- und Fernmeldewesen," pp. 54–55.

56. Dr. Horst Hauthal mentions that F. H. Hinsley et al., *British Intelligence in World War II*, Vol. 3, pt. 1, stated that the Allies decrypted versions of the T-52 by using more than four hundred people and a "rapid calculating machine which used at that time more than 2400 [vacuum] tubes." He maintains, however, that the official history does not mention the Auswärtiges Amt's connection using the T-52 between Berlin and Madrid. Hauthal, "Beitrag zur Geschichte...," pp. 52–53; Paschke, "Das Chiffrier- und Fernmeldewesen," p. 69.

57. See, for example, decrypts of this Berlin-Madrid Auswärtiges Amt line in the National Archives, RG 457 HCC Box 192 NR 899 – "Intelligence Summaries – Blue."

58. Flicke, *War Secrets*, 2:156–158. This does not, however, demonstrate that the Germans had cracked the Japanese diplomatic cipher, although some contend the Pers Z cracked the sophisticated cipher machine, nicknamed "Purple" by U.S. cryptanalysts. This contention remains unproved. Some historians have suggested to me that a German agency bugged the Japanese embassy. See J. Rohwer, "International Historiography about Signals Intelligence," *Enigma Bulletin* 2 (May 1997): 3–16.

59. KTB/Skl – 19 December 1941, 28:200.
60. The Allies recognized the need for cooperation across traditional lines, and the U.S. Navy's Japanese Intelligence section readily passed Oshima's signals to the Anglo-American European section. These reports to Tokyo were well informed and a great boon to the Allies. See Carl Boyd, *Hitler's Japanese Confidant* (Lawrence: University Press of Kansas, 1993); and Oshima's decrypted report in *ULTRA, MAGIC and the Allies*. T. Mulligan, ed. (New York: Garland, 1989).
61. NSA: DF 187D (Fenner), p. 10.
62. See Klaus-Jürgen Müller, *Armee, Politik und Gesellschaft in Deutschland 1933–45* (Manchester: Manchester University Press, 1987), passim; Hans-Ulrich Wehler, *The German Empire 1871–1918*, trans. K. Traynor (New York: Berg Publishers, 1985) (German original 1973), p. 159; Craig, *The Politics of the Prussian Army 1640–1945*, pp. 218, 425–426.
63. KTB/Skl – 22 May 1940, 9:191.
64. I am indebted to Timothy Mulligan for his insights into the German Marine, its personnel, and its culture.
65. Increased signaling increases the risk of successful enemy cryptanalysis and of exposure to locating devices. The World War II belligerents knew each other capable of locating the source of radio signals through direction finding, locating a signal by triangulation – the longer and more frequent the signals, the more likely the enemy's location efforts will succeed. Also, increased signals mean more material for enemy cryptanalysts.

## 4. THE WORK OF STATION X

1. Although during the war, GC&CS's name changed to Government Communications Headquarters (GCHQ), the old name will be used here throughout.
2. They had considerable success against other nations' cryptosystems as well, including some American systems. Allied successes against nations other than Germany are beyond the scope of this work. For successes against neutral nations, see David Alvarez, *Secret Messages: Codebreaking and American Diplomacy, 1930–1945* (Lawrence: University Press of Kansas, 2000); against other Axis systems, see Steven Budiansky, *Battle of Wits: The Complete Story of Codebreaking in World War II* (New York: The Free Press, 2000); against Japanese and other Asian systems, see Alan Stripp, *Codebreaker in the Far East* (Oxford: Oxford University Press, 1989).
3. Room 40 had cracked German naval codes using codebooks salvaged from the captured German ship *Magdeburg* in August 1914. See Patrick Beesley, "Das Signalbuch der 'Magdeburg' half den Ersten Weltkrieg zu gewinnen," *Marine Rundschau* 78, no. 5 (1981): 273–276.
4. To name just two examples, intelligence from decrypts helped save the British Home Fleet from being completely surprised in the Battle of Jutland in 1916 and, with its deciphering of the Zimmermann telegram, brought the United States

into the war firmly on Britain's side. For the section's history, see Patrick Beesley, *Room 40* (New York: Harcourt Brace Jovanovitch, 1982).

5. 1 April 1922. PRO: HW 3/16 – Historical memos by W. F. Clarke, p. 7. Also, William Clarke, "GC&CS," *Cryptologia* 11, no. 4 (Oct. 1987): 221.

6. In Britain's naval intelligence during the interwar period, the entire staff served as civilians, except for the naval officer in charge. PRO: ADM 223/84: NID 0135/37 – Report on Operational Intelligence by W.M.J., 11 February 1937.

7. Wesley Wark, *The Ultimate Enemy: British Intelligence and Nazi Germany 1933–1945* (Ithaca, NY: Cornell University Press, 1985), p. 188; and Smith, *The Ultra Magic Deals*, p. 21.

8. Smith, *The Ultra Magic Deals*, pp. 26–27 (see Introduction, n. 9).

9. Richard Woytak, *On the Border of War and Peace*, p. 76. See also Kozaczuk, *Enigma*, pp. 261, 269. On the Polish contribution, see also Gustave Bertrand, *Enigma ou la plus grande énigme de la guerre 1939–1945* (Paris: Plon, 1973); Bloch, *Enigma avant Ultra*, Garlinski, *The Enigma War*; Linda Y. Gouazé, "Needles and Haystacks: The Search for Ultra in the 1930s" (MA thesis, Naval Postgraduate School, 1983); and Irene Young, *Enigma* (Edinburgh: Mainstream Press, 1990).

10. Marian Rejewski believed that, with more personnel, they could have easily read 90 percent of the signals. Kozaczuk, *Enigma*, p. 265.

11. Bloch, *Enigma avant Ultra*, p. B5.

12. *Informationheft*, 1940, quoted in Wilhelm Agrell and Bo Huldt, eds. *Clio Goes Spying* (Lund, Sweden: University of Lund, 1983), p. 12.

13. NARA: RG 457 HCC Box 1126 NR 3620 – E Operations of the GC & CS at Bletchley Park, p. 2.

14. See Calvocoressi, *Top Secret ULTRA*, p. 45; F. H. Hinsley et al., *British Intelligence in World War II*, abridged ed. (London: HMSO, 1990), p. 117. Permanent GC&CS staff "grew from 168 in 1939 to 3789 in 1945 … [B]y the end of the war the annual cost of [just the temporary staff] had reached the considerable sum of 220,000." Eunan O'Halpin, "Financing British Intelligence," in *British and American Approaches to Intelligence*, ed. K. G. Robertson (London: Macmillan Press, 1987), p. 203.

15. NARA: RG 457 SRH 364, p. 89.

16. Carman Blacker, for example, "Recollections of *Temps perdu* at Bletchley Park," in *Codebreakers: The Inside Story of Bletchley Park*, ed. F. H. Hinsley and Alan Stripp (Oxford: Oxford University Press, 1993), pp. 300–305.

17. PRO: ADM 223/84: NID 0135/37 – Report on Operational Intelligence by W.M.J., 11 February 1937.

18. Although no documents explicitly state Marlowe worked in intelligence, since J. Leslie Hotson's analysis of the Privy Council Register entry on Marlowe's conduct, historians generally accept this explanation. See J. Leslie Hotson, *The Death of Christopher Marlowe* (New York: Russell & Russell, 1925), pp. 58, 62, 67; and Charles Nicholls, *The Reckoning: The Murder of Christopher Marlowe* (New York: Harcourt Brace, 1992).

19. Christopher Andrew, *Her Majesty's Secret Service* (New York: Viking, 1986), p. 25; and Richard Deacon, *A History of the British Secret Service* (London: Frederick Muller Ltd., 1969), p. 125.

20. Christopher Andrew, "F. H. Hinsley and the Cambridge Moles," in *Diplomacy and Intelligence*, ed. R. Langhorne (Cambridge: Cambridge University Press, 1985), notes that dons were official "decyphers" in the seventeenth and eighteenth centuries (p. 33).

21. I am grateful to German historian Eberhard Jäckel for pointing out the significance of this location and to Anthony Adamthwaite for the information on the "Golden Triangle."

22. In spite of the infamous 1933 Oxford Union vote to fight for neither king nor country, "the Admiralty [had] a list of 'gentlemen who had offered their services to the Admiralty in the event of hostilities'." Calvocoressi, *Top Secret Ultra*, p. 12.

23. A. G. Denniston, "The Government Code and Cypher School Between the Wars," in *Codebreaking and Signals Intelligence*, ed. Christopher Andrew (London: Frank Cass, 1986), p. 52. See also, W. F. Clarke's comments in PRO: HW 3/16, chapter V, p. 8.

24. NARA: RG 457 HCC Box 1417 NR 4633 – Col. McCormack's trip to London 1943, p. 1.

25. NARA: RG 457 HCC Box 1126 NR 3620 – E Operations of the GC & CS at Bletchley Park, p. 70; Bennett, *Ultra in the West*, p. x. Jones's directives fill entire files at the PRO: e.g., HW 3/123 and 124.

26. Ibid. McCormack himself was formerly a New York lawyer; by 1943 he served on the General Staff Corps and would become director of Intelligence.

27. While the same skill might be required of all students of languages, "modern linguists tended to be used rather for [pure] translation work." Patrick Wilkinson in Hinsley and Stripp, *Codebreakers*, p. 63. Eric Birley drew on his academic research on the Imperial Roman Army's order of battle to reconstruct the Wehrmacht's order of battle and to educate other intelligence officers in uncovering and updating the German military structure. Interview with Professor Ralph Bennett; Robert Slusser in Hinsley and Stripp, pp. 74–75. Professor Birley later told students of his wartime use of Roman military history – without mentioning Ultra, of course. Interview with Prof. A. Adamthwaite.

28. Interview with Ralph Bennett.

29. Hinsley and Stripp, *The Codebreakers*, p. 113.

30. Christopher Andrew, "F. H. Hinsley," pp. 35–36.

31. NARA: RG 457 HCC Box 1368 NR 4276 – US Cryptographic Queries and Information, Provided ONI 1920–1941 – 19 June 1934 letter to Lieutenant W. W. Bayley, USN (ret) referring to "the Friendly Group," which became the American Cryptogram Association.

32. Interview with Alan Stripp.

33. In Britain, once accepted to, say, Cambridge, one's university "finances were almost assured." Interview with Alan Stripp. Naturally, this system still favored certain classes and abilities and made little compensation for the early effects of poverty and lack of opportunity. Deborah Thom, "The 1944 Education Act: The 'Art of the Possible'?" in *War and Social Change: British Society in the Second World War*, ed. Harold Smith (Manchester: Manchester University Press, 1986), p. 101.

34. Deacon, *A History of the British Secret Service*, p. 187.

35. In World War II, unlike World War I, women were subject to full military discipline in the auxiliaries, although they did not need to handle lethal weapons "unless they signified willingness to do so in writing." Arthur Marwick, "Problems and Consequences of Organizing Society for Total War," in *Mobilization for Total War* (Ontario: W. Laurier University Press, 1981), p. 3; Harold L. Smith, "The Effect of the War on the Status of Women," in *War and Social Change*, pp. 212–214.

36. Diana Payne, in Hinsley and Stripp, *The Codebreakers*, p. 137.

37. NARA: RG 457 HCC Box 1026 NR 3283 – History of Converter M-134-C, Vol. 3, p. 188.

38. Daphne Humphreys Baker papers, Imperial War Museum, p. 9. American women served as the first US "computer," performing all the countless calculations needed for the A-bomb research in Los Alamos, NM. NPR's "Morning Edition," 14 July 1994.

39. Aileen Clayton, *The Enemy Is Listening* (London: Hutchinson & Co., Ltd., 1980), p. 323. She tells of women working as intercept operators in various theaters, combat zones, even bombing raids, and one who was killed in action.

40. Calvocoressi, *Top Secret ULTRA*, p. 61.

41. Clarke, "BP 1941–45," *Cryptologia* 12 (April 1988): 93. For further examples of women working on Ultra, see Denniston in *British and American Approaches to Intelligence*, p. 127; and the collected papers of various women's auxiliary participants at the Imperial War Museum, London.

42. Peter Twinn in Hinsley and Stripp, *The Codebreakers*, p. 130. "Cribs" referred to a short list of likely combinations or solutions to a coded message, usually based on analysts' past experience with a particular operator or message type. See also accounts in *Action This Day*, eds. R. Erskine and M. Smith (London: Bantam Press, 2001); and Penelope Fitzgerald, *The Knox Brothers* (Washington, DC: Counterpoint, 2000).

43. Hodges, *Alan Turing*, p. 195. Hilary Brett-Smith also joined Hut 8. Her name's uncertain (to the British) gender gave her a man's salary. David Kahn, *Seizing the Enigma* (Boston: Houghton Mifflin, 1991), pp. 138–139.

44. NARA: RG 457 HCC Box 1424 NR 4685 – History of Hut Eight 1939–1945 by A. P. Mahon, p. 31.

45. NARA: RG 457 HCC Box 1417 NR 4633 – Col. McCormack's trip to London 1943, p. 1. See also PRO: HW 14/99.

46. NARA: RG 457 HCC Box 1417 NR 4633 – Col. McCormack's trip to London 1943, p. 1. See also his response to the letter of complaint by BP staff, reproduced in *Intelligence and National Security* 1, no. 2 (May 1986): 272–276.

47. Hinsley and Stripp, *The Codebreakers*, p. 57. Americans "too were temporarily mobilized civilians." Calvocoressi, *Top Secret ULTRA*, p. 63.

48. Smith, *The Ultra Magic Deals*, pp. 150–152, citing NSA Cryptologic History, p. 125.

49. William Bundy. "Some of My Wartime Experiences," *Cryptologia* 11, no. 2 (April 1987): 65–77, 69; interview with Sir Edward Thomas.

50. Ronald Lewin, *Ultra Goes to War* (New York: McGraw-Hill, 1978), p. 140. See the description of these lieutenants in the next chapter's discussion of Special Liaison Units.

51. NARA: RG 457 SRH 364, p. 93.

52. Bennett interview.

53. Thomas interview; Bundy, "Some of My Wartime Experiences," p. 69.

54. NARA: RG 457 HCC Box 699 NR 1707 – TDY Report of Capt. Vogel, p. 4; see also at PRO: HW 3/166 memo from Denniston and HW 14/62 doctor's memo.

55. PRO: HW 14/5 23 May 1940 memo "to all" from Denniston.

56. Direction Finding (D/F – later HF/DF or Huff Duff, for High Frequency Direction Finding) and traffic analysis provided valuable information from otherwise unintelligible signals. The latter allowed the Allies to pinpoint the origin of a message and hence to attack its senders, a U-boat, Bomber squadron, Panzer division, or Army field command.

Traffic Analysis required greater effort. By knowing the origin, length, and number of a day's or week's messages and comparing these facts with past experience, an alert intelligence officer could tell when a bombing raid, new offensive, or strategic retreat was on the horizon.

57. PRO: HW 3/17, p. 3.

58. PRO: HW 3/124 – Directive #339a, 26 April 1943. Note that Jones previously worked as an executive with a textile company and according to William Friedman exuded "a decided impression of great ability, force, and decisive power." NARA: RG 457 HCC Box 1126 NR 3620 – E Operations of GC&CS at Bletchley Park, p. 70.

59. PRO: HW 3/124 Directive 373, 16 May 1943.

60. PRO: HW 3/124 Directives 356 and 373, 16 May 1943.

61. NARA: RG 457 HCC Box 1429 NR 4729 – German Traffic Analysis in Sixta, p. 6.

62. The primary exception was the nonmachine diplomatic and commercial ciphers located at Berkeley Street in London.

63. PRO: HW 3/124 Directive 373, 16 May 1943.

64. NARA: RG 457 HCC Box 1429 NR 4729 – German Traffic Analysis in Sixta, pp. 24–25.

65. The training described in this paragraph appears in NARA: RG 457 HCC Box 1429 NR 4729 – Traffic Analysis in Sixta, Supplement.

66. PRO: HW 14/28 Welchman letter, 2 February 1942, p. 3.

67. NARA: RG 457 HCC Box 1429 NR 4729 – German Traffic Analysis in Sixta, p. 50. The British referred to cryptanalysts and cryptanalysis as cryptographers and cryptography.

68. Ibid., p. 53.

69. Ibid., pp. 49–50.

70. Ibid., Supplement.

71. NARA: RG 457 HCC Box 1429 NR 4729 – German Traffic Analysis in Sixta [Six T. A.], p. 6.

72. Many of these exploits, large and small, are detailed in the literature on Ultra intelligence, e.g., Calvocoressi, *Top Secret ULTRA*; Hinsley and Stripp, *Codebreakers*; Kahn, *Seizing the Enigma*; Welchman, *The Hut 6 Story*.

73. "W/T I, that is, information, intelligence, or inference based solely upon W/T [wireless traffic] studies." NARA: RG 457 HCC Box 1126 NR 3620 – E Operations of the GC&CS at Bletchley Park, by Friedman, p. 30.

74. Intercipher information appears to mean information from decrypts of different grades of ciphers as well as from the ciphers of different units and different services.

75. PRO: HW 14/28 Letter from W. G. Welchman to Commander Travis, 2 February 1942, p. 3.

76. NARA: RG 457 HCC Box 1126 NR 3620 – E Operations of the GC&CS at Bletchley Park, by Friedman, p. 33. Emending meant, essentially, cleaning up the text, which generally arrived a bit garbled from imperfect reception, so that it looked as it presumably had when sent.

77. NARA: RG 457 HCC Box 699 NR 1707 – TDY Report of Capt. Vogel – (Hut 3), 26 July 1944–18 May 1945, p. 4.

78. NARA: RG 457 HCC Box 1126 NR 3620 – E Operations of the GC&CS at Bletchley Park, by Friedman, pp. 32–33.

79. Ibid., p. 82.

80. By 1943, virtually all Enigma intercepts came by teletype. Kozaczuk, *Enigma*, p. 305.

81. PRO: HW 14/30 "No. 6. I.S.," 1 March 1942, p. 3. This system emerged after a strongly worded tussle over control of interception. See memos in HW 14/19.

82. NARA: RG 457 HCC Box 1417 NR 4633 – Col. McCormack's trip to London, [April] 1943, p. 1.

83. NARA: RG 457 HCC Box 1417 NR 4633 – "Cooperation between Intelligence and Operations," p. 1.

84. Stripp interview.

85. See, however, NARA: RG 457 HCC Box 1424 NR 4683 – Memo for Major Robert M. Slusser, MIS, 19 December 1945, which reports Mr. Birch's objections to Mr. Lucas' Hut 3's History.

86. PRO: HW 3/135 Miss Seynard's history of German Naval section, p. 13.

87. Bundy, "Some of My Wartime Experiences," p. 75. Also Thomas interview and 1943 BP organization chart showing chains of command and communication between the Huts and the machine section. NARA: RG 457 HCC Box 808 NR 2336 – British Communications Intelligence Chart II and Box 1424 NR 4683.

88. NARA: RG 457 HCC Box 808 NR 2336 – British Communications Intelligence, p. 50.

89. PRO: HW 14/28.

90. PRO: HW 14/87, p. 9 – "Liaison with Hut 8."

91. PRO: HW 14/98 Memo to Travis, 25 February 1944, from Milner-Barry (Hut 6), J. Clarke (Hut 8), and Jones (Hut 3), which notes that as of February 1944, "there has not yet been any case of failure to reach agreement" in these meetings.

92. NARA: RG 457 HCC Box 1424 NR 4683 – Memo for Major Robert M. Slusser, MIS, 19 December 1945, p. 2.

93. PRO: HW 14/27 – Report on Military intelligence at the GC&CS by Brigadier W. E. van Cutsem.

94. Derek Taunt in Hinsley and Stripp, *The Codebreakers*, p. 103.

95. Henry Dryden in Hinsley and Stripp, *The Codebreakers*, p. 201.

96. PRO: HW 14/30 "No. 6. I.S.," 1 March 1942, p. 3.

97. Calvocoressi, *Top Secret ULTRA*, p. 64.

98. F. H. Hinsley et al., *British Intelligence in World War II*, 4:181.

99. Garlinski, *The Enigma War*, p. 20.

100. The Post Office lent two automation experts: T. G. Flowers and Jack Good. See their articles in *Cryptologia*; Cipher A. Deavours and Louis Kruh, *Machine Cryptography and Modern Cryptanalysis* (Dedham, MA: Artech House, 1985).

101. NARA: RG 457 SRH 003 and Colin (Brad) Burke, paper at Seventh Annual Cryptologic History Symposium, October 26, 1995. This trend has intensified as our intelligence agencies increasingly turn to commercial operations for expertise and resources. Because of the small runs needed, commercial production of top-secret cryptology has not proved feasible, so the U.S. government manufactures its own top-secret computer chips. I am indebted to the NSA's History Center and David Hatch for a tour of this lab.

102. NARA: RG 457 HCC Box 808 NR 2336 – British Communications Intelligence, e.g., p. 47.

103. The full explanation for this move lies beyond the scope of this work and requires further research into the personal and political issues surrounding Commander Denniston and the reorganization of GC&CS in 1942.

104. PRO: HW 3/17, p. 3.

105. Calvocoressi, *Top Secret ULTRA*, pp. 14–15.

106. NARA: RG 457 HCC Box 1126 NR 3620 – E Operations of the GC&CS at Bletchley Park, by Friedman, p. 80.

107. NARA: RG 457 HCC Box 808 NR 2336 – British Communications Intelligence, p. 30.

108. PRO: HW 14/29, February 1942 RAF Section memo.

109. PRO: HW 14/62, 29 December 1942. For a wonderful (fictionalized) example of the role weather codes played, see Robert Harris's novel, *Enigma* (New York: Random House, 1995). See also NARA: RG 457 HCC Box 808 NR 2336 – British Communications Intelligence.

110. See Bennett and Noskwith, in Hinsley and Stripp, *The Codebreakers*, pp. 33, 120–122, as well as Erskine in Erskine and Smith, *Action This Day*, chap. 4.

111. PRO: HW 14/62, 29 December 1942, p. 13.

112. Ibid.

113. NARA: RG 457 HCC Box 880 NR 2612 – Capt. Walter J. Fried Reports/SSA Liaison with GC&CS, p. 4.

114. PRO: HW 14/17 "The Problem," July 1941, p. 3.

115. PRO: HW 14/62 Appreciation of the "E" Situation December 1942, p. 3. Complete key repeats did appear elsewhere occasionally; on 21 December 1942 Goldfinch repeated the entire Bullfinch of 21 November (ibid., p. 4). Code names for Enigma nets followed a precise, if "whimsical," pattern:

| | |
|---|---|
| Luftwaffe keys | Colors (Red, Blue, etc.) |
| Luftflotte and Fliegerkorps | Insects (Cockroach, Wasp) |
| Geschwader and other operations | Animals: Badger, Civet |
| Luftgau | Flowers: Daisy, Daffodil |
| Weather | Vegetables: Leek, Garlic |
| Army | Birds: Sparrow, Falcon |
| S. S. | Fruit: Orange, Quince |
| Police Playfair | Games: Rummy, Poker |

NARA: RG 457 HCC Box 1009 NR 3175, p. 10.

116. NARA: RG 457 HCC Box 880 NR 2612 – Capt. Walter J. Fried Reports/SSA Liaison with GC&CS, 4 June 1944, p. 2.

117. NARA: RG 457 HCC Box 1009 NR 3175 – Cryptanalytic Report on the Yellow Machine, p. 80.

118. Another "quadrilateral" ran between Primrose, Brown, Osprey, and Orange. NARA: RG 457 HCC Box 1126 NR 3620 – E Operations of the GC&CS at Bletchley Park, p. 40.

119. PRO: HW 14/30 – Appreciation of Present Position of "E," p. 6.

120. PRO: HW 14/62 – Appreciation of the "E" Situation December 1942, p. 3.

121. Or from "Scorpion," PRO: HW 14/62, 29 December 1942, p. 13.

122. NARA: RG 457 HCC Box 880 NR 2612 – Capt. Walter J. Fried Reports/SSA Liaison with GC&CS – Hut 6 report on Compromise of Red, 13 July 1944.

123. Derek Taunt in Hinsley and Stripp, *The Codebreakers*, p. 103.

124. Britain apparently guided the signals intelligence operations of its Commonwealth countries, particularly Canada and Australia (see, e.g., NARA: RG 457 HCC Box 1369 NR 4279 – Collaboration between U.S. Army Comint and

Foreign Comint units, World War 2, p. 3 of Tab D, but this special relationship lies outside the scope of this work.

125. PRO: HW 14/1 – note to Denniston. The Poles arrived by 1 October 1939; see Gouazé, *Needles and Haystacks*, p. 59. The story of the escape to France can be found in Kozaczuk, *Enigma*.

126. See, for example, PRO: HW 14/4 "Expansion of Anglo-French Co-operation in Naval Work." Ironically, the cipher used on these teleprinter lines was Enigma itself. The Poles were certain that the Germans would never suspect their own machine. Kozaczuk, *Enigma*, pp. 85, 87. One French decipherer always ended his messages "Heil Hitler." Bloch, *Enigma avant Ultra*, p. E9.

127. Kozaczuk, *Enigma*, pp. 84, 96.

128. See memos in PRO: HW 14/3 (January 1940).

129. PRO: HW 14/11 Report on German Section No. 4 I.S., p. 2. The U.S. Army and Navy, in a largely political compromise, followed the same practice with Purple; see David Kahn, "Roosevelt, Magic and Ultra," *Cryptologia* 16, no. 4 (October 1992): 289–319.

130. Kozaczuk, *Enigma*, pp. 108–114. During this period, the Polish cryptanalysts also attacked their own cipher machine, Lacida or L.C.D., and found it wanting, pp. 133–135.

131. In the second half of the war, the French Army could not even "be allowed to suspect the existence of ultra." NARA: RG 457 HCC Box 1417 NR 4630 – Practices in the Dissemination of COMINT, p. 20.

132. By 1945, the Army and Navy began officially coordinating cryptology (NARA: RG 457 HCC Box 1112 NR 3551 – Establishment of Army-Navy Communication Intelligence Board); in 1952 the National Security Agency emerged, reporting to the director of the Central Intelligence Agency. The CIA still does not contain all U.S. intelligence services. The National Security Council, however, appears to do the sort of coordination that GC&CS (now GCHQ) has accomplished for Britain.

133. For the story of the various U.S. cryptologic agencies before 1945, see NARA: RG 457 SRH 364 and Benson, *A History of U.S. Communications Intelligence during World War II*.

134. Colonel G. S. C. Alfred McCormack, "Origin, Functions and Problems of the Special Branch, M.I.S.," in *Ultra, Magic and the Allies*, ed. Timothy Mulligan (New York: Garland, 1989), pp. 38–39.

135. PRO: HW 14/7 Denniston letter of 1 October 1940.

136. PRO: HW 14/8 Telegram, 5 November 1940.

137. PRO: HW 14/8 Letter to the Director, 15 November 1940. GC&CS still remembered that in the last war the United States sent "the now notorious Colonel Yardley," who then published his experiences.

138. NARA: RG 457 HCC Box 1417 NR 4632 "Report of Technical Mission to England," 11 April 1941; PRO: HW 14/12, 14/60; NSA: Sinkov oral history; Ralph Erskine, "From the Archives: What the Sinkov Mission Brought to Bletchley

Park," *Cryptologia* 27, no. 2 (April 2003): 111–118. The Americans, Captain Abraham Sinkov, Lt. Leo Rosen, Lt. Robert Weeks, and Ensign Prescott Currier, were sworn to secrecy about Enigma and not given time to take notes. Later GC&CS agreed Russian intelligence officers should visit Britain but should not learn of Bletchley Park. PRO: HW 3/166.

139. NARA: RG 457 HCC Box 1417 NR 4632, "Report of Technical Mission to England," 11 April 1941.

140. PRO: HW 14/19 handwritten note; HW 14/62 "Future of Cryptography in Canada."

141. PRO: HW 14/60 has several memos on this fracas.

142. Thomas interview.

143. PRO: WO 208/3478. Minutes of meeting, 16 June 1943.

144. PRO: HW 3/166, 22 May 1943; HW 14/8; HW 14/12.

145. Calvocoressi, *Top Secret ULTRA*, p. 63; PRO: WO 244/128, "Lessons from Operations in the Italian Campaign." The strength of this cooperative effort can be measured by its many personal mergers. Barbara and Joe Eachus's marriage (she was British, employed by the Foreign Office, he was with the U.S. Navy) was only one of the many trans-Atlantic pairings stemming from BP. Interview with the Eachuses, 26 October 1995.

146. NARA: RG 457 HCC Box 1369 NR 4279 – Collaboration between U.S. Army Comint and Foreign Comint units, World War II, p. 3 of Tab D.

147. Ibid.

148. NARA: RG 457 SRH 364, p. 110, and Smith, *The Ultra Magic Deals*, pp. 92–93. Radio interception was also centralized: Bainbridge Island, Washington, received all the Pacific theater material, while Cheltenham (England) collected and forwarded all the Atlantic intercepts (pp. 36, 110, 120).

149. McCormack, *Ultra, Magic and the Allies*, pp. 38–39.

150. NARA: RG 457 HCC Box 1369 NR 4279 – Collaboration between U.S. Army Comint and Foreign Comint units, World War II, p. 3 of Tab D.

151. NARA: RG 457 HCC Box 1328 NR 4013 – US/British Agreements on Comint Effort 1942–43.

152. NARA: RG 457 HCC Box 880 NR 2612 – Capt. Walter J. Fried Reports/SSA Liaison with GC&CS, for example.

153. NARA: RG 457 HCC Box 1328 NR 4022 – Cryptanalytic Technical Exchanges between SSA and GC&CS.

154. NARA: RG 457 HCC Box 623 NR 1690 – COMINCH File of Memoranda Concerning U-boat Tracking Room Operations and SRMN 32.

155. For example, decrypts in Hinsley, Vol. 3, pt. 2, Appendices 5, 7.

156. Richard Overy, *Why the Allies Won* (New York: Norton, 1995), has examples of not just the wealth of resources which the United States offered but also the swift, efficient, awesome manufacturing of the materials for war.

157. NARA: RG 457 HCC Box 808 NR 2336 – British Communications Intelligence, p. 33.

158. See Welchman's description in *The Hut Six Story*, pp. 75–77.

159. NARA: RG 457 HCC Box 880 NR 2612 – Capt. Walter J. Fried Reports, 29 June 1944, p. 2.

160. NARA: RG 457 HCC Box 1126 NR 3620 – E Operations of the GC&CS at Bletchley Park, p. 92.

161. The apparently last remaining Navy Bombe resides in the National Cryptologic Museum, Fort Meade, Maryland. Many were dumped in the sea after the war.

162. Scritchers recovered a key when the reflector wheel was not known. NARA: RG 457 HCC Box 580 NR 1417 – Tentative list of Enigma and other Machine usages; Crawford and Fox, ed., "The Autoscritcher and the Superscritcher," *IEEE Annals of the History of Computing* 14, no. 3 (1992): 9–22.

163. Hinsley et al., *British Intelligence in World War II*, 2:57.

164. NARA: RG 38 Crane collection CBSG 5750/176 OP-20GM-6/GM-1-C-3/GM-1/GE-1/GY-A-1 Daily War Diary CNSG LIB Box 102.

165. Commander J. Russell, "Ultra and the Campaign Against the U-Boats," in *Ultra, Magic and the Allies*, p. 6. The same level of cooperation did not occur with other Allies. The British and Americans had evidence that insecure ciphers plagued the Russians, French, and Chinese. Stalin was notorious for his secrecy and had rejected a British offer of cryptanalytic cooperation. Smith, *The Ultra Magic Deals*, p. 135.

166. NARA: RG 457 HCC Box 804 NR 2323 – M-228 Converter (Information sent to British), p. 1 [brackets in original].

167. In May 1944 a formal study on sharing SIGABA reiterated the ban on British use (let alone inspection) of the machine. NARA: RG 457 HCC Box 804 NR 2323 – M-228 Converter (Information sent to British), p. 1 and notes following p. 18. The final report (Box 1025 NR 3281) replaces SIGABA with SIGCUM.

168. NARA: RG 457 HCC Box 804 NR 2323 – M-228 Converter (Information sent to British), June 1942 memo from the SSA Chief to the Army Communications Branch Chief.

169. NARA: RG 457 HCC Box 804 NR 2323 – M-228 Converter (Information sent to British), p. 9.

170. Ibid., p. 11.

## 5. PROTECTING BONIFACE

1. NARA: RG 457 HCC Box 1429 NR 4729 – German Traffic Analysis in Sixta, pp. 4–5.

2. Ibid., p. 50.

3. See Aileen Clayton's account in *The Enemy Is Listening*.

4. PRO: HW 14/59, 22 November 1942.

5. PRO: HW 14/12, 3 February 1941.

6. PRO: HW 14/59, 22 November 1942 mentioning the MI8 arrangement with DDMI(O). Personnel could be loaned, of course, as in the case of Alan Turing's work with Bell Labs.

7. With the obvious exceptions of secure briefings.

8. Lewin, *Ultra Goes to War*, p. 17 (see chap. 4, n. 50). Presumably he did not tell her even then.

9. Vicki Moeser, "Unlocking Enigma's Secrets," *Cryptologia* 14, no. 4 (October 1990): 366.

10. The Americans, as well, used informal appeals to national security to great effect. The 1944 Republican presidential candidate, Thomas E. Dewey, somehow learned of Ultra's existence, and the military feared he would mention Ultra in the course of his campaign. General Marshall sent his personal representative to Dewey with a letter outlining Ultra's importance and the damage from any public mention of this valuable source. Dewey agreed to silence and never spoke of Ultra again. Lewin, *The American Magic*, chap. 1.

11. See the discussion in NARA: RG 457 HCC Box 1424 NR 4686 Brig Williams and Group Capt. Humphreys Reports, p. 4.

12. David Kahn, *Seizing the Enigma*, p. 140. When R. V. Jones and his staff saw the Bombes, their escort explained, "if any one of them ever dared to open his mouth on this particular subject, he ought to be boiled in oil." PRO: HW 14/27.

13. See PRO: AIR 41/48, for example.

14. Donald McLachlan. *Room 39: Naval Intelligence in Action 1939–45* (London: Weidenfeld and Nicolson, 1968), p. 14. Of course the front lines could move suddenly, and Bletchley's longest-serving members knew the Germans had already captured Polish and French men with Ultra experience.

15. PRO: HW 1/1393, 20 February 1943.

16. PRO: HW 1/1469, March 1943.

17. PRO: HW 3/166 Heads of Sections meeting, 13 March 1943. See also PRO: HW 1/1469, 1/1470, 1/1511.

18. BA/MA: RM7/105. Smith, *The Ultra Magic Deals*, p. 191, says French ciphers were made secure in September 1944; Bletchley remained worried.

19. PRO: HW 1/1822.

20. NARA: RG 457 HCC Box 1277 NR 3731–NR 3732 – Memo from Colonel C. B. Brown, 11 January 1945, p. 1.

21. NARA: RG 457 HCC Box 1277 NR 3732 – Liaison with French on Signals Intelligence Matters – Annexure "A," 6 February 1945.

22. See, for example, PRO: HW 1/1662, 3 May 1943 and more specifically, C's note to Churchill in HW 1/1134, 22 November 1942. Apparently, John Cairncross passed some Ultra material to the Soviet Union. Hugh Skillen, *Enigma and Its Achilles Heel*, n.p., p. 106.

23. Eunan O'Halpin, "Financing British Intelligence," in *British and American Approaches to Intelligence*, p. 203.

24. There was apparently one significant lapse during the war, when an indoctrinated man mentioned his BP contribution at a Cambridge College dinner table. His colleagues around the table, both indoctrinated and not, hushed him and no further damage was done (Calvocoressi, *Top Secret ULTRA*, p. 66). Cambridge scholars describe a similar breach in an Oxford commons room, which may be the same story. Alan Stripp interview.

25. For example, "Fred" referred to Fred Winterbotham, who organized the SLU system from Bletchley Park.

26. PRO: HW 14/4, 8 April 1940.

27. David Dilks, "Flashes of Intelligence," in *The Missing Dimension*, ed. C. Andrew and D. Dilks (London: Macmillan, 1984), p. 103. GC&CS itself had various pseudonyms such as the Golf Club and Chess Society (Julian Rathbone, *A Spy of the Old School*, New York: Pantheon, 1982, p. 163), and the existence of "C," GC&CS's head, received official recognition only in the early 1990s. About the same time, Britain officially admitted the existence of a Secret Intelligence Service (MI 6).

28. PRO: HW 14/13, 23 March 1941.

29. PRO: HW 14/10 Memo from Commander Saunders, 20 January 1941.

30. Ibid. Such precautions probably account for the popular myth that Churchill "sacrificed" Coventry for Ultra, not warning the city of a major bombing raid for fear of exposing the intelligence source. In fact, neither Churchill nor Bletchley's Hut 3 knew Coventry was the target until the beams went on just scant hours before the raid. See F. H. Hinsley et al., 1:316–18.

31. Interview with Ralph Bennett. Bennett mentions another cover name of "Agent OL" in *Ultra and Mediterranean Strategy*, p. 21. See also the terms Orange Leonard (PRO: HW 14/13 Telegram, 8 March 1941) and "OL messages" (PRO: HW 14/18 Winterbotham memo, 8 August 1941). "Leonard" was the special setting for Typexes encrypting Ultra intelligence on SLU nets (NARA: RG 457 HCC Box 1370 NR 4287 – British Administrative History of the Special Liaison Units, p. 15). St. Boniface christianized Germany.

32. PRO: HW 1/1714, 21 May 1943; NARA: RG 457 HCC Box 699 NR 1707 – TDY Report of Capt. Vogel, p. 4.

33. PRO: HW 1/203, 20 November 1941; HW 1/1526.

34. PRO: HW 1/1164, 24 November 1942; HW 1/1148, 20 November 1942.

35. NARA: RG 457 HCC Box 1417 NR 4633 – Col. McCormack's trip to London, p. 11.

36. A Foreign Office cryptanalyst from long before the war, de Grey became Assistant Director (S), 4 February 1942. PRO: HW 14/28.

37. PRO: HW 14/62 Letter, 29 December 1942.

38. Direction Finding (D/F – later HF/DF or Huff Duff, for High Frequency Direction Finding) is the process of locating the origin of a signal using triangulation.

39. PRO: HW 1/1470 SCU Algiers memo, 13 March 1943, for example.

40. PRO: HW 14/13, "JQ Information to Middle East," 1 March 1941.

41. PRO: HW 1/1075, for example.
42. PRO: HW 1/1164, emphasis in the original.
43. PRO: HW 14/28, 2 February 1942.
44. PRO: WO 106/3867.
45. PRO: HW 1/203, 20 November 1941.
46. PRO: WO 244/72 – Signal Procedure.
47. Calvocoressi, *Top Secret ULTRA*, p. 49.
48. Hinsley, 2: Appendix I (ii), p. 645, quoting a Cabinet Office file 82/43/1, Part 2, PM's personal telegram T/851, 23 November 1941.
49. PRO: HW 3/165, p. 4.
50. PRO: HW 3/96, p. 10.
51. PRO: HW 3/165, p. 2, which dates the start to April 1941, whereas HW 3/96, p. 8, says June 1941.
52. PRO: HW 1/1393 says 80 miles from the North African front.
53. PRO: HW 3/165, pp. 3, 15, 33. SSOs, the American version of SLUs in the Pacific, used Sigaba.
54. When misused, one-time pads (OTP) can be and have been broken in practice. For example, the Venona decrypts of KGB agents allowed the United States to discover atomic bomb spies, such as the Rosenbergs. See Venona decrypts in the NSA library and several recent books, such as Robert Louis Benson and Michael Warner, eds., *Venona* (Washington, DC: NSA, 1996); and John Earl Haynes and Harvey Klehr, *Venona* (New Haven, CT: Yale University Press, 1999).
55. See the chapters on German cryptanalytic successes and on Allied communications security, as well as NARA: RG 457 HCC Box 1429 NR 4726 – "CHARTS."
56. PRO: HW 14/18 Memo, 9 August 1941, Security and Distribution.
57. PRO: HW 3/165, pp. 2, 6, 32.
58. PRO: HW 3/165, pp. 17–18.
59. PRO: HW 3/165, p. 67.
60. PRO: HW 14/18 Memo, 9 August 1941, Part 2.
61. PRO: HW 3/165, p. 3.
62. PRO: HW 3/165, Story of the SLUs. Chapter X, p. 2.
63. PRO: HW 3/96, p. 10.
64. PRO: HW 3/165, p. 6.
65. Calvocoressi, *Top Secret ULTRA*, p. 60.
66. PRO: HW 3/165, p. 3.
67. NARA: RG 457 HCC Box 1370 NR 4287, British Administrative History of the Special Liaison Units, p. 7.
68. Churchill got his own SLU staff when he was abroad. NARA: RG 457 HCC Box 1370 NR 4287 – British Administrative History of the Special Liaison Units, p. 24.
69. PRO: HW 3/96, p. 8; HW 3/165, Chapter X, p. 65.
70. PRO: HW 3/165, pp. 65–66.

71. PRO: HW 3/165, p. 15.
72. Bennett suggested his own return from the Middle East on 30 December 1942. PRO: HW 14/62 Bennett telegram from Cairo.
73. PRO: HW 3/165, p. 21. The United States adopted SSOs modeled on the SLU system for the Pacific theater. Still the British continued to worry about American openness and downright carelessness – with some reason. In 1944, the *Washington Post* not only reported the disastrous results of a test of Arlington Hall's security but detailed exactly how the "infiltrators" had gained access to classified areas, counterfeited security badges, and stolen top secret documents from desktops and wastebaskets. NARA: RG 457 HCC SRMA-011.
74. PRO: HW 3/165, pp. 15, 46.
75. PRO: HW 14/10 Memo from Hut 3, 20 January 1941.
76. PRO: HW 14/55, 13 October 1942 memo.
77. Hinsley et al., *British Intelligence in World War II*, 2:400, 414. Sadly, Winterbotham's colorful tale in *The Ultra Secret* of a thank-you telegram to Naples dockyard workers has no corroboration.
78. Because POWs often served as cover for Ultra, the same warnings for requirements of disguise and paraphrasing appear on surviving interrogation reports in the PRO: WO 208/4000 series. See WO 208/4117, for example.
79. PRO: HW 14/55, 13 October 1942 memo.
80. Sonar was then called ASV (antisurface vessel) radar.
81. McLachlan, *Room 39*, p. 112 (see chap. 5, n. 14).
82. NARA: RG 457 HCC SRH-024 (reprinted as *Ultra in the Atlantic*, Vols. 1–6 [Laguna Hills, CA: Aegean Park Press, 1994] 4:49); Hinsley et al., *British Intelligence in World War II*, 2:563.
83. Hinsley et al., *British Intelligence in World War II*, 2:177.

## 6. THE ILLUSION OF SECURITY

1. NARA: RG 457 HCC Box 1282 NR 3806.
2. Herbert Dammert and Franz Kurowski, *Adler Ruft Führerhauptquartier*, p. 18.
3. Groadmiral Karl Dönitz ordered the Marine Nachrichtendienst (MND) (Intelligence Service) to turn over everything it had at its disposal at the war's end. Dönitz made this order to prove that his beloved Marine had not sullied its hands in the Nazi Final Solution, whose horrors were just emerging. The truth of his claims lies beyond the scope of this volume, except insofar as Dönitz unwittingly aided future researchers and that his orders explain the dominating presence of naval examples in this and other accounts of Enigma.
4. NARA: RG 457 HCC Box 1098 NR 3448 – [German] Analysis of the Cipher Machine "ENIGMA," Type K.
5. The affordability of Enigma also offset this disadvantage. NARA: RG 457 HCC Box 579 NR 1400 – Results of the Work of the Italian Crypto Unit at Rome, dated November 1944, p. 3.

6. NARA: T-1022/3979 (microfilm) KTB/BdU, 10 September 1939; 11 September 1939, re: machine lost in North Africa; BA/MA: RM7/107, p. 29.

7. BA/MA: RM7/103, pp. 53–54, 62–63. Kapt. zur See Stummel signed these reassurances. Note that U-26 was not in fact lost or captured at this point, although the Marine believed her to be.

8. The Allied convoy ciphers were upgraded several times, usually foiling the B-Dienst only temporarily. See chap. 7.

9. BA/MA: KTB/Skl: 173, 21 August 1940.

10. NARA: T-1022/4063 PG 30287, 18 April 1941. The Wehrmacht also shrank access to Enigmas on land. See n. 20.

11. NARA: T-1022/4063 PG 30287, 18 April 1941. According to the official history, this new key, Triton, went into effect 1 February 1942. Ralph Erskine, a specialist in the Marine Enigma, disagrees, stating that Triton actually appeared 5 October 1941 in three-rotor form and that the 1 February 1942 change was an upgrade. (F. H. Hinsley et al., *British Intelligence in World War II*, 2:667; J. Rohwer personal papers, Bibliothek für Zeitgeschichte, Stuttgart; personal communication with R. Erskine, 11 January 1999).

12. NARA: T-1022/4063 PG 30297, 16 September 1941.

13. NARA: T-1022/2310 PG 34534 Flottenkommando 1941, Akte Gkdos 31 "Taktik, Mob. Angl.," p. 5.

14. Ibid., p. 6.

15. NARA: T-1022 (German Navy records 1850–1945) PG 34534 Flottenkommando 1941, Akte Gkdos 31 "Taktik, Mob. Angl.," p. 2.

16. Ibid., pp. 8, 12–13.

17. Ibid., p. 13.

18. NARA: T-1022/1721 (microfilm) PG 32164, 16 July 1942.

19. NARA: T-1022/3103, 29 September 1941.

20. NARA: T-1022/3103, 22 August 1941, and a long series of inspection reports on T-1022/2373 PG 37374. The inspectors generally reported no significant violations and after July 1942 mention of the raids disappears.

21. NARA: T-1022/1724 and BA/MA: RM7/845. Timothy P. Mulligan of National Archives discusses this investigation in "The German Navy Evaluates Its Cryptographic Security, October 1941." *Military Affairs* 49, no. 2 (April 1985): 75–79. I am indebted to Mulligan for his assistance with records, translations, and military details through the years.

22. NARA: T-1022/1724, p. 188.

23. Ibid., p. 189.

24. Ibid., p. 198.

25. Ibid., p. 205.

26. U-570 did aid Bletchley Park's breaking of Enigma M and by October 1941 the British were decrypting and translating Enigma M messages within roughly twenty-four hours of their original transmission, quickly enough to route ships

around U-boat patrol lines. Hinsley et al., *British Intelligence in World War II*, 1:337–339; 2:174–175; Kahn, *Seizing The Enigma*.

27. With the exception of the "spare" Enigma M rotors which Kahn says came from U-33. See *Seizing the Enigma*, chapts. 8, 9; and Hinsley et al., *British Intelligence in World War II*, Vol. 3, part 2, p. 957. These rotors were added to Enigma M in part because of the loss of U-26 (see above) and the potential compromise of the three-rotor Enigma M. Ironically, the new rotors were also on U-26 and were assumed to have fallen, along with the regular Enigma, into British hands. KTB/Skl, vol. 1, p. 47.

28. NARA: T-1022/1724, p. 205.

29. Ibid., 18 October 1941.

30. KTB/Skl, vol. 28, p. 218, 21 December 1941. Nonetheless, the British passed the Americans six boxes of copied material from U-570, now in NARA: RG 38 Boxes 1404–1409.

31. In fact, the shift to the four-rotor Enigma put Bletchley Park in the dark until December 1942. This darkness was partially illuminated by the submarine tracking room's expert extrapolation from other signals, based on previous experience with Marine movements.

32. Hinsley, Vol. 2, Appendix 8. Only the "critical convoy battles" of March 1943 came close to these totals, when U-boats sank 95 ships for a loss of six boats. In May 1943, in contrast, they sank far fewer ships for a loss of twenty-eight U-boats.

33. Evidence that January's losses were the trigger are in the BdU log (NARA: RG 457 HCC Box 808 NR 3775, German Navy: U-boat Logs) for 28 January 1943. The Allies had again been reading the Marine's Enigma since December 1942, rarely within a day, but generally in time for convoys to avoid set patrol lines. See Hinsley et al., *British Intelligence in World War II*, 2:559–560.

34. BA/MA: RM7/107, pp. 4, 25. The B-Dienst was still reading the Allied (No. 3) convoy ciphers – Hinsley et al., *British Intelligence in World War II*, 2:553–554, 559, citing Jürgen Rohwer's presentation to the U.S. Naval Academy.

35. BA/MA: RM7/107, pp. 14–15. The report focused on signals sent 22, 23, 24, 25, 26, 28 January 1943.

36. BA/MA: RM7/107, pp. 10–12. "Officer-only" messages were encrypted in a separate cipher before being enciphered by Triton.

37. With considerable delays during a nine-day "blackout" in the beginning of March 1943. Robert Harris's novel *Enigma* (see chap. 4, n. 109) vividly describes the panic this blackout created at BP.

38. NARA: RG 38 (Crane files) CNSG Lib Box 102 CNSG 5750/176 OP-20GM-6/GM-1-C-3/GM-1/GE-1/GY-A-1 Daily War Diary, with thanks to Steven Budiansky. The 23 January keys may not have ever been broken. Things got better in February; on 25 February, the U.S. team recovered the Stecker setting by 1430, sent these to the British 1510. The first crib came out at 1525, the

second at 1625. These results led to the recovered Grundstellung by 1640, which went to the British before 5 p.m.

39. BA/MA: RM7/107, p. 4.

40. BA/MA: RM7/107, p. 33. The Germans were right to be concerned about Italy's ciphers, which were being cracked by the Allies as successfully as Enigma was.

41. BA/MA: RM7/107, p. 13.

42. Ibid.

43. Although the possibility appears in BA/MA: RM7/107, p. 17.

44. Hinsley et al., *British Intelligence in World War II*, 2:560.

45. BA/MA: RM7/107, p. 5.

46. Ibid., p. 13.

47. Ibid., p. 12.

48. Bletchley Park occasionally cracked the coordinates ("by ad hoc research") before early 1944, when the code's fixed principle was partially reconstructed. The codebook was finally captured with U-505 in 1944. Hinsley et al., *British Intelligence in World War II*, 2:552.

49. The British frequently overestimated German production capabilities in general: for planes, see W. Wark, *The Ultimate Enemy* (Ithaca, NY: Cornell University Press, 1985); for U-boats, see D. McLachlan, *Room 39: Naval Intelligence in Action 1939–45*, chap. 6, etc. No one has mentioned that the Allies might *add* to the numbers mentioned by Ultra or captured documents but would *never* subtract from them.

50. NARA: RG 38 Box 49 File 3840/20 – COMINCH U-BOAT SUMMARIES 1 January–31 March 1943 – daily submarine estimate for 16 January 1943.

51. NARA: RG 38 Box 49 File 3840/20 – COMINCH U-BOAT SUMMARIES 1 January–31 March 1943 – Memo on the Daily Submarine Situation Report in reference to the COMINCH 061852, January 1943.

52. There were some cases of underestimation, for example a report of five U-boats when there were actually ten. Coordinates for these U-boats were also clearly incorrect. This episode requires further research (17 January 1943) BA/MA: RM7/107, p. 11.

53. In 1942 a similar incident occurred in Norway when the RAF went looking for the light cruiser *Nürnberg* at its predetermined destination, only to discover that bad weather had forced the ship to anchor before reaching its base. The Germans discounted this blunder by assuming agents had revealed the ship's movements. Hinsley et al., *British Intelligence in World War II*, 2:528.

54. NARA: RG 38 Crane files CNSG LIB Box 102 CBSG 5750/176 OP-20GM-6/GM-1-C-3/GM-1/GE-1/GY-A-1 Daily War Diary. January 1943 proved a difficult month for Bletchley. Apparently a few days – 2, 16, 19, 23 January – never did yield to Hut 8. Early in the month Hut 8 recovered an occasional key within forty-eight hours, but more often took much longer. By the third week of the month, the pace picked up. Four keys came out on 24 January (17, 18, 21,

and 22 January), and the next seven days saw six more keys emerging. Thus by 29 January, Bletchley had in fact recovered the key for 24 January and would read those for 25 and 26.

55. BA/MA: RM7/107, p. 17.
56. Bletchley did read the signals of 25 January on 29 January (see previous note), although probably too late in the day for the day's submarine situation report.
57. BA/MA: RM7/107, p. 17.
58. Hinsley et al., *British Intelligence in World War II*, 2:552.
59. Bonatz, *Marine Funkaufklärung*, p. 87. (Note his surprise at French and British cryptanalysts – probably Alan Turing – collaborating.) This Marine report claims the French could not yet crack the 1935 Enigma and blames Allied information on the Italians. BA/MA: RM7/103, 19 September 1940, pp. 118–121. See also the [German] Naval Historical Teams' assessment of these documents: NARA: RG 457 HCC Box 743 NR 1860 – Radio Intercept and Cryptanalysis (German), p. 20.
60. Bonatz, *Marine Funkaufklärung*, p. 87.
61. BA/MA: RM7/107, 5 February 1943, p. 31.
62. Ibid., p. 33.
63. Ibid., p. 13.
64. Ibid., p. 13. As the Germans themselves readily admitted, both the British and American machine ciphers were never broken.
65. BA/MA: RM 7/108, pp. 19–21. The details of how the Marine designed and implemented these checks have not emerged in declassified records.
66. Ibid. Note the Allies used the inverse of the letter frequency method – knowing that *e* is the most common letter in German and that Enigma could not replace a letter with itself, they focused on where *e* did not appear.
67. Author's correspondence with Timothy Mulligan, 7 July 1996, as well as subsequent discussions.
68. PRO: ADM 223/505, p. 6.
69. *German Radio Intelligence and the Soldatensender*, introd. John Mendelsohn (New York: Garland 1989); National Archives, RG 338, Manuscript. P-038, General A. Praun, p. 147.
70. The Metox countered Allied Mark II meter radar found by the Germans in a downed bomber in spring 1942. It could detect a radar sweep before the sweep found the sub because when radar returns to its origin for interpretation, its signal loses half its strength. Thus the Metox, under ideal conditions, noted the radar signal at twice the strength (and twice the distance) as the original sender read the return pulse. See Brian McCue, *U-Boats in the Bay of Biscay* (Washington, DC: National Defense University Press, 1990), p. 25.
71. PRO: AIR 41/48, p. 39.
72. NARA: T-1022/4064, p. 38, 23 March 1943.
73. PRO: AIR 41/48, pp. 39–40.

74. Conceivably, the Magic Eye might have been able to detect Allied 10 cm radar (Metox could not), but *only* when the Eye happened to be directed precisely toward the oncoming radar. The 10 cm radar came into use in the Atlantic in spring 1943, so U-382 might have seen the new radar. PRO: AIR 41/48, p. 40; NARA: T-1022/4064, May 1943. See also McCue, *U-Boats*, pp. 25–27.

75. NARA: T-1022/4064, 25 April 1943, p. 39.

76. NARA: T-1022/4064 KTB/BdU, 31 July 1943, p. 50.

77. Ibid.

78. PRO: AIR 41/48, p. 173. The pilot has never been identified. No further information about his account has emerged. Historians speculate that he was inventing what his captors wanted to hear. Technically, saying anything other than name, rank, and serial number directly violated RAF orders.

79. While British cryptanalysts at each of these points were reading the U-boat cipher, at other times, notably the sinking of the *Bismarck*, the information had come from an Enigma cipher used by another division of the German military.

80. NARA: RG 457 HCC Box 808 NR 3775. BdU Log 1–15/8/43. Note that the leak comes from the Americans, not Bletchley Park.

81. The following paragraphs rely on this log, available at NARA: RG 457 HCC Box 808 NR 3775.

82. NARA: RG 457 HCC Box 192 NR 908, 27 August 1943, p. 2.

83. Ibid., p. 7.

84. Red did not follow this pattern in July 1944, perhaps because of the introduction of the pluggable Umkehr Walz D. See NARA: RG 457 HCC Box 880 NR 2612 – "Compromise of Red."

85. The British discuss this 1944 report in PRO: ADM 223/505. My thanks to Colin (Brad) Burke for help on this topic as well.

86. BA/MA: RM7/107, pp. 4, 9, 30.

87. Bletchley Park did rely on such carelessness; see above, as well as Calvocoressi, *Top Secret ULTRA*; Gordon Welchman, *The Hut 6 Story*; Erskine and Smith, eds., *Action This Day*; and Hinsley et al., *British Intelligence in World War II*.

88. PRO: HW 14/55.

89. PRO: HW 14/55 Copy of signal 5/9/42.

90. Nor did the Allies successfully infiltrate spies into Germany until the last days of the war. Joseph E. Persico, *Piercing the Reich* (New York: Viking, 1979).

91. The British continue to maintain that this agent (Cicero) did not seriously compromise any Allied intentions.

92. The most devastating case being that of U.S. Army attaché Colonel Feller, whose regular and detailed reports to Washington went just as regularly to the Wehrmacht, who swiftly deciphered them with the help of the pilfered codes. "Feller's reports" appear frequently in the KTB/Skl after mid-April 1942. See above.

93. BA/MA: RM7/104, p. 16, 18 January 1941 re: English diplomats in Sweden. PRO: Monitored POW conversations SRA 35, 23 February 1940.

94. NARA: T-1022/2178/PG 36734, 23 June 1941, 4 October 1941. W. Agrell in *Clio Goes Spying* (Lund, Sweden: University of Lund, 1983), pp. 112–119, discusses the causes for this partially justified paranoia about the proliferation of agents in occupied territory.

95. Many Americans do not realize that in Europe ownership of ordinary radios, as well as ham radios and later TVs, VCRs, and answering machines, has always required registration with the state and an annual fee. This regulation did not start as an oppressive Nazi tactic but was already in place across Europe and continues, albeit with frequent disregard, today.

96. NARA: T-1022/1668/PG 32046, 2 October 1941.

97. KTB/Skl, vol. 28, p. 242, 24 December 1941.

98. PRO: Monitored POW conversation SRA No. 4, 1 March 1940.

99. He told a fellow POW that the Allies got information "through agents and spies, workshop spies and in all sorts of ways. Just in the same way that we also have got everything." PRO: Monitored POW conversations SRA 35, 23 February 1940.

100. Gustav Eigner, Letter to the Editor, *Internationale Wehrrevue* 9, no. 5 (Oct. 1976): 861. He admits the possibility that the more primitive Marine hand ciphers (the "Greek" cipher) did succumb to enemy decipherment. His explanations for the Allied success without Ultra include radar.

101. See Richard Gehlen, *The Service* [*Der Dienst*], trans. David Irving (New York: World Publishing, 1972), p. 48; Paul Leverkühn, *Der Geheime Nachrichtendienst* (Frankfurt: Verlag für Wehrwesen B & G, 1957), p. 149; Gert Buchheit, *Spionage in zwei Weltkriegen* (Landshut: Verlag politisches archiv gmbh, 1975). I have also been told of such betrayals by General Fellgiebel, Himmler, Canaris, and other high-ranking Wehrmacht officers, albeit always without corroborating evidence.

102. For instance, Albert Speer's memoirs, p. 399 and throughout.

103. Hinsley et al., *British Intelligence in World War II*, 2:577, 716.

104. Interview with Dr. Prof. Jürgen Rohwer.

105. 23 March 1943, Helmut Heiber, *Hitler's Lagebesprechungen* (Stuttgart: Deutsche Verlags-Anstalt, 1962), p. 931.

106. NARA: T-1022/3103, 30 October 1940.

107. Flicke, *War Secrets in the Ether*, 2:285.

108. The Allies put POWs from different services together so that they would have to explain their jobs, technical abilities, equipment, and objectives to their cellmates – and the microphone.

109. Unfortunately, many POW interrogations, especially those conducted by the British, remain classified. But see NARA: RG 457 HCC Box 770 NR 2012 for a thorough description of Enigma from a POW in 1943.

110. NA: RG 165, Box 727 "Interrogation of E. Höller," 5 August 1943, p. 14. This belief has not disappeared and serves as the basis for many denials of Ultra's existence. See, for example, Radio operator H. Dammert and Franz Kurowski's *Adler ruft Führerhauptquartier* (Leoni am Starnberger See: Druffel, 1985).

111. NARA: RG 165, Box 666.

112. German officers all learned codes which would inform their commands as to whether they had had time to destroy all Enigmas and relevant documentation before capture. They wove these signals into their Red Cross letters from POW camps to family in Germany. The family knew to turn them over to their sons' and fathers' headquarters. (Interview with Dr. Prof. J. Rohwer. Reference to one such letter appears in NARA: T-1022/3103 PG 33325, 8 November 1939.) Such a letter explains Dönitz's (apparently mistaken) assurances to his superiors that all "secret material, codes and recognition signals of [captured] submarine U-570" were destroyed." (KTB/Skl vol. 28, p. 218, 21 December 1941).

113. Hinsley et al., *British Intelligence in World War II*, 2:565–66.

114. Tony Devereux considers the Allied advantage minimal; see *Messenger Gods of Battle* (London: Brassey's, 1991). Others mention not only British wartime radar advances but also the advantage of a global empire for interception. See, for example, R. V. Jones and Aileen Clayton, among others.

115. NARA: RG 457 HHC Box 743 NR 1860 – Radio Intercept and Cryptanalysis (German) – report by former Skl officers dated 18 September 1950, p. 9.

116. Hinsley et al., *British Intelligence in World War II*, 2:567, puts the beginning of the offensive stage in May 1943.

117. The destruction of a single tanker U-boat could disrupt Dönitz's entire Atlantic U-boat plans for months. See Commander J. Russell in *Ultra, Magic and the Allies*, ed. T. P. Mulligan (New York: Garland, 1989).

118. NARA: RG 457 HCC Box 1405 NR 4541 – Codes and Ciphers: Germany, KTB July 1943.

### 7. A LONG-STANDING ANXIETY

1. William Clarke, "GC&CS." *Cryptologia* 11, no. 4 (Oct. 1987): 222.

2. Ibid.

3. NARA: RG 457 HCC Box 808 NR 2336 – British Communications Intelligence appendix.

4. PRO: HW 14/60. The minutes note MI8's responsibility "for the world-wide Military wireless intelligence organisation," i.e., signaling and interception. MI8 advised "on the security aspect of Signal Procedure and the method of maintaining wireless and line security in the light of experience gained from the interception of enemy communications."

5. F. H. Hinsley, letter to the author, 10 May 1994.

6. See, for example, PRO: ADM 223/2, 7 August 1941.

7. Andrew and Dilks, eds. *The Missing Dimension: Governments and Intelligence Communities in the Twentieth Century*, p. 109.

8. Although the American Sigaba machine cipher did not actually fall into enemy hands, the worldwide system was declared compromised in February 1945. See below and NARA: RG 457 HCC Box 1024 NR 3268 – Annual Report of

Cryptographic Material Branch FY 1945, p. 35; Box 1026 NR 3283 – History of Converter M-134-C (SIGABA) Vols. I–III, p. 71ff; Box 1370 NR 4290 – Signal Security Agency (SSA) Staff Group studies.

9. F. H. Hinsley, et al., *British Intelligence in World War II*, Vol. 2, Appendix I(i), p. 633.

10. The Germans clearly followed this line of reasoning when they upgraded and split the U-boat cipher from the main Marine cipher in February 1942. If so, they reasoned correctly as the increased difficulty and decreased signal load kept BP from reading the improved U-boat cipher for nine months.

11. McLachlan, *Room 39*, p. 391.

12. PRO: HW 14/28 and WO 244/72 – Signal Procedure.

13. PRO: HW 14/28, 14 February 1942.

14. PRO: ADM 223/2 – ZIP/ZG/25, 4 July 1941.

15. Hinsley et al., *British Intelligence in World War II*, 2:554.

16. NARA: RG 457 HCC Box 1277 NR 3733 – Signal Information and Monitoring, 1944–45, History of SIAM, p. 4.

17. See, for example, PRO: HW 14/28, 12 February 42, Report "Inspection of RAF Wireless Intelligence "Y" Service," p. 2.

18. NARA: RG 457 HCC Box 1277 NR 3733 – Signal Information and Monitoring, 1944–45, History of SIAM, p. 8.

19. NARA: RG 457 HCC Box 1277 NR 3733 – Signal Information and Monitoring, 1944–45, History of SIAM.

20. NARA: RG 457 HCC Box 1277 NR 3733, 23–29 June 1944 report. Padding consists of nonsense elements that disguise the message's true length and reduce the possibility of cribs.

21. PRO: ADM 223/2 – ZIP/ZG/25, 4 July 1941.

22. PRO: WO 244/128 – Lessons from Operations in the Italian Campaign, pp. 11, 64.

23. See W. Kozaczuk, *Geheimoperation WICHER* (Koblenz: Bernard & Graef, 1989), chap. 2, and footnote 19.

24. NARA: RG 457 HCC SRMA 011 – "Signal Security Service Staff Meeting Minutes," 4 July 1944.

25. NARA: RG 457 HCC Box 1019 NR 3242 – Weekly Notes on Cryptanalytic Efforts Against U.S. Equipments, 1943–45.

26. NARA: RG 457 HCC Box 1124 NR 3609 – Research and Development of Cryptographic Equipments 1918–45.

27. See the 1943 reports in NARA: RG 457 HCC Box 1019 NR 3242 – Weekly Notes on Cryptanalytic Efforts.

28. NARA: RG 457 HCC Box 1370 NR 4285 – Signal Security Agency Summary Annual Report (1944), p. 106.

29. See, for example, the plaque outside the Frank Rowlett building at the U.S. National Security Agency, Fort Meade, Maryland.

30. NARA: RG 457 HCC Box 804 NR 2323 – M-228 Converter, p. 14.

31. NARA: RG 457 HCC Box 1019 NR 3242 – Weekly Notes on Cryptanalytic Efforts Against U.S. Equipments, 1943–45, 27 March–1 April 1944.

32. Ibid. Report for 27 November–2 December 1944.

33. Ibid., 22–27 January 1945.

34. Ibid., particularly 3 July 1944 and 22 January 1945.

35. Ibid., 12 November 1945.

36. NARA: RG 457 HCC Box 804 NR 2323 – M-228 Converter, p. 3. See German assessments of Typex in BA/MA: RM7/104, 28 February 1941.

37. Emphasis in original. NARA: RG 457 HCC Box 804 NR 2323 – M-228 Converter (Information sent to British), p. 12.

38. For more on Sigaba's design and theoretical security, see Stephen J. Kelley, "Big Machines: The Relative Cryptographic Security of the German Enigma, the Japanese PURPLE, and the U.S. SIGABA/ECM cipher machines in World War II," unpublished manuscript, pp. 212–220.

39. Even the ones shown to me in the National Cryptologic Museum had their wiring cut.

40. NARA: RG 457 HCC Box 1026 NR 3283 – History of Converter M-134-C. 3 vol. III:7–8; Box 1278 NR 3755 – Cipher Machines.

41. See also their monitoring of German messages about Allied location devices in Bray, ed., *Ultra in the Atlantic* (NARA: RG 457 HCC SRH-024) 3:14.

42. NS (Naval Section) III and the research section of NS XI, among others. NARA: RG 457 HCC Box 808 NR 2336 – British Communications Intelligence, pp. 65–67.

43. Hinsley et al., *British Intelligence in World War II*, Vol. 2, Appendix I (ii), p. 643. See also memo by Charles R. Gajan (1943) in NARA: RG 457 HCC Box 833 NR 2445.

44. PRO: ADM 223/2, 2 August 1941, p. 2, and 20 August 1941.

45. Numerous accounts have appeared explaining how the Allies came to realize Col. Fellers's code was being read. They tend to fall into two categories. One claims that in the early summer of 1942, an Italian intelligence employee (or military attaché) let slip "in his always-readable code that Rommel was so successful because he was receiving the American military attaché's daily reports" (for example, Papers of Erich Hüttenhain, p. 10). Another version reports that the Ultra analysts responsible for North Africa became suspicious that Rommel's 'intuition' about his enemy's moves actually stemmed from intelligence, and so they persuaded their superiors to trace the leak. The first tale tends to appear in Axis accounts and the second in Allied versions.

46. PRO: HW 1/636.

47. Some insist that German intelligence deciphered Fellers's signals (Bradley F. Smith, *The Ultra Magic Deals*, pp. 111–12). Ralph Bennett says the Italian secret service stole Fellers's codes; see *Behind the Battle*, p. 92.

48. PRO: DEFE 3/771.
49. Hinsley et al., *British Intelligence in World War II*, 2:414, footnote, citing a decrypt of 11 September 1942.
50. General A. Praun, in *German Radio Intelligence and the Soldatensender*, p. 53. The restrained silence impressed the Germans.
51. Hinsley et al., *British Intelligence in World War II*, 2:554.
52. Hinsley et al., *British Intelligence in World War II*, vol. 2, Appendix I (i). Unfortunately the Allies' own cipher systems and changes lie under stricter security than the Enigma and Purple. Thus few details of these changes can be found in declassified sources.
53. For details below, see NARA: RG 457 HCC SRH-024.
54. NARA: RG 457 HCC SRH-024, III:43. For Allied inability to identify specific dispatches compromised, see pp. 44–45.
55. NARA: RG 457 HCC SRH-024, III:53.
56. Ibid., 50–51.
57. Ibid., 45.
58. Ibid., VI:195–199.
59. Hinsley et al., *British Intelligence in World War II*, Vol. 2, Appendix I (i).
60. NARA: RG 165, Box 2061 "P" File: District Three Security Intelligence Report, 8 December 1944.
61. Harry Hinsley orchestrated "snatches" of German weather ships and their cipher materials for just this reason. Kahn, *Seizing the Enigma*. See Harris, *Enigma*, for a vivid fictional account of the subsequent breaks.
62. NARA: RG 457 HCC Box 1119 NR 4633 – McCormack's Trip to London, p. 22.
63. PRO: ADM 223/2 – ZIP/ZG/25, 4 July 1941.
64. PRO: WO 244/128 – Lessons from Operations in the Italian Campaign, p. 11.
65. NARA: RG 457 HCC Box 1119 NR 3601 – Indications of the German Offensive of December 1944 (Ardennes).
66. NARA: RG 457 HCC Box 1123 NR 3606 – Plans for Research and Development of Cryptographic and Cryptanalytic Machinery, 18 September 1942, pp. 1, 4.
67. NARA: RG 457 HCC SRMA-011, 12 February 1945. See also HCC Box 1370 NR 4290.
68. Presumably the pluggable rotor. NARA: RG 457 HCC Box 1024 NR 3268 – Annual Report of Cryptographic Material Branch FY 1945, p. 35.
69. NARA: RG 457 HCC Box 1026 NR 3283 – History of Converter M-134-C (SIGABA), p. 74. In the process the military discovered that the average female auxiliaries wired rotors two to three times faster than the average man. Ibid, p. 188.
70. NARA: RG 457 HCC Box 1024 NR 3268 – Annual Report of Cryptographic Material Branch FY 1945 Memo, 12 March 1945.
71. NARA: RG 457 HCC Box 1024 NR 3268 – Annual Report of Cryptographic Material Branch FY 1945 Memo to General Bissell, 16 April 1945, p. 2.

72. Commander J. Russell, "Ultra and the Campaign Against the U-Boats..." in Mulligan, *Ultra, Magic and the Allies*, p. 5.

73. Hinsley et al., *British Intelligence in World War II*, 2: Appendix I, pp. 636–640.

74. BA/MA: RM7/104, p. 40.

75. Clarke, "GC&CS," p. 222.

76. Wark, *The Ultimate Enemy*, p. 174, citing Berlin Embassy minutes, 31 December 1935, C61/4/18, OF 371/19883.

77. Hinsley et al., *British Intelligence in World War II*, 2:554.

78. See the exchange in PRO: HW 14/5 Letter 19 June 1940 to Air Commodore A. R. Boyle; HW 14/6 Letter to Head of GC&CS from DDMI (O), 5 July 1940 and following.

## 8. DETERMINED ANSWERS

1. PRO: ADM 223/505, p. 6.

2. NARA: RG 457 HCC Box 625 NR 1695 – German Naval Communications Intelligence, p. 41.

3. NARA: RG 457 HCC Box 1400 NR 4644 – The Cryptologic Service in World War II, p. 23. (emphasis mine)

4. NARA: RG 457 HCC Box 594 NR 1515 – German Operational Intelligence, pp. 87–90.

5. General Albert Praun notes Hitler and General Jodl "showed a lack of confidence in communication intelligence, especially if the reports were unfavorable." He quotes Hitler as saying "Only men of genius can recognize the enemy's intentions and draw the proper military conclusions..." in "German Radio Intelligence," in *Intelligence, Counterintelligence and Military Deception During the World War II Era*, pp. 77, 134, 240. See also Michael Geyer, "National Socialist Germany: The Politics of Information," in *Knowing One's Enemies*, ed. Ernest May (Princeton, NJ: Princeton University Press, 1984).

6. Indeed, by the end of 1942, after just one year at war, the United States outproduced not just the Reich but all of the Axis powers combined. See Overy, *Why the Allies Won*, p. 192 and chap. 6.

7. Omar Bartov, *Hitler's Army* (Oxford: Oxford University Press, 1991).

8. The BBC series *The World at War* depicts this German tragedy vividly.

9. NARA: RG 457 HCC Box 743 NR 1862 – German Navy's Use of Special Intelligence, p. 53.

10. NARA: RG 457 HCC Box 625 NR 1695 – German Naval Communications Intelligence, p. 41.

11. This paragraph from NARA: RG 457 HCC Box 743 NR 1862 – German Navy's Use of Special Intelligence, pp. 46–47, 74, 78.

12. NARA: RG 457 HCC Box 625 NR 1695 – German Naval Communications Intelligence, p. 42.

13. NARA: RG 457 HCC Box 743 NR 1862 – German Navy's Use of Special Intelligence, p. 80; XB-Bericht 45/42, pp. 33–38, citing signals from Naval Command Oran and from Admiral Darlan to Petain.

14. NARA: RG 457 Entry 9003 Bericht 24/44, pp. 6–7.

15. NARA: RG 457 Entry 9003 Bericht 45/42, 2.–8.11.42, p. 19.

16. See, for example, NARA: RG 457 Entry 9003 Bericht 43/42 19.–25. Oktober 1942, p. 14, and RG 457 HCC Box 743 NR 1862 – German Navy's Use of Special Intelligence, pp. 78–81.

17. This deception (Fortitude) explained D Day as merely a feint prior to "real" assaults on Calais and Norway. See F. H. Hinsley et al., *British Intelligence in World War II*, especially vol. 5; Anthony Cave Brown, *Bodyguard of Lies* (New York: Harper & Row, 1975); John Masterman, *Double Cross System* (New York: Avon, 1972); James R. Koch, "Operation Fortitude: the Backbone of Deception," *Military Review* 73, no. 3 (1992): 66–77; Ralph Bennett, "Fortitude, Ultra and the 'Need to Know'," *Intelligence and National Security* 4, no. 3 (July 1989): 482–502.

18. Hinsley et al., *British Intelligence in World War II*, 5:199. Germany's designation of Sunday as a day of rest largely survived even Albert Speer's move toward a "total war" footing. Even in the twenty-first century, most commercial activity remains illegal on Sundays.

19. NARA: RG 457 HCC Box 743 NR 1860 – Radio Intercept and Cryptanalysis (German), p. 15.

20. See the story of Menzer's security messages in chap. 4, for example. Weather codes also allowed breaks into the highly secure Enigma M, see David Kahn, *Seizing the Enigma*, pp. 189–190, and Hinsley et al., *British Intelligence in World War II*, vol. 2, *passim*.

21. See chap. 6: The Allied Reality II.

22. Note that a 1944 Marine report mentions a warning from the OKH about "weak points in the use of machine cyphers in the Army sphere." The Marine disregarded these concerns as not pertinent to naval enciphering methods. PRO: ADM 223/505, pp. 20–21.

23. NARA: RG 165 Box 666: Lt. Gen. Schimpf interrogation 20 March 1945.

24. Gellermann, . . . *und lauschten*, p. 35.

25. NARA: RG 457 HCC Box 1400 NR 4644 – The Cryptologic Service in World War II, pp. 20–21, 45.

26. NARA: RG 457 HCC Box 604 NR 1571 – History of the German Naval Radio Intelligence Service, p. 6.

27. NARA: RG 457 HCC Box 1400 NR 4644 – The Cryptologic Service in World War II, p. 41.

28. BA/MA: RW 4/v. 777 – Vortragsnotiz.

29. BA/MA: RM 7/104, 18 and 28 February 1941.

30. BA/MA: RM 7/105, 9 March 1942.

31. NARA: RG 457 HCC Box 743 NR 1860 – Radio Intercept and Cryptanalysis (German), p. 26.

32. Flicke, *War Secrets in the Ether*, 1:153.

33. Gellermann, . . . *und lauschten*, pp. 57–58. In the Netherlands, they did use Dutch National Socialist interceptors; however, these regional stations were

presumably intercepting signals from local Party enemies rather than from enemies of the state, so even if they passed material to the Allies, it would be of little value.

34. NARA: RG 457 HCC Box 1405 NR 4541 – Codes and Ciphers: Germany, German Cryptanalytic Documents Inspk. 7 KTB May 1943. Possibly Mettig was after that promotion.

35. Gellermann, . . . und lauschten für Hitler, pp. 39, 44.

36. NARA: RG 457 HCC Box 1400 NR 4644 – The Cryptologic Service in World War II, pp. 40–41.

37. Cremer, U-Boat Commander, p. 117.

38. Including the Ettinghausen brothers, German Jews who worked on Ultra at Bletchley; Edward Teller worked on the top secret Manhattan Project in the United States.

39. One historian puts Germany's move to Total War at July 1943, when Albert Speer became head of War Production (Bennett, Behind the Battle, p. 138).

40. BA/MA: RH 44/506, p. 29. The Heer's radio station worked no later than 7 p.m. until 29 March 1943, when their workday lengthened to 9:15 p.m.; 8 May 1943 they worked as late as 22:15. The Allies had moved to twenty-four hour, seven-day-a-week shifts almost immediately.

41. BA/MA: RM 7/104, 14 December 1942. At this time they were using Hollerith machines to attack U.S. strip ciphers.

42. The maneuvers of March 1943. Flicke, War Secrets in the Ether, 2:204.

43. NARA: RG 457 HCC Box 769 NR 1995 – Interrogations, p. 13.

44. Gellermann, . . . und lauschten, p. 32.

45. See Toliver and Hanns Scharff, The Interrogator (Fallbrook, CA: Aero, 1978).

46. Gellermann, . . . und lauschten, p. 32.

47. German Military Intelligence, Military Intelligence Division, U.S. War Department, April 1946 (Frederick, MD: University Publications of America, 1984), p. 143.

48. Ibid., p. 280.

49. The Navy drew its officers from the middle class, particularly the upper middle class. T. P. Mulligan, Neither Sharks Nor Wolves (Annapolis, MD: Naval Institute Press, 1999), pp. 31–32. See also Craig, The Politics of the Prussian Army 1640–1945; Demeter, The German Officer-Corps in Society and State 1650–1945; Martin Kitchen, A Military History of Germany from the Eighteenth Century to the Present Day (Bloomington: Indiana University Press, 1975); Müller, The Army, Politics and Society in Germany 1933–45.

50. Gordon Welchman foresaw this problem with Enigma decrypts and set up an excellent production process at Bletchley Park. See Welchman's The Hut 6 Story: Breaking the Enigma Code, passim; NARA: RG 457 HCC Box 1126 NR 3620 – E Operations of the GC&CS at Bletchley Park; Box 880 NR 2612 – Capt. Walter J. Fried Reports; and PRO: HW 14 passim, and chapters above. Because the Germans did not see this possibility for their own decryption, presumably they never

imagined the enemy producing anything so massive as Bletchley's production system.

51. Bonatz, *Marine Funkaufklärung*, p. 28.
52. Gellermann, *...und lauschten*, p. 115.
53. Praun, *German Radio Intelligence*, p. 77.
54. NSA: DF 187C (Fenner) p. 4; Gellermann, *...und lauschten*, pp. 21–23. Mettig of OKH also transferred to the front in 1943 (see above).
55. NARA: RG 457 HCC Box 625 NR 1695 – German Naval Communications Intelligence, p. 58. Marine communications in the Black Sea apparently had more independence, passing results from Russian naval traffic "immediately to the local naval command" before forwarding them to headquarters; ibid., p. 65.
56. NARA: RG 457 HCC Box 1400 NR 4644 – The Cryptologic Service in World War II, p. 12.
57. NARA: RG 457 HCC Box 604 NR 1571 – History of the German Naval Radio Intelligence Service, p. 5.
58. Note that this negative attitude in sigint contrasts with Dönitz's acceptance of the U-boat technician's creation of the Magic Eye (see below). Perhaps the technician's work came close enough to his assigned tasks or perhaps such a technical development was seen as distinctly different from the type of work required for cryptology.
59. NARA: RG 457 HCC Box 625 NR 1695 – German Naval Communications Intelligence, p. 57.
60. Ibid., p. 58.
61. Granted, the last suggestion brings with it an increased danger of duplicate messages that could provide cribs for previously unbroken systems and so would have required tightening standard cryptologic procedures.

## 9. ENTER THE MACHINES

1. Bonatz, *Marine Funkaufklärung*, p. 105.
2. NARA: RG 457 HCC Box 189 NR 894 – SIGESO 56 Report, 19/10/45, p. 2 and pp. 9–10.
3. This animosity appears throughout Fritz Ringer's work *The Decline of the German Mandarins: The German Academic Community, 1890–1933* (Cambridge, MA: Harvard University Press, 1969). After 1848, German professors largely retreated from politics and civil life. Hitler's suspicion of intellectualism would only deepen the division between military and academia. See also Craig, *The Germans*, pp. 173–178.
4. While the same could be said for the Allied signals intelligence effort's emphasis on results, the cryptanalysts at Bletchley Park did mention that "the problem [of Enigma ciphers] was an interesting and amusing one.... [offering] the pleasure of playing an intellectual game." NARA: RG 457 HCC Box 1424 NR 4685 – History of Hut 8, Conclusion. See also U.S. long-term research in chap. 7.

5. NSA: DF 187 (Fenner), p. 9. The broader topic of Nazi ambivalence about technology requires further research and lies beyond the scope of this work.

6. See, for example, Tom Bower, *The Paperclip Conspiracy: The Battle for the Spoils and Secrets of Nazi Germany* (London: Joseph, 1987); and Linda Hunt. *Secret Agenda: The United States Government, Nazi Scientists, and Project Paperclip, 1944–1990* New York: St. Martin's Press, 1991).

7. NARA: RG 457 HCC Box 189 NR 894 – SIGESO, 19/10/45, p. 3.

8. Ibid., pp. 4, 6.

9. Cremer, *U-Boat Commander*, p. 163; and NARA: RG 457 HCC Box 189 NR 894 – SIGESO 56 19/10/45, p. 4.

10. NARA: RG 457 HCC Box 189 NR 894 – SIGESO 19/10/45, p. 4. Many continued unaware of the effort. Professor Bechert did not know he was the adviser in Theoretical Physics until an Allied officer told him after V-E day; ibid., p. 7.

11. Cremer, *U-Boat Commander*, p. 164. Note the distinction between "technical inferiority" and tactical and strategic superiority.

12. NARA: RG 457 HCC Box 189 NR 894 – Report on German Electronics and Signals Organizations, 19/10/45, p. 4; also 5/3/46, sheet 2.

13. Göring's Reichforschungsamt proved a partial exception to this rule and in postwar Allied analyses came closer to exploiting the potential of its scientific staff. Postwar interrogators determined that this system of division should continue in post-Reich Germany as it rendered scientists "harmless." NARA: RG 457 HCC Box 189 NR 894 – Report on German Electronics and Signals Organizations, 6/2/46, sheet 13; 19/10/45, p. 10.

14. NARA: RG 457 HCC Box 189 NR 894 – Report on German Electronics and Signals Organizations, 19/10/45, pp. 9–10; 6/2/46, sheets 11–13.

15. Cremer, *U-Boat Commander*, p. 167. In interviews, J. Rohwer and T. P. Mulligan have described Admiral Dönitz meeting with each returning commander alone.

16. NARA: RG 457 HCC Box 189 NR 894 – SIGESO, 19/10/45, p. 8.

17. Dr. Erich Hüttenhain in NARA: RG 457 HCC Box 1006 NR 3142 – Statements by POWs, p. 5.

18. BA/MA: RM7/104 3./Skl p. 40, 28 February 1941; PRO: ADM 223/505, p. 8.

19. BA/MA: RM 7/104 3./Skl, 29 February 1941, p. 40.

20. Dr. Erich Hüttenhain, chief cryptanalyst at OKW/Chi. NARA: RG 457 HCC Box 1006 NR 3142 – Statements by POWs, p. 5. (emphasis in original)

21. See discussion of the Enigma machine in chap. 1 and of the machine's theoretical strengths in "How Statistics Led the Germans to Believe Enigma Secure and Why They Were Wrong," *Cryptologia* 27, no. 2: 119–131; and Miller's pamphlet, "The Cryptographic Mathematics of Enigma."

22. NARA: RG 457 HCC Box 1006 NR 3142 – Statements by POWs re: Work on American and British Systems, p. 5. In fact, Bletchley's cryptanalysts constructed catalogues of all the possible permutations of *eins* [one] and then tried the results against suspected cribs. Thus they combined statistical methods with their knowledge of the Wehrmacht's practices.

23. See Marion Rejewski's appendix in Garlinski's *The Enigma War*; and Hodges, *Alan Turing: An Enigma*.

24. *NOVA* "The Codebreakers." Germany used similar machines, which they called Holleriths, in cryptology and also in the logistics of the relocation and extermination of those the Nazis deemed "undesirable." See the permanent display in the Holocaust Museum (Washington, DC).

25. Kozaczuk, *Enigma*, Appendix E, "The Mathematical Solution of the Enigma Cipher by Marian Rejewski," pp. 272–291.

26. Ibid., p. 290, Appendix E.

27. Ibid., p. 28.

28. Burke, paper at Seventh Annual Cryptologic History Symposium, October 26, 1995.

29. H.-R. Schuchmann, "ENIGMA Variations," No. 194 in Cryptography, *Lecture Notes in Computer Science* (Berlin: Springer-Verlag, 1982), pp. 65–68. Note that this date is six months before the MARK I's first operation and two years before ENIAC. T. H. Flowers, "The Design of Colossus," *Annals of the History of Computing* 5, no. 3 (July 1983): 238–253. See also Hinsley and Stripp, *Codebreakers*, pp. 141ff; and Erskine and Smith, eds., *Action This Day*, chap. 18.

30. NARA: RG 457 HCC Box 1405 NR 4541 – Codes and Ciphers: Germany, March 1943; however, this comment focuses on Hollerith machines again.

31. David Kahn, "Codebreaking in World Wars I and II," in *The Missing Dimension*, citing OKW memo of 29 Nov 1937: Wi/IF 5.2150 in Freiburg.

32. Paschke, "Das Chiffrier- und Fernmeldewesen im Auswärtigen Amt." p. 73.

33. Ibid., pp. 73–74.

34. Ibid., p. 155.

35. NARA: RG 457 HCC Box 1369 NR 4282 chart.

36. BA/MA: RM 7/105, 27 April 1942.

37. Paschke, "Das Chiffrier- und Fernmeldewesen," p. 73.

38. NARA: RG 457 HCC Box 1369 NR 4282 chart. For more on the effort to apply scanning and detection technology to film for cryptanalytic purposes, see Colin B. Burke, *Information and Secrecy* (Metuchen, NJ: Scarecrow Press, 1994).

39. Hüttenhain's papers have a description of these ciphers.

40. NSA: DF 187A (Fenner), p. 27.

41. Bonatz, *Die Deutsche Marine Funkaufklärung*, p. 105.

42. NSA: DF 187 (Fenner), pp. 18–19.

43. NSA: DF 187 (Fenner), pp. 18–19 (italics added).

44. NSA: DF 187A (Fenner), p. 27.

45. BA/MA: RM 7/105, 27 April 1942.

46. NSA: DF 187 (Fenner), p. 13.

47. NSA: DF 187A (Fenner), p. 18.

48. Konrad Züse's obituary, 20 December 1995. Associated Press.

49. Richard Stevens, *Understanding Computers* (Oxford: Oxford University Press, 1986), cited in Devereux, *Messenger Gods of Battle*, p. 306 footnote. After the war,

Züse described his machine to his Allied captors and offered both his machine and his expertise to the Americans. NARA: RG 338 290/56/2/1 – Records of BIOS subcommittee reports, Box 48 – BIOS/IR/47 #1–835 Miscell. Interrogation of K. Züse.

50. NSA: DF 187A (Fenner), p. 27.

51. Bonatz, *Marine Funkaufklärung*, p. 105.

52. NARA: RG 457 HCC Box 1419 NR 4645 – Tentative Brief Descriptions of Cryptanalytic Equipment For Enigma Problems; Box 1369 NR 4282 RAM Chart; and David J. Crawford and Philip E. Fox, "The Autoscritcher and the Superscritcher: Aids to Cryptanalysis of the German Enigma Cipher Machine, 1944–1946," *IEEE Annals of the History of Computing* 14, no. 3 (1992): 9–22, and with thanks to Phil Fox.

## CONCLUSION: RECOGNIZING THE END OF SECURITY

1. From Charles Mann's profile of Bruce Schneier, "Homeland Insecurity," *The Atlantic Monthly* (September 2002): 81–102.

2. For more information on the Pacific theater, see such works as Richard Aldrich, *Intelligence and the War Against Japan* (Cambridge: Cambridge University Press, 2000); Budiansky, *Battle of Wits*; Edward J. Drea, *MacArthur's Ultra* (Lawrence: University Press of Kansas, 1992); Lewin, *The American Magic*; and Stripp, *Codebreaker in the Far East*.

3. *German Military Intelligence.* [Military Intelligence Division, U.S. War Department. April 1946.] (Frederick, MD: University Publications of America, 1984), p. 147.

4. For more on this social and political revolution, which paralleled uprisings around Europe in 1848, see such works as Craig's *The Germans* and his *Politics of the Prussian Army 1640–1945* and Fritz Ringer's *The Decline of the German Mandarins*, among others. For the number of professors driven from their posts, see Charles E. McClelland, *State, Society, and University in Germany 1700–1914* (Cambridge: Cambridge University Press, 1980), p. 357.

5. See von Lingen's description of the Luftwaffe's Eastern Front operation, for example. NARA: RG 457 HCC Box 1400 NR 4644, p. 41.

6. I am indebted to Robert J. Hanyok of NSA for this point.

7. *Die deutsche Luftwaffe: 1941–1945*, 1976 issue. A scientist, K. Becker, was also rumored to have committed suicide, "because he could not produce what Hitler wanted." NARA: RG 457 HCC Box 189 NR 894 – SIGESO 56 Report on German Electronics and Signals Organizations – Vol. 1, 6/2/46 report.

8. The literature on the military under the Third Reich fills many shelves. See, for example, Demeter, *The German Officer-Corps in Society and State 1650–1945* (German original 1962); Klaus-Jürgen Müller, *The Army, Politics and Society in Germany 1933–45* (Manchester: Manchester University Press, 1987); Albert Seaton, *The German Army 1933–45* (London: Weidenfeld and Nicolson, 1982).

9. Flicke, *War Secrets in the Ether*, p. v. The British called their evaluators analysts.

10. Mulligan, *Neither Sharks Nor Wolves*, p. 53; Jordan Vause, *U-Boat Ace* (Annapolis, MD: Naval Institute Press, 1990).

11. PRO: ADM 223/505 – Security of Allied Communications May–June 1945, p. 1.

12. Irving Janis, *Victims of Groupthink: A Psychological Study of Foreign-Policy Decisions and Fiascoes* (Boston: Houghton Mifflin Company, 1972).

13. On the significance of the 1940 torpedo failure investigation and the legacy of the mutiny, I am indebted to both Dr. Timothy Mulligan and Professor Dr. Jürgen Rohwer. German sailors played a highly visible role in the mutinies which helped drive out Imperial Germany's regime in October/November 1918.

14. NARA: RG 457 HCC Box 808 NR 3775. BdU Log 1–15/8/43.

15. The German Enigma company had purchased the patents of a Dutch commercial inventor.

16. NARA: RG 457 HCC Box 1405 through Box 1409 NR 4541 – Codes and Ciphers: German Cryptanalytic Documents Folder 3, October, November 1943 on Inspk. 7's work; Paschke, "Das Chiffrier- und Fernmeldewesen im Auswärtigen Amt: Seine Entwicklung und Organisation" A.A. Aktengruppe VS Band 6025 discusses the Pers Z work, pp. 54ff. See also Ralph Erskine's discussion in Erskine and Smith, *Action This Day*, chap. 19.

17. The Allies also failed to readjust their assumptions in vital areas – most notoriously, neither the British insistence on the effectiveness of widespread bombing nor the American obsession with precision bombing were supported by the known results – even during the war. See Harold L. Wilensky, *Organizational Intelligence: Knowledge and Policy in Government and Industry* (New York: Basic Books, Inc., 1967), chap. 2; Wark, *The Ultimate Enemy*; Sir Charles Webster and Noble Franklin, *Strategic Air Offensive Against Germany 1939–1945*. 4 vols. (London: HSMO, 1961); and Janis, *Victims of Groupthink*.

18. Dr. Erich Hüttenhain, chief cryptanalyst at OKW/Chi. NARA: RG 457 HCC Box 1006 NR 3142 – Statements by POWs, p. 5.

19. See, for example, the presentations given at the conference on Ultra intelligence in Stuttgart and Bad Godesberg in 1978. E. Jäckel and J. Rohwer, eds., *Die Funkaufklärung im Zweiten Weltkreig* (Stuttgart: Motorbuch Verlag, 1978).

20. David Kahn, *The Codebreakers: The Story of Secret Writing* (New York: Scribner, 1996), p. 973.

21. NARA: RG 457 HCC Box 1112 NR 3551 – Establishment of Army-Navy Communication Intelligence Board, Memo 2 March 1945, on establishing the board from Major General Clayton Bissell to Deputy Chief of Staff.

22. The list of operations includes intentional capture of German vessels to acquire Enigma materials, the planting of mines at sea to crack German coordinate codes, and the U.S. Navy's famous Midway signal requesting water to prove that JN25's "AF" stood for that island, as well as direction of elements of deception

plans such as 'Fortitude' and 'Mincemeat' (known as "The Man Who Never Was").

23. The Americans ignored this principle more than once, most notably with the shootdown of Admiral Yamamoto and attacks on Atlantic U-boat tankers. These lapses infuriated the British.

24. Many myths about this sacrifice have surfaced since 1974. Most famously, F. W. Winterbotham claimed that Churchill had "sacrificed" Coventry; that is, refused to warn the city of an impending bombing and thereby allowing unsuspecting hundreds to die where a warning would have saved them. (Hinsley et al., *British Intelligence in World War II*, effectively refute this story.) Other tales of doomed airplane reconnaissance flights hold more credence. The theme of unheralded sacrifice to preserve the secret of Ultra recurs in nearly every account of Allied intelligence from the deprivations and dangers suffered by SLUs to Dillwyn Knox's death from exhaustion, attempting new solutions to the end (e.g., Fitzgerald, *The Knox Brothers*, pp. 247–251).

25. For more on the development and adoption of Operations Research, see authors such as Erik P. Rau, "The Adoption of Operations Research in the United States during World War II," in *Systems, Experts and Computers*, eds. Agatha C. Hughes and Thomas P. Hughes (Cambridge, MA: MIT Press, 2000).

26. The story of the American cracking of a Soviet OTP, code-named Venona, became public in the 1990s. See such works as Benson and Warner, *Venona*, and Haynes and Klehr, *Venona*.

27. Bruce Schneier quoted in Charles C. Mann's profile "Homeland Insecurity," *Atlantic Monthly* (Sept. 2002): 81–102.

# BIBLIOGRAPHY

In citing archival documents, I have used those abbreviations found in the indexes to the documents. In the footnotes, I have abbreviated the U.S. National Archives' and Records Administration as NARA and the UK's Public Record Office as PRO. The National Archives' documents are by record group, abbreviated RG. The documents from the German Bundesarchiv Militärarchiv (BA/MA) use the following abbreviations:

RHD – Reichsheer (the army's documents)
RL – Reichsluftwaffe (the Luftwaffe's documents)
RM – Reichsmarine (the navy's documents)
RW – Reichswehrmacht (the armed forces command documents)

The collections in BA/MA, PRO, and NARA overlap, but do not completely duplicate each other.

### ARCHIVAL SOURCES

**Bundesarchiv/Militärarchiv, Freiburg**

Seekriegsleitung Kriegstagebuch [War diaries] (Note: the KTB are being published and are also available on microfilm, most in English translation, at
NARA and the PRO)

Chronik Marine Nachrichtenschule (2 volumes)

Note: nearly all of the following are also available in National Archives, College
Park, MD U.S.A., Record Group 457
H. Dv. g. 89 – "Feindnachrichtendienst" – 1941
RHD 5/92 – Teil 1 – "Handbuch für die Generalstabsdienst im Kriege" – 1.8.39
RHD 7/29/1 – "Verstöße gegen die Geheimhaltung im Nachrichtenverkehr" –
24.6.44

RM 7/98 – 1./Skl – Teil B V – Anlagen Allgemeinen Inhalts 6/43–12/43
RM 7/100 – "Vernehmigung des Funkers…"
RM 7/103 – 2./Skl – Sept 1939–16.2.40; 15.3.40–6.12.40
RM 7/104–7/108 – B-Dienst records 1941–1945
RMD 4/6 (Vorschrift für den Funk- und U.T. Dienst in den Reichsmarine)
RL 14/91 HDv.g. 89 and 92
RW 4/v. 910 "Arbeitsunterlagen der Nachrichten Truppe"
RW 4/v. 777 – Vorlage and some C.V.s

### Bibliothek für Zeitgeschichte, Stuttgart, Germany

Personal papers of Dr. Prof. Jürgen Rohwer – Referate, Correspondence, Tagung
    documents
Papers of Dr. Erich Hüttenhain
Papers of Wilhelm Fenner

### Auswärtiges Amt, Politisches Archiv, Bonn, Germany

Adolf Paschke, "Das Chiffrier- und Fernmeldewesen im Auswärtigen Amt Seine
    Entwicklung und Organisation. Eine historische Studie von Adolf Paschke
    Vortragender Legationsrat a.D." Bonn 1957. Aktengruppe VS, Band 6025
    (2 volumes)
Horst Hauthal, Aktengruppe VS, Band 6025, "Beitrag zur Geschichte des
    Chiffrierwesens im Auswärtigen Amt – 1939–1945."

### Office of Public Records in Kew, England

ADM 199, 223 (the Admiralty's documents)
AIR 41/48
DEFE 3
CAB 81/132
FO 371
FO 935
HW 1–16
PREM 3, 4, 13
WO 106, 165, 169, 199, 201, 208, 244

### Imperial War Museum, London, England

Papers of Colonel R. T. Jenks
Papers of Mrs. M. Ackroyd
Papers of Daphne Humphreys Baker
Papers of J. R. Vezey

## National Archives and Records Administration, Washington, DC and MD

RG 165, Box 2061 "P" File: District Three Security Intelligence Report; Boxes 666 and 727, POW Interrogations

RG 331, Box 3

RG 457 Special Research Histories (SRH), such as SRH-112 "Post-Mortem Writings on Indications of the Ardennes Offensive," 1945; SRH-024 "Ultra in the Atlantic," 1944–1945. 6 volumes (citations are from published version, see Bray below); SRH-364 "History of the Signal Security Agency"; SRH-365 "History of the Signal Intelligence Division of the Signal Officer AFMIDPAC, 1941–1945."

RG 457 SRMA 4–11 U.S. Army Records Relating to Cryptology 1927–1985

RG 457 SRMN 30–33 Navy Records Relating to Cryptology 1918–1950

RG 457 Entry 9003 German Navy Reports of Intercepted Radio Messages – the B-Dienst Berichte, microfilm and hard copy. Duplicate set of originals also in Freiburg RM 7 collection.

RG 457 Historic Cryptographic Collection Pre–World War I through World War II (HCC) (1479 boxes)

T-1022 series – (microfilm) Captured German Naval documents, including war diaries (KTB) of the Marine Command (Skl) and of the Commander of Uboats (BdU). [T-1022/4063 and T-1022/4064 are KTB/BdU; T-1022/2310/PG 34534 – Flottenkommando documents on Taktik, Mob.-Angl.]

American records on Japanese ciphers can be found through the Military Records department of the National Archives.


## National Cryptologic History Museum, National Security Agency (NSA), Fort Meade, MD

DF 187 (187A, 187C, 187D) [Memoirs of Wilhelm Fenner]

Abraham Sinkov oral history

"European Axis Signal Intelligence in World War II as Revealed by TICOM Investigations and by other Prisoner of War Interrogations and Captured Material." volumes 1–2

MDR #42585, 27 March 2003 "Report on the Interrogation of Five Leading Germans at Nuremberg on 27th September 1945."


### UNPUBLISHED SOURCES

Burke, Colin (Brad). Paper at Seventh Annual Cryptologic History Symposium, October 26, 1995.

Erskine, Ralph. "The Development of Typex" (unpublished paper).

Kelley, Stephen J. "Big Machines: The Relative Cryptographic Security of the German Enigma, the Japanese PURPLE, and the U.S. SIGABA/ECM cipher machines in World War II" (unpublished manuscript). A published version is now available.

Papers of Timothy P. Mulligan.

Personal correspondence with Prof. F. H. Hinsley, Wladyslaw Kozaczuk, Wolfgang Mache, Michael van der Meulen, and Heinz Ulbricht.

Interviews by the author with Ralph Bennett, Barbara and Joseph Eachus, William F. Filby, Christian Gellrich, Arthur Levinson, Brian McCue, Cecil and Nancy Phillips, Jürgen Rohwer, Alan Stripp, James F. Thacher, and Edward Thomas.

Stripp, Alan. "Reflections on British Wartime Codebreaking." Paper delivered at The Significance of Secret Intelligence in World War Two, Institute of Anglo-American History, University of Cologne, June 24–25, 1994.

PUBLISHED SOURCES

Agrell, Wilhelm, and Bo Huldt, eds. *Clio Goes Spying: Eight Essays on the History of Intelligence.* Lund, Sweden: University of Lund, 1983.

Albrow, Martin. *Bureaucracy.* New York: Praeger, 1970.

Aldrich, Richard J. *Intelligence and the War against Japan: Britain, America and the Politics of Secret Service.* Cambridge: Cambridge University Press, 2000.

Alvarez, David J., ed. *Allied and Axis Signals Intelligence in World War II.* London: Frank Cass, 1999.

  *Secret Messages: Codebreaking and American Diplomacy, 1930–1945.* Lawrence: University Press of Kansas, 2000.

  *Nothing Sacred: Nazi Espionage against the Vatican, 1939–1945* (with Robert A. Graham, SJ). London: Frank Cass, 1997.

  "Diplomatic Solutions: German Diplomatic Cryptanalysis, 1919–1945." *International Journal of Intelligence and Counterintelligence* 9 (Summer 1996).

Andrew, Christopher, ed. *Codebreaking and Signals Intelligence.* London: Frank Cass, 1986.

  "F. H. Hinsley and the Cambridge Moles." *Diplomacy and Intelligence during the Second World War*, ed. R. Langhorne. Cambridge: Cambridge University Press, 1985.

  *Her Majesty's Secret Service.* New York: Viking, 1986.

  "Historical Research on the British Intelligence Community." In *Comparing Foreign Intelligence*, ed. Roy Godson. New York: Pergamon-Brassy's, 1988. pp. 43–64.

  "How the Russians Cracked Enigma." *Daily Telegraph*, 20 January 1988.

Andrew, Christopher, and David Dilks, eds. *The Missing Dimension: Governments and Intelligence Communities in the Twentieth Century*. London: Macmillan, 1984.

Andrew, Christopher, and Jeremy Noakes, eds. *Intelligence and International Relations, 1900–1945*. Exeter: University of Exeter, 1987.

Ansens, André. "The Netherlands Military Intelligence Summaries 1939–1940." *Military Affairs* 50 (Oct. 1988): 190–199.

Arnold-Forster, Mark "Playing the deadliest numbers game." *The Guardian* (18 October 1977): 4.

Atha, Robert I. "Bombe! 'I Could Hardly Believe It!'" *Cryptologia* 9, no. 4 (October 1985): 332.

Barnett, Correlli, ed. *Hitler's Generals*. New York: Grove Weidenfeld, 1989.

Bartov, Omar. *Hitler's Army*. Oxford: Oxford University Press, 1991.

Bar-Zohar, Michael. *Arrows of the Almighty*. New York: Macmillan, 1985.

Bauer, Friedrich L. "Cryptology: Methods and Maxims." In *Cryptography*, ed. Thomas Beth. *Lecture Notes in Computer Science* No. 149, ed. G. Goos and J. Hartmanis. Berlin: Springer, 1982. pp. 32–46.

Beck, Earl R. *Under the Bombs: The German Home Front 1942–1945*. Lexington, KY: University Press of Kentucky, 1986.

Beesly, Patrick. "Convoy PQ17: A Study of Intelligence and Decision Making." *Intelligence and National Security* 5, no. 2 (April 1990): 292–322.

    *Room 40*. New York: Harcourt Brace Jovanovitch, 1982.

    "Das Signalbuch der "Magdeburg" half den Ersten Weltkrieg zu gewinnen." *Marine Rundschau* 78, no. 5 (1981): 273–276.

    *Very Special Intelligence: The Story of the Admiralty's Operational Intelligence Center, 1939–1945*. New York: Doubleday, 1978.

Beesly, Patrick, and Jürgen Rohwer. "'Special Intelligence' und die Vernichtung der 'Scharnhorst'." *Marine Rundschau* (October 1977): 563ff.

Behrendt, Hans-Otto. *Rommel's Intelligence in the Desert Campaign*. London: William Kimber, 1985 (German edition by Rombach, 1980).

Bennett, Ralph. *Behind the Battle: Intelligence in the War with Germany, 1939–45*. London: Sinclair-Stevenson, 1994.

    "Fortitude, Ultra and the 'Need to Know'." *Intelligence and National Security* 4, no. 3 (July 1989): 482–502.

    "Intelligence and Strategy: Some Observations on the War in the Mediterranean, 1941–45." *Intelligence and National Security* 5, no. 2 (April 1990): 444–464.

    *Ultra and Mediterranean Strategy*. London: H. Hamilton, 1989.

    *Ultra in the West: The Normandy Campaign: 1944–1945*. London: Hutchinson, 1979.

"World War II Intelligence: The Last 10 Years' Work Reviewed." *Defense Analysis* 3, no. 2 (June 1987): 103–117.

Benson, Robert Louis. *A History of U.S. Communications Intelligence during World War II: Policy and Administration*. Fort Meade, MD: National Security Agency, 1997.

Benson, Robert Louis, and Michael Warner, eds. *Venona: Soviet Espionage and the American Response 1939–1957*. Washington, DC: National Security Agency, 1996.

Berkowitz, Bruce. "National Security: Secrecy and National Security." *Hoover Digest* (2004): 3.

Bertrand, Gustave. *Enigma ou la plus grande énigme de la guerre 1939–1945*. Paris: Plon, 1973.

Best, Richard A., Jr. "Intelligence Community Reorganization: Potential Effects on DOD Intelligence Agencies." *CRS Report for Congress* (Order Code RL32515).

"The National Intelligence Director and Intelligence Analysis." *CRS Report for Congress* (Order Code RS21948).

Blau, Peter M. *The Dynamics of Bureaucracy: A Study of Interpersonal Relations in Two Government Agencies*. Chicago: University of Chicago Press, 1955.

Bloch, Gilbert. *Enigma avant Ultra*. Paris: 1985.

Blumenson, Martin. "Will 'Ultra' Rewrite History?" *Army* 28, no. 8 (August 1978): 42–48.

Böll, Heinrich. *The Casualty*. trans. Leila Vennewitz. New York: Farrar Straus Giroux, 1986. pp. 83–85.

Bonatz, Heinz. *Die deutsche Marine Funkaufklärung*. Darmstadt: Wehr & Wissen, 1970.

*Seekrieg im Äther: die Leistungen der Marine-Funkaufklärung 1939–1945*. Herford: E. S. Mittler, 1981.

Bontilier, James A. *The Royal Canadian Navy in Retrospect, 1910–1968*. Vancouver: 1982.

Bower, Tom. *The Paperclip Conspiracy: The Battle for the Spoils and Secrets of Nazi Germany*. London: Joseph, 1987.

Boyd, Carl. *Hitler's Japanese Confidant*. Lawrence: University Press of Kansas, 1993.

Brammer, Uwe. *Spionageabwehr und Geheime Meldedienst*. Heraus. Militärgeschichtliches Forschungsamt. Freiburg: Rombach GmbH & Co., 1989.

Bray, Jeffrey K., ed. *Ultra in the Atlantic*. [SRH-024 (1944–5)] Vols. 1–6. Laguna Hills, CA: Aegean Park Press, 1994.

Breitman, Richard. *Official Secrets: What the Nazis Planned. What the British and Americans Knew*. New York: Hill and Wang, 1998.

Brennecke, Jochen. *The Hunters and the Hunted.* London: Burke, 1958.

Brissaud, André. *Canaris: The Biography of Admiral Canaris, Chief of German Military Intelligence in the Second World War.* New York: Grosset & Dunlap, 1974.

   *The Nazi Secret Service.* trans. Milton Waldman. New York: Norton & Company, 1974.

Brown, Anthony Cave. *Bodyguard of Lies.* New York: Harper & Row, 1975.

   *"C": The Secret Life of Sir Stewart Menzies.* New York: Macmillan, 1987.

Buchheit, Gert. *Der deutsche Geheimdienst: Geschichte der militärischen Abwehr.* München: List, 1966.

   *Spionage in zwei Weltkriegen: Schachspiel mit Menschen.* Landshut: Verlag politisches archiv gmbh, 1975.

Budiansky, Stephen. *Battle of Wits: The Complete Story of Codebreaking in World War II.* New York: The Free Press, 2000.

Bundy, William P. "Some of My Wartime Experiences." *Cryptologia* 11, no. 2 (April 1987): 65–77.

Burke, Colin B. *Information and Secrecy.* Metuchen, NJ: Scarecrow Press, 1994.

Calvocoressi, Peter. *Top Secret ULTRA.* New York: Pantheon Books, 1980.

Calvocoressi, Peter, Guy Wint, and John Prichard. *Total War: The Causes and Courses of the Second World War.* London: Penguin, 1989.

Chalou, George C. *The Secrets War: The Office of Strategic Services in World War II.* (Proceedings of July 11–12, 1991 Conference.) Washington, DC: National Archives and Records Administration, 1992.

Clarke, William. "Bletchley Park 1941–1945." *Cryptologia* 12, no. 2 (April 1988): 97–99.

   "GC&CS." *Cryptologia* 11, no. 4 (October 1987): 221.

Clayton, Aileen. *The Enemy Is Listening.* London: Hutchinson & Co., Ltd., 1980.

Cline, Ray. *Secrets, Spies and Scholars: Blueprint of the Essential CIA.* Washington, DC: Acropolis Books, 1976.

Constantinides, George C. *Intelligence and Espionage: An Analytical Bibliography.* Boulder, CO: Westview Press, 1983.

Craig, Gordon A. *The Germans.* New York: Putnam, 1982.

   *The Politics of the Prussian Army 1640–1945.* Oxford: Oxford University Press, 1955.

Crawford, David J., and Philip E. Fox, eds. "The Autoscritcher and the Superscritcher: Aids to Cryptanalysis of the German Enigma Cipher Machine, 1944–1946." *IEEE Annals of the History of Computing* 14, no. 3 (1992): 9–22.

Cremer, Peter. *U-Boat Commander: A Periscope View of the Battle of the Atlantic.* trans. Lawrence Wilson. Annapolis, MD: Naval Institute Press, 1984.

Dallek, Wolfgang. *Marine Nachrichten Schule.* Flensburg: n.p., 1989.

Dammert, H., and Franz Kurowski. *Adler ruft Führerhauptquartier: Führungsfunk an allen Fronten: 1939–1945.* Leoni am Starnberger See: Druffel, 1985.

Davies, D. W., and D. A. Bell. "The Protection of Data by Cryptology." *National Physical Laboratory Report* 68 (Jan 1978).

Davies, Donald W. "The Bombe: A Remarkable Logic Machine." *Cryptologia* 23, no. 2 (April 1999): 108–138.

Deacon, Richard. *A History of the British Secret Service.* London: Frederick Muller, 1969.

Deavours, Cipher A., and Louis Kruh. *Machine Cryptography and Modern Cryptanalysis.* Dedham, MA: Artech House, 1985.

Demeter, Karl. *The German Officer-Corps in Society and State 1650–1945.* Introduction by Michael Howard. New York: Praeger, 1965 (German original 1962).

Denniston, A. G., "The Government Code and Cypher School Between the Wars." In *Codebreaking and Signals Intelligence,* ed. Christopher Andrew. London: Frank Cass, 1986. pp. 48–70.

Devereux, Tony. *Messenger Gods of Battle.* London: Brassey's, 1991.

*Die deutsche Luftwaffe 1941–1945.* [magazine] (1976).

Donini, Rear Admiral (disch.) Luigi. "Cryptographic Services of the Royal (British) and Italian Navies." *Cryptologia* 14, no. 2 (April 1990): 97–127.

Dönitz, Großadmiral Karl. *10 Jahren und 20 Tagen.* Bonn: Athenäum, 1958.

Drea, Edward J. *MacArthur's Ultra: Codebreaking and the War against Japan, 1942–1945.* Lawrence: University Press of Kansas, 1992.

*Das Dritte Reich.* Hannover: Verlag für Literatur & Zeitgeschehen, 1963.

Duffy, James P. *Hitler Slept Late and Other Blunders That Lost Him the War.* New York: Praeger, 1991.

Dulles, Allen. *The Craft of Intelligence.* New York: Harper & Row, 1963.

Eigner, Gustav (Former Abwehr personnel), Letter to the Editor, *Internationale Wehrrevue* 9, no. 5 (Oct. 1976): 861.

*Entwicklung, Planung und Durchführung operativer Ideen im Ersten und Zweiten Weltkrieg.* ed. Militärgeschichtlichen Forschungsamt. Herford & Bonn: E. S. Mittler, 1989.

Erskine, Ralph. "From the Archives: GC&CS Mobilizes 'Men of the Professor Type'." *Cryptologia* 10, no. 1 (January 1986):50–59.

Erskine, Ralph, and Gilbert Bloch. "Enigma: The Dropping of the Double Experiment." *Cryptologia* 10, no. 3 (July 1986): 97–108.

"Naval Enigma: An Astonishing Blunder." *Intelligence and National Security,* 11, no. 3 (July 1996): 468–473.

Erskine, Ralph, with Frode Weierud. "Naval Enigma: M4 and Its Rotors." *Cryptologia* 11, no. 4 (October 1987): 235–244.

"A Signal-Intelligence War." *Journal of Contemporary History* 16 (1981): 501–512.

"The Soviets and Naval Enigma: Some Comments." *Intelligence and National Security* 4, no. 3 (July 1989): 503–511.

Erskine, Ralph, and Michael Smith, eds. *Action This Day*. London: Bantam Press, 2001.

Eurich, Claus. *Tödliche Signale: Die kriegerische Geschichte der Informationtechnick*. Frankfurt: Luchterhand, 1991.

Fitzgerald, Penelope. *The Knox Brothers*. Washington, DC: Counterpoint, 2000.

Flicke, Wilhelm F. *War Secrets in the Ether*. 2 vols. Laguna Hills, CA: Aegean Park Press, 1977.

Flowers, T. H. "The Design of Colossus." *Annals of the History of Computing* 5, no. 3 (July 1983): 238–253.

Foot, M. R. D. *S.O.E. in France*. London: Frank Cass, 1966.

Friedmann, William F. Patent 2,028,772, issued 28 January 1936.

———. *Synoptic Tables for the Solution of Ciphers and a Bibliography of Cipher Literature*. Geneva, IL: Riverbank Laboratories, Dept. of Ciphers, 1918.

Garlinski, Józef. *The Enigma War: The Inside Story of the German Enigma Codes and How the Allies Broke Them*. New York: Scribner & Sons, 1979.

*Die geheimen Tagesberichte der deutschen Wehrmachtführung im Zweiten Weltkrieg 1939–1945*. hrsg. von Kurt Mehner. 10 Bände. Osnabrück: Biblio, 1984.

Gehlen, General R. *The Service*. [*Der Dienst*] trans. David Irving. New York: World Publishing, 1972.

Gellermann, Günther. *...und lauschten für Hitler: Geheime Reichssache: Die Abhörzentralen des Dritten Reiches*. Stuttgart: Bernard & Graefe, 1991.

*German Military Intelligence*. [Military Intelligence Division, U.S. War Department. April 1946.] Frederick, MD: University Publications of America, 1984.

*German Radio Intelligence and the Soldatensender*. Introduction by John Mendelsohn. New York: Garland, 1989 (National Archives, Record Group 338, Mans. P-038, General A. Praun).

Giessler, Helmuth. *Der Marine-Nachrichten und Ortungsdienst*. München: J. F. Lehmanns, 1971.

Gouazé, Linda Y. *Needles and Haystacks: The Search for Ultra in the 1930s*. MA thesis, Naval Postgraduate School, Monterey, CA, 1983.

Goulter, Christina. "The Role of Intelligence in Coastal Command's Anti-Shipping Campaign, 1940–45." *Intelligence and National Security* 5, no. 1 (January 1990): 84–109.

Groehler, Olaf. "Die Erforschung der Geschichte des zweiten Weltkrieges Stand und Aufgaben." *Zeitschrift für Geschichtswissenschaft* 33, no. 4 (1985): 316–322.

Groscurth, Helmut. *Tagebücher eines Abwehroffiziers 1938–1940*. H. Krausnich und H. C. Deutsch, eds. Stuttgart: Deutsches Verlags-Anstalt, 1970.

Gudgin, Peter. *Military Intelligence: The British Story*. New York: Sterling Publishers, 1989.

Guske, Heinz F. K. *The War Diaries of U-764: Fact or Fiction?* Gettysburg, PA: Thomas Publications, 1992.

Habatsch, Walter, ed. *Hitlers Weisungen für die Kriegführung 1939–1945*. Herford: Mittler & Sohn, 1983.

Halder, Franz. *KTB: Tägliche Aufzeichnungen des Chefs des Generalstabes des Heeres 1939–1942*. Hans-Adolf Jacobsen, ed. Stuttgart: Kohlhammer, 1962–1964.

Hamel, Georg. "Mathematisches Gutachten über die Chiffriermaschine Kryha." *Sitzungsberichte der Berliner Mathematischen Gesellschaft* 26 (1927).

Hanyok, Robert J. *Eavesdropping on Hell: Historical Guide to Western Communications Intelligence and the Holocaust, 1939–1945*. Fort Meade, MD: Center for Cryptologic History, 2005.

Harris, Robert. *Enigma*. New York: Random House, 1995.

Haynes, John Earl, and Harvey Klehr. *Venona: Decoding Soviet Espionage in America*. New Haven, CT: Yale University Press, 1999.

Heiber, Helmut. *Hitlers Lagebesprechungen*. Stuttgart: Deutsche Verlags-Anstalt, 1962.

Heldt, Siegfried. *Militärisches Nachrichtenweser*. Berlin: Militärverlag der Deutschen Demokratischen Republik (VEB), 1987.

Hepp, Generalleutnant a.D. Leo. "Fernmeldewesen." *Wehrwissenschaftliche Rundschau* 4, no. 9 (1954): 432–434.

"Die Funkabwehr." *F-Flagge* (May 1986): 9–15.

"Funktäuschung: Ein Hilfsmittel der operativen Führung." *Wehr-Wissenschaftliche Rundschau* 4, no. 3 (März 1984): 116–123.

"Der Geheime Nachrichtendienst." *Wehrkunde* 24, no. 6 (June 1975): 299–301.

Hessler, Günter. *Uboat War in the Atlantic*. London: HMSO, 1989.

Hinsley, F. H. "The Cambridge-Bletchley Line." *The Cambridge Review* (March 1990).

Hinsley, F. H., and Alan Stripp. *Codebreakers: The Inside Story of Bletchley Park*. Oxford: Oxford University Press, 1993.

Hinsley, F. H., E. E. Thomas, C. F. G. Ransom, and R. C. Knight. *British Intelligence in World War II*. 5 vols. London: Her Majesty's Stationery Office, 1979–1990.

Hitchcock, Walter, ed. *The Intelligence Revolution: A Historical Perspective*. Proceedings of the Thirteenth Military History Symposium. October 1988. Lt. Col. Walter Hitchcock, Washington, DC: U.S. Air Force Academy, 1991.

Hodges, Andrew. *Alan Turing: An Enigma*. New York: Simon & Schuster, 1983.

Hohne, H. *The General Was a Spy.* New York: Coward, McCann & Geoghegan, 1971.

Hotson, J. Leslie. *The Death of Christopher Marlowe.* New York: Russell & Russell, 1925.

Hunt, Linda. *Secret Agenda: The United States Government, Nazi Scientists, and Project Paperclip, 1944–1990.* New York: St. Martins Press, 1991.

Irnberger, Harald. *Nelkenstrauß ruft Praterstern.* Wien: Libera Press Verlagsgesellschaft m.b.H., 1981.

Irving, David. *The Destruction of Convoy PQ-17.* New York: Richardson & Steirman, 1987.

Jäckel, E. *Hitlers Herrschaft. Vollzug einer Weltanschauung.* Stuttgart: Deutsche Verlags-Anstalt, 1986.

Jäckel, E., and J. Rohwer, eds. *Die Funkaufklärung und ihre Rolle im Zweiten Weltkrieg.* Stuttgart: Motorbuch, 1978.

Janis, Irving L. *Victims of Groupthink: A Psychological Study of Foreign-Policy Decisions and Fiascoes.* Boston: Houghton Mifflin, 1972.

Jones, R. V. *Reflections on Intelligence.* London: Heinemann, 1989.

   *The Wizard War* (published in the U.K. as *Most Secret War*). London: Hamish Hamilton, 1978.

Jukes, Geoff. "More on the Soviets and Ultra." *Intelligence and National Security* 4, no. 2 (April 1989): 374–384.

Kahn, David. *The Codebreakers: The Story of Secret Writing.* New York: Scribner, 1996.

   "The Forschungsamt – Nazi Germany's Most Secret Communications Intelligence Agency." *Cryptologia* 2, no. 1 (1978): 12–19.

   *Hitler's Spies.* New York: Macmillan, 1978.

   *Kahn on Codes.* New York: Macmillan, 1983.

   "Roosevelt, Magic and Ultra," *Cryptologia* 16, no. 4 (October 1992): 289–319.

   *Seizing the Enigma.* Boston: Houghton Mifflin, 1991.

Karski, Jan. *Story of a Secret State (Poland).* Boston: Houghton Mifflin, 1944.

Kasiski, Friedrich. *Die Geheimschriften und die Dechiffrierkunst* [Codes and the Art of Deciphering]. 1863.

Kitchen, Martin. *A Military History of Germany from the Eighteenth Century to the Present Day.* Bloomington: Indiana University Press, 1975.

Knightley, Phillip. *The Second Oldest Profession.* London: Deutsch, 1986.

Koch, James R. "Operation Fortitude: The Backbone of Deception." *Military Review* 73, no. 3 (1992): 66–77.

Kozaczuk, Wladyslaw. *Bitwa o tajemnice.* Warszawa: Verlag Ksiazka i Wiedza, 1967.

   *Enigma: How the German Machine Cipher Was Broken and How it Was Read by the Allies in World War Two.* Frederick, MD: University Publications of America, 1984.

   *Geheimoperation WICHER.* Koblenz: Bernard & Graef, 1989.

"Intelligence and Strategy: Some Observations on the War in the Mediterranean, 1941–45." *Intelligence and National Security* 5, no. 2 (April 1990): 444–464.

"World War II Intelligence: The Last 10 Years' Work Reviewed." *Defense Analysis* 3, no. 2 (June 1987): 103–117.

Kullback, Soloman. *Statistical Methods in Cryptanalysis*. Laguna Hills, CA: Aegean Park Press, 1982.

Langhorne, R. ed. *Diplomacy and Intelligence during the Second World War: Essays in Honour of F. H. Hinsley*. Cambridge: Cambridge University Press, 1985.

Laqueur, Walter. "The Future of Intelligence." *Society* 35, no. 2 (Jan–Feb. 1998): 301–311.

*The Terrible Secret*. London: Weidenfeld and Nicolson, 1980.

Layton, Edwin T. *"And I Was There": Pearl Harbor and Midway – Breaking the Secrets*. New York: Morrow, 1985.

Leverkühn, Paul. *Der Geheime Nachrichtendienst der Deutschen Wehrmacht im Krieg*. Frankfurt: Verlag für Wehrwesen B & G, 1957.

Lewin, Ronald. *The American Magic: Codes, Ciphers and the Defeat of Japan*. New York: Farrar Straus Giroux, 1982.

*Entschied Ultra den Krieg?* München: Bernard & Graefe, 1981.

*ULTRA Goes to War*. New York: McGraw-Hill, 1978.

"A Signal-Intelligence War," *Journal of Contemporary History* 16(1981): 501–512.

Lüdtke, Alf. "'Coming to Terms with the Past': Illusions of Remembering, Ways of Forgetting Nazism in West Germany." *Journal of Modern History* 65, no. 3 (1993): 542–572.

Mann, Charles C. "Homeland Insecurity" (profile of Bruce Schneier), *Atlantic Monthly* (September 2002): 81–102.

Masterman, John. *The Double Cross System*. New York: Avon, 1972.

May, Ernest. *Knowing One's Enemies: Intelligence Assessment Before the Two World Wars*. Princeton, NJ: Princeton University Press, 1984.

McClelland, Charles E. *State, Society, and University in Germany 1700–1914*. Cambridge: Cambridge University Press, 1980.

McCue, Brian. *Uboats in the Bay of Biscay: An Essay in Operations Analysis*. Washington, DC: National Defense University Press, 1990.

McGeoch, Ian. "Enigma Variations." *Army Quarterly & Defence Journal* 123, no. 1 (Jan. 1993): 88–89.

McKee, Alexander. *Dresden, 1945*. New York: E. P. Dutton, 1982.

McLachlan, Donald. *Room 39: Naval Intelligence in Action 1939–45*. London: Weidenfeld and Nicolson, 1968.

Mehner, Kurt, ed. *Der Geheimetagesberichten der deutschen Wehrmachtführung im Zweiten Weltkrieg: 1939–1945*. Osnabrück: Biblio Verlag, 1985.

Meinicke, Friedrich. "Kausalitäten und Werte in der Geschichte," *Historische Zeitschrift* 137 (1927–1928): 1–27.

Mendelsohn, John. J. *Intelligence, Counterintelligence and Military Deception during the World War II Era*. Series: Covert Warfare. New York: Garland Publishing, 1989.

Metropolis, Nicholas, J., Howlett, and Gian Carlo, Rota, eds. *A History of Computing in the Twentieth Century*. New York: Academic Press, 1980.

Millar, George Reid. *The Bruneval Raid*. Garden City, NY: Doubleday, 1974.

Miller, Ray A. "The Cryptographic Mathematics of Enigma." Fort Meade, MD: NSA, n.d.

Milner-Barry, P. S. "Review of Kozaczuk's *Enigma* (1984)." *International History Review* (Simon Frasier U.), 8, no. 1 (1986).

Moeser, Vicki. "Unlocking Enigma's Secrets," *Cryptologia* 14, no. 4 (October 1990): 366.

Montagu, Ewen. *The Man Who Never Was*. London: Evans Brothers, 1953.

*Beyond Top Secret U*. London: P. Davies, 1977.

Mosse, George L. *The Crisis of German Ideology: Intellectual Origins of the Third Reich*. New York: Grosset & Dunlap, 1964.

Müller, Klaus-Jürgen. *The Army, Politics and Society in Germany 1933–45*. Manchester: Manchester University Press, 1987.

Mulligan, Timothy. "Battleship *Bismarck*: The Most Powerful Warship Not Ready for Action." *Naval History* 15, no. 1 (February 2001): 20–26.

"The German Navy Evaluates Its Cryptographic Security, October 1941." *Military Affairs* 49, no. 2 (April 1985): 75–79.

"German U-Boat Crews in World War II: Sociology of an Elite." *Journal of Military History 56*, no. 2 (1992): 261–281.

*Neither Sharks Nor Wolves*. Annapolis, MD: Naval Institute Press, 1999.

ed., *Ultra, Magic and the Allies*. New York: Garland, 1989.

Murphy, Walter. *The Roman Enigma*. New York: Macmillan, 1981.

Neilson, Keith, and B. J. C. McKercher, eds. *Go Spy the Land: Military Intelligence in History*. Westport, CT: Praeger, 1992.

Nicholl, Charles. *The Reckoning: The Murder of Christopher Marlowe*. New York: Harcourt Brace, 1992.

O'Neill, James E., and Robert, W. Krauskopf. *World War II: An Account of Its Documents*. Washington, DC: Howard University Press, 1976.

O'Toole, G. J. A. *The Encyclopedia of American Intelligence and Espionage from the Revolutionary War to the Present*. New York: Facts on File, 1988.

Overy, Richard. *Why the Allies Won*. New York: Norton, 1995.

Paillole, Paul. *Notre Espion Chez Hitler*. Paris: Robert Laffont, 1985.

Parrish, Thomas. *The Ultra Americans: The U.S. Role in Breaking the Nazi Codes*. New York: Stein & Day, 1986.

Perrault, Gilles. *The Red Orchestra*. trans. Peter Wiles. New York: Simon and Schuster, 1967.

Persico, Joseph E. *Piercing the Reich*. New York: Viking, 1979.

Pfeifer, Jochen. *Der deutsche Kriegsroman 1945–1960: Ein Versuch zur Vermittlung von Literatur und Sozialgeschichte*. Königstein/Ts: Scripton, 1981.

Picker, Dr. Henry. *Hitlers Tischgespräche im Führerhauptquartier*. Stuttgart: Seewald Verlag, 1976.

Ponting, Clive. *Secrecy in Britain*. Oxford and Cambridge, MA: Basil Blackwell, 1990.

Popov, Dusko. *Spy-Counterspy*. New York: Grosset & Dunlap, 1974.

Ratcliff, R. A. "How Statistics Led the Germans to Believe Enigma Secure and Why They Were Wrong: Neglecting the Practical Mathematics of Cipher Machines." *Cryptologia* 27, no. 2 (April 2003): 119–131.

"Searching for Security: The German Investigations into Enigma's Security." *Intelligence and National Security* 14, no. 1 (June 1999).

Rathbone, Julian. *A Spy of the Old School*. New York: Pantheon, 1982.

Rau, Erik P. "The Adoption of Operations Research in the United States during World War II." *Systems, Experts, and Computers: The Systems Approach in Management and Engineering, World War II and After*. Agatha C. Hughes and Thomas P. Hughes, eds. Cambridge, MA: MIT Press, 2000.

"Technological Systems, Expertise, and Policy Making: The British Origins of Operational Research." *Technologies of Power: Essays in Honor of Thomas Parke Hughes and Agatha Chipley Hughes*. ed. Michael Thad Allen and Gabrielle Hecht. Cambridge, MA: MIT Press, 2001.

Riefenstahl, Leni. *Triumph of the Will* [film, 1934].

Ringer, Fritz K. *The Decline of the German Mandarins: The German Academic Community, 1890–1933*. Cambridge, MA: Harvard University Press, 1969.

Robertson, K. G., ed. *British and American Approaches to Intelligence*. London: Macmillan Press, 1987.

Rohwer, Jürgen. *Axis Submarine Successes 1939–1945*. Annapolis, MD: Naval Institute Press, 1983.

*The Critical Convoy Battles of March 1943*. Annapolis, MD: Naval Institute Press, 1977; London: Allen, 1977.

"Der Einfluss Der Alliierten Funkaufklärung auf den Verlauf des Zweiten Weltkrieges." *Vierteljahrshefte für Zeitgeschichte*: 325–369.

"Entwicklungsprobleme einer historischen Specialbibliothek", *Arbeitsgemeinschaft der Spezialbibliotheken*. (Kiel, 1967): 87–100.

"Die Funkführung der deutschen U-Boote im Zweiten Weltkrieg: Ein Beitrag zum Thema Technik und militärische Führung, Funkpeilung von Bord," *Wehrtechnik* 1 (1969): 324–328, 360–364.

"Funkaufklärung und Intelligence in dem Entscheidungs-prozessen des Zweiten Weltkrieges." *Festschrift für Eberhard Kessel* (1983): 330–364.

*Die U-Boot-Erfolge der Achsenmachte, 1939–1945.* Hrsg. von der Bibliothek fur Zeitgeschichte. München: J. F. Lehmann, 1968.

"War 'Ultra' Kriegsentscheidend?" *Marine Rundschau* 76 (1979): 29–36.

Rosen, Stephen Peter. *Winning the Next War: Innovation and the Modern Military.* Ithaca, NY: Cornell University Press, 1991.

Rosengarten, Adolf G., Jr. "With Ultra from Omaha Beach to Weimar, Germany – A Personal View." *Military Affairs* 42, no. 3 (October 1978): 127–132.

Rowlett, Frank. *The Story of Magic.* Laguna Hills, CA: Aegean Park Press, 1998.

Runyan, Timothy J., and Copes, Jan M. *To Die Gallantly: The Battle of the Atlantic.* Boulder, CO: Westview Press, 1994.

Rusbridge, James. "The Sinking of the "Automedon," the Capture of the "Nantun": New Light on Two Intelligence Disasters in World War II." *Encounter* (May 1985): 8–14.

Salewski, Michael. "Das Kriegstagebuch der Deutschen Seekriegsleitung in Zweiten Weltkrieg." *Marine Rundschau* 64 (June 1967): 137–145.

Santoni, Antonio. "Der Einfluß von 'Ultra' auf den Krieg im Mittelmeer." *Marine Rundschau* 78, no. 9 (1981): 503–512.

Schellenberg, Walter. *Aufzeichnungen des letzten Geheimdienstchefs unter Hitler.* London: André Deutsch, 1956.

Schickel, Alfred. "Verlor Deutschland den Zweiten Weltkrieg durch Verrat?" *Information für die Truppe* (1968): 211–228.

Schlee, Major a. D. Hans. *Entwicklung und Verwendung der Funktechnik bei der deutschen Armee.* n.p.

Schramm, Percy Ernst, ed. *Kriegstagebuch des Oberkommandos der Wehrmacht (Wehrmachtführungsstab) 1940–1945.* Frankfurt: Bernard & Graefe, 1961–1965.

Schramm, Ritter von. *Verrat im Zweiten Weltkrieg.* Düsseldorf and Wien: 1967.

Schuchmann, H.-R. "ENIGMA Variations." In *Cryptography. Lecture Notes in Computer Science* No. 194. Berlin: Springer, 1982. pp. 65–68.

Scott, K. "Window of Deceit." *Army Quarterly and Defence Journal 123*, no. 1 (January 1993): 39–42.

Seaton, Albert. *The German Army 1933–45.* London: Weidenfeld and Nicolson, 1982.

Silverman, David. *The Theory of Organizations: A Sociological Framework.* New York: Basic Books, 1971.

Sinclair, Andrew. *The Red and the Blue: Cambridge, Treason and Intelligence.* Boston: Little, Brown, 1986.

Skillen, Hugh. *Enigma and Its Achilles Heel*. Bath: Hugh Skillen, 1992.

Smith, Bradley F. *The Ultra Magic Deals*. Novato, CA: Presidio, 1993.

Smith, Harold L., ed. *War and Social Change: British Society in the Second World War*. Manchester: Manchester University Press, 1986.

Soltikow, M. G. *Ich war mittendrin – Meine Jahre bei Canaris*. Wien: Paul Neff Verlag, 1980.

    *The Spy Factory and Secret Intelligence*. Introduction by Bradley F. Smith. New York: Garland, 1989.

Stevens, Richard. *Understanding Computers*. Oxford: Oxford University Press.

Stripp, Alan. *Codebreaker in the Far East*. Oxford: Oxford University Press, 1989.

Strumph-Woytkewicz, Stanislaw. "Die Enigma." *Radar: Jugendzeitschrift aus Polen. Warschau* 1 (1979): 29–31.

*Stuttgart Im Zweiten Weltkrieg*. Gerlinger: Bleicher, 1989.

Taylor, A. J. P. *The Origins of the Second World War*. New York: Fawcett, 1961.

Toliver, Raymond, and Hanns J. Scharff. *The Interrogator: The Story of Hanns Scharff, Luftwaffe's Master Interrogator*. Fallbrook, CA: Aero, 1978.

Tompkins, Peter. "Are Human Spies Superfluous? The Secrets War." Washington, DC: National Archives, 1992.

Topp, Erich. *The Odyssey of a Uboat Commander*. trans. Eric C. Rust. New York: Praeger, 1992.

Trenkle, Fritz. *Die deutschen Funknachrichtenanlagen bis 1945*. Heidelberg: Hüthig, 1990. Band 2: Der Zweite Weltkrieg.

    *Die Deutschen Funk-Navigations- und Funkführungsverfahren bis 1945*. Stuttgart: Motorbuch, 1979.

Trevor-Roper, Hugh Redwald. *Hitler's War Directives 1939–1945*. London: Pan Books, 1966.

    *Ultra and the History of the U.S. Strategic Air Force in Europe v. the German Air Force*. Frederick, MD: University Publications of America, 1980.

Van der Vat, Dan. *The Atlantic Campaign: World War II's Great Struggle at Sea*. New York: Harper Smith & Row, 1988.

Vause, Jordan. *U-Boat Ace*. Annapolis, MD: Naval Institute Press, 1990.

von Thilo, Bode. "Die Schlüsselknacker von Bletchley Park." *Suddeutsche Zeitung* (Samstag/Sonntag, 25/26. Nov. 1978): 3.

Wark, Wesley K. *The Ultimate Enemy: British Intelligence and Nazi Germany 1933– 1945*. Ithaca, NY: Cornell University Press, 1985.

Webster, Charles, and Noble Franklin. *Strategic Air Offensive against Germany 1939–1945*. 4 vols. London: HMSO, 1961.

Wehler, Hans. *The German Empire 1871–1918*. trans. K. Traynor. New York: Berg Publishers, 1985.

Weinberg, Gerhard L. "Some Thoughts on World War II." *Journal of Military History* 56 (Oct. 1992): 659–668.

Welch, David. *Propaganda and the German Cinema, 1933–1945.* Oxford: Clarendon Press, 1983.

Welchman, Gordon. *The Hut 6 Story: Breaking the Enigma Code.* New York: McGraw-Hill, 1982.

Whitaker, Paul, and Louis Kruh. "From Bletchley Park to Berchtesgarden." *Cryptologia* 11, no. 3 (July 1987): 129–141.

Whitemore, Hugh. *Breaking the Code.* [play]

Wichman, Herbert. *45 Jahre Danach.* München: Verlagsagentur Walther Angerer, 1981.

Wilensky, Harold L. *Organizational Intelligence: Knowledge and Policy in Government and Industry.* New York: Basic Books, 1967.

Winks, Robin W. *Cloak and Gown: Scholars in the Secret War, 1939–1961.* New York: Morrow, 1987.

Winterbotham, F. *The Nazi Connection.* New York: Dell, 1978.
  *The ULTRA Secret.* New York: Dell, 1974.

Winton, John. *ULTRA at Sea: How Breaking the Nazi Code Affected Allied Naval Strategy during World War II.* New York: W. Morrow, 1988.

Wohlstetter, Roberta. *Pearl Harbor: Warning and Decision.* Stanford, CA: Stanford University Press, 1962.

Woytak, Richard. *On the Border of War and Peace: 1937–1939 and the Origin of the Ultra Secret.* New York: Columbia University Press, 1979.

Yardley, Herbert O. *The Chinese Black Chamber: An Adventure in Espionage.* Boston: Houghton Mifflin, 1983.

Young, Irene. *Enigma Variations.* Edinburgh: Mainstream Press, 1990.

Zetzsche, Hansjürgen. "Alliierte Geleitzugsoperationen im Eismeer während des Zweiten Weltkrieges." Magisterarbeit der universität Hamburg, 1983.

# INDEX